PRODUCING INDIA

CHICAGO STUDIES IN PRACTICES OF MEANING

Edited by Jean Comaroff, Andreas Glaeser, William Sewell, and Lisa Wedeen

MANU GOSWAMI

PRODUCING INDIA

From Colonial Economy to National Space

The University of Chicago Press   *Chicago & London*

MANU GOSWAMI is assistant professor of history and East Asian studies at New York University.

The University of Chicago Press, Chicago 60637
The University of Chicago Press, Ltd., London
© 2004 by The University of Chicago
All rights reserved. Published 2004
Printed in the United States of America

13 12 11 10 09 08 07 06 05 04   5 4 3 2 1

ISBN (cloth): 0-226-30508-2
ISBN (paper): 0-226-30509-0

Library of Congress Cataloging-in-Pubication Data

Goswami, Manu.
    Producing India : from colonial economy to national space / Manu Goswami.
      p. cm. — (Chicago studies in practices of meaning)
    Includes bibliographical references and index.
    ISBN 0-226-30508-2 (cloth : alk. paper) — ISBN 0-226-30509-0 (alk. paper)
    1. India—History—British occupation, 1765–1947. 2. India—Historical
geography. 3. Nationalism—India—History. 4. India—Economic conditions.
I. Title. II. Series.
    DS463.G687 2004
    954.03'5—dc22

                                                      2003019956

For Mummy and Tannia

In love and gratitude

CONTENTS

ACKNOWLEDGMENTS

N obody should have to write a book alone, and nobody actually does. This project has received more support than I fear it actually warrants. It assumed initial form at the University of Chicago, where the scholarship, pedagogy, and buoyant patience of my teachers made graduate school an uncommon and unexpected joy. Bernard Cohn taught all his students about the inseparability of politics and scholarship and, with singular insight and drollness, warned us about writing history in the facile mode of "Lucy Lacuna" and "Fillias Fillagap." Arjun Appadurai provided benevolent instruction, acute comments, and careful counsel with characteristic graciousness. Moishe Postone tirelessly prodded me to examine my basic assumptions and kept me alert to the challenge of overcoming conceptual conundrums. Susanne Rudolph offered crucial support and advice at different junctures. Dipesh Chakrabarty has long urged me to attend to the inner logics of everyday practices, exhibiting, at every turn, much intellectual generosity. I owe my deepest debt to Bill Sewell. His wise and gentle mentorship, astute criticism, and expansive spirit have sustained various incarnations of this project. And his friendship and everyday practice have represented an inspired instance of how to be in the world.

The conceptual roots of this project reside in the many interdisciplinary reading groups and weekly workshops that frame and distinguish intellectual life at the University of Chicago. I am particularly grateful to the members of the Red Line Working Group and participants of the Social Theory, Comparative Politics/Historical Sociology, South Asia/Middle East, and Nations and Nationalism workshops for indulging early stabs at this project. Different pieces of this work were presented at conferences and workshops at the University of Chicago, University of California, Santa Cruz, University of Michigan, Harvard University, New York University, and Middlebury College. I thank the participants for their helpful comments.

This book took final shape at New York University, where the learning begun at Chicago has continued. My colleagues in the departments of History and East Asian Studies have been closely engaged in the final stages of this project, proffering both inspiration and invigorating discussion. Harry Harootunian has been a storehouse of intellectual ingenuity, iconoclastic insight, and boundless energy. Special thanks to Frederick Cooper, Jean Comaroff, Prasenjit Duara, David Ludden, and Molly Nolan for providing perceptive, painstaking, and generously detailed responses on recent drafts of this work. Many thanks also to Julia Adams, Sumathi Ramaswamy, George Steinmetz, James Scott, Louise Young, and Marilyn Young for their suggestive and spirited comments on earlier versions of the book as a whole.

I am grateful to Sugata Bose, Ayesha Jalal, and Thomas Trautmann for their encouragement, comments, and intellectual advice. In addition to those already mentioned, the following individuals have shared valuable comments and criticisms on different sections of this work: Benedict Anderson, Tom Bender, Neil Brenner, Rogers Brubaker, Craig Calhoun, Michel Callon, Partha Chatterjee, Fernando Coronil, Nicholas Dirks, Mamadou Diouf, Nicholas De Genova, Greg Grandin, Gary Herrigel, Sudipta Kaviraj, Rebecca Karl, Yanni Kotsonis, Robin Kelley, Timothy Mitchell, Hyun Ok Park, Veena Oldenburg, Lulu Roy, Ajay Skaria, Ron Suny, Ann Stoler, Lisa Wedeen, and Gary Wilder. Conversations with many others, too many to fully record, but especially Billy Armshaw, Laura Bear, Indrani Chatterjee, Maggie Clinton, Faisal Devji, Sasha Disko, Debbie Gould, Walter Johnson, Tristan Kirvin, Uday Mehta, Osamu Nakano, Kristin Ross, Anna Tsing, Sinclair Thompson, and Xudong Zhang, opened up insights whose traces inform this work. My apologies to those I have inadvertently overlooked.

Funding for research in India and Britain and subsequent writing support was enabled by generous grants, including the Harry Frank Guggenheim Dissertation Fellowship, the MacArthur Scholars Dissertation Fellowship (Council for Advanced Studies in Peace and International Cooperation, University of Chicago), the IDRF Fellowship from the Social Science Research Foundation, and the University of Chicago Mellon Dissertation Writing Fellowship. A year's leave in 1999–2000, generously granted by the University of California, Santa Cruz, and spent at the International Center for Advanced Study at New York University, provided much needed time to rethink my dissertation thesis. I am grateful to the publishers of *Comparative Studies in Society and History* for their permission to use in this book sections from my previously published articles: "Rethinking the Modular Nation Form: Towards a Sociohistorical Understanding of Nationalism," 44, 4 (2002): 770–99; and "From Swadeshi to Swaraj: Nation, Economy, Territory in Colonial South Asia, 1870–1907," 40, 4 (1998): 609–36.

I thank Doug Mitchell of the University of Chicago Press for his editorial wisdom, unwavering cheer, and many lovely lunch conversations about jazz. Tim McGovern ably guided the completion of this project. Kathryn Gohl exhibited exemplary fortitude in clearing the thickets of my prose.

Neil Brenner has been a source of varied learning, comradeship, and a great deal more for many years. I could not have weathered Chicago winters, or much else since, without the friendship of Urmi Bhowmik, Ian Barrow, Nicholas De Genova, Lulu Roy, Anjali Singh, and Gary Wilder. Through gentle nudging and example, Greg Grandin has encouraged me to embrace the present and tame, in the fashion of Buffy, my inner slayer.

This project has meant a long absence from the everyday rhythms of my parents and of Maharani and Pradeep Prasad in Delhi. This book neither is nor could be an adequate recompense for all the riotous merriment that I have missed and the familial sorrows that I only felt at a remove. It is dedicated to my mother and sister who, with their rare talent for love, have helped me imagine many possible futures. It is from my mother's stories for children that I first learnt about the power of words to make old worlds new. My sister, Tannia, took much of the heat for my waywardness growing up and, ever generous, has now once more kindly assented to share the blame for the inadequacies of this work.

INTRODUCTION

Often, as I wandered from meeting to meeting, I spoke to my audience of this India of ours, of *Bharata*, the old Sanskrit name derived from the mythical founders of the race. . . . I spoke of this great country for whose freedom we were struggling, of how each part differed from the other and yet was India, of common problems of the peasants from north to south and east to west, of the *Swaraj* that could only be for all and every part and not for some. I told them of my journeying from the Khyber Pass in the far north-west to *Kanya Kumari* or Cape Comorin in the distant south, and how everywhere the peasants put to me identical questions, for their troubles were the same — poverty, debt, vested interests, landlords, moneylenders, heavy rents and taxes, police harassment, and all these wrapped up in the structure that the foreign government had imposed upon us — and relief must also come for all.

— Jawaharlal Nehru, *Discovery of India*, 1946

C entral to the project of nationalism is making the nation appear natural. Written in the early 1940s, from the confines of a colonial prison — the most compressed of the spaces of colonial domination — Jawaharlal Nehru's *Discovery of India* illustrates how persuasively, almost with the transparency of the self-evident, the conception of India as a bounded national entity was popularized.[1] Like many other elite nationalists, Nehru had devotedly followed Gandhi's exhortation to spend extended time in rural India. In an effort to make peasant audiences think "of India as a whole" along with the wider world of which it was a fundamental expression, Nehru cited contemporary struggles in "China, in Spain, in Abyssinia, in Central Europe, in Egypt and the countries of Western Asia" and extolled the "wonderful changes in the Soviet Union and of the great progress made in America" (60). The "task" of rendering concrete the idea of India as at once a singular "whole" and an integral part of the "wide world" was not as difficult as he had initially assumed. For "our ancient epics and myths and legends, which they knew so well" had vouchsafed a tangible sense "of their country." What is more, many others had either "traveled far and wide to the great places of pilgrimage situated at the four corners of India" or served as soldiers "in foreign parts in World War I or other expeditions." Even the seemingly esoteric references to foreign countries had, he noted, been "brought home to them by the consequences of the great depression of the thirties" (60).

Instructing peasant audiences on *swaraj* or self-rule — one of the foundational categories of Indian nationalism — Nehru affirmed its universalistic signification for "all and every part" of India and its people. This task was not as easy as he had supposed:

> Sometimes as I reached a gathering, a great roar of welcome would greet me: *Bharat Mata ki Jai* — Victory to Mother India! I would ask them unexpectedly what they meant by that cry, who was this *Bharat Mata*, Mother India, whose victory they wanted? My question would amuse them and surprise them, and then, not knowing exactly what to answer, they would look at each other and at me. I persisted in my questioning. At last a vigorous *Jat*, wedded to the soil from immemorial generations, would say that it was the *dharti*, the good earth of India, that they meant. What earth? Their particular village patch, or all the patches in the district or province, or in the whole of India? And so question and answer went on, till they would ask me impatiently to tell them all about it. I would endeavor to do so and explain that India was all this that they had thought, but it was much more. The mountains and the rivers of India, and the forests and the broad fields, which gave us food, were all dear to us, but what counted ultimately were the people of India, people like them and me, who were spread out all over this vast land. *Bharat Mata*, Mother India, was essentially these millions of people, and victory to her meant victory to these people. You are parts of *Bharat Mata*, I told them, you are in a manner yourselves *Bharat Mata*, and as this idea slowly soaked into their brains, their eyes would light up as if they had made a great discovery. (60)

The elusive amplitude of the ideal of *swaraj* and its relation to the national whole encoded in *Bharat Mata* had mandated a more insistent, even tedious, series of specifications. And it had demanded the appearance of a dialogic authoring of nationalist categories threaded across from the "great roar of welcome" to the quiet collective epiphany of nationalist discovery. The nationalist project of teaching the nation, often saturated with the elite paternalism that imbues Nehru's narrative, involves transforming the abstract categorical conception of the nation into a taken-for-granted frame of reference. It involves fixing collective identities in place and refashioning local and regional solidarities in accord with a larger national whole. It entails the institution of a lived equivalence between the individual and the nation and the forging of a deeply interiorized affiliation among a particular national space, economy, people, and state.

Nehru, who would become the first prime minister of postcolonial India and a chief architect of the left and liberal anti-imperial national developmentalist models elaborated by third world states at the Bandung Conference in 1955, has long been regarded as the incarnation par excellence of the modernizing, rationalist, and secular imperatives of institutional nationalism. A modernist master-builder, Nehru had little public time for the popular sentiments of iconic Indian nationhood. Indeed, his deep personal ambivalence toward the affective resonance and force of communalism — that is, sociopolitical and religious conflict between Hindus and Muslims — was more than offset by his faith in its scheduled transcendence in a postcolonial Indian state. Despite the nativist slide from nation to Hindu deity condensed in the conception of India as *Bharat Mata* (Mother India), Nehru held up the universalistic project of national development as embodied in "a heavy engineering and machine-making sector, scientific research institutes, and electric power" as the "temples" of India's future (410).[2] In the early twentieth century, anticolonial nationalists in India, as elsewhere, had sought in the reconstituted particularism of the nation-state the guarantee of a secular modernity.

In the early twenty-first century, we are heirs to the promise of democratic self-determination and economic autonomy — bequeathed as the legitimating mission of anticolonial nationalist movements — which a sovereign nation-state was to secure. Yet we are also witness in contemporary India to a profound crisis of democracy, developmentalism, and the nation-state. The signs and effects of this multidimensional crisis resist simple cataloging in a headline-driven register. But its concrete expressions include the pervasive institutionalization of the violent and exclusionary "alphabet-soup" of organizations (BJP, RSS, VHP) associated with the hegemonic project of Hindu nationalism; the apparent success of this movement in shaping political subjectivities oriented, in equal parts, to the consumption of a militant Hinduness or *Hindutva* and a naturalized theology of economic accumulation; the proliferation of nativist ideologies in tandem with widening socioeconomic disparities; and numerous regionally grounded nationalist movements (from Kashmir to Assam) that seek to re-order the existing configuration of national space. The embrace of neoliberal strategies by successive governing regimes in recent decades has effected a turn away from the Nehruvian developmentalist imperative of equalizing growth across disparate regions, of overcoming the inherited economic cartography of colonial space, and of abating, even if only in a formal sense, the expressions and effects of socioeconomic and religious polarization. Not only has the grand dream of realizing economic sovereignty and overcoming communalism been put on hold, but the very claim of an emancipatory nationalist project has been hollowed out. The decades after the nationalization of political space have seen not the anticipated eclipse of communal conflict but its intensification. They have witnessed not the actualization of the promise of democratic autonomy and collective development, but its radical attenuation.

It would appear, at first blush, that the impassioned politics of cultural authenticity have triumphed over the disenchanted, prosaic Nehruvian project of national developmentalism. Yet current claims about the resurgence and ubiquity of communalism and nativist ideologies in South Asia, like earlier sweeping claims of their eventual demise, obscure more than they reveal. They occlude the long-run internal tensions within Indian nationalism and the categorical kinship between the political economy of nationhood and nativist cultural projects. They bracket the historically constituted affinity between Nehru's simultaneous appeal to *Bharat Mata* — the master trope, then as now, of popular organicist and nativist figurations of national space — and the imperative of forging an autarkic, self-sufficient national economy. The elision of this particular historical problematic has been enabled, as this work suggests, by a pervasive methodological nationalism that has imbued both the scholarship on Indian nationalism and the wider interdisciplinary literature on nationalism. I define *methodological nationalism* as entailing the common practice of presupposing, rather than examining, the sociohistorical production of such categories as a national space and national economy and the closely related failure to analyze the specific global field within and against which specific nationalist movements emerged.

Many scholars, within and beyond the field of South Asian studies, have interpreted contemporary neoliberal trends — the accelerated integration of financial, labor, and capital markets on global and subglobal scales; the reorganization of the international division of labor; the circulation of aesthetics, images, and cultural flows; the rise of a host of supranational regulatory regimes (World Bank, International Monetary Fund) and related policies of stabilization and structural adjustment — as posing a fatal challenge to the nation form as such.[3] Others have emphasized the continued force of nationalism across diverse regional political landscapes.[4] Both sides in this debate assume, in varying timbres, the radical novelty of the present conjuncture between processes of nationalization and the proliferation of profoundly uneven yet densely intertwined supranational, regional, and lo-cal processes of capitalist restructuring and intra- and interstate dynamics. In an anxious attempt to fix the future of the nation form in general and of India in particular, contemporary debates have pushed aside the *longue durée* of the internal relations between nationalism, the contradictory dynamics of global capitalism, and the relational character of intra- and interstate fields.

This book traces the sociocultural, political, economic, and global trans-formations that made possible nationalist imaginings of India — or, more specifically, *Bharat*, the dominant Hindu-Hindi term for the nation and the constitutional name for postcolonial India — as a bounded national space and economy, ca. 1858–1920. By exploring this question, this work devel-ops a novel account of the emergence, trajectory, and contradictory charac-ter of Indian nationalism. I argue that a tension between a universalistic conception of national development and a particularistic, specifically Hindu understanding of nationhood was built into Indian nationalism. On the one hand, nationalism sought to inscribe the imagined nation within a univer-salistic framework of national development and an idealized space-time that was understood as outside of and prior to colonial space. Yet, at the same time, it delimited a hierarchical order of national subjects along exclusion-ary lines of territorial and sociocultural origin in order to preserve the imag-ined nation against contamination from both the perceived abstraction of the colonial present and the particularistic foreign body of the Muslim. Both the secular self-understanding of institutional nationalism (associated with the Indian National Congress, established in 1885) and the particular-istic ideology of Hindu nationalism rest on a notion of a Hindu majority and a Muslim minority bound together within a single spatial whole, India. My analysis suggests that the very idea of India as a bounded national space and economy, as first elaborated in the last third of the nineteenth century, has made possible both a universal language of national unity and development and engendered terrifying violence and social conflict.

Rather than replicating the "misplaced concreteness" of nationalist no-tions of India, this book explores the multiple, overlapping, and densely in-tertwined socioeconomic and cultural processes — from the globally scaled to the mundane scapes of the everyday — by which the conception of India as a bounded national space and economy was brought into being histori-cally.[5] It suggests that social spaces — colonial and national, political and economic, material and imagined — do not emerge from self-evident geogra-phies, nor do they exist in mutual isolation. Rather, they are co-constituted through the complex "superimposition and interpenetration" of socioeconomic structures, state practices, cultural forms, and collective agency on multiple spatiotemporal scales.[6] By placing Indian nationalism within and against the wider historical-geographical field of its emergence, this study underscores the long-run historical dynamic between processes of global restructuring and nationalization and elucidates the global and regional coordinates of apparently discrete local formations.

My analysis of Indian nationalism is motivated by the conviction that the emergence, dynamics, and trajectory of specific nationalist movements are best understood from a global and historical-geographical perspective. Yet it is also impossible to grasp nationalism, let alone politically engage it, as Benedict Anderson suggests, in "any but particular terms."[7] This paradox — intrinsic to the nation form — poses key theoretical and methodological challenges. It necessitates a doubled perspective, one that pays equal attention to the simultaneously universal and particular character of nationalism in the modern era. It requires as well a sustained elaboration of the dialectical relationship between material, social, and cultural fields and the experiential contradictions and lived practices of individuals and social groups. It demands, in other words, a framework that speaks to the lived interdisciplinarity of everyday life.

This book situates and addresses these theoretical and methodological concerns — the task of demonstrating the intrinsic relationship between sociohistorical forms, categories of understanding, and forms of subjectivity and of integrating apparently distinct spatial scales and temporalities — in historical and analytical practice. In this respect, the nonlinear narrative structure of the book, its focus on the differential logics and effects of political-economic and cultural processes on multiple spatiotemporal scales, its attempt to weld together "thick description" and wider analytical frames, and its emphasis on the joint determinations between shifts in meaning and materiality are as important as its explicit theoretical content.

More than fifty years after the realization of *swaraj* (self-rule), India remains the locus of a desperately felt, and increasingly bloody, argument. In light of the brutalization of everyday social and political life, the violence that attended the territorial partition of colonial India into the mutually exclusive sovereign nation-states of India and Pakistan in 1947–48 appears less as a discrete event than as an interminable condition. These developments have lent urgency to a critical rethinking of the distinctive dynamics, form, and trajectory of Indian nationalism. This book recasts the complex dynamic between colonialism and nationalism from a historical-geographical and global perspective in order to gain analytical leverage on a contradictory present in which the past is not yet past.

THE ARGUMENT OF THE WORK

The conception of India as a spatially bounded and singular national entity served as the starting point of late-nineteenth-century nationalism. From the moment of its emergence in the 1870s, nationalist discourse both pre-supposed an already given national space and sought to institute a spatial coincidence between the imagined nation's history, culture, people, and economy. The reconfiguration of colonial space as national space in the late nineteenth century represented a radical socioepistemological break from received conceptions of historicity, space, political subjectivity, and sover-eignty. Yet despite this historical novelty, the historiography on Indian na-tionalism and colonial South Asia has presupposed rather than examined the sociohistorical production of nationalist and popular conceptions of In-dia as an externally distinctive national space and economy.[8] The effort to excise nationalist assumptions from analyses of nationalism has not yet ex-tended to such categorical conceptions as a national space and economy. It is a testament to the naturalization of the nation form that these assumptions have for so long passed unquestioned. Indeed, they have acquired the fixity of common sense.

Against the limits of methodological nationalism, this work explores the reciprocal determination between the production of particular political-economic and social spaces and the forging of such categories as a national space and economy in a specific historical conjuncture and global field. In so doing, my analysis reworks the dominant periodization of Indian nation-alism in South Asian scholarship that locates the 1885 establishment of the Indian National Congress as the ground zero of origin. It also departs from the more common focus on nationalist movements and discourses after 1905 (the beginning of the *swadeshi* movement) or during the 1920s as the roots of the internal tensions of nationalism, especially with respect to the problem of "communalism." This periodization ignores the dynamic interplay be-tween the profound restructuring of social space and time in late colonial In-dia and the emergence of specifically modernist, nativist, and organicist spa-tiotemporal discourses condensed in the conception of India, or more specifically, *Bharat,* as a bounded national entity between 1860 and 1880.

My focus on the production of an internally uneven colonial space and its reconstitution as national space presents specific historiographical and ana-lytical challenges. It entails moving beyond narrowly construed institutional histories of nationalism as well as discursivist frameworks that track shifts in ideology and subjectivity without a simultaneous focus on specific social transformations, historical conjunctures, and global political-economic dynamics. It also demands an account of historical change in terms at once more differentiated and more fundamental than the single-stranded chronology that nationalist discourse gave itself and that subsequent scholarship has either reproduced or left unexamined. Only then can we begin to show the multiply-refracted concrete effects of colonial practices, intra- and interstate dynamics, and processes of global restructuring in the reworking of received cultures of reference, in the forging of novel epistemological categories of space and time, and in the emergence of a nativist, organicist, and idealist vision of nationhood. And only then can we begin to account for the production and taken-for-granted character of figurations of national space encoded in such foundational categories of Indian nationalist practice as *Bharatvarṣh* and *Bharat Mata* as well as the transnational constitution and transposition of such categories as a national economy.

But I am getting ahead of my argument, whose concrete narration actually begins with the transfer of power from the East India Company (EIC) to the British Crown in 1858. The assumption of direct Crown rule of colonial India followed the brutal repression of the rebellion of 1857 or what colonial discourse named the "Mutiny." The suppression of the rebellion of 1857 marked the end of the protracted denouement of the EIC as a governing apparatus and consolidated the shift from mercantile to territorial colonialism. It also inaugurated a spectacular reworking of the institutional, political-economic, and spatial coordinates of the colonial state, its technologies of power, and its material and epistemological modes of reproduction.

Drawing on Henri Lefebvre's theory of the production of social space and of the modern state as a "spatial framework of power," the first four chapters of this work explore the production and representation of what I call a colonial state space during the post-1857 era.[9] The term *colonial state space*, as employed in this work, denotes the complex ensemble of practices, ideologies, and state projects that underpinned the restructuring of the institutional and spatiotemporal matrices of colonial power and everyday life. The post-1857 formation of a distinctive colonial state space was effected in and through a range of institutions, representational artifacts, and regulatory practices. The modalities of spatialization included the institution and workings of a massive web of transportation and irrigation structures that integrated and demarcated colonial India as a unit of state governance and the shifting coordinates of a distinctive political economy of empire as forged by various colonial officials and British economists from John Stuart Mill to John Maynard Keynes. The material homogenization of financial space and official representations of the colonial economy as a bounded totality occurred simultaneously. This process was concretized in the generalization of state-issued "pure" (nonconvertible) paper currency, the hierarchical consolidation of distinct monetary forms and institutions on different spatial scales of the imperial economy, the reconfiguration of financial instruments (*hundis* or bills of exchange), the 1862 introduction of a single, annual state budget, and the standardization of accounting procedures. The making of colonial state space and the lived geographies it generated during the post-1857 era — from railway journeys to the circulation of ever-more-reified money forms to the racialization of the labor force to the localization of colonial pedagogical practices — framed the experience of colonial-domination-as-lived for the vast majority of colonial subjects in colonial India.

Yet, rather than a unitary or homogenous whole, colonial state space was a contradictory force-field, shot through with both everyday and spectacular tensions. The production of a colonial state space was made and marked by an immanent contradiction: the very practices that homogenized social relations also engendered new forms of differentiation and deepened socioeconomic and cultural unevenness. This was manifest not only in the consolidation of colonial India as a hierarchically subordinate space within the Britain-centered globally organized imperial economy but in the emergence and deepening of new forms of socioeconomic inequality (devastating famines, rising rural indebtedness, widening urban–rural differentiations) and spatiotemporal unevenness within colonial India. Although the phenomenon of unevenness — uneven development, the presence of contending temporalities and spaces, the phenomenological experience of the "synchronicity of the non-synchronous" — is intrinsic to capitalism, it assumed an exaggerated form in a colonial context.[10] Indeed, this book emphasizes how the articulation of sociocultural and political-economic relations was overlaid, even overburdened, by the fractious interplay between received and transposed practices and imaginaries in colonial India.

The production of colonial state space transformed the socioeconomic geography of colonial India, consolidated modalities of state power, and deepened the reach of state-generated classificatory schemes. It also spurred a profound reworking of popular practices of subjectivity and categories of understanding, one in which received conceptions of temporality, space, and sovereignty were assailed and could no longer be presupposed. The materialization of colonial space in everyday landscapes made possible emergent popular imaginings of colonial India as a temporally dynamic and spatially bounded entity. Yet the contradictions of colonial space also enabled popular conceptions of colonial space as specifically nonnational, as constituted by a non-isomorphism between political and economic structures and by a disjuncture between the space of the production of value and the imperial scale of its realization. Concretized in novel experiences of space-time, repertoires of collective action, and conceptions of history, territory, and economy, this multidimensional process pervaded, if in an uneven fashion, both elite and subaltern worlds. The last four chapters of this work trace this complex playing out in diverse political-cultural fields and social arenas, specifying their relationship to both the internal tensions of colonial practices and wider processes of global restructuring from the 1860s until 1920, the beginning of the noncooperation/*khilafat* movement.

Through a detailed analysis of an unexplored archive of vernacular geographical and historical texts produced by an ascendant upper-caste Hindu middle class during the late 1860s and 1870s in northern colonial India, I provide a critical account of the reconstitution of colonial India as the locus of a distinct national space, of India as *Bharat*. This novel terrain of spatial and temporal imaginings—which include the first systematic history of India written in Hindi (1864), popular pamphlets, plays, novels, folk songs, and geographical and historical textbooks explored in chapter 6—was concretized across various educational fields. The conception of India as *Bharat* and gendered figurations of *Bharat Mata*—given voice in a range of vernacular pedagogical debates and enacted in popular cultural forms and practices—heralded a radical re-signification of previously dominant categories of spatial and temporal understanding (explored in chap. 5) and their self-conscious placement under the sign of "tradition." It marked the formation of a specifically modernist and historicist discourse of nationhood, one that I call territorial nativism. Territorial nativism was predicated on a doubled movement of the territorialization of history and the delimitation of organically conceived core nationals from the standpoint of territorial origin and a fictive unity between the past and present. It identified upper-caste Hindus as the organic, original, core nationals with an intimate and unmediated relationship to the imagined nation. Within this schema, Muslims were figured either as a problematic particularity against the self-understood universality of an organic whole or as the foreign body within the internal space of the nation. Territorial nativism haunted and undermined subsequent anticolonial projects and movements, especially the Indian National Congress's project of societal unification and economic development.

Deeply engraved within everyday practices and interpretive frames, the conception of India as a bounded national space gradually acquired a self-evident givenness. Indeed, by the late 1870s and early 1880s, a distinctly nationalist episteme emerged—a dominant and authoritative frame of reference—within which the meanings of history, territory, and economy were articulated and empowered. The experiential and structural contradictions of colonial space, in tandem with key global developments, reinforced and consolidated territorial nativist conceptions of economy and space from the late 1870s onward. Specifically, I elaborate the eventful convergence of the multiply-refracted effects of colonial space and global processes of restructuring and show how they made the contradictions of colonialism both more apparent and acute. The challenges posed to Britain's global hegemony by the counterhegemonic formation of state-centric developmentalist imaginaries in Europe, the United States, and Japan shaped the shifting forms and targets of state practices within colonial India, intensified modalities of financial domination in an era beset by devastating famines, deepening impoverishment, and high inflation, and sharpened the lived unevenness of colonial space.

It was during this historical conjuncture that middle-class intellectuals and activists such as M. G. Ranade, Dadabhai Naoroji, G. V. Joshi, G. K. Gokhale, and Romesh Chunder Dutt—many of whom became central figures in the Indian National Congress—summoned the analytical and normative categories of a specifically national developmentalist framework to ground their doubled critique of both colonial rule and classical political economy. The formation of a strongly autarkic, idealist, and idealizing nationalist political economy—one that enriched the political signification of the central concepts of the German historical school of political economy, especially the work of Friedrich List—constituted the positive content of the economic critique of colonialism and the normative basis for institutional nationalism (associated with the Indian National Congress). It also spawned a radical politics of autonomy that demanded an absolute congruence between the territory, history, and economy of the imagined nation.

During the last decades of the nineteenth century and the early ones of the twentieth, the dizzying expansion of the field of Indian economics, as embodied in a range of experimental economic institutions and works by Vaman Govind Kale, Radhakamal Mukherjee, and Bipin Chandra Pal, among others, did more than merely excoriate inflated official claims of material and moral progress. The authors of Indian economics—an anticolonial disciplinary formation rooted in the everyday experience of colonial unevenness—anticipated twentieth-century dependency frameworks forged by Latin American intellectuals and authored a conception of the nation as the natural scale of capital accumulation and the institutional means for overcoming the problem of colonial unevenness. They also, as elaborated in chapter 7, explicitly thematized the intrinsic links between the epistemological coordinates of classical political economy and the ideological underpinnings of colonial rule, thus presaging contemporary debates about the relationship between colonial epistemologies and modalities of rule.

The early-twentieth-century *swadeshi* (indigenous manufactures) movement was the first systematic campaign to incorporate and mobilize the "masses" within the elite structure of institutional or Congress nationalism. It was the crucial relay for the generalization and radicalization of both the economic critique of colonialism and popular nativist imaginings of India on the terrain of the everyday. The multiple practices and imaginaries that marked and made the movement, as elaborated in chapter 8, sought to actualize the presumed organic character and imagined singularity of an autonomous national space and society. *Swadeshi* practices fused together a universalistic conception of national economic development with a particularistic, organicist, and idealist vision of national space as specifically Hindu. Expressed in a high philosophical nativist idiom, *swadeshi* projects and discourses attributed an ontological privilege to Hinduism (in its late-colonial objectified form) as the very sign of a unique universality and the very substance of nationhood. The idealist and organicist longings that imbued *swadeshi* practices and imaginaries gave expression to the lived temporality of estrangement, of socioeconomic and spatial unevenness constitutive of colonial space. Yet the territorial nativist episteme that underpinned *swadeshi* nationalism also violently shaped the sharper crystallization of the conflictual and hierarchical elaboration of the relational categories of Hindu, Muslim, and India as *Bharat*.

My analysis seeks to render palpable the historically constituted kinship between the universalistic political economy of nationhood as forged by the first generation of Congress nationalists and territorial nativist conceptions of India as a bounded and organically constituted national space and economy. Against dominant readings of anticolonial nationalism, I argue that territorial nativism, as exemplified by the *swadeshi* movement, was not produced within an autonomous domain, nor did it represent the upsurge of atavistic tradition in the face of an abstractly conceived process of modernization. Rather, the movement's idealist and nativist particularism was conditioned by the perceived threat of the deterritorializing dynamic of colonial and capital expansion. For Indian nationalists, the simultaneous homogenization and differentiation of socioeconomic and cultural relations—which defined the lived experience of colonial space—could only be overcome through the wholesale nationalization of political-economic and cultural space. Indian nationalism was, in this regard, irreducibly part of a wider dynamic between processes of global restructuring and nationalization in the late nineteenth and early twentieth centuries. The deterritorializing dynamics of capitalism and the reterritorializing strategies of nationalist practices were intrinsically interrelated moments. Although territorial nativism was articulated within the terms of a locally specific argot of autonomy, it was neither exclusive to Indian nationalism nor simply an expression of its particularistic dimension. Rather it was a symptom of the immanent contradictions of the nation form in a specific global field and historical conjuncture.

The analytical path I tread in the chapters that follow navigates key methodological divides and theoretical conundrums that have beset debates on nationalism and colonialism. In the remainder of this introduction, I delineate the conceptual scaffolding of my analysis of the dialectical relationship between colonialism, anticolonial nationalism, and processes of global restructuring, specifying some of its key categories: nation form, historical-geographical field, national space, and anticolonial nationalism.

BEYOND METHODOLOGICAL NATIONALISM: RETHINKING THE NATION FORM

One of the central aims of this book is to integrate and treat as analytically inseparable the objective and subjective dimensions of nationalism as a modern social form. If this is a familiar call, it is also one more honored in the breach than in the observance. A number of social theorists have long stressed the limits of this canonical opposition and identified its socially generated character.[11] However, theoretical discussions about the problem of mediating between objectivist and subjectivist modalities and the literature on nationalism have tended to operate as parallel rather than intersecting fields of inquiry. Nowhere is this more apparent than in the deepening cleavage between objectivist and subjectivist approaches to nationalism and the related rift between scholars in quest of a general theory of nationalism as such and those wedded to the localized, contingent, and singular aspects of nationalist movements.

In a programmatic review of the extensive literature on nationalism, Geoff Eley and Ronald Suny identify a fundamental methodological reorientation from "structural and materialist" to "cultural studies" perspectives on nationalism.[12] Notwithstanding significant exceptions to this trend away from "structural and materialist" approaches among state-centric and neo-institutionalist sociologists,[13] their mapping of nationalism research captures its recent trajectory especially among historians and literary-critical and cultural theorists. In relative decline, if not uniform retreat, are objectivist frameworks that sought to uncover the origins or first causes of nationalism and that primarily focused on the long-run social processes and historical transformations that conditioned the emergence of nationalism as a world-historical phenomenon. Within this broad framework, nationalism has been variously understood as the product of expanding communication and transportation networks;[14] as a functional requirement of modernization;[15] as a legitimating ideology of class domination;[16] as an outgrowth of the homogenizing practices associated with the creation of centralized, unitary territorial states;[17] and as a separatist response of peripheral regional elites against centralizing states and processes of uneven development.[18] Objectivist analyses of nationalism have tended to pay less attention to the emotive power of nationalism, its capacity to summon affective attachment and collective sacrifice, the discursive practices that help secure a tie between individuals and an abstract national collectivity, and "eventful" transformations of its meaning.[19]

The "cultural turn" in nationalism research has sought to repudiate objectivist readings of nationalism by focusing attention on its diffuse, contingent character, its inner incoherence, its constitutive ambiguity, and its lack of discursive closure.[20] Conscious of the ideological circularity of nationalist discourse with its self-referential and self-serving claims, various recent works have argued, from different analytical and disciplinary perspectives, that nationalism resists not only a priori, positivist, and abstract definitions but all definitional attempts.[21] For many recent scholars of nationalism, the apparent incommensurability between cultural and ideological articulations of nationalisms, across divergent historical and regional contexts, is conclusive.[22] In its most popular variant, this acute perception of the multivalent character of nationalism has taken the form of substituting for the sociohistorical problematic of nationalism its symbolic, semantic, and discursive aspects.[23]

Condensed in this methodological shift from nationalism as a sociohistorical problematic to the view of the nation as a discursive formation is a consequential, if subtle, eclipsing of the sociohistorical processes and institutional constraints that condition the global (re)production of the universally legitimate form of the nation. The recent emphases on the promiscuous plurality and unruly dissemination of the concept nation usefully caution us against "substantialist" rendering of nations as "real, enduring collectivities" that organized many objectivist accounts of nationalism.[24] "Cultural" or subjectivist studies of nationalism have also enriched our understanding of the constructed character of discourses of nationhood,[25] the internal tensions within nationalism concretized in the fraught management of race, gender, and class differences, the dispersed disciplinary regimes that shape nationalist practices, and the interpellation of individuals and collectivities into normative national subjects.[26] However, these works have paid less attention to the ways in which broader social processes and institutions — such as the dynamics of the interstate system, the expansive logic of capital, the institutionalized tie between nationhood and statehood — shape the political-economic and discursive structure of nationalism. By relegating nationalism to a discursive domain, these works repeat, rather than overcome, such classical dichotomies as objectivity/subjectivity and universality/particularity. The conceptual challenge posed by nationalism lies in placing the interlinked objective/subjective and universal/particular dimensions of nationalism in a single analytical field, treating them as "two translations of the same sentence."[27]

The protean character of nationalism as at once irredeemably particular and solidly universal renders a general or comprehensive theory of nationalism as such illusory. Yet, at the same time, the multidimensional character of nationalism calls for analytical lexicons attentive to its simultaneously singular and plural character, its instantiation as a dominant political form, and its status as an authoritative everyday frame of reference for modernity-as-lived. In an astute aside, Etienne Balibar reminds us that nationalisms "do not work everywhere the same way: in a sense they must work everywhere in a different way, this is part of the 'national identity.'"[28] A central aspect of the modern nation form is its doubled character as at once universal/particular and objective/subjective. By the late nineteenth and early twentieth centuries, nationalism became in Latin America, East Asia, South Asia, and Europe not only one of the most universally legitimate articulations of collective identity (either in conjunction with imperial projects or as a repudiation of empire), but also one of the most pervasive and entrenched forms of modern particularism. The representational complex of modern nationalism indexed, then as now, a doubled understanding of identity and difference. Nationalist discourses, across regional and cultural contexts, worked in and through the simultaneous assertion of their similarity with and difference from other nation-states and nations. Nationalist movements and nationalizing states presented themselves as universalistic within the spatial confines of a particularized national community, but as particularistic without, that is, in relation to other nations and nation-states. The doubled character of the nation form mirrored, in this respect, the spatial partitioning of the modern interstate system into a series of mutually exclusive, formally equivalent, sovereign states. Nationalist claims of particularity and the imagined singularity of national formations only become intelligible against and within a global grid of formally similar national communities and states. It is precisely the doubled character of the nation form as simultaneously universal and particular that allows both for objectivist programmatic theories of nationalism as well as for subjectivist denunciations of such attempts.

An exclusive focus on the particularistic aspects of specific nationalist movements reproduces, albeit in a different register, claims of singularity dear to nationalist discourses as such. It renders invisible the historically constituted family resemblances, in both an institutional and ideological sense, between nationalist movements, despite highly variegated sociocultural and political-economic contexts of production. During the late nineteenth and early twentieth centuries, these family resemblances included the incipient formation of the tie between nationhood and statehood; the emergence of the idea of territorial nationality and formal juridical sovereignty; the articulation of conceptions of a common territory, history, culture, and economy as the "frontier signs" of a modern nation;[29] a novel emphasis on a territorial correspondence between people, culture, economy, and state; ritualized claims of a shared past and a linear, developmentalist conception of the future; and the concept of "direct membership," according to which individuals were understood as formally, if not substantively, equivalent within a national collective.[30]

In order to deepen our understanding of the historically specific "family resemblances" between nationalist movements without sacrificing their particular, contingent, and local contours, this study emphasizes the dynamic affiliation between Indian nationalism and the wider historical-geographical field of its constitution. I employ the term *field* in both a spatiotemporal and organizational sense. Three further specifications are necessary here. First, the term *historical-geographical field*, as used in this work, refers to the multiform, differentiated, and profoundly uneven global space-time engendered by the deepening and widening of colonial territorial and capitalist expansion during the last third of the nineteenth century. Second, this field was an arena of both material and symbolic struggles. A particularly remarkable aspect of this field was the transposition of a range of modern social forms (territorial states, nation form), ideologies (developmentalism, imperialism, nationalism), and categories (national economy, national space) across regional contexts in tandem with the growing discursive overlap of nationalist discourses. And third, this field was defined by structured interdependencies insofar as the reproduction of particular imperial nation-states, colonial formations, and nationalist movements came to rest on the complex, radically relational dynamics of the field as a whole.[31] It was in this specific global field, as elaborated in the chapters that follow, that the nation form came to be viewed as promising an institutional mediation between the global (the world economy and the interstate system) and the local (the internal lines of difference) in both a structural and discursive sense. Against the perceived deterritorializing force of processes of global restructuring, discourses of Indian nationhood presented the nation as historically continuous, spatially bounded, and internally homogenous. The nation was increasingly figured, although not precisely lived, by nationalists in colonial India as elsewhere as a "still point in a turning world."[32]

A focus on the historically constituted family resemblances among nationalist movements and the dynamics of specific global fields is crucial for overcoming the embedded problem of methodological nationalism. As noted some pages earlier, the problem of methodological nationalism has shaped the specific literature on Indian nationalism. It has also imbued the wider and highly sophisticated literature on nationalism. It informs even self-consciously social-constructionist approaches that have sought to disassemble the so-called myths that surround nationalism, especially claims of an ancient origin, a linear, continuous, organic tradition, and a homogenous, enclosed national people. Paradoxically, it informs even those works on nationalism that have explored the territoriality of national imaginings, emphasizing the symbolic modalities through which national boundaries anchor difference from without and identity within an imagined national community.[33] Recent works on the territorial dimensions of nationalism have elaborated the role of cartographic mappings and iconic representations of national territory,[34] the generalization of modern geographic and archaeological discourses,[35] and the discursive formation of culturally delimited frontiers in forging an identity between place and people.[36]

Yet despite significant differences in conceptual orientation and interpretation, common to these analyses is a focus on the discursive effects and meaning of national territory and the narrowing of the concept of national space to that of metaphor or physical territory. Recent works on national territoriality have deepened our understanding of the representational practices, which help establish an identity, however uneven and contested, between a particular place and people; but more often than not, they have focused one-sidedly on the circulation and effects of particular representational artifacts (e.g., maps, print media) and geographical discourses of national territory. Indeed, with few exceptions, the analytical concept of national space continues to be treated, in both historical and sociological works, either in metaphoric terms or as a self-evident reference to physical-geographical terrain.[37]

In contrast, the category of space, as employed in this work, owes its broad conceptual coordinates to the work of the social philosopher Henri Lefebvre and recent debates in critical geography that have emphasized the material production of space, scale, and place. I conceive of space as a dynamic social product and as a constitutive dimension of social relations. Against conceptions of space as a pregiven container or physical-geographical location of social relations and representational perspectives of space as an ontological horizon or discursive effect, I follow Lefebvre's account of social space as at once the locus, medium, and outcome of complex, superimposed social relations that are always already also temporal.[38]

Works that focus on the representational poetics of national territory without considering the production of national space, sidestep several questions central to an understanding of nationalism. Which social processes and historical transformations made possible understandings of territory, economy, and history as fundamental signs of nationhood? Why is the nationalist preoccupation with societal homogenization—the unification of a people, economy, and culture—articulated with direct reference to a national-territorial whole as opposed to other spatial scales and forms? How does the spatiotemporal form of the nation-state differ from other modern state-territorial forms such as the colonial state? What is the historical specificity of such conceptions—in both social-scientific and lay discourse—as a national space and economy? What historical processes made possible the constitution and global articulation of a political-economic space, designated as national by collective actors, and organized in terms of an inside and outside? How do we account for the remarkable convergence, across regional contexts and among disparate nationalist movements, of the interlinked themes of spatial, cultural, and economic closure and the demand for a spatial coincidence between people, economy, culture, and state? In sum, how do we account for the ideological and "institutional materiality" of the nation as a global sociospatial *form?*[39]

These questions are inseparably epistemological and historical. They cluster around the distinctive spatiotemporal, institutional, and ideological *form* of the modern nation.[40] None of these questions can be adequately addressed unless we cast aside the tendency to presuppose the nation form and delimit the spatial referents of our analyses of nationalist movements to particular national boundaries. In excising scales of analysis other than the national and the local, accounts of nationalism presuppose precisely what must be accounted for, namely, the historical constitution of the nation form as a distinct scale of socioeconomic institutions, everyday practices, ideologies, aesthetics, and affective identification. The making of particular national spaces in the late colonial era—rather than physical-territorial boundaries or metaphorical geographies—only becomes intelligible through a focus on the differentiated, multiscalar, and multitemporal historical geography of colonial and capitalist expansion and the consolidation of the interstate system.[41]

Studies of nationalism that fail to explore the production of the spatiotemporal matrix of the nation form remain hostage to the reifying assumptions of nationalist discourse. In effect, such works treat what Rogers Brubaker calls nationalist "categories of practice" as "categories of analysis."[42] Methodological nationalism is part of a broader nation-state centric bias. Nation-state centric frameworks—the conflation of society and nation-state, the exaggerated privilege accorded to the national scale as a unit of analysis—are an entrenched legacy, as various works have argued, of late-nineteenth-century sociological and philosophical paradigms.[43] Dominant methodological protocols have reinforced this equation of society with the boundaries established by modern nation-states, thereby begging questions of the historical production of national space. This internalist schema masks the ways superimposed local, regional, and global processes help structure the national scale as a distinct, though not exclusive, site of social relations, economic processes, and affective solidarity. Because of the just sketched internalist and methodological nationalist bias—the conflation of society and state-territorial boundaries, operative conceptions of spatial closure, and the conflation of nationalist categories of practice as analytical categories—society, territory, and economy have long been conceived, especially in the orthodox social sciences, as spatially coincident and as self-evidently national.

The interpenetration of nationalist categories of thought and social-scientific analyses is not just an intellectual mistake. The reification of the nation form—and the presumed territorial coincidence between national economies, national states, and national societies—is a social process. The persistent overlap between nationalist categories and social-scientific analyses is rooted in and reinforced by the routine practices and institutions of the modern nation form; by the organization of the interstate system as a series of mutually exclusive, formally similar, bounded nation-states; and by the pervasively institutionalized tie between nationhood and statehood.

I suggest here that the taken-for-granted character of nationalist categories of practice attests to the status of the nation form as a paradigmatic "deep structure" in three interlinked respects.[44] First, the nation form underlies and has spawned a range of practices, institutions, and meanings that structures everyday life. Examples include the practices, meanings, and in-

stitutions associated with national economies (regimes of economic planning, national taxation and welfare systems, national currencies, tariffs, import quotas, national banks, national debts, and the like); national cultural
fields (standardized languages, educational institutes, museums, the sys-
tematization of expressive and folk traditions, national public spheres and
literary traditions); the regulation of cultural and political belonging on a
national scale (citizenship, passports, borders); and national built environments (national capitals, memorials) that serve as the territorial locus of
state-mediated collective memory and commemoration. Second, the status
of the nation form as an enduring "deep structure" derives not only from the
fact that it has been, from the mid-twentieth century, the dominant political
framework on a global scale, but in the ways nationalist categories of understanding permeate everyday interpretive frames, classificatory schemes,
and social practices. Third, the depth and durability of the nation form stem
from the fact that many of the practices, institutions, and conceptual categories associated with it have become second nature, that is, they have acquired a self-evident facticity. It is precisely because of the intrinsic ties between processes of nationalization and naturalization that the conflation of
nationalist categories of practice as analytical categories represents more
than just a problem of essentialism. In order to move beyond the horizon of
the nation form, we need to reconstruct the "historical labour of dehistori-
cization" that has enshrined the nation form as natural, has authorized the
incarceration of multiscalar processes within state-delimited territorial
boundaries, and has engendered an entrenched nation-state centric bias.[45]
Rather than presupposing such nationalist categories of practice as a national economy and a national space, we need to provide a sociohistorical
account of their constitution.

The chapters that follow extend and concretize the excursion begun here
into the epistemological issues raised by nationalism, specifying in historical
practice the complex entanglement between colonialism, Indian nationalism, and the formation of an uneven, differentiated, and contradictory
global space-time. To avoid the trap of methodological nationalism, this
study explores the complex links between the production of conceptions of
India as a bounded national space and economy and the global field of the
late nineteenth and early twentieth centuries. Can we account for the
specificity of anticolonial nationalism within an analytical framework that
emphasizes the dynamics of global fields, historically constituted family resemblances among nationalist movements, and the systemic dimensions of
the nation form? It is to this question, and related issues that surround it,
that I now turn.

THE PROBLEMATIC OF ANTICOLONIAL NATIONALISM

My analysis of anticolonial nationalism at once builds on and departs from the dominant historiographical narrative on Indian nationalism associated with the post-Gramscian turn in subaltern studies. Taken as a whole, subalternist historians have wrought a profound transformation in the historiography on colonialism, anticolonial nationalism, and modernity both within and beyond the field of South Asian history.[46] From the moment of its emergence in the early 1980s, the subaltern studies collective has enlarged our sense of the political by eschewing narrowly institutional and formalistic conceptions of political forms, subjectivities, and struggles that structure dominant strands of modern historical thought. In their effort to re-presence, rescue, and redeem subaltern subjects as more than just the invisible watermarks that haunt the colonial archive, subalternist historians have forged fresh textual and conceptual techniques for re-reading the colonial archive against the grain. In so doing, they have sharpened our sense of the multiple violations — epistemological and sociopolitical — effected by colonialism on subaltern social groups, deepened our understanding of the multifarious agency of the colonized, and have underscored the limits of ideal-typical and teleological understandings of modernity in grasping the sociocultural dynamics of colonized societies.

These productive interventions have been especially apparent in the work of Partha Chatterjee. His highly acclaimed studies of anticolonial nationalism have presented a profound challenge to both the hagiography of Indian nationalism authorized by the postcolonial Indian state and the reductionism of dominant approaches to anticolonial nationalism in the Western academy. No study of anticolonial nationalism, much less Indian nationalism, can overlook the conceptual ingenuity and consistently ethical impulse of Chatterjee's widely influential studies. Indeed, many of the thematic and analytical concerns that have animated analyses of anticolonial nationalism in recent decades, including the present study, owe their inspiration to his brilliant 1986 work, *Nationalist Thought and the Colonial World*. In this work, Chatterjee refocused attention on the dialectical relationship between colonialism and nationalism, emphasizing the unresolved epistemological tensions that beset anticolonial nationalism.

His analysis lambasted both sociological determinist accounts of anticolonial nationalism as flawed replicas of European models and normatively conceived renderings of it as a dangerous problem in the world at large.[47] Taking as his object of analysis the inner tensions of anticolonial nationalism, Chatterjee sought to explain how and why Indian nationalism legitimized its claims of cultural particularity within the terms of a universalistic postenlightenment discourse that was indissolubly tied to colonial domination. He argued "that there is . . . an inherent contradictoriness in nationalist thinking, because it reasons within a framework of knowledge whose representational structure corresponds to the very structure of colonial power nationalist thought seeks to repudiate" (38). Chatterjee identifies postenlightenment universalistic epistemologies as the very substance of colonial domination. From this perspective, in order for anticolonial nationalism to be authentically anticolonial it would have had to liberate itself from postenlightenment rationalistic frameworks of thought or the "cunning of reason." Its relationship to colonial discourse would have had to take the form of a determinate negation. But therein lay the rub. Chatterjee claims in no uncertain terms that despite liberal-rationalist assertions, "the Cunning of reason has not met its match in nationalism. On the contrary, it has seduced, apprehended and imprisoned it: this is what this book is about" (17).

Starting from this arresting, if politically bleak, premise, Chatterjee narrates the relationship between the colonial "cunning of reason" and nationalism as a tragedy in an almost classical sense. His analysis underscores the "fatal" failure of Indian nationalism in general and such nationalists as Jawaharlal Nehru in particular to think beyond the horizon of colonial discourse. This failure is what Chatterjee calls the "blocked dialectic" between nationalism and colonialism (169). The indelible stain of colonial discourse imparted, he argues, a particular social and ideological cast to the transition from the colonial to the postcolonial national state in India. Indian nationalism established and sought the nationalization of the colonial state without attempting a substantive transformation of its administrative, juridical, pedagogical, and institutional structure, and without mounting a radical challenge to existing class configurations. Although bourgeois nationalists, from Gandhi onward, found it necessary to mobilize the largest popular element of the colonized — the peasants — against the colonial state, they did so without handing over effective sovereignty to those in whose name they spoke. Thus, rather than establishing a form of universality grounded within the national-popular (i.e., the peasantry), the profoundly statist and reformist orientation of bourgeois Indian nationalism merely reproduced the global union between "Reason and capital" and authorized the continued marginalization of subaltern social groups in the postcolonial national era (168).

Chatterjee's analysis of the failure of Indian nationalism to wrest free of the hegemony of colonial discourse, and by extension of postenlightenment universalistic epistemologies, represented a political intervention in an unhappy present. Motivated by an acute unease with the inequities of the contemporary Indian nation-state, *Nationalist Thought and the Colonial World* is both an argument for and an example of a critical history of nationalism. Chatterjee's narrative of the "blocked dialectic" between colonialism and nationalism brought home, in both an analytical and political sense, the enduring continuities between colonial and national forms of domination.[48] This keenly felt indictment of Indian nationalism bears more than a passing resemblance, in this respect, to Frantz Fanon's prophetic gloom about the social consequences of the "sterile formalism" of bourgeois nationalism in colonized worlds.[49]

There is, however, a central tension within Chatterjee's analysis of anticolonial nationalism. On the one hand, he locates the contradictions of nationalism in terms of the hegemony of postenlightenment universalistic epistemologies that are seen as constitutive of colonial domination. Yet he criticizes specific nationalists for remaining within the hegemonic sway of colonial/postenlightenment discourse. Such a framework of analysis presupposes, without accounting for, the possibility that we can think ourselves outside of the dialectic of universality and particularity that structures the doubled character of the modern nation form. By identifying the problem of nationalism only in terms of the formal constraints of its discursive content, Chatterjee overlooks the wider sociohistorical and historical-geographical context of its production. His reading of the "logical sequence in the evolution" of nationalism's "ideological structure" as moments within a "blocked dialectic" does not differentiate between a logical, deductive sense of necessity (e.g., certain premises have strict logical entailments) and a nondeterministic, historically specific conception of necessity.[50] The problem, I suggest, consists in a one-sided formalistic reading of the tensions of anticolonial nationalism. By analyzing the inner tensions of nationalism only in relation to a reified conception of postenlightenment epistemologies, his account ignores the ways in which the contradictions of anticolonial nationalism were embedded within a specific social and historical configuration. Such a narrowly discursivist reading of anticolonial nationalism ultimately renders arbitrary the internal tensions of nationalism. For they are conceived as a discursive effect of the hegemony of European/colonial frameworks of thought rather than as socially embedded within the contradictions of the late colonial era.[51]

Chatterjee's later work, *The Nation and Its Fragments*, which signaled a broader shift within subaltern studies from Gramscian to Foucauldian frameworks, attempts to undo the theoretical impasse of the "blocked dialectic" between colonialism and nationalism that his earlier work presented. In this work, Chatterjee locates the emergence of Indian nationalism within an "inner spiritual" realm that bears an ambiguous relationship at best to what he calls a "material" colonial domain.[52] The exact relationship between colonialism and nationalism is left ambiguous because there is a slippage in Chatterjee's work between an ontological claim about the existence of separate material/colonial and spiritual/indigenous domains and an analysis of this opposition in terms of the conceptual idioms and performative self-fashioning of colonized elites against colonial rule. Whereas his first work on nationalism castigated Indian nationalists for remaining within the framework of colonial discourse, his second work posits a pure, autonomous, "spiritual" domain apparently untrammeled by colonialism and capitalism. Although this might appear to cleanse anticolonial nationalism from the stigmata of its "derivative" character as posited in his first work, it does so only at considerable conceptual expense. Chatterjee's second work tends to reify an indigenous domain as the repository of a pure difference. But there are good empirical and conceptual reasons to question the claim of a static and pure indigenous sphere untouched by colonial and capitalist transformations. Chatterjee's theory of anticolonial nationalism fails to take into account fully the contradictory re-articulations and qualitative reconstitutions of social practices and imaginaries during the late colonial era.

In Chatterjee's schema, however, lies the basis for a more historically specific approach to anticolonial nationalism. In a striking passage, which contravenes the overarching thrust of his argument, Chatterjee asserts:

> If there is one great moment that turns the provincial thought of Europe to universal philosophy, the parochial history of Europe to universal history, it is the moment of capital—capital that is global in its territorial reach and universal in its conceptual domain. It is the narrative of capital that can turn the violence of mercantilist trade, war, genocide, conquest and colonialism into a story of universal progress, development, modernization, and freedom. (235)

An acknowledgment of the imbrication of modes of colonial domination and forms of anticolonial nationalism within the global history of capitalism poses a major methodological challenge. This recognition would make it impossible to restrict analysis to discursive domains divorced from structuring social practices and socioinstitutional contexts. It challenges conceptions of sociospatial categories and forms (colonial/material versus indigenous/spiritual) as self-enclosed, hermetically sealed units. Chatterjee, however, only gestures toward this alternate approach; it does not inform his larger argument. Instead, his analysis tends toward an embrace of a particularistic difference (variously coded as an "inner sphere," "spiritual domain," and a logic of community grounded in the vernacular imagination of *jati*) conceived as outside the historically constituted field of colonial sociospatial relations.

Positioned against various modes of "elitist historiography" in the South Asian context and Eurocentric epistemologies in the Western academy, the subaltern studies project of rendering tangible the uneasy coexistence of historically constituted forms of difference signifies a vital political intervention in the contentious field of knowledge production. An emphasis on the specificity of colonial and postcolonial societies represents a crucial corrective over accounts insufficiently attentive to or straightforwardly contemptuous of difference. Yet attention to historical and cultural particularity does not require the strong claim of a radical, pregiven, or static field of difference. In the last decade, there has been a discernible proliferation of claims of an incommensurable "difference" registered in the shifting categorical fortunes of the term *subaltern* that has long lost its initial Gramscian sociohistorical referent and increasingly stands in as a sign of untranslatable alterity and incommensurability as such.[53] Yet such claims not only risk a general inaudibility in political terms but are ultimately unintelligible even to themselves. The subaltern studies collective has sought to revise "elitist historiography" from what Gyan Prakash has called the "place of 'otherness.'"[54] However, many subalternist historians either explicitly assert or presume that forms of sociocultural difference and the otherness of the "other" were pregiven rather than a dialectical product of the protracted encounter between colonialism and received practices, subjectivities, and categories of understanding. Instead of either presupposing an autonomous sociocultural domain exempt from colonial and capitalist mediation or positing indigenous practices as untranslatable in any but local terms, this study argues that colonial and nationalist forms, although distinguishable, were not separable. They were, I propose, coproduced within a common, if asymmetrically structured, social field. To intimate otherwise would be to flatten the dialectical relationship between identity and difference that underwrote the contentious process of translation and, more precisely, the transformation of received worlds of value and meaning in the colonial era.

Anticolonial nationalism cannot be rendered intelligible as a particular instance of a hegemonic Euro-American social form or as an autonomous, indigenous domain, much less as an instance of a distinct "Indian modernity."[55] To do so either abstracts analysis from the complexity of modern colonialism or posits a separation between colonial and so-called indigenous domains that is belied by their intimate interlinking in practice. What is more, it presupposes precisely what must be accounted for, that is, the sociohistorical constitution of notions of India as a bounded national space and economy and nationalist claims that India after colonial rule would exemplify and fashion a distinctive form of modernity. In contrast, this work argues that the ideologies and practices of anticolonial nationalism were forged within rather than outside the contradictory interstices of colonial practices. The contradictory form of colonial practices—the tension between its simultaneously homogenizing and differentiating character—in tandem with key global developments made possible the reconfiguration of colonial space as national space. The nationalist critique of colonialism, the emergence of notions of India as a bounded nation, and *swadeshi* conceptions of a distinct Indian modernity were rooted within rather than outside the experiential and structural contradictions of colonial domination.

An exclusive focus on the particular, local, and singular aspects of nationalism cloaks the constitutive force of global processes in the making of local and regional worlds. A one-sided emphasis on the cultural autonomy and radical difference of anticolonial nationalisms threatens to render inaudible the testimonies of late-nineteenth-century liberal nationalists such as Mahadev Govind Ranade, Dadabhai Naoroji, Romesh Chunder Dutt, and Radhakamal Mukherjee as well as later radical critics of empire. Despite differences in conceptual and political emphases, late-nineteenth-century Indian nationalists as well as such twentieth-century critics of empire as M. N. Roy, Frantz Fanon, C. L. R. James, and Amilcar Cabral, among others, sought not just to recover, much less simply celebrate, a realm of cultural difference but sought rather to overcome the differentiating effects of colonial capitalism. These critics of empire voiced a profound impatience with both sociosymbolic practices of particularization and the structured inequalities endemic to colonial worlds. Yet many of them also articulated a deeply held faith in the universalistic promise that sovereign nationhood, underwritten by a self-sufficient industrial-economic complex and practices of sociocultural homogenization, was supposed to deliver. Anticolonial nationalist thought and practice were born and borne across a single, if unequal, global space. It would be an empirical and conceptual mistake, then, to confine the cognitive map of anticolonial nationalists to the proximate geographical boundaries of colonial India. It would be even more problematic to claim that the world of anticolonial thought and practice was forged in a space of cultural autonomy that was outside of, beyond, or untouched by colonial and capitalist transformations. It is precisely because the imaginative geography of anticolonial nationalism was irreducibly material and global—in both its origins and scope—that this study charts the multiple contexts of its production.

A HISTORICAL-GEOGRAPHICAL PERSPECTIVE

While focused on the intimacies between colonialism and nationalism in a specific regional and historical context, this book sets its theoretical sights more widely in three interlinked respects. First, and at the most fundamental level, this work enlarges and deepens the historical and geographical referents of dominant approaches to the colonial state and anticolonial nationalism. Against internalist approaches to the colonial state that ignore the transnational coordinates of state practices, I argue that, in the late nineteenth and early twentieth centuries, colonial practices of spatial and political-economic restructuring were indissolubly tied to broader processes of global restructuring whose pervasive if uneven effects were articulated on multiple spatial scales. Although this study contains a strong plea for heeding what one historical sociologist has called "big structures, large processes, huge comparisons," it attempts to show that this line of interpretation need not return us to the realm of sociological metanarratives characterized by a disregard for the everyday negotiations, expressive actions, and creative agency of modern subjects.[56] Quite the converse; by recasting the relationship between colonialism and anticolonialism in historical-geographical terms, this work seeks not only to emphasize the dense interleave between local, regional, and global processes but to render palpable the mutual constitution of forms of objectivity and subjectivity, of material transformations and shifts in meaning. By placing the making of colonial space and the spatiotemporal matrix of nationalist imaginings in a single analytical field, this work illuminates the dialectical relationship between the social production of particular political-economic spaces and the formation of such taken-for-granted categories as a national space and economy.

Second, this book is intended not only as a history of the radically relational production of particular spaces (colonial and national, political-economic and cultural) and spatial categories (national space and national economy) but also as a spatialized history, that is, one that takes space as well as time seriously. The chapters that follow mobilize recent debates within sociospatial theory, studies of nationalism, and historical political economy toward a reading of global space-time as radically relational (i.e., defined by systemic interdependencies between its various parts), multispatial (i.e., composed of distinct yet entwined spaces and scales), multitemporal (constituted by different temporalities and time horizons), and endemically uneven (i.e., constituted by the structurally engendered process of uneven development).[57] In so doing, this study reframes the vexed question of modernity and difference that has animated historiographical debates on colonial South Asia and driven recent efforts to rethink global history outside modernization, Eurocentric, and historicist paradigms.[58] My analysis departs from the grand historiographical narrative, which in liberal historiography, Weberian historical sociology, as well as in the dominant traditions of Western Marxism has tended to ignore the global formation of capitalist modernity by delimiting it within Euro-American parameters. The interpretation of modernity as an autochthonous formation that developed within particular self-enclosed regions, and subsequently extended outward to so-called late developers forever doomed to play a game of catch-up not of their making, pervades both modernization and Marxian accounts of transitions to capitalism in non-Western societies. Within this framework, the world placed outside Euro-America seems destined to replicate processes that have always already occurred elsewhere and against which they can only signify, as Dipesh Chakrabarty argues in his forceful critique of historicism, insufficiency, belatedness, and lack.[59] Such narratives have tended to assume, in Harry Harootunian's apt formulation, that "true time was kept by the modern West" and that colonized societies and so-called late developers exist in a "temporality different from the modern."[60] The denial of the spatial and temporal simultaneity of colonized and so-called peripheral spaces, within both Marxian and modernization approaches, stems from unexamined normative conceptions of capitalism as a unilinear, evolutionary, and noncontradictory process. This has been reinforced, as Fernando Coronil suggests, by the prevalent territorialization of modernity as an intra Euro-American process and its figuration as the "offspring of a self-propelled West."[61] Such cognitive mappings have long authorized conceptions of capitalism as impinging on so-called peripheral societies and territorial statehood from some putative outside rather than constituting them from within.

An emphasis on what Henri Lefebvre calls the "superimposition and interpenetration" of social spaces within a single, yet uneven, global space-time unsettles narratives that delimit the modern within a particular geographical arena and that posit global capitalism as a process external to so-called peripheral states and societies.[62] It does so, however, without claiming the existence of a privileged point outside, whether in the form of inner spiritual sphere, nontranslatable alterity, irreducible difference, or an "alternative modernity," as advanced in recent works.[63] Such conceptions unwittingly preserve, even as they attempt to overcome, the ideological coding of the Anglo-European world as the hegemonic site of a noncontradictory and undifferentiated modernity.[64]

Third, the following analysis of colonialism departs more generally from ascendant frameworks in South Asian historiography and colonial studies that have tended to focus almost exclusively on the discursive formation of colonial governmentality, thereby bracketing questions of the transnational and structural determinants of colonial domination.[65] Contemporary colonial studies has been marked by a pronounced shift away from an older fixation on uneven development, structured dependencies, center–periphery relations, and material exploitation toward a focus on colonial dialogics, forms of representational violence, cultural hybridity, and symbolic politics. The move away from economistic readings of colonialism has immeasurably enriched our understanding of the sociocultural complexities of colonial societies. Yet, at the same moment, it is important to recall that the conceptual template of uneven development, structured dependencies, and the like articulated the lived experience of colonial unevenness and forms of domination for many colonial subjects. The normative and analytical power of these frameworks derives, in part, from the improvisational work and practice of many anticolonial intellectuals who grappled with the complex historical geographies of colonial domination by forging conceptually innovative and concretely political projects that were resolutely materialist and translocal in texture and scope. In pointed contrast, the recent course of colonial studies attests to the growing analytical dominance of what Jean and John Comaroff aptly name the "voice-over of a postcolonial discourse" that has been beset by the conviction that attention to large-scale socioeconomic processes and the material underpinnings of colonialism serves only to legitimate Euro-American imperial narratives.[66] Against the representational glare of this discursivist turn, this study aims to show that a focus on the historical geography of capital does not require us to reify the economy, to treat it as an ontological given, as a self-regulating, autonomous sphere, or as determinative in some dreaded last instance.[67]

The discrediting of the teleological and Eurocentric axioms of many iterations of dependency frameworks, world-systems theory, and structural Marxism need not sink us into the paradoxical postmodern predicament of excising the socioeconomic coordinates of colonialism. Such attempts not only fly in the face of the lived testimonies of anticolonial intellectuals and activists but overlook the dialectical relationship between colonialism and capitalism as global social forms. They paradoxically have acquired ascendancy in a historical moment—saturated as it is by the "global babble" of an emergent neoliberal order—that is uncannily similar to that of the late-nineteenth and early-twentieth-century colonial era.[68]

Colonial and capitalist expansion were epochal historical processes: literally and symbolically world making in scope and scale. But it would be a mistake to attribute a single logic, emanating from on high, to colonialism and to narrate the progression of capitalism as "empty, homogenous time," as a linear pathway to an already known social landscape peopled with cultural dupes in a bleak, and fantastically scholastic, Althusserian world of overdetermination.[69] The lived complexity of unevenness that typified colonial worlds cannot be grasped through a linear, bottom-line causal narrative comprised of single determinations. In order to do justice to the proliferation of spatialities and temporalities that defined colonial fields, this work emphasizes the tangled causal relationships between political-economic and sociocultural processes on multiple spatial scales. The chapters that follow aim to show how, and to what multifarious effects, the contradictions of colonial practices, in tandem with wider socioeconomic dynamics, produced a world that was at once structurally interdependent, fragmented, and endemically uneven.

CHAPTER ONE

GEOGRAPHIES OF STATE TRANSFORMATION: THE PRODUCTION OF COLONIAL STATE SPACE

T he unprecedented expansion of the scope and scale of the colonial state followed the brutal repression of the rebellion of 1857–58 and the formal incorporation of colonial India into the British Crown. The post-1857 colonial regime was the locus of a spectacular restructuring of political-economic, administrative, and military structures that wrought a profound transformation in the spatiotemporal matrices of everyday categories of understanding, political-economic institutions, and modalities of state power. Committed to spreading its authority evenly throughout the territory, to filling up the geographic space of colonial India with its authoritative presence, the post-1857 colonial regime made territorially comprehensive claims to rule. Territorial consolidation involved the attempted monopolization of regulatory powers by an increasingly centralized apparatus, the development of an elaborate, hierarchical bureaucracy that surveyed, mapped, and measured both land and people, the deepening and widening of the administrative and military reach of the state, and a determined reinvestment in epistemic modalities of rule.

Bernard Cohn — the historian par excellence of the political imaginary of the colonial absurd — has elaborated a central paradox constitutive of the post-1857 colonial regime. The officially enunciated policy of nonintervention in local social practices, expressed in Queen Victoria's proclamation of 1858, was belied by the development of institutions and practices with an invasive, tentacular reach. The post-1857 colonial regime simultaneously sought to modernize the social body and keep intact its imagined traditional lineaments, what Victoria identified as its "ancient rights, usages, and customs."[1] Following Bernard Cohn's pioneering analysis of the co-constitution of a distinctive "colonial sociology of knowledge" and modalities of rule, historians and historical anthropologists, working within diverse conceptual frameworks, have taken as their point of departure the gap between the stated policy of preserving existent practices and the proliferation of disciplinary regimens that profoundly reworked sociocultural practices in multiple arenas.[2] The focus on colonial epistemologies and modalities of rule has more recently found fresh impetus in the burgeoning literature on colonial governmentality that has animated recent historiographical debates on late colonial India.[3] My analysis of the making of a distinctive colonial state space in the post-1857 era builds on the many insights proffered by these intersecting literatures, especially the dense articulation between colonial sociologies of knowledge and modalities of rule. Yet it also departs from the currently ascendant literature on colonial governmentality in two interlinked respects. First, it explicitly focuses on the structural contradictions rather than discursive tensions of colonial practices and political rationality by specifying the dynamic relationship between the political-economic and epistemological coordinates of late colonial rule. Second, my account breaks from the "internalist" focus of the literature on colonial governmentality that neglects the global field of spatial-economic restructuring within and against which novel institutional and disciplinary forms took shape in late colonial India. By broadening the spatial referents of dominant approaches to the colonial state and economy, I attempt to specify the historicity of colonial space and show the "interpenetration and superimposition" of apparently distinct spaces (imperial and national, political-economic and ideological) within a specific global field.[4]

Building on Henri Lefebvre's conception of the state as a "spatial framework" of power (281), I delineate in this chapter the complex ensemble of institutions, practices, and ideologies that marked and made colonial state space and underwrote the transition from mercantile to territorial colonialism. The making of a colonial state space was inseparably part of a broader imperial *scale*-making project, one that sought to secure and maintain a Britain-centered and globe-spanning imperial economy.[5] The territorialization of colonial state power in the decades after 1857 was premised on, enabled by, and constitutive of the expansion of a Britain-centered global economy. I take as my point of departure an often-noted yet underdeveloped (in both a historiographical and theoretical register) aspect of the late colonial state: the fact that its spatiality literally and institutionally exceeded state territorial boundaries. A constitutive aspect of the colonial state lay in the institutionalization of a disjuncture between political and economic structures, between the space of the production and the realization of value. By exploring the making of colonial political-economic space in a specific global field, I seek to specify the radically relational character of sociospatial formations and to historicize such categories as national and colonial, and internal, domestic versus external, international economy.

The analysis that follows emphasizes the internal relations between the territorialization of colonial state power in colonial India, the expansion of a Britain-centered global economy, and the initial consolidation and later unmaking of Britain's hegemony. To claim a historically specific internal relation between processes that have been either ignored or analyzed as distinct and autonomous does not reciprocally imply that either the Britain-centered global economy or colonial state space was a unitary formation. Indeed, a chief analytical burden of this chapter is to elucidate the ways in which both colonial state space and the Britain-centered global economy were multiplex and contradictory force-fields.

The first half of this chapter develops an analytical vocabulary attuned to the overlapping political imaginaries and material geographies that helped forge a distinctive colonial state space. Toward this end, I appropriate key concepts and categories from Henri Lefebvre's theorization of the production of an uneven and differentiated global space-time and the relationship between state and space. The second half of this chapter elaborates the organizing categories, ideologies, and institutions that forged a distinctive state space in the post-1857 period. I argue that the territorialization of colonial state power contained an immanent contradiction: the very practices that homogenized sociospatial relations also produced internal differentiation and fragmentation. The territorialization of colonial state power in the post-1857 period occurred initially under conditions of the expansion and consolidation of a Britain-centered global economy. However, the rise of nationalist, neomercantilist, and state-centric models of development in diverse regional contexts from the late 1870s challenged the self-evident status of a Britain-centered global system of financial and economic liberalism. The reconfiguration of political-economic space along self-consciously national developmentalist and statist principles, during the late 1870s and 1880s, not only entailed a crisis for Britain's global hegemony but made the contradictions of colonial practices both more apparent and acute. The concluding section of this chapter discusses the shifting forms and targets of colonial state practices in the context of the challenges posed to Britain's hegemony during the 1870s and 1880s by the intensification of interimperial conflict and the ascendancy of nationalist forms of territorial-economic regulation. The contradictory logic of colonial practices together with these global developments enabled, as subsequent chapters elaborate, the radical resignification of popular understandings of space, temporality, and economy.

THE PRODUCTION OF GLOBAL SPACE-TIME

We are confronted not by one social space but by many — indeed, by an unlimited multiplicity or uncountable set of social spaces. . . . No space disappears in the context of growth and development: the *worldwide does not abolish the local.* . . . Considered in isolation, such spaces are mere abstractions. As concrete abstractions, however, they attain their "real" existence by virtue of networks and pathways, by virtue of bunches or clusters of relationships. . . . *Social spaces interpenetrate one another and/or superimpose themselves upon one another.* They are not *things,* which have mutually limiting boundaries and which collide because of their contours.

—Henri Lefebvre, *The Production of Space,* 1978

In a densely philosophical work, *The Production of Space,* Henri Lefebvre opens with a wide-ranging critique of territorialist, ontological, and discursive conceptions of space. Against conceptions of space as a pregiven container, a physical-geographical location, a neutral backdrop of social relations, an ontological horizon, and a discursive effect, Lefebvre argues that space is a constitutive dimension of social relations, that it is at once a central "field of action" and "a basis for action."[6] This relational and processual conception of space resonates with sociotheoretical understandings of social structure as simultaneously the locus, medium, and product of social relations and collective agency.[7] Space, in this view, is not the static "container" of social relations, nor is it opposed to, much less ontologically privileged over, time and historicity. Rather, Lefebvre emphasizes the temporal dynamic of spatialization as a matrix of social relations and as an intrinsically historical phenomenon.

This account of space-as-process, of its social and historical embeddedness, fundamentally differs from narrowly representational and ontological perspectives. Lefebvre self-consciously differentiates his theory of social space from, for instance, Foucault's metaphorical and representational perspective. His account also challenges transhistorical conceptions of space whether in the form of Heidegger's phenomenological ontology or Durkheim's sociologization of Kantian categories in *The Elementary Forms of Religious Life,* where space and time are posited as basic categories of thought but in a way that elides their historical constitution.[8] Despite substantive differences, these perspectives bracket in common the sociohistorical production of space and the historical specificity of particular spatial practices, representations, and formations. Recent analyses of colonial and postcolonial space, much of them grounded in an explicitly Foucauldian perspective, have likewise elided the production of space in favor of an exclusive focus on spatial representations or conceptions of space as a discursive effect and site for the articulation of power *dispositifs*.[9] I turn to Lefebvre's account of modern spatiality here for the insights it provides into the uneven and differentiated character of global space, the reciprocal liaison between spatial practices and representations, and the dynamic relationship between the modern state and space.[10]

Of particular importance in this regard is Lefebvre's analysis of the space generated by the expansive and universalizing dynamic of capitalism, that is, "abstract, homogenous space." Akin to the commodified form of labor power, "abstract, homogenous space" has a formal, quantitative, measurable, and interchangeable quality; it is "produced and reproduced as reproducible."[11] The formation of a global abstract space, like its dialectical twin, "empty, homogenous time," hinges on specific material and ideological foundations that condition its appearance as abstract and homogenous. There is a strong resonance between Lefebvre's emphasis on the appearance of space as abstract as a historically specific misrecognition rooted in the phenomenological experience of capitalism and Walter Benjamin's reading of "empty, homogenous time" as the utopian self-presentation of capital and associated teleological images of progress.[12] Lefebvre and Benjamin, in common, seek to embed the appearance of abstract homogenous time and space in social processes of reification and a specific experience of modern space-time wherein, as Lefebvre argues, the "conflicts and contradictions," that is, the "heterogeneity," of social space do not "appear as such."[13] Lefebvre's claim that ontological and representational understandings of space reproduce rather than challenge the ideological self-presentation of capitalism accords with Benjamin's critique of a traditional historiography that uncritically replicates the closed and evolutionary self-presentation of capital by ignoring the heterogeneous character of temporality.

More specifically, Lefebvre locates abstract space-time in the "capitalist trinity," that is, the production and circulation of land (rent), labor (wages), and capital (profits) and the generalization of form-determined capitalist social relations (282). On a concrete terrain, it is fashioned through the attempted imposition of a formally similar grid of property relations and property markets across diverse contexts through the aegis of a regulating state agency, and the statist mobilization of space whereby each states "maps out its own territory, stakes it out and signposts it" through the creation of juridical-political grids, territorialized administrative structures, built environments, and economic complexes (341–42, 278–82). Of particular importance to the issues central to this work is Lefebvre's characterization of modern capitalist space-time as simultaneously "global, fragmented and hierarchical" (282).

Lefebvre deploys the category "global" here not in a physical-territorial sense but in a qualitative sense. The making of a global space-time is not reducible to the physical-geographical expansion of capitalism alone. Rather it signifies the formation of relations of interdependence, as differentiated from external linkages or interconnections, between multiple spatial scales (e.g., local, regional, imperial) and temporalities (e.g., the multiple temporalities of everyday life, the different temporalities of capital accumulation, including short-term financial, medium-term industrial, and long-term infrastructural). The global whole becomes increasingly present, Lefebvre suggests, through internal relations at the "micro level," the "local and localizable," and the "sphere of everyday life" (366).[14] This conception of global space-time rejects the attribution of methodological and causal primacy to any one spatial scale in an a priori fashion (88). It marks a sharp departure, for instance, from world-system theory that privileges the global scale as causally determinative in the modern era. Lefebvre emphasizes that global space produces rather than subsumes, generates rather than negates, the local, regional, and national.

> The local does not disappear . . . it is never absorbed by the regional, national or even worldwide level. The national and regional take in innumerable "places"; national space embraces the regions; and world space does not merely subsume national space, but even precipitates the formation of national spaces through a remarkable process of fission. All these spaces, meanwhile, are traversed by myriad currents. The hypercomplexity of social space should now be apparent . . . [it] means that each fragment of space subjected to analysis masks not just one social relationship but a host of them. (88)

Lefebvre does not specify the "remarkable process of fission" that subtends the proliferation of multiple spatialities and temporalities within and against a global space of coexistence. However, the principle of the "interpenetration and superimposition of social spaces" suggests that the very appearance of national, regional, and local spaces as bounded and mutually exclusive depends on a dense network of overlapping, intertwined, and dynamic interrelations.

The "hypercomplexity" of global space-time and the radically relational character of spaces, as elaborated by Lefebvre, present a challenge to dominant contemporary analyses of "globalization" as a process of homogenization and to those that conceive global space as a homogenous unity. In contrast, Lefebvre suggests that global space is hierarchically organized and internally differentiated in the specific sense that the relations between particular spaces — metropole and colony, urban and rural, local and national and the like — are shot through with power inequalities and unevenness. By conceiving unevenness as constitutive of global space, this formulation counters approaches that conflate the structural tendency of capital toward homogenization with its actual historical realization. Such approaches reiterate, as Lefebvre observes, "extreme" forms of "reductionism," itself generated by the contradictions of capitalism, that entail the "reduction of time to space, the reduction of use value to exchange value, the reduction of objects to signs," the "movement of the dialectic" to a transhistorical "logic," and "social space to a purely formal mental space" (296). In contrast, he foregrounds the dialectic between the homogenizing orientation of capital and its uneven historical actualization:

> Abstract space is *not* homogenous; it simply has homogeneity as its goal, its orientation, its "lens." And, indeed it renders homogenous. But in itself it is multiform. . . . Thus to look upon abstract space as homogenous is to embrace a representation that takes the effect for the cause, and the goal for the reason why that goal is pursued. A representation which passes itself off as a *concept*, when it is merely a . . . mirage; and which instead of challenging, instead of refusing, merely *reflects*. (287)

A critical understanding of capital as not natural, unitary, or impelled by a unilinear logic demands equal attention to capitalism's own history, namely, its contradictory historical forms and the multiple space-times it generates.

A conception of capitalist space-time as a global, differentiated, and hierarchical totality also underscores the limits of the enduring conceptual grammar forged by Althusserian Marxism and its strong echoes in a range of self-understood poststructuralist perspectives, that is, the notion of distinct economic and non-economic spheres and levels of determination. The division of the social world into economic and non-economic spheres/levels is economistic not in the last instance but in the very first. By relegating capitalism to a distinct economic domain and focusing on the external rather than the internal relations between apparently distinct and mutually exclusive spheres of the "social," "political," and "economic," such perspectives reproduce the forms of reification associated with capitalism.[15] They not only frustrate attempts at developing genuinely transdisciplinary categories of analysis adequate to the task of grasping a differentiated global totality but obscure the lived interdisciplinarity of social life.

Finally, of particular importance to the issues at stake in this work is

Lefebvre's account of the role of the modern state in shaping social space, establishing the spatiotemporal matrices for everyday life, and naturalizing everyday state epistemologies. Echoing Max Weber's classic account of the state's monopolization of legitimate violence over a delimited political-geographical space, Lefebvre argues that the modern state is a "spatial framework" of power marked and made by the foundational violence it directs toward things and peoples in space.[16] His portrayal of the "fetishization of space in the service of the state" directs attention to the diverse modalities through which the modern state inscribes its authority in a continuous body of bounded territory and constructs specific spatiotemporal and institutional structures (21). These include the demarcation and mapping of boundaries; the appropriation and designation of natural resources (forest lands, oil, mines) as sovereign state space; the expansion and interpenetration of society by institutions such as the army, schools, bureaucracies with their distinct temporal rhythms and spatial practices; the formation of vast networks of communication and infrastructural complexes such as roads, railways, bridges, canals, post offices, and the like; forms of economic planning wherein the unit of development is delimited by state territorial boundaries; and the construction of capitals, monuments, and museums, which constitute places of collective, state-mediated memory and commemoration. Yet rather than a unitary, homogenous configuration, state space is shot through with contradictions. The contradictions internal to capitalism and the multiple ideologies, practices, and institutions that comprise state space continually beset, undermine, and constrain the attempted homogenization of state space and the naturalization of everyday state epistemologies. These include, but are not limited to, the contradiction between exchange-value and use-value, production and consumption, work and leisure, need and desire, dominant and dominated spaces, and that between the mobility of capital and the generation of value through the fixing of capital and geographies of allegiance within particular spaces.[17]

Lefebvre's theorization of the modern state as a "spatial framework" is explicitly elaborated in relation to the modern nation form as distinct from imperial formations or colonial states. However, it provides key insights for understanding the relational character of colonial state space and for elucidating both its similarities with and distinctions from national space, and its particular integration of violence and spectacle. It suggests, at the outset, that we neither can nor should incarcerate analyses of sociohistorical processes in the modern global era within fixed, preconstituted, a priori state territorial boundaries. Building on this methodological injunction, I conceive colonial state space and the imperial space economy as hierarchically interrelated, interlocking "spatial frameworks" of power. Rather than mutually exclusive, bounded entities, the imperial economy and colonial state space were both embedded within a single and profoundly uneven global space. The precise ensemble of practices and institutions that defined colonial state space only becomes intelligible, as I suggest later in the chapter, within and against this broader historical-geographical context.

Before turning to this specific question, I specify further some of the implications of Lefebvre's theorization for rethinking the late-nineteenth- and early-twentieth-century era. I suggest here that the emergence of what Lefebvre identifies as a global space-time cannot be understood apart from the late-nineteenth and early-twentieth-century context of the consolidation of a world market, imperial expansion, and interimperial conflict, and the institution of novel communication and infrastructural technologies. These developments were concurrent, interlinked phenomena that helped forge denser networks and interdependencies among societies on multiple spatial scales and fields. The making of a global space-time was a dialectical, contradictory, and doubled process. It was generated by and expressive of the simultaneous "deterritorialization" (the acceleration of what David Harvey has identified as "space-time compression") and "reterritorialization" (the production of relatively fixed sociospatial organizations from material infrastructures to state forms that enable the accelerated temporal circulation of capital) of multiple socioeconomic fields and cultural imaginaries.[18]

The production of a global space-time during this era was, in part, an expression of the universalizing drive of capitalism succinctly voiced in Marx's statement that "the tendency to create the world market is directly given in the concept of capital itself."[19] However, it did not mean, neither then nor now, the realization of a unified and homogenous globalized space-time. This was a consequence of both the internal contradictions within capitalism that impose structural limits on the homogeneity toward which the value form tends—extended commodification necessitates the increasing socialization of certain institutions and practices as evident, for instance, in the gendered severing of domestic versus value-producing labor—and the efficacy of historically diverse and multiple forms of resistance to capitalism. Lefebvre's claim that abstract space carries within itself the principle of its own negation echoes Marx's assertion of the historically doubled dynamic of capital. On the one hand, capital, as Marx argued, drives "beyond national barriers and prejudices as much as beyond nature worship, as well as all traditional, confined, complacent, encrusted satisfactions of present needs, and reproduction of old ways of life." Yet, as Marx continues, "from the fact that capital posits every such limit as a barrier and hence gets *ideally* beyond it, it does not by any means follow that it has *really* overcome it, and since, every such barrier contradicts its character, its production moves in contradictions which are constantly overcome but just as constantly posited." The internal contradictions of capitalism or the "barriers in its own nature" continually engender new forms of spatiotemporal difference (410). These forms of unevenness and distinctions are, as David Harvey insists, "actively reconstituted features" rather than "historical residuals" of an anterior space-time.[20] From this perspective, a central task concerns excavating, as Peter Osborne suggests, the nonfunctionalist "transformation and contradictory reintegration" of heterogeneous social and cultural forms (whose internal dynamics are framed by but not reducible to a capital logic) "to the destructuring with which the expansion of the value form threatens them."[21]

An emphasis on the production of an uneven global space-time departs from orthodox Marxian assumptions of the linear, homogenous progress of capital that carry, as Dipesh Chakrabarty argues, untenable historicist implications and that ignore at different levels of analysis, as Frederick Cooper shows, the internal tensions that beset historical forms of colonial capitalism.[22] Yet it also enables us to foreground the dynamic and contradictory historical geography of capitalism without insisting on an absolute opposition between what Chakrabarty names as "History 1" (universal logic of capital) and "History 2" (histories shaped by but outside the logic of capital).[23] A conception of global space-time as hierarchical and differentiated rather than unified and homogenous foregrounds the ongoing creation of unevenness (economic and cultural, spatial and temporal) as the internal supplement of the universalizing orientation of capital. It suggests that the universalizing dynamic of capital develops unevenly across space and time and that it actively generates new forms of sociospatial and sociocultural unevenness. From this perspective, History 2 represents an internal dimension of History 1, not an absolute outside that episodically interrupts the supposedly homogenous, linear progression of an abstract logic of capital as such. We need, then, to distinguish between the inflated, utopian self-presentation of capital as abstract and homogenous and the contradictions internal to historical capitalism that produce a global, differentiated, and hierarchical space-time.

AN IMPERIAL FORMATION

The last half of the nineteenth century was characterized by a radical restructuring of political, economic, and social space on a global scale. The spatial widening and deepening of the world economy along with colonial territorial expansion yoked together diverse communities, regions, and places into a complex space of coexistence and interdependence.[24] The interpenetration of socioeconomic processes, during this period, was part and parcel of the consolidation of Britain's global hegemony as defined by its welding together, as Giovanni Arrighi argues, of "territorialist and capitalist logics of power" on a historically novel worldwide scale.[25] In contrast with previous hegemonic formations, Britain was simultaneously the center of a global empire and a global economy.[26]

The constitution of a Britain-centered global economy (unlike the multicentric character of the contemporary global economy) and the attendant formation of a global space-time were rooted in colonial territorial expansion, the development of novel communication and transportation structures coupled with new systems of credit, corporate forms of organization, and technological and organizational innovations in production. These complex, interlinked formations helped constitute a densely interwoven network of connections and flows on a global scale. Before this period, the scope of Britain's economy, and therefore of the global economy, was limited. Between 1800 and 1830, international trade increased by a modest 30 percent, but between 1840 and 1860 it increased fivefold, and by 1870 tenfold.[27] By 1870, Britain produced half of the world's iron, coal, and lignite and manufactured half of the world's supply of cotton textiles. More generally, the volume of British industrial production was greater than that of the next "two powers [United States and Germany] combined."[28] The Britain-centered global economy was organized, to employ a key categorization of Lefebvre's, at once "territorially (in terms of flows and networks) and politically (in terms of centers and peripheries)."[29] The structure of global interdependencies and unevenness took the form of a specific international division of labor, one shaped by a Britain-centered world economy.

The expansion and reconstitution of the interstate system, under Britain's hegemony, was marked by the emergence of a novel perception of a world market that operated above and beyond the arena of interstate relations.[30] The conception of the economy as an ontologically distinct entity endowed with self-regulating powers was pervasively institutionalized in the practices and ideologies of the British imperial regime. The chief regulatory institutions of Britain's hegemony — the system of free-trade imperialism and the International Gold Standard — embodied conceptions of the economy as a self-regulating force beyond politics. This global regulatory order, shaped by the theories of such classical economists as Adam Smith and David Ricardo, articulated a robust faith in the capacity of an unfettered market to

affect the universal expansion of wealth. The core principles of classical exchange theory, the Ricardian law of comparative costs, assumed that all
states would in time benefit from trade. If for Adam Smith the pursuit of individual interests resulted in collective welfare, the pursuit of free trade
within classical economics was assumed to bring universal and uniform
benefits.[31] The envisioning of political-economic space in terms of universal
harmonies repressed the fact of uneven development and growing inequalities in favor of a quasi-sacral faith in eventual even growth.

In a manner uncannily akin to the planetary spread of neoliberal ideologies in recent decades, it was widely assumed that the efficiency of an unfettered market would enhance and expand wealth everywhere, or more
specifically, within Europe and North America. Britain's unilateral adoption
of free trade in the 1830s and 1840s created geographically expansive networks of financial and economic interdependencies that reinforced the
claim that the growth of Britain's imperial economy served not just particular but universal interests.[32] The historical geography of capitalism was, until the 1870s and 1880s, wrought by a set of institutions, practices, and ideas
that were inseparably tied to the consolidation of Britain's global hegemony,
and the expansion of the imperial space economy.

Within the hierarchical "ensemble of places, institutions, and functions,"
to borrow a phrase from Lefebvre, that comprised the global regulatory order of the British imperial regime, colonial India came to occupy a crucial
place in relation to military and infrastructural resources and the representational logic of an expansive imperial imaginary.[33] This dynamic and multidimensional relationship framed the specific spatial and institutional form
of the colonial state.

The Colonial Political Economy of Space

We are determined as long as the sun shines in heaven to hold India. Our national character, our commerce, demand it; and we have, one way or another, two hundred and
fifty millions of English capital fixed in the country.

—Lord Mayo, viceroy and governor-general of British India,
to Sir A. Buchanan, September 26, 1869

From 1858 until 1869, colonial India was the target for more than 21 percent of all British capital invested outside the United Kingdom and nearly
55 percent of all British capital invested in the empire as a whole. Of the
capital invested, 72 percent was in the transportation sector (mainly rail-

ways), a figure that represented nearly 94 percent of all British capital invested in this sector.[34] Both the India Office in London and the colonial state played central roles in securing, channeling, and regulating the conditions of what was the "largest single unit of international investment in the nineteenth century."[35] The unprecedented magnitude of the flow of capital to colonial India was set in the immediate context of the transfer of power from the East India Company to the British Crown.

The transfer of power from the East India Company to the post-1857 colonial state consolidated the shift, begun in the late 1830s, from mercantile to territorial colonialism. This transition was linked to a range of convergent processes, including the ascendancy of utilitarianism, the end of the East India Company's trade monopoly, and the formation of a political economy of empire within both popular and scholarly discourse.[36] From the late 1830s, the lineaments of a political economy of empire had begun to crystallize. Particularly influential in the constitution of this new imperial imaginary was the work of Edward Wakefield and his influence on Jeremy Bentham and so-called Benthamite radicals, including William Molesworth, Charles Buller, and John Stuart Mill.[37] What has been characterized as the mid-nineteenth-century "Benthamite ideology of colonialism" was grounded on Wakefield's advocacy of colonization based on the "expansion of the field of production" rather than "investitures in trade" (515). In a number of works, including *A Letter from Sydney* (1829), *England and America* (1833), and *The Art of* Colonization (1849), Wakefield refuted Say's law that general overproduction was impossible and thematized the recurrent problem of overproduction that drove down the rate of profit and spawned economic crises. In light of the "superabundance of capital," he urged the expansion of the "field of employment for capital and labour" (quoted at 515). Against Ricardian notions of production as only limited by the extent of capital, Wakefield argued that land was the "chief element of production" and the "field of employment for capital itself" (515–16). Territorial expansion and formal colonialism were seen, then, as a potential solution to the problem of over accumulation:

> The whole world is before you. Open new channels for the most productive employment of English capital. Let the English buy bread from every people that has bread to spare. Make England, for all that is produced by steam, the workshop of the world. If, after this, there be capital and people to spare, imitate the ancient Greeks; take a lesson from the Americans, who as their capital and population increase, find room for both by means of colonization. (517)

By employing surplus capital and labor and increasing rates of profits and wages at home, territorial colonialism would abate the "bad blood between the two classes" and "prove that masters and servants have one and the same interest" (518).

This thesis found strong echoes in John Stuart Mill's highly influential *Principles of Political Economy* (1848) as well as in works by Robert Torrens, who advocated, as early as 1844, a neomercantilist imperial economy grounded on an "imperial Zollverien."[38] Mill's work, written during his period of employment by the East India Company at the India Office in London from 1823 to 1858, was mandatory reading for subsequent generations of colonial administrators and officials in colonial India. Explicitly invoking Wakefield, Mill approved an understanding of "colonization, in the present state of the world" as the "best affair of business, in which the capital of an old and wealthy country can engage."[39] Mill argued that the "perpetual overflow" and exportation of capital into colonies were among the "counter-forces which check the downward tendency of profits," for capital export via colonization was not only an "agent of great efficacy in extending the field of employment" but a crucial measure to defer the coming of what classical economists called the "stationary state" (741–42, 748, 749). He observed, "as long as there are old countries where capital increases very rapidly, and new countries where profit is still high, profits in the old countries will not sink to the rate which would put a stop to accumulation" (746).

The combination of colonial expansion and redirection of capital to places outside of Britain was not novel in itself. The point here concerns the difference between mercantilism and territorial colonialism as a historically specific "spatial fix" in both a discursive and institutional sense.[40] Whereas mercantilism sought an expansion of trade through the export of surplus capital as a means of payment to purchase excess commodities produced in Britain, territorial colonialism mandated the generation of new spaces for the reproduction of capital. Colonies were increasingly conceived not as extraterritorial zones for mercantilist trade and the provision of raw materials but rather as substantively and functionally internal supplements of a globe-spanning and hierarchically configured imperial space economy. John Stuart Mill's argument that colonies are "hardly to be looked upon as countries, carrying an exchange of commodities with other countries, but more properly, as outlying agricultural or manufacturing estates belonging to a larger community" typifies the new imperial episteme that placed colonial spaces within rather than outside the larger British-imperial whole.[41] He argued that colonial spaces were inner supplements of the "larger community" forged by English "productive" capital. Because all the "capital employed is English capital" and "almost all the industry is carried on for English uses," the trade between Britain and its colonies "is hardly to be considered an external trade, but more resembles the traffic between town and country." Articulated during an era of aggressive capital expansion and the consolidation of Britain's hegemony, Mill's formulation underscores the naturalization of uneven development (the traffic between town and country) on a globally organized imperial scale.

This distinctive imperial political economy shaped the reconfiguration of the relationship between state and space in colonial India. A central aspect of the transition to territorial colonialism in colonial India, and the making of colonial state space, concerned the mechanisms, modes, and forms of state intervention in sociocultural and economic domains. The mercantilist regime of the East India Company was grounded on the extraction of tribute (the few plantations notwithstanding), the expansion of trade, and the maintenance of order through largely expedient, defensive, and piecemeal measures. In contrast, the post-1857 colonial regime hinged on "occupying space, producing space."[42] Instead of generating revenue through the extraction of tribute and the expansion of trade, the post-1857 colonial regime sought to transform the geographical space of colonial India into a commodified, "second-order" space embedded within rather than merely tied to the broader imperial economy through external relations. From the late 1830s until 1857, the East India Company regime, for instance, had invested only 1.43 million pounds or approximately 1 percent of its average revenues of 20 million pounds a year in social and physical infrastructures.[43] In contrast, the post-1857 colonial state increasingly mobilized both direct and indirect techniques of spatial, economic, and social intervention and massively extended investments in both productive and unproductive sectors. In the majority of cases, state debt was the major channel for investments in social and military infrastructures. Furthermore, central state apparatuses increasingly took over the role of the overall management and production of crucial social infrastructures. The development of a massive network of communication and transportation structures — railways, bridges, irrigation projects, ports, canals, telegraph networks, postal services — marked the shift from the mercantilist policies of the East India Company to a new colonial political economy of space and state in the post-1857 era. The production, ordering, and maintenance of a vast network of social and physical infrastructures not only required the establishment of new hierarchically interlaced institutions but was premised on, and constitutive of, a new colonial state form.

A Categorical Imperative: State Works and the Making of State Space

In an attempt to differentiate itself from both the Mughal Empire and the mercantilist East India Company, the post-1857 state presented itself as a historically unique modernizing state. Queen Victoria's famous proclamation of 1858 announced the new order of things: "It is our earnest desire to stimulate the peaceful industry of India . . . to promote works of public utility and improvement, and to administer its government for the benefit of all our subjects resident therein. In their prosperity will be our strength, in their contentment our security, and in their gratitude our best reward."[44] John and Richard Strachey, prominent colonial officials during the late nineteenth and early twentieth centuries, articulated the modernist self-understanding of the colonial state with particular force.[45] Writing in 1882, they observed:

> The territorial expansion of the Empire during the last forty years has been enormous. Five great provinces have been added to, with an area almost equal to that of France and the German Empire put together. . . . After [the mutinies of 1857] the change went on with enormously accelerated speed. Ten thousand things were demanded which India had not got, but which it was felt must be provided. The country must be covered with railways and telegraphs, and roads and bridges. Irrigation canals must be made. . . . Barracks must be built for a great European army. . . . In fact the whole paraphernalia of a great civilized administration, according to the modern notions of what that means, had to be provided. (1–3)

The colonial state performed its rule over space and society through a spectacular display of its authoritative presence, from the staging of elaborate political rituals and events to the construction of a vast network of dazzling "state works," the visible, material embodiments of its authority and "civilizing" modernity.

Within post-1857 official discourse and practice, the broad rubric of "state works" occupied a privileged place. State works were divided into three categories. The first included the built environment of all official buildings from courts to district provincial offices to prisons to railway stations and military barracks. The second category embraced railways, canals, roads, lighthouses, postal services, telegraphs — that is, all projects that "provided transport and communications." The third category — which had direct reference to the self-understood status of the colonial regime as the supreme, ideal landlord—consisted of irrigation projects. Presented as the concrete incarnation of a modernizing colonial political economy, state works were deemed essential for "the advancement of the moral and material prosperity of the people."[46] They were constructed and construed as magical technological and engineering feats that would domesticate, discipline, and modernize a barbarous population, tame its prejudices, and elicit its loyalty.

Within official discourse, railways were a privileged sign of a colonial modernizing project. Edward Davidson, the chief consulting engineer for railways, observed in 1869:

> Railways, which had gone far in England to annihilate distance, were in India to . . . vivify and give such a bias to the character of the peoples of India, as ages had not effected, and ages would not efface. . . . *Railways, in short, have placed upon the country itself the broad and indelible stamp of England:* laws could be abrogated, education could be neglected, and even roads might be obliterated or canals choked up; but . . . change what may, they [railways] will remain firm and altered memorials of British rule.[47]

Inscribed on the landscape of colonial India, state works were to speak for themselves in the language of objective reality: they would stand as the incontrovertible evidence of the modernizing project of the colonial state.

The campaign for state-financed and state-directed railway investment in colonial India illustrates the organizing ideologies of the postmercantilist colonial political economy of space. The campaign for building railways in colonial India crystallized in the late 1840s, that is, during the speculative frenzy associated with the railway mania of 1844–47. It originated, as Daniel Thorner has shown, not with the East India Company but with "manufacturers and Members of Parliaments from Manchester, pivotal City figures, the *Times*, and James Wilson [the founder-editor of the *Economist*, who became the first finance minister for colonial India in 1858]."[48] It emerged, in other words, from the very center of laissez-faire Britain. The largest of the railway companies—the East India Railway (EIR) and the Great Indian Peninsular Railway (GIPR)—had been established in Britain during the railway mania of the late 1840s. A range of financial and shipping interests that sought to penetrate the interior markets of colonial India advocated the EIR. The GIPR Company, which aimed to construct a railway line from the port of Bombay to the cotton-producing districts of Nagpur in the Central Provinces, was supported by Lancashire mill owners.[49] Long before the actual stoppage, during the American Civil War years of 1860–66, of the raw cotton imported from the southern United States, Lancashire manufacturers warned against the dangers of depending exclusively on American raw cotton and sought to break the monopolistic prices of American producers. The proposed line from Bombay to the cotton districts, for instance, was regarded, in the words of a contemporary pamphlet, "as nothing more than an extension of their own line from Manchester to Liverpool." Such a project, it was proclaimed, "would be a great national object. . . . If we had the Bombay railway carried into the cotton country it would be the great work which Government is capable of performing with a view to this end" (quoted at 14). Railways would eliminate spatial barriers to circulation and production by opening up new sources for raw materials and markets for British manufactures.

The expansion of the imperial space economy hinged on the creation of a vast, spatially integrated transportation system fixed within a particular geographical space. Hyde Clark, a prominent railway economist in late-nineteenth-century Britain, concisely articulated this line of argument. Clark observed that "the excitement of railway construction in India, will, of itself, cause an increased demand for English goods, so that at each step one operation will be found harmonising and cooperating with another, like a well planned and highly finished train of wheel work."[50] He made clear that the colonial regime, in subsidizing such a project, was not departing from the fundamental principle of "self interest." There was, he stated, "no instance upon record of civilized government taking the initiative in a grand scheme for the amelioration of the condition of a barbarous people, for the mere sake of doing good." The "real operation," Clark noted with candor, "was to make the Hindoos form the railways, and enable us to reap a larger portion of the profits" (178). But this statement was qualified with a broader assertion of progressive development, grounded on classical assumptions that trade based on "naturally" given comparative costs would benefit all concerned. The "wretchedness of the natives of India" would not last long:

> When improved facilities of communication have brought these benighted people and their ways under the observation and influence of the civilized world. . . . any measures which would promote the sale and transmission of the raw productions, particularly the staples of wool, silk, dyes, rice, sugar, etc., to the steam manufactories of England, would at once improve the condition of the country in the most legitimate way, namely, by encouraging to the fullest extent the cultivation of the soil, now so direfully neglected. Once this was accomplished, it

would be no hardship to the Hindoos to be compelled to receive their cottons in a manufactured shape, at a less exchangeable cost of labour than they could make themselves.[51]

The proposed transportation system would bring previously inaccessible products and resources into the network of exchange, open up colonial India as a market for British manufactures, and consolidate the emergent international division of labor. The assumptions that animated the railway campaign prefigure the ways in which colonial spatial-economic practices entailed the transformation of the geographical space of colonial India into an internal component of the imperial economy.

A pamphlet written by the board of the East India Railway and sent to British Prime Minister Lord John Russell argued that railways were indispensable "not to the improvement, but to the very establishment of commercial and industrial enterprise" in colonial India. For without an adequate transportation system, the "door is closed which might admit capital, and a vast empire containing the most useful and various productions, most of them susceptible of indefinite increase, is available neither as a market to sell or to buy."[52] The formation of a comprehensive transportation grid would increase the demand for British manufactures, set idle productive capacity to work, and create a space for the expansion of capital. The pamphlet figured railways as literal portals toward bourgeois individualism, economic rationality, and free-market competition. It argued that the establishment of railways "by private enterprise would put the people into a principle of association by which they might all be effected. This is a matter of extreme importance in India, where the energy of individual thought has long been cramped by submission to despotic governments, to irresponsible and venal subordinates, to the ceremonies and priesthood of a highly irrational religion, and to a public opinion founded not on investigation, but on traditional usages and observances." The untutored masses of colonial India, laboring under the nightmarish burdens of an "irrational religion," would receive "in their minds a portion of that energy which characterizes us as a nation . . . arousing a spirit of active emulation."[53] The posited equivalence between the British nation and the regime of capital powerfully expresses dominant figurations of railways as magical tools for economic growth and as privileged instruments for making manifest the virtues of private enterprise and competition.

Railways were also crucial instruments for the consolidation of political and military domination within colonial India. Lord Dalhousie, the governor-general of the East India Company, in his famous minute of 1853, captures in a distilled form the potent mix of economic and political imperatives that animated the campaign. He argued:

> A single glance cast upon the map recalling to mind the vast extent of the Empire we hold . . . will suffice to show how immeasurable are the political advantages to be derived from a system of internal communications which would admit of full intelligence of every event being transmitted to the Government under all circumstances, at a speed exceeding five-fold its present rate; and would enable the Government to bring the main bulk of its military strength to bear upon every point, in as many days as it would now require months. . . . The commercial and social advantages . . . are beyond all present calculation. Great tracts are teeming with produce which they cannot dispose of. Others are scantily bearing what they would carry in abundance, if only it could be conveyed whither it is needed. England is calling aloud for the cotton which India does already produce in some degree, and would produce sufficient in quality, and plentiful in quantity, if only there were provided the fitting means of conveyance to it from distant plains, to the several ports adopted for its shipment. Every increase of facilities for trade has been attended . . . with an increased demand of European produce in the most distant markets of our empire. . . . Ships from every part of the world crowd our ports in search for produce which we have or could obtain in the interior, but which at present we cannot possibly fetch to them, and new markets are opening to us on this side of the globe under circumstances which defy foresight of the wisest to estimate their probable value, or calculate their future extent. . . . The first object must be, then, to lay down the great trunk lines, with a view to the broadest future ramification, and on a principle that shall ensure the most profitable permanent working of the lines generally, bearing upon the intercourse of India with Europe.[54]

Dalhousie's minute illustrates the pervasive force of classical economic understandings that unfettered markets would produce sustained growth and economic sameness. Railways, he remarked, "would surely and rapidly give rise within this empire to the same encouragement of enterprise, the same multiplication of produce, the same discovery of latent wealth, and to the similar progress in social improvements, that have marked the introduction of improved communications in the western world" (88). The underlying assumptions of the universalizing force of new technologies and the reproducibility of uniform economic growth at once expressed and helped reproduce the ideology of an expansive, triumphant imperial capitalism. As the former director of the British Board of Trade during the height of the speculation spurred railway mania in the 1840s, Dalhousie spoke with an authoritative voice. The rebellion of 1857–58 reinforced the political and military necessity of railways, and the question of investment in colonial India acquired an unprecedented urgency. The massive expansion of transport and communication structures occurred under the novel and distinctive spatial and economic planning regime of the post-1857 colonial state.

As the most privileged of all "state works," railways were constructed at an astonishing pace. Between 1860 and 1920, an average of 594 miles of railways were constructed each year, a pace that far exceeded that of Britain and France during the same period.[55] By 1860, colonial India had the ninth largest railway system in the world, by 1890 the seventh largest, and by the turn of the century the fourth largest system. By 1900, colonial India had a higher rail density (the percentage of tracks to area) than South America, the rest of Asia, as well as Russia, Canada, and Australia. Of regions of comparable size, only the United States had a denser network.[56] This massive railway grid represented the largest single investment undertaken by the British imperial regime in any colony. British investments in transportation structures in Australia, during this period, were 50 million pounds, and only 25 million in Canada.[57] By 1900, investment in railways in colonial India totaled 200 million pounds, of which some 95 million were invested by 1875. Because the shares were sold and loans floated in the City (the financial district in London), approximately 99 percent of the total capital was raised in Britain. Of the fifty thousand individual shareholders of Indian railroads in 1868, only four hundred were colonial subjects.[58]

Until the early 1870s, when the colonial state assumed the direct production and management of railways, British railway companies were responsible for their construction. They did so under a state-guaranteed return of 5 percent on total capital expended. The guarantee system marked a radical departure from state policies on railways within Britain and sparked considerable debate. However, the opposition mounted did not stem from the usual suspect of classical economic theory, which suggested that the modern state merely secured the legal and administrative conditions for the free play of the market, that it framed but did not fashion the economic field. In Britain, among the most consistent campaigners for state ownership of railways in colonial India was Thomas Bazley, an ardent Cobdenite and the head of the Manchester chamber of commerce. In a memorandum to the secretary of state, Lord Mayo, he stated: "I am strongly in favor of all the public works of India being established as government property."[59] With particular reference to railway policy in colonial India, Julian Danvers, the secretary for railways in the Public Works Department, attested to the British Parliament that colonial practices could not "be defended on the abstract principles of political economy."[60] In an influential memorandum, Louis Mallet, the financial secretary, underscored the ways the colonial state marked the limits of practices of laissez-faire. He argued that not only were the "strict rules of economic and financial science" inapplicable to colonial India but that such an attempt would transform the governance of colonial India into "little less than the venture of a gambler, with the empire for the stakes." The government of India, he said,

> is an audacious experiment, conceived and executed in defiance of all prudence and of all principle. . . . My personal prepossessions in favour of the principles of laissez faire in matters of State economy are well known, but in India it is simply impossible and illogical to press this policy. . . . In its execution it will be found that the first step which would be necessary would be that of leaving the country.[61]

There was a frank recognition that the increasingly interventionist thrust of colonial practices was the very condition of possibility of rule. The deepening imbrication of the state within the political-economic field was nowhere more apparent than in the grand orchestration of a massive ensemble of state works.

Under the guarantee system, the colonial state acquired the land required for railway construction and right-of-way and leased it to the railway companies free of rent, guaranteed a return of 5 percent on total capital expanded, and secured the right to purchase railway lines after twenty-five years. The state had full access to all the accounts, proceedings, and minutes of the railway companies, and the state official on the board of every railway company had the right of ultimate veto in all proceedings.[62] The Land Acquisition Act as it was applied to the purchase of land and the right-of-way for railways did not allow landholders to contest the choice of routes for lines or challenge the appropriation of their lands for state works. In Britain, the legal costs to private companies from individual landholders formed a substantial percentage of the average cost of railway construction, and from the 1840s onward various provisions had been established that enabled landholders and residents to protest choice of lines and practices of land acquisition.[63] However, the Railway Acts of 1854, 1871, and 1890 in colonial India did not include such concessions. Government gazettes notified the public that land was reserved for railway construction. In order to receive compensation, landowners had to submit legal documents and titles of deeds confirming ownership to state agencies. For the vast majority of nonliterate communities involved, this policy (an expression of the brutality of accumulation) effectively amounted to unilateral forfeiture.

The guarantee system, although initially formulated with respect to railways, was extended to the numerous port development companies that mechanized, extended, and developed port facilities in Bombay, Calcutta, Madras, and Karachi.[64] There was a simultaneous expansion of communication structures from a postal service directly under the colonial state to the construction of a dense network of telegraph lines and submarine cables underwritten by the state guarantee system. By 1880, more than twenty-five thousand miles of telegraph lines and submarine cables linked the major urban centers in colonial India to financial and political centers in London, a development that was part of the wider consolidation of a globally organized British imperial communications network.[65] As a result, market information, prices, orders, and delivery rates could be passed instantly between the City and the main financial centers in India, which were linked to smaller trading posts. The telegraph industry made possible the integration of localities and regions within emergent international markets, that is, where the buy and sell prices of commodities were posted in more than one place. This communication infrastructure proved of fundamental importance during the last quarter of the century, when the market in currencies and, more specifically, remittances by the colonial state to Britain assumed increasing importance. Technological innovations in communications networks deepened the state's infrastructural capacity and, by accelerating the circulation of capital, enhanced the integration of colonial India within the broader imperial space economy.

The third category of state works comprised irrigation projects. The first canal projects such as the Grand Anicut on the Kaveri Delta, built in 1846, and the gigantic Upper Ganges Canal, which opened in 1854 (the largest canal in the world), were constructed during the East India Company's rule, through loans raised in London.[66] However, the massive expansion of canal irrigation occurred during the post-1857 period under the aegis of the newly founded Public Works Department. Like the railway system, these large-scale irrigation projects were grand technological and engineering feats, and had the quality of a spectacular display. They were as well, on the whole, extremely profitable investments. The largest of the irrigation and canal projects yielded high annual rates of return on investment, amounting to 23.5 percent (Cauveri), 45 percent (Godavri), 16 percent (Krishna), and 30 percent (Western Jumna Canal). The return for irrigation projects, as a whole, was 7.3 percent (1875–76), 5.13 percent (1876–77), and 5.15 percent (1877–78).[67] Until the late 1860s, irrigation works were constructed under the guarantee system. However, from the late 1860s onward the colonial state directly undertook irrigation projects in northern, northwestern, and southeastern colonial India by earmarking, on an annual basis, a half million pounds from ordinary revenue and two million pounds obtained through loans raised in London.[68] Lord Canning, the first viceroy and governor-general of the post-1858 state, stressed that "the interference of Government in the management of these works must be close and constant, call it if you will, so vexatious and intolerable . . . the management must not merely be controlled by Government, but must be taken entirely into its hands."[69] Over the next decade (1871–80), the colonial state directed 9.2 million pounds toward the construction of a number of irrigation projects, on the basis of the strict criterion of their productivity. The new irrigation projects constructed and financed by the colonial state included the Lower Jhelum and Lower Chenab Canals (Punjab), the Lower Ganges Canals (North-Western Provinces), Jamrao and Nira Canals (Bombay Presidency), the Son Canal (Bihar), and Periyar and Kumol-Chuddap Canals (Madras Presidency).[70] By 1903, 42 percent of all irrigated land (approximately 18.5 million acres) within colonial India had been brought under canal irrigation.[71]

Elizabeth Whitcombe's classic analysis of colonial irrigation works in the United Provinces, as well as more recent studies, has argued that irrigation canals were highly contested sites of struggle between the modernizing designs of colonial engineers and entrenched local modalities of managing irrigation works.[72] In the post-1857 period, water distribution and access, for instance, came to be regulated by abstract principles of productivity and efficiency rather than by embedded social hierarchies, local patronage networks, and conceptions of privilege that bore the imprint of earlier moments of colonial land settlement.[73] The creation of an elaborate irrigation bureaucracy entailed the institutional exclusion of local social groups from the everyday administration of canals. Whereas local hierarchies and power relations had previously shaped access to irrigation, the new regime of canal administration enshrined abstract principles of productivity and efficiency as the regulating principles that determined the spatial distribution of canal outlets and the temporal regulation of irrigation.

The apparent departure from classical political economy signaled by direct state investment and construction of state works was inextricably tied to the self-understanding of the colonial state as the supreme, ideal landlord. In making the case for the establishment of an agricultural department in

1869, Lord Mayo articulated the entrenched official understanding of the relationship between the state and space. He declared that

> [t]he Government of India is not only a Government, but the chief landlord. The land revenue, which yields 20 millions of our annual income, is derived from that portion of the rent which belongs to the State and not to individual proprietors. There can be no doubt that throughout the greater part of India, every measure which can be taken for the improvement of the land, and for increasing its productive powers, immediately enhances the value of property of the State. . . . The duties which in England are performed by a good landlord fall in India, in a great measure, upon the government. Speaking generally, the only Indian landlord who can command the requisite knowledge is the state.[74]

The specificity of the "system of administration" in colonial India was, as W. W. Hunter argued, "based upon the view that the British power is a paternal despotism, which owns, the entire soil of the country, and whose duty it is to perform the various functions of a wealthy and enlightened proprietor."[75] The self-understanding of the colonial state as the supreme landlord, continually reiterated within official discourse, coexisted with the intensified commodification of space, the extension of the regime of private property, and a phenomenal increase in rural indebtedness in the last half of the nineteenth century.[76] Although the Ricardian conception of land revenue as rent was, by the turn of the century, recast in official discourse as a tax on agricultural production, the conception of the state as the "universal landlord" continued to haunt colonial discourse and practice.[77] The colonial state's appropriation of an ultimate right of ownership of land was not just a regulating fiction that unwittingly expressed envy for imagined despotic regimes conjured by Orientalist imaginaries. It was rendered socially effective in the enduring practice of "hypothecation," whereby the state reserved a supreme claim to land by selling land deeds at public auction in the event of a failure to pay the cash revenues in time.[78]

B. H. Baden-Powell's magisterial 1892 manual for aspiring colonial officials, titled *The Land Systems of British India*, expressed the centrality of land and land revenue in the fashioning of colonial state space. Baden-Powell (a leading authority on land revenue policies, a chief architect of colonial forest policies, and the founder of the Boy Scouts) claimed:

> The State derives its principal revenue from the land; it has done so at all times, and the people are accustomed to pay it; it is with them the

very nature of things. The collection, when once the assessment is arranged for a term of years, is effected without inquisitorial proceedings
and without trouble, or extortion. The population is so largely agricultural, and the different classes so wedded to custom, that the speculative administrator who should conceive the idea of getting rid of the
land-revenue would soon find himself in a position of difficulty which
language could hardly do justice do. (25)

With an ease peculiar to late-nineteenth-century official discourse, Powell
rendered the novel spatiotemporal regime of the colonial state as an archaic
order and erased the long history of violent agrarian struggles and the profoundly uneven power relations that defined colonial space. However, this
is a point not just about representational violence but about the status of
land and land revenue as a cultural dominant in the colonial political economy of space. A "speculative" administrative official would find himself in a
"position of difficulty that language cannot do justice to" precisely because
the statist production and mobilization of space represented the constitutive
limit of the colonial state episteme (25).

The conception of land as state property was a structuring dimension of
colonial state space in both a discursive and institutional sense. Enshrined
as doxa within official discourse, the colonial imagination of space as state
property profoundly shaped the administrative hierarchy and internal organization of the state. It informed the stunning post-1857 expansion of
cadastral surveys of land (village-by-village and plot-by-plot) and the determination of landed rights, and made the "record of everything which concerns the agricultural and social habits of the people" into "an immense business" (25). Baden-Powell illustrates the intimate connections between the
collection of the land revenue and the organization of state space:

> The collection of the land-revenue, and the management of all the af-
> fairs that are connected with the maintenance of the land-holders in
> prosperity . . . naturally becomes the *basis of the entire administrative sys-
> tem.* Considerations connected with it find their way into every depart-
> ment, the Post-office, the Irrigation department, the Public Works and
> many others. . . . The administration has to take a sort of paternal or
> "lord of the manor" interest in the whole range of agricultural condi-
> tions. . . . In order that the revenue may not be reduced below what a
> prosperous country should yield, the State officers — among whom the
> District officer or Collector vested with magisterial powers, is the most
> prominent — have continually to watch the state of the country . . . to

watch the state of crops, the failure of rain, the occurrence of floods, lo-
custs and blight, the spread of cattle-disease . . . they have to repress
crime and other sources of social disturbance, which demoralize and
tend to pauperize the people; to consider how estates may be improved
and protected against famine, by studying the requirements of the district in respect of communications which improve the market, of canals
which render the waste cultivable, of drainage and embankment works.
(26–27)

The self-understanding of the state as an ideal landlord found institutional
expression in diverse arenas. It underwrote the establishment of technical
and research institutes (e.g., the Imperial Council of Agricultural Research)
that sought to enhance agricultural productivity by developing commercial
crops such as sugarcane, cotton, tea, and the like; the sponsorship of agricultural shows in towns and villages intended to foster the use of new agricultural techniques and machinery; the organization and financing of
geological and coal-mining explorations; the training of a veritable army of
civil engineers, economic botanists, agricultural chemists, land surveyors,
and the like; and the construction of a vast network of "state works."[79]
The actual workings of these institutions were marked, as David Ludden
has argued, by a sharp disjuncture between statist projects and local realities.[80] Yet they nonetheless reveal the close intimacy between the self-
understanding and practices of a state that construed itself as the collective,
ideal landlord.

The colonial "rule of property," inaugurated in Bengal with the Permanent Settlement of 1793 and brilliantly analyzed by Ranajit Guha, had entailed the introduction of private property in land and the transformation of
previous systems of landownership and holdings as revenue collectors were
turned into land holders and landownership and taxation was disarticulated
from group claims and community rights.[81] In a second round of sociospatial restructuring, the post-1857 colonial state appropriated all natural resources and uncultivated land. Through a series of legislative acts and decrees, during the 1860s and 1870s, natural resources such as minerals,
mines, timber, and the like and all uncultivated land, drainage runs for irrigation tanks, public space in towns, villages, and cities, seashores, and
riverbeds were delimited as state property.

Among the most dramatic instances of the authoritative appropriation
and delimitation of land as state space concerned the institutionalization of
the novel category of state forests.[82] The 1864 foundation of a separate Forest Department was driven by a combination of revenue needs, the expan-

sion of specialized agricultural production, the development of the mining industry, and the growing need for timber to construct railways and to fuel steam engines. The Indian Forest Act of 1878, formulated by Baden-Powell (and which remains in force in the contemporary period), represented the culmination of colonial practices of appropriating and integrating forest, waste, and all uncultivated land in general into the productive sector.[83] The Forest Act of 1878 established state ownership of forests by employing the principle of eminent domain, whereby the colonial state, drawing on European jurisprudence, claimed to be acting in the public interest. The act sought to ground its legitimacy by evoking such precolonial practices as the delimitation of certain lands and groves as royal preserves. Baden-Powell, the architect of the Forest Act of 1878, proclaimed that "the right of the state to . . . waste and forest area is among the most ancient and undisputed features in Oriental Sovereignty."[84] In its attempt to legitimate what were radically novel measures, the colonial state glossed over the highly localized and exceptional character of such received practices.

The principle of eminent domain in its strict sense implied a legal obligation to provide compensation for customary rights to forest and waste lands lost in the appropriation of land as state space. However, this obligation, as K. Sivaramakrishnan has shown, was effectively nullified through a range of procedural sleights.[85] The Forest Act, for instance, codified a distinction between those rights, inscribed in the settlement record or obtained through grants and licenses, that could not be abrogated without compensation and those customary rights that, because unrecorded, were recast as alienable privileges that could be terminated without compensation. In short, existing customary rights and practices were redefined as "alienable privileges."[86] These included grazing, pasture, grass cutting, lopping boughs, gathering leaves, rights to decayed leaves and wood for manure, hunting and fishing, and the like. In a process that mirrored the acquisition of land for railway construction, a simple gazette notification stating that forest and wastelands were reserved as "state forests" effectively erased all such customary rights. Because claims on forest and wastelands had to be grounded in legal records of ownership, the vast majority of nonliterate subaltern communities were simply dispossessed of their lands.[87]

Following the principles of German forestry science, adopted in a number of late-nineteenth-century states, the colonial Forest Department severely restricted physical access to forests and transformed the composition of forests through the homogenization of biological diversity.[88] During the last quarter of the century, with the transformation of forests from habitats for subsistence farming to the center of commercial agricultural production, net revenues from state forests increased fourfold, from five million pounds in 1880 to more than twenty million in 1920.[89]

State works at once expressed and helped concretize the novel spatial and institutional form of the colonial state. An official report identified the determining criterion for the selection and planning of state works:

> The obligation on the Government in respect of the construction of these Works is essentially based on the idea of their being *profitable* in a pecuniary point of view; not of necessity to the Government as capitalists, *but to the entire body politic of the State*. If it cannot be reasonably be predicted that a work will be *profitable* in this sense, it should not be undertaken.[90]

With the inscription of a vast network of state works on the physical-territorial space of colonial India, the "entire body politic of the state" was increasingly framed, in both material and discursive terms, as colonial state space.

HOMOGENIZATION AND DIFFERENTIATION

The spatial morphology of the railway grid, organized in terms of the imperial space economy, spawned a new uneven economic geography. The major trunk lines of the railway system, constructed before 1870 under the state guarantee system, were built from the raw product–producing interior to the major port cities: Bombay, Calcutta, Madras, and Karachi. Lines deemed crucial from a strategic-military perspective were not undertaken until the early 1870s, when the colonial state directly assumed the construction of railways. By 1867, of the twenty urban centers in colonial India (according to the census of 1872), nineteen were on railway lines. The regions most densely traversed by rail lines—from Karachi and Surat in the northwest into the Punjab through the Indus river basin, from Calcutta across the Gangetic plain into Punjab, and down the western coast from Bombay and Madras and inland into present-day Maharashtra, Karnataka, and the Deccan—became the dominant economic regions. The urban corridor from Calcutta in the east to Karachi in the west came to hold a "preponderance of imperial personnel and assets . . . [and] became the imperial heartland and the central zone for state-sponsored agricultural development."[91] The mapping of transportation networks cut across existing trade and commercial routes, which clustered around inland river junctions and trade marts, and profoundly altered the spatial organization of production.

Received regional mosaics and patterns of unevenness congealed into new and more systematic forms of socioeconomic and cultural polarization.

A particularly stark instance of socioeconomic polarization was the increasing differentiation between the eastern and western regions of the United Provinces (UP). Until the 1850s, eastern UP, which lay astride the Ganges River route to Calcutta, had been the dominant economic region in terms of agricultural production, indigenous financial and merchant networks, and handloom weaving centers within the United Provinces. With the institution of railways, which skirted past this region, inland river trading and financial centers declined and specialized, export-oriented agricultural production shifted westward into the new canal tracts established in the Upper Doab areas.[92] The eastern UP regional economy, which had the highest population densities in the mid-nineteenth century, became increasingly isolated during the last decades of the century. From a dominant agricultural center it became the paradigmatic site for subsistence agricultural production, a recurring arena for devastating famines, and the source of a massive deterritorialization of peoples. Landless indentured laborers from this region comprised the majority of the thirty million migrants shipped out via Madras and Calcutta to the Caribbean (especially Trinidad and Guyana) to substitute for the labor of emancipated slaves on sugar plantations, to Malaya and East Africa to work in mines, plantation and railway-building projects, and to smaller British colonies such as Fiji and Mauritius.[93] The scope and structure of colonial migration were part of the evolving scale of the imperial space economy, creating and reproducing uneven development over ever wider geographical arenas.

By contrast, the Upper Doab region, which was the target of large-scale irrigation projects as well as an extensive railway network, became a chief growth pole for specialized agricultural production.[94] From an economically peripheral subregion of the UP, during the early nineteenth century, the Upper Doab area became the center for export-oriented agricultural production, a focal point for the employment of migrant workers, and a central node within the new, territorially expansive markets in agricultural commodities.[95] On a broader scale, industrial (cotton and jute mills) and financial enterprises (joint stock-companies and managing houses) clustered in the urban port centers, and the proximate hinterlands were characterized by a phenomenal growth in agricultural production, aided by such state works as canal and irrigation projects.[96] The hierarchical, uneven, and differentiated economic geography materialized by colonial practices remains "visible" in the contemporary period "in the routes of the main trunk lines, in the location of national capitals, and in the central place hierarchy, as well as in the geographical distribution of wealth and political power."[97]

A range of microlevel practices reinforced the mapping of infrastructures with reference to the spatial scale of the imperial economy. Consider, in this respect, the structure of railway rates. As John Hurd has shown, railway rates in colonial India were both extremely high—in comparison with regions of comparable size such as the United States and Continental Europe—and set against inland trade. Rates for long-haul freight were much lower than for shorter-haul freight, and rates to and from port cities were significantly lower than for comparable inland distances. Charges for shipping British-made matches, for instance, from Bombay to Delhi were the same as those for shipping matches manufactured in Ahmadabad to Delhi, even though Ahmadabad was 483 kilometers closer. Another example of the skewed structure of railway rates was the prohibitively high cost of coal, which disproportionately burdened local and regional industrial enterprises.[98] Coal was expensive in colonial India because of the high railway rates to the interior, where coalmines were located, and not because of the costs of production. This shaped not only the port-city and urban-centered economic cartography of industrial enterprises but ensured that British coal imports remained competitive until the 1920s.

Colonial spatial-economic structuring was distinguished by its privileging of infrastructures of circulation over production. During the last quarter of the nineteenth century, railways were chief instruments of national-economy making in the United States, Germany, France, Russia, and Japan. In these contexts, massive state investments in railroads, ports, canals, and educational systems and the proliferation of protective tariffs entailed the reorganization of economic space into distinct national blocs and a general movement toward autarkic, protectionist, and closed national economies.[99] What set apart the organization and planning of railways in colonial India was not only its orientation toward the broader imperial space economy, but the blocking of complementary industrial (e.g., coal, steel, locomotive production) and financial enterprises (indigenous joint-stock companies and financial capital). As early as 1865, for instance, railway workshops in colonial India had begun manufacturing competitively priced locomotives. However, the operative imperial purchase policy of the colonial state ensured that between 1865 and 1941, railway workshops in colonial India produced only seven hundred locomotives. From the late 1860s until the early 1940s, more than 22 percent of British-produced locomotives, for instance, were sold to colonial India. The various forms of discriminatory practices instituted by the colonial state were expressed in the ways in which more than two-fifths of the capital invested in railways in colonial India was actually expended in Britain. All the equipment and skilled labor — from engineers, engine drivers, down to plate-layers — were, until the close of the century, brought from Britain. Rails, points, fishplates, locomotives, machinery, even sleepers and coal, were imported almost exclusively from Britain until the 1930s.[100] The production of colonial India as an internal component of the imperial economy was pronounced: by the turn of the twentieth century, Britain supplied more than 80 percent of all imports to colonial India.

The spatial morphology of the transportation system, the structure of railway rates, and the location and planning of large-scale irrigation works privileged export-oriented agricultural production. In the post-1857 period, more than 60 percent of the freight carried by the railway network consisted of agricultural goods for export markets.[101] Before the constitution of a vast railway grid, only an insignificant proportion of agricultural production had been exported. In contrast with the indigo and opium exports from plantations of the early and mid-nineteenth century, the dominant export staples of the railroad era were, as B. R. Tomlinson notes, both more "firmly rooted" in the peasant economy and more generalized over colonial India as a whole.[102] Exports of indigo and opium gave way to a range of new products, most notably raw jute, food grains (rice and wheat), oilseeds, tea, and raw cotton. These export staples, a product of the last third of the nineteenth century, secured colonial India's structural location within the emergent global market for primary commodities. By the late 1920s, "62% of the cotton crop, 45% of the jute crop, 23% of wheat, and 20% of the groundnut crop were exported, with a further percentage sold in processed form" (59). Colonial India also became, after the late 1850s, the single most-important market for British cotton textiles. In the 1830s, colonial India absorbed only 6 percent of cotton exports from Britain, in 1840 it absorbed 22 percent, by 1851 it took in 31 percent, and by 1873 it took in more than 50 percent of cotton textiles.[103] The geographic space of colonial India was transformed into a "second-order" produced space for the production of raw materials — tea, wheat, oil seeds, hides and skins, indigo, raw silk, cotton, jute, opium — and as a massive captive market for industrial manufactures.

The production of novel communication and transport networks did enable the formation of an increasingly uniform space of production, circulation, and exchange.[104] Yet what distinguished the produced space of colonial India was the emergence of a distinct set of regional, urban, and local markets that were more tightly interwoven with imperial markets than with each other.[105] Some of the most dramatic effects of this unevenness were expressed during the devastating famines of 1876–79, whose estimated mortality figures ranged, depending on the source, from 6.1 to 10.3 million.[106] During that period, agricultural goods produced in the Punjab and the western districts of the UP were shipped by rail to Karachi and by steamer to England, but wheat did not reach the rural famine-stricken areas outside the transportation grid.[107] The official policy of nonintervention in famines, especially with regard to relief works, was as much a species of the prevailing fetish for free-market harmonies — self-consciously abrogated with "state works" but upheld rhetorically and institutionally in famine policy — as it was an embedded effect of the imperial scale-making orientation of colonial spatial and economic cartography.

The question of peasant indebtedness and its attempted resolution exemplifies the contradictory movement toward the simultaneous homogenization and differentiation of sociospatial relations. Colonial spatial-economic restructuring led to a sharp increase in the value of land, triggering both increased speculation as well as higher land revenue assessments. The higher assessed value of the land, the generalized pressure to grow commercial crops, the rising burden of various forms of direct and indirect taxation, and the like led to an unprecedented growth of peasant indebtedness across diverse regional contexts.[108] The political implications of the spread and rise of peasant indebtedness were not lost on the colonial state, which regarded and presented itself as the ideal landlord. The rise of rural indebtedness presented a central challenge to the self-presentation of the colonial regime as the custodian of its tenant-subjects.

Within official discourse, the structurally generated problem of peasant indebtedness — an expression of deepening urban-rural polarization — was displaced onto the figure of the indigenous moneylender and/or urban financier, who was seen as an alien intruder in the imagined timeless space of a central invention of the "colonial sociology of knowledge," that is, the traditional village republic.[109] The conception of colonial India as spatially ordered in the form of a series of self-sufficient, corporately organized, and static village republics was a foundational tenet of colonial administrative discourse and practice.[110] From Charles Metcalfe's influential minutes on village republics in the 1830s to Henry Maine's and B. H. Baden-Powell's magisterial surveys in 1870 and 1892, respectively, the image of colonial India as made up of bounded village republics acquired a self-evident status. Rendered an abstract "ideal-type," it became, as Bernard Cohn argues, the basis for the construction of "evolutionary stages . . . which could be used to compare similar developments or stages in other parts of the world."[111] The conception of the village republic as the spatiotemporal essence of India was incorporated as common sense in nineteenth-century European social-scientific and philosophical discourse through the works of John Stuart Mill, Karl Marx, and Max Weber, as well as later nationalist discourse.

Official concern about the perceived erosion of what was assumed to be the pure, enclosed, and static space of the village republic sharpened with wide-spread peasant insurgencies in the 1860s and 1870s, the alienation of land, the growing masses of landless laborers, and ineffectual famine relief policies in the Madras and Bengal presidencies, the United Provinces, and the Punjab. The colonial state ignored popular demands — rooted in the contradictions of social practices — for the reduction of land revenue assessments and water taxes, the organization of rural credit associations, and the reorientation of irrigation and railway projects. Instead, it instituted a series of legislative acts inhibiting and proscribing the sale of land to what were identified as "non-agricultural castes" and "urban interests."[112] However, this often meant simply that landowners themselves increasingly took on the role of financiers, and the position of the actual cultivator or tenant did not improve.[113] Although colonial practices incorporated subaltern classes into the universalized social relations entailed in commodity production for the world market, they also at the same time objectified and bound particular social groups in a territorial and social particularity. The homogeneity toward which colonial spatial and economic practices tended contained their own negation in the form of intensified differentiation and unevenness.

Colonial state space was predicated upon a territorial noncorrespondence between economic and political structures and a "rule of difference" that mandated the continual performance of the nonidentity between the state and its colonized subjects.[114] Colonial practices enhanced the physical-territorial boundedness of colonial India, enabled the infrastructural integration of diverse communities and regions, and shored up political and military domination. However, although the colonial state directed the production of a massive network of state works fixed within the territorial boundaries of colonial India, these boundaries did not carry an exclusive or primary economic significance. To the extent that it makes sense to speak of a territorialized conception of the economy, during this period it corresponded to the globally organized Britain-centered imperial scale. Although colonial practices produced an increasingly centralized state structure, the regulatory order of the imperial regime as a whole militated against the formation of territorial-bounded economic structures as expressed, for instance, in the privilege accorded to infrastructures of circulation (e.g., railways, telegraphs, and ports) over those of production. Imagined as a hierarchically embedded component of the imperial economy, colonial practices only become legible with reference to the scale of the imperial economy.

Just as the production and circulation of fixed capital investments, with a long turnover time, represent the futural anticipation of "further labor as a counter-value," the financing of such investments through state debt hinges on the anticipated power of the state to tax surplus value production.[115] The extent of the latter was staggering. During the first thirty years of railway construction, for instance, some fifty million pounds of tax revenues were raised in colonial India to meet the guarantee.[116] However, the productivity of state-directed investments was realized not on what nationalists would come to imagine and claim as the space of a national economy but on the scale of the imperial economy. This disjuncture between the scale of the production of value and the scale of its realization was a structuring dimension of colonial state space. By the last decades of the nineteenth century, the territorial noncorrespondence between the scales of accumulation, of political structures, and of the production of value became a central element of the nationalist argument against colonialism.

From the late 1860s onward, the colonial state began engaging in the direct production of railways that were deemed important from a military and security perspective, especially along the northwest frontier. The state took over most of the largest railway companies, including the highly profitable East India Railway network that extended from the Punjab to Bengal, and was most densely spun in the United Provinces. This was part of a broader trend toward greater state intervention and greater state investment in unproductive expenditures. During this period, state expenditures on the army, which had never fallen below 25 percent of total revenues, soared even higher with the costs of the Afghan war in the late 1870s. By the mid-1870s, however, colonial India was the target of only 6.9 percent of British capital invested outside the United Kingdom, and by 1890 it received less than 5 percent of the total.[117] This was conditioned by the fall in profit in railways and particular agricultural commodities; the reduction of the guaranteed interest rate to 3.5 percent, with the colonial state appropriating 60–75 percent of the surplus; and growing financial and monetary uncertainty rendered real by periodic state fiscal crises (44). More generally, it was a consequence of broader transformations of the global economy and the redirection of British capital toward North America and Europe.

A "GLOBAL, FRAGMENTED, HIERARCHICAL" WORLD

Cecily, you will read your Political Economy in my absence. The chapter on the fall of
the Rupee you may omit. It is somewhat too sensational. Even these metallic problems
have their melodramatic side.

— Oscar Wilde, *The Importance of Being Earnest*, 1895

With the widening and deepening of a Britain-centered global economy, the
tensions between homogenization and differentiation acquired an enlarged
field of play over an ever more differentiated global space. The space embraced by the world market, as Marx observed, is where "production is
posited as a totality together with all its moments, but within which, at the
same time, all contradictions come into play"; the world market forms both
the "presupposition of the whole as well as its substratum."[118] This formulation points to the limits of conceptions of global space-time as the sum of
mutually exclusive, bounded economic spaces across which a supposedly
teleological process of development and/or underdevelopment occurs. The
fashioning of a global space-time—the deepening of transnational interdependencies, the subjection of local and regional economies to a global
rhythm, the entwinement of multiple spaces and histories in an uneven contradictory whole—was coextensive with the emergence of novel forms of
socioeconomic polarization and unevenness. Although the crisis of 1847–
48, for instance, was delimited to Europe, the "depression" of 1873–94 was
worldwide in scope. It spread with uneven effects over an increasingly differentiated globe. This extended economic crisis, which signaled a crisis in
Britain's hegemony, led to the rearticulation of the relationship between
colonial India and the imperial space economy.

By the mid- to late 1870s, it became increasingly apparent that the claims
of universal and uniform progress embodied in Britain's global regulatory
regime did not hold. During the 1870s and 1880s, in an attempt to afford
protection to local industries and capture world market share controlled by
Britain, states such as Germany, the United States, France, Russia, and Japan became increasingly autarkic and protectionist. There was a conscious
attempt, through a variety of policies, to fabricate a state-protected economic space and effect a degree of closure from a Britain-centered global
economy. These included the erection of protectionist barriers through import tariffs and quotas in order to protect internal capital accumulation from
outside competition; massive state investments in social and physical infrastructure such as transportation and communications; the formation of centralized banking systems; the creation of national systems of labor disci-

pline; and state-sponsored education.[119] The intensification of global economic competition was inseparably part of the new form of nationally regulated capitalism that developed, most notably in such rising imperial and industrial powers as the United States, Germany, and Japan.[120] It signaled the emergence of what Karl Polanyi famously called the countervailing "great transformation"—the rise of protectionist regulatory frameworks in response to Britain's attempt to institute a self-regulating world market through imperial expansion and trade liberalization.[121]

Although the specific state strategies, political cultures, and institutional complexes of these states were distinct, there was a broad "family resemblance" in the political-economic and spatial imaginary of state-centered developmentalism. It represented a form of autarkic development that rested upon a strong conceptual and institutional divide between an internal, national economic space enclosed within the borders of the state and a foreign, international economy that existed beyond state territories. The emergence of these state forms, what Max Weber called the "closed national state which afforded to capitalism its chance for development," both presupposed and made possible a configuration of state-capital relations, in an era of intensified interstate competition for mobile capital, premised, at least rhetorically, on the principle of nationality.[122] This principle entailed a conception of the state as the state of and for a particular, bounded society, economy, and citizenry. The institutional and ideological coordinates of national developmentalism hinged on the interlinked principles of territorial isomorphism, closure, and homogenization. First, national developmentalism was distinguished by its privileging of the national-territorial scale as the fundamental matrix for social relations, political projects, and economy planning. A central objective of national developmentalism was not only the extension of economic and social infrastructures within a state-defined space but the attempted integration of circuits of production and realization within a state-territorial delimited space. Second, national developmentalism was premised on various practices of spatial and economic closure, including the proliferation of protectionist import tariffs and quotas, the spread of economic repertoires of collective action such as mass-scale boycotts of foreign commodities, and the growing role of states as custodians of the "principle of social protection," even while rising imperial and industrial powers extended their spatial boundaries.[123]

It is important to emphasize here that the emergence of national developmentalism proceeded in tandem with the intensification of interimperial rivalry among European powers and the expansion of colonies during the 1880s and 1890s. The partitioning of the globe among European states found its most obvious expression in the reconstitution of the world map of domination.[124] Paradoxically, the growing prevalence of national representations of economic and political space proliferated in the era of "high imperialism" and the consolidation of an interdependent yet profoundly differentiated global economy shaped by rising intra-imperial economic and political competition (62). Not only did the map of world domination change beyond recognition during the last decades of the nineteenth century, but the global growth in production and commerce between 1880 and 1900 was distinctly higher than it had been during the decades of free trade.[125] Just as the constitution of colonial state space hinged on the expansion of the Britain-centered global economy, the rise and consolidation of national developmentalism presupposed the increasing interdependence of economic relations. By 1900, not only was most of the world formally bound into rival blocs carved out by European colonial powers but more and more of the world's populations and resources were drawn into a geographically specialized and polarized global economy.[126] Processes of nationalization and capitalist global restructuring were complexly intertwined, mutually constitutive processes.

From the last quarter of the nineteenth century onward, the monetary surpluses generated by colonial India became central for the survival of Britain's imperial economy in an era of intensified imperial rivalry and economic competition. Colonial India assumed, during this period, "the role of a chief protagonist of the international settlement system."[127] The scaffolding of international settlements until the First World War rested on two chief bases: "the first was that of India's balance of payments deficit to Britain and the surpluses with other countries with which this deficit was financed, the second the trading balances between Britain, Europe and North America."[128] Britain's largest deficits, during this period, were with the United States (£50 million) and continental Europe (£45 million), and its largest surplus with colonial India (£60 million). Great Britain employed the favorable balance of payments with colonial India to settle more than a third of its deficits with the United States and Europe.[129]

Whereas British exports to Europe, the United States, and South America were crippled by increasing tariff protection, colonial India's balance-of-payments surplus was drawn from the export of agricultural commodities that did not encounter the same high tariffs. Colonial India's deficit with Great Britain consisted of the imports of manufactured goods, largely from Britain, and the interests, dividends, and remittances that comprised the annual so-called home charges from the colonial state in sterling to the India Office in London. This financial structure explains, in part, why colonial India was kept out of the protectionist imperial customs union, formulated in the 1880s and 1890s, which granted fiscal autonomy and protection for nascent industries in settler colonies, that is, Australia, New Zealand, South Africa, and Canada.[130] The formation of an imperial customs union was a powerful instance of the ways in which the British imperial regime pursued autarky within a closed empire. However, not only was the produced space of colonial India denied fiscal autonomy and barred from adopting protective tariffs, but it was coercively maintained as a market for British manufactures and as a source of agricultural commodities and raw materials. Lord Hamilton, the secretary of state for India, justified this scheme of differentiation with reference to the long-run interests of the imperial economy as a whole. He argued that "we are not only a great manufacturing nation but England, in addition, is an enormous exchange market, and free trade in this respect specially benefits us . . . the foundation of our industrial edifice lies in the constant and large supply of cheap food and raw materials." Thus any "encouragement of industrial enterprises" within colonial India would entail the "colony gaining at our expense" and the dismantling of the very "edifice" of Britain's industrial supremacy. More generally, with reference to the empire as a whole, it was held that the "interests of different localities and colonies would be placed in antagonism one to another." In short, the establishment of "local industry" within colonial India, and its inclusion within the protectionist scheme of imperial preferences, would be "detrimental in every way to our broad commercial and industrial interests."[131]

Far from being residual to the growth of the global economy, colonial-produced spaces were central to it.[132] The large surpluses in the colonial Indian balance of payments, for instance, were a crucial source for sustaining London as the center of world finance.[133] Britain's financial hegemony hinged on its monopoly over "world money" or universally accepted means of payment. Whereas Britain pushed the gold standard elsewhere, a sterling exchange standard—a system based on rupee paper currency maintained artificially at par with gold through sterling reserves kept in London—was forcibly retained in colonial India under the aegis of the India Office. Under the sterling exchange standard—whose chief architects and defenders included such figures as Lionel Abraham, Basil Blackett, and John Maynard Keynes at the India Office, London—the colonial state held sterling reserves in London as backing for rupee issue in colonial India.[134] These reserves provided, as Marcello de Cecco argues, "a large masse de manoeuvre which British monetary authorities used to supplement their own reserves and to keep London the center of the international monetary system."[135]

During the last quarter of the nineteenth century, the exchange value of the rupee began to fall steadily against currencies that had moved onto a gold standard, and especially against the pound. With the demonetization of silver in Germany (1873), the Scandinavian countries (1874), and subsequently the Latin Union, Belgium, France, United States, Netherlands, and Spain, the transition from silver to gold in the dominant core was completed. This change, coupled with the enormous increase in the output of silver from new mines, led to a sharp fall in the price of silver from 58 pennies in 1875 to 37.5 pennies in 1879 to 28 pennies in 1894. By the 1890s, colonial India absorbed more than a third of the world's output of silver, and the gold value of the rupee fell from 2s. in 1871 to 1s.2d. in 1892.[136] The depreciation of the rupee not only spawned spiraling inflation but exacerbated the annual politically established "home charges," that is, the colonial state's sterling obligations to Great Britain. Despite the existence of large export surpluses from the late 1860s onward, there was a net outflow of capital from colonial India. For Indian nationalists in the 1870s and 1880s, the key to this apparent disjunction lay, in part, in the unilateral transfer of funds remitted to Britain—what came to signify and embody a "national drain." These charges included the debt incurred on capital investments in public works, salaries and pensions of officials, the purchase of manufactures in Britain, the expenses of the India Office, the entire imperial army, and the War Office. The annual home charges, which ranged from 5 to 6 percent of the "total resources of India," increased significantly during the 1880s.[137] This increase, financed by increased land revenue charges and taxation, was set in the context of devastating famines, the slump of agricultural prices, rising rural indebtedness and inflation, and widening spatial and socioeconomic polarization within colonial India.

The intensification of the financial domination of the produced space of colonial India cannot be understood apart from the challenges posed to Britain's hegemony by the rise of developmentalist, neomercantilist, and nationalist state forms and practices. On a conceptual register, the dynamic, intersecting geographies of regional and global shifts suggest the limits of "internalist" analyses that delimit political and economic processes within the boundaries of particular states. As a consequence of this embedded methodological nationalist bias, global structures of interdependencies are all too often represented as "economic" transfers and flows between sovereign, self-contained spaces. As the preceding analysis has sought to show, it is impossible to grasp the dynamic contradictions of colonial practices without placing them in relation to globe-spanning sociopolitical imaginaries and the uneven historical geography of capitalism.

CONCLUSION

When I hear the employment of British capital in India deplored, I feel tempted to ask where, without it, would have been Calcutta? Where would have been Bombay? Where would have been our railways, our shipping, our river navigation, our immense and prosperous trade? . . . I would say to the people of this country — if my words would have the slightest effect — look facts in the face. Recognize that capital does not wrap itself in the flag of any country. It is international. It is like the wind that bloweth where it listeth, and comes and goes as it will. The whole industrial and mercantile world is one great field for the tiller to till; and if the man who lives on the spot will not cultivate it with his own spade, then he has no right to blame the outsider who enters it with his plough.

— Lord Curzon, governor-general and viceroy of colonial India

Capital in our time, is no doubt "international"; and the "whole industrial and mercantile world is one great field for the tiller to till"; but it cannot pursue its own object without regard to the supreme economic, industrial, and political interests of the different peoples among whom history has parceled out this "great field." British capital cannot work in South Africa, or Russia or even in China, in the same way as it has and is doing in India. If Lord Curzon's theory of the international character of capital be correct, one might ask, why should not German capital be admitted into Great Britain . . . or into India upon the same terms and with the same measure of freedom, as British capital is employed or admitted?

— Bipin Chandra Pal, *swadeshi* nationalist

The remarkable "exchange" between Lord Curzon and Bipin Chandra Pal quoted in the epigraphs above — which occurred at the turn of the century — anticipates key elements of the larger argument of this work as a whole.[138] The idiom of this exchange was shaped by the specific context of the *swadeshi*-era radicalization and generalization of the economic critique of colonialism. The lived experience of the unevenness of colonial state space, and the growing visibility of its relationship to an imperial scale-making project, generated a range of contending spatiotemporal imaginaries. Curzon's identification and endorsement of the "international" dynamic of capital and Bipin Pal's insistence on the difference between state regulatory practices in colonial versus national spaces contain, in condensed form, key conceptual insights for understanding the making and unmaking of colonial spaces in the late nineteenth and early twentieth centuries.

It suggests that neither the making of a colonial state space nor a "global, fragmented and hierarchical" space-time can be grasped as autonomous formations. Each was what it was historically only by virtue of its relation to the other, and must be conceptualized accordingly. Instead of confusing physical-territorial boundedness with substantive closure, we need to examine the radically relational articulation of apparently distinct spatial formations and socioeconomic processes. It makes little empirical or conceptual sense to view processes of global capitalist restructuring—whether in the late-nineteenth and early-twentieth-century era or at present—as encroaching on territorial statehood and/or so-called peripheral societies from some imagined outside. Rather, the multiple relations and processes subsumed under the singular rubric of the "global" must be conceived as taking effect within and shaped by local, regional, and everyday spaces and relations. It is through the intersections of multiple geographies that specific spaces—colonial and national—acquire both their singularity and interdependence in the modern global era.

The following chapters explore, on a more concrete terrain, how new forms of political struggle, subjectivities, and everyday categories of understanding emerged not just in response to but on the very basis of the experiential tensions of colonial state space. For to suggest that colonial state space was the locus of contradictory practices of homogenization and differentiation is only to set the stage, establish the framework, for an analysis of its multiply refracted social and cultural effects.

CHAPTER TWO

ENVISIONING THE COLONIAL ECONOMY

Argument: The Indian Government being minded to discover the economic condition of their land, sent a committee to inquire into it; and saw that it was good.

Before the beginning of years
There came to the rule of the State
Men with a pair of shears
Men with an Estimate

. . . .

And the bigots took in hand
Cess and the falling of rain,
And the measure of sifted sand
The dealer puts in the grain —
Imports by land and sea,
To uttermost decimal worth,
And registration — free —
In the houses of death and of birth . . .
With the Armed and the Civil Power,
That his strength might endure for a span —
From Adam's Bridge to Peshawur,
The Much Administered Man.

— Rudyard Kipling, "The Masque of Plenty," 1885

A distinctive feature of the colonial accumulation of knowledge, during the last third of the nineteenth century, was that it was state-territorial in focus. The geographic space of colonial India became the territorial unit and organizing frame for bureaucratic statistical labor, plans, and programs as well as official representations of economic relations and flows. A range of official practices, during the post-1857 era, fostered the appearance of colonial India as a bounded and relatively homogenous transactional and financial space, a space defined and delimited by state and statewide political, social, and economic institutions and processes.

This chapter argues that colonial state space became the locus of a com-

plex ensemble of official representational and regulatory practices that profoundly altered the spatiotemporal coordinates of financial and monetary
practice. It also charts, albeit in an impressionistic fashion, how these practices enabled the envisioning of the colonial economy as a territorially
bounded and temporally dynamic whole. Concerned primarily with everyday state practices and economic categories of understanding, I focus on
two interlinked fields: the official imaginary of the colonial economy and the
homogenization of financial space. The first section explores various practices that helped conjure colonial state space and the colonial economy as a
homogenous totality from the standardization of accounting procedures, to
the formation of a single, temporally calibrated state budget for colonial India as a whole, to the orchestrations of a "masque of plenty" encoded in the
annual *Moral and Material Progress Report*. These representational artifacts
and practices repressed internal differences and unevenness through a
metonymic logic wherein parts stood in for wholes and through a logic of
equivalence that rendered concretely unequal transactions and objects as
abstract equivalents. Yet they also unwittingly provided the basis for new
imaginative geographies and an insurgent vocabulary of political economy.
The second section of this chapter explores the emergence of a novel monetary framework and the progressive homogenization of financial space.
The emergence of a state-regulated financial space hinged on specific developments during the post-1857 era. These included the circulation of
state-issued paper currency or fiduciary money, the coalescing of interdependent yet hierarchically organized financial and monetary agencies and
practices on different spatial scales, and the informal assimilation of indigenous financial instruments and practices into the codified principles established for transactions in colonial India. The attempt to homogenize financial space in colonial India, as elsewhere, required continual navigation of
the underlying contradiction between the financial system and its monetary
basis and between the role of money as a measure of value and as a medium
of exchange. In colonial India, this contradiction acquired a highly particular and particularizing form—one that not only enabled the envisioning of
a bounded economic space but rendered visible its imbrication within a
wider imperial economy.

"THE MASQUE OF PLENTY":
REPRESENTING COLONIAL ECONOMIC SPACE

The expansion of colonial state space was concomitant with the consolidation of its institutional reflexivity, that is, the generation and reflexive use of

a body of discursive knowledge for the reproduction of state power.[1] What scholars have variously identified as the colonial "regimen of numbers,"[2] the "rule by record,"[3] the consolidation of an "official sociology of knowledge,"[4] and an "ethnographic" statist imaginary[5] can be understood as elements of this broader process. The deepening of the state's "institutional reflexivity" proceeded in tandem with the expansion of its reach into society and the reconfiguration of state–economy relations during the post-1857 era.

A central mandate of the newly instituted and reconstituted state departments (e.g., Revenue, Agriculture, and Commerce; Public Works; Finance) was the accumulation of specialized agricultural, commercial, and financial statistics that were systematized over time in district, provincial, and imperial gazetteers. The innumerable statistical records and surveys were integral to the consolidation and legitimization of colonial practices of restructuring wherein an ever-wider range of transactions were enveloped within the fold of the colonial economy and subjected to the regulatory practices of the colonial state. The production of a distinctive state space required and generated comprehensive data about market structures, productive expenditures, property relations, agricultural production, cropping patterns, practices of consumption, and the like. The modalities of information gathering, in turn, shored up the institutional-territorial reach of the state into divergent social domains. The colonial accumulation of knowledge in the post-1857 period did not simply service internal statist functions, nor was it impelled by an economistic utilitarian function alone, for statistics of economic transactions were widely disseminated in an effort to make visible official claims of "material and moral progress." What is more, the intensified accumulation of knowledge was rooted in the transformation of colonial India into a second-order space welded to a globally organized imperial economy. In the context of the expansion and consolidation of Britain's economic hegemony, there was a sustained effort by the colonial state to record, classify, and determine the range of agricultural raw materials, economic resources, and industrial products on a local, provincial, and all-India basis. The proliferation of multivolume commercial dictionaries and agricultural glossaries, compiled by George Watt, William Crooke, and B. H. Baden-Powell, among others, on the resources and products of various regions attests to the mediation of official representational forms and practices in colonial India by imperial geographies of power and the imperial space economy.[6]

Colonial representational practices effected the subsumption of everyday, dispersed, and concretely unequal objects and economic transactions into the emergent all-India representational scale of state–economy relations. One of the most dramatic expressions of this process was the introduction and public circulation of an annual, comprehensive, all-India budget that, along with other cognate developments, made possible a macroeconomic aggregative envisioning of the colonial economy and helped foster a novel public discourse on state expenditures, investments, taxation, debt, and transactions. From the late 1850s onward, under the direction of James Wilson — the first secretary of the new Finance Department located at the India Office in London and the founder-editor of the *Economist* — fiscal accounting systems were rationalized on an annual and an all-India basis. Officials of the Department of Finance argued that "the most important step toward securing financial economy will be the establishing of a system whereby a Budget of Imperial Income and Expenditure shall be prepared annually, so that the financial estimates for each year may be arranged, considered and sanctioned by the supreme government of India before the year commences. The system prevails in England; and it will now be introduced and rigidly carried out in India."[7] The reworking of accounting procedures and systems began in 1860–61, and the resultant artifact in 1862 was a single and "general budget for the whole of India . . . showing in abstract the revenue and expenditure of the whole empire and the estimated receipts and expenditure of the Home Government as furnished by the Secretary of State . . . such that in one view would be displayed the whole Revenue and Expenditure of India, both here and at home."[8]

"Each Presidency, each local government, each department under the Supreme Government" was directed to transmit uniformly organized, temporally calibrated budgets crafted in the prescribed methods of double-entry bookkeeping to the newly constituted Central Revenue Department located in Calcutta.[9] The Central Revenue Department was charged with analyzing, recording, and compiling a general, abstract statement for the whole of colonial India. The system of fiscal accounting and annual budgets, fashioned in accordance with those prevailing in Britain, marked a sharp departure from the practices of the East India Company. Under the previous system, multiple and diverse sets of accounts, including separate commercial and political books, had prevailed, and the central concern had been to accurately record bullion imports and ensure equivalence of gold worth. During the tenure of the East India Company, accounts had been organized on a provincial and local basis, with each provincial administration employing, until 1858 when the Bengal system of accounts was introduced across colonial India, different systems of accounting.[10] These accounts were neither temporally calibrated with each other nor organized with reference to colonial India as a whole. For instance, under the earlier system, a twofold system of accounts had prevailed in which the first set consisted of the

> [a]ctual payments, including adjusted and unadjusted. The Second, which always lags a year or two behind the other, contains only such expenditure of the year as has been audited. The first is incorrect, because it contains a large number of payments which on audit may be reflected or adjusted to other heads. The second account is incorrect, because it only includes such expenditure as has been finally audited, and rejects payments amount to very considerable sums, which for some informality have, after payment, been kept in the Inefficient balance.[11]

Before the inaugural general budget of 1862, there had "never been . . . any accounts representing the real Expenditure of the entire country, for any one year" (39). Even the consolidated set of accounts of the East India Company, derived from statements of receipts and expenditures from Bombay, Madras, and Bengal (the three presidencies), did not separately demarcate the colonial India account from other commercial accounts (e.g., the East India Company trade with China) but rendered the "East Indies" as a single unit. The novel system of a single, annual budget for colonial India as a whole enabled "the Supreme Government to have better means than heretofore of regulating the Revenues of the State in all parts of the empire, both here and at home" (13). It was precisely the unprecedented expansion of state fiscal activities in the post-1857 era and the incorporation of the second-order produced space of colonial India into an imperial economy that rendered previous practices of fiscal representation inadequate. Moreover, as the ways and means of daily life came increasingly to emanate from the colonial economy, a regular, standardized, and spatiotemporally comprehensive form of accounts became necessary.

Under Act X of 1866 and the Indian Company Act of 1882, the new form of fiscal and statistical accounting was extended to private capitalist enterprises operating within colonial India.[12] The successive acts of 1866 and 1882, directed at private firms, made it mandatory for joint-stock companies with limited liability to formally present statements of their income and expenditures and provide a balance sheet in the prescribed format that prevailed in state agencies. Professional auditors, regulated by the colonial state, were given the task of certifying whether the accounts submitted were accurate and constituted complete balance sheets. The revised act of 1882 explicitly incorporated statutory amendments passed in England since 1860 that regulated joint-stock companies. This was driven, in part, by the speculation-fueled boom in cotton commodity markets and the proliferation, during the 1860s and 1870s, of joint-stock companies that quickly went bankrupt, revealing the lack of adequate juridical protection for shareholders. But it was also enacted on the grounds that the "laws relating to such a subject as mercantile companies should be as nearly as possible the same in India as in England."[13] The institution in colonial India of legal codes and procedures related to companies in Britain expressed the necessity of establishing uniformity in company law throughout the globally organized imperial economy, within which colonial state space was a distinct but hierarchically subordinate complex.

The production and circulation of a single all-India budget, the rationalization of state fiscal and accounting procedures on various spatial scales of the imperial economy, and the assimilation of British company law symbolized the growing consolidation of colonial state space and its representational and material incorporation into the financial landscape of the imperial economy. On a wider scale, these developments were bound up with the transregional consolidation of rational large-scale capitalist enterprises. Unlike mercantilist enterprises concerned primarily with questions of buying and selling, industrial capitalist firms undertook large fixed capital investments predicated on an extended temporal horizon or turnover time. The accounting procedures of modern firms and developmentalist states of the latter half of the nineteenth century were concerned with the calculation of future growth, the anticipation of future profits, the minimization of risk, and long-term investment planning. They were oriented, in other words, toward a qualitatively novel spatiotemporal matrix. Although earlier mercantilist enterprises had recorded profits and losses on an annual basis, the conception of the long-term growth and development of the enterprise as a whole, and related accounting innovations, was specific to the temporal and scalar matrix of industrial capitalism and the related expansion of state fiscal activities and regulatory practices.

For Max Weber, the emergence of double-entry bookkeeping was an iconic expression of the progressive rationalization (the ascendancy, in particular, of formal instrumental rationality) of everyday practices under modernity.[14] Recent works, in a Foucauldian vein, have emphasized the close affinities between the evidentiary protocols of modern social science and those vouchsafed by statistical and accounting discourses and procedures of the mid- and late nineteenth century, through a focus on the internal representational logics of new disciplines.[15] Yet statistical and accounting discourse and representational forms such as state budgets and capital accounting must also be read as a sign of a specific historical conjuncture, that is, beyond the internal and formal constraints of their own logics. The totalizing ambitions and scientific self-understanding of such representational forms and discourses were shaped by the spatiotemporal matrices specific to the era of industrial capitalism and intensified geopolitical economic competition for increasingly mobile capital. Oriented toward the expanded reproduction and accumulation of capital, the production process of capitalism is characterized, as Nicos Poulantzas observes, by a distinctive temporal matrix or "a segmented, serial, equally divided, cumulative and irreversible time . . . which has an orientation and a goal but no fixed limit." A corollary of the production of a segmented and serialized time was its second-order "unification and universalization" through a single homogenous measure capable of assimilating the "multiple temporalities (workers' time and bourgeois time, the time of the economic, the social and the political)" that marked differential moments within a single temporal matrix.[16] The relationship between the materiality of capitalist time (serial, cumulative, irreversible) and the representation forms (double-entry bookkeeping, temporally calibrated and spatially comprehensive state budgets, novel procedures for capital accounting) that capitalist time occasioned cannot be understood in terms of a mechanical causality or historical precondition. Rather, the relationship between the material and the representational matrix was one of a historically constituted reciprocal determination. It is in this sense, then, that the formation of a single, temporally calibrated, all-India budget presupposed a specifically capitalist system of general exchange and the attendant logic of equivalency between the universal and the particular, the local and global, insofar as it meant the transformation of qualitatively disparate localized transactions into quantitative equivalents on a state-delimited territorial scale. What made state budgets possible was the representation of qualitatively diverse transactions and stocks (plant and equipment, fixed and circulating capital, assets and liabilities) as quantitatively homogenous equivalents. What made them necessary was the re-articulation of state–economy relations. The system of accounts that prevailed under the East India Company was no longer adequate, in an institutional and representational sense, to the task of capturing the reconfigured scope and scale of state–economy relations that subtended the consolidation of the post-1857 colonial state. The cumulative effect of the transposition of modern forms of capital accounting and the generalization of notions of cash flow, investment, and capital stock was the growing intelligibility of the colonial economy as a temporally dynamic and territorially distinct totality.

The ideology of colonial state space was shot through with a modernist representational logic of "readability-visibility-intelligibility."[17] The modernist logic of visualization mandated the making public, rendering visible and generally known the claims of moral and material progress. This was concretely expressed in the dissemination of official statistical and economic figures and representations through gazetteers and the numerous agricultural and industrial exhibitions organized by various state agencies that conjured, in specular fashion, a vast collection of commodities as metonymic of a dynamic and improving colonial economy. Yet given the fact that subjects not citizens inhabited colonial state space and that the colonial state continually attested to a nonidentity with the people, the logic of visualization worked as a simulacrum of political consensus. It displaced the question of popular political-economic sovereignty onto the dramaturgical and specular terrain of colonial state space. This specific logic assumed concrete shape in a range of practices and forms. Central among them was the socio-encyclopedic annual *Moral and Material Progress Report.* These massive volumes published by the India Office in London were made publicly available in gazetteers and provincial and local publications in colonial India. Along with numerous departmental records, these massive volumes contained information on the development of infrastructural and communication technologies and programs of agricultural development as well as statistics on population, production, wages, trade guilds, prices, bank assets, soil types, village boundaries, tax liability, mortality, morbidity, industrial output, railway traffic, and imports and exports, based on the territorial and institutional reach of the colonial state. By the turn of the century, the colonial state had, as David Ludden suggests, "the power to value, demarcate, judge, and survey assets, transactions, and conflicts in every corner of British India; it had rendered India systematic."[18] The expansion of state information apparatuses over ever-wider spheres of social and economic activity proceeded apace with the deepening of its regulatory capacity.

The volumes of data collected and circulated had a seemingly extra-referential status. Indeed, as Arjun Appadurai observes, "the sheer vastness of the numbers involved in major policy debates in the nineteenth century often made their strictly referential or informational dimension unmanageable."[19] Yet despite the questionable accuracy of vast bodies of official data, state-generated economic categories and classifications were pervasively institutionalized. They were deployed in the classification and demarcation of urban, provincial, district, and local spaces; the delimitation of property rights; the planning and location of state works; the demarcation of state forests; and the formulation of economic and social policies and the like. The accumulation of statistical and informational data was a constitutive aspect of the colonial political imaginary, the essential fuel for extensive, wide-ranging policy debates, and the reproduction of colonial rule.

Colonial representational practices, based on an attempt to achieve "mathematical precision" over a circumscribed territory, presented a unified pan-Indian political-economic space.[20] Statistical aggregates and data on trade, production, circulation, and investment along with averages of prices, wages, and the like were calculated with reference to a bounded geographical-political space and over time, thus enabling conceptions of the economy as a dynamic whole. Such practices operated through a metonymic logic wherein the territorial whole was rendered equivalent to the sum of its statistical parts. Aggregates of imports and exports and averages of exchange rates, capital flows, and the like were defined and measured to capture economic transactions within a state-delimited economic space. What is more, official representations of colonial state space were based on a sharp distinction between an internal-domestic and an external-foreign political-economic space. This was nowhere more apparent than in the practices for recording and measuring trade and production statistics. From the late 1860s onward, uniform rules and regulations were established for the registration and compilation of statistics of land and seaborne trade for the "whole of India."[21] This ambitious scheme had two principal objects. First, it sought to "diffuse trade knowledge, with reference to the trade of India for both the Supreme Government as well as the common population of India, both European and native." Second, the scheme sought to indicate the "extent of the market for the products of the UK among the common population of India."[22]

The registration of trade was organized to facilitate "comparisons with other countries . . . for it is obviously very desirable that returns of trade of one country be comparable to those of another." Within the delimited space of colonial India, it was declared that the returns of trade should be framed in a uniform fashion that "admits of the publication of general results on one homogenous system. . . . It enables inquirers to trace country merchandise from the place of production to that of consumption within India; or the seaport when intended for export, and imported merchandise from the seaport to the place of consumption, or to the frontier when re-exported by land."[23] What was especially remarkable about the registration of trade and products was the operative division between an internal-domestic and external-foreign economic space.[24] According to the official guidelines for the registration of trade, "the external, foreign trade comprises the traffic which is conveyed outside the boundaries of British India. . . . In a certain sense the traffic with the French and Portuguese possessions, and the native territories in the center of India, may be reckoned as external trade, but for statistical and registration purposes it is to be classified as internal."[25] The external physical-territorial boundaries of colonial India constituted the principle of division between internal-domestic and external-foreign transactions. In fact, princely states or so-called native territories were subsumed within the overarching classificatory scheme of internal, domestic trade. This occurred not only in the case of princely states that were geographically embedded within particular British provincial and presidency boundaries but extended to all princely states and non-British colonial territories within the boundaries of colonial India.

This scheme of representation necessitated the meticulous marking of the geographical origin of commodities based on an internal-domestic versus external-foreign division. Colonial officials in charge of compiling and recording statistical data were instructed that the "distinction . . . between articles of Indian and foreign production be given particular prominence."[26] This scheme, employed at local, provincial, and all-India scales, tracked the relative consumption and production of "native" versus foreign (which effectively meant British) manufactures and agricultural commodities and directed the organization and planning of various state works and policies. Such practices helped forge and sustain the reification of state boundaries as the appropriate container of economic flows.

A central tenet of colonial ideology was that "native thought" was defined, as John Strachey claimed, by an intrinsic "lack of precision in magnitude, number, and time."[27] Colonial departmental records resound with the entwined themes of the imperative of data gathering, the presumption of local deception, and the pedagogical value of such efforts. With reference, for instance, to the system of registration posts established for classifying the direction, course, and specificity of the circulation of commodities and goods, colonial officials were continually cautioned "to exercise great discretion . . . in the mode of obtaining information." This generalized injunction had particular relevance for "measures of a novel kind. . . . For the natives have to be continually divested of the idea that . . . inquiries are always undertaken merely with a view to increased taxation." To combat this prevailing assumption, local and provincials officials were instructed to actively encourage "natives to take an intelligent interest in the matter . . . [for this] would have the double value of giving to the government and commercial men the knowledge of important facts, and, at the same time, of affording to the people the most valuable and practical kind of education."[28]

This process of "officialization," enacted within a geographically delimited political-economic space, was double-edged.[29] The dissemination of colonial representational forms led to the formation of a common cognitive frame, a standardized scheme of socioeconomic discourse, and categories of perception and evaluation. They enabled the possibility of grasping colonial India as a bounded, singular political and economic entity in a manner that erased internal differences and unevenness. However, rather than simply dazzling or passively instructing colonized subjects, statist representations of the colonial economy became the locus of intense conflict. The unintended consequences of colonial spatial-economic restructuring, as well as the logic of visualization, inform the comments of the viceroy, Lord Ripon:

> The very fact that we have established a central government for India and that with the present facilities for communication and the spread of news and information, the eyes of men, from the Punjab to Adams Bridge and from Bombay to Madras, are turned upon the Supreme Government as the final and evident arbiter of their fate, brings them more together among themselves, and gives, as it were, a common center for their political thoughts, and a rallying point for their political action. The Government of India is constantly struggling against this tendency . . . but the force of things is too strong for them, and the welding process will go on, whether we like it or not.[30]

Colonial practices spawned conceptions of political-economic processes as definitionally coextensive with the state. However, official representations of colonial India as a bounded space ran up against the lived experience of colonial unevenness, the palpable actuality of the "superimposition and interpenetration" of socioeconomic networks and flows that were not contained within state-territorial boundaries.[31] What is more, the sharp division posited, within official representational discourse, between an internal-domestic and an external-foreign space unwittingly secured the legitimacy of evaluations of colonial state practices from an India-wide standpoint.

An early illustration of this unintended consequence was an article from 1868 in *Oudh Akhbar*, published from Lucknow, that drew attention to the apparent "anomalies" of the colonial regime of "moral and material progress." It caustically pointed out that no "attention has been paid to the material conditions of the people." Official claims of bringing the "light of civilization to a benighted populace" amounted to a façade, "for mental and moral progress is of no avail to a people who have been reduced to poverty."[32] Colonial economic policies were, in this reckoning, a mere spectacle that presented the illusion of progress. A related article published in *Nur-ul-Absar* contested claims that the colonial state "has been educating its subjects for their enlightenment and civilization." It suggested that "the enlightenment we have thus gained is merely external." Building on this argument, the article concluded by noting:

> When we want clothes, we get them from English manufacturers; when we travel, we surrender ourselves hopelessly to English engineers; when we fall ill, we use English medicines. . . . Dependent are we for everything upon the arts and manufactures of foreign lands . . . can it not be said then that the time has arrived when Government can safely leave us to educate ourselves?[33]

What distinguished these imaginings of the colonial economy was the critical revaluation by colonial subjects of official schemas. An editorial published in 1870 in the *Taj-ul-Akhbar* suggested that a "mere glance at official documents," especially those relating to trade and production, proved that "native commerce, industry, and art have entirely decayed and that India now depends upon Europe for the supply of all articles of daily consumption and use." Such apparently mundane data as railway and seaborne trade returns were held up as indices of the fact that "English ships now daily empty their cotton goods, glass wares, liquors, and other manufactures, on the shores of India, and carry away our silver in return." With reference to the annual state budget, it noted that "after defraying the ordinary expenses of the state, the majority of revenues ultimately goes to enrich European manufacturers, and the remainder is sent to England in the form of home charges." Although the article proclaimed that "natives would fare far better if all foreign merchants and goods were forbidden entry within India," it acknowledged that such a scheme was impossible under "present circumstances." Instead, it urged the reorientation of colonial projects toward the "teaching of industrial arts in India . . . just as the Supreme Government has done for its own countrymen in England . . . so that natives may carry out commerce with greater parity, and native manufactures may find a secure place on the European market."[34]

In an extraordinary travelogue from the 1860s (which appeared in serial form in the London *Saturday Evening Post* from 1860 to 1866 and was published in book form in 1869), Bholanauth Chunder, a resident of Calcutta, traversed the main trunk lines of the railway grid in northern colonial India. While traveling through the North-Western Provinces (later designated the

United Provinces), he noted that sitting down to dinner at his local hosts in Agra, the

> conversation turned upon the principal subject of the day — Income Tax. Throughout Hindoostan it is regarded as a national mulct for the rebellion. The mysterious "wants of the State" are incomprehensible to the popular understanding . . . the annual income or expenditure of the State . . . its "chronic deficits." . . . Never before was the national debt known in India. . . . Not more is the national debt foreign to the ideas of the North-Westerns than is the Income Tax.[35]

Chunder continually interspersed his travel narrative with a lament for the "passing off of the manufactures of our country into foreign hands" and hoped that

> our sons and grandsons will emulate our ancestors to have every *dhooty*, every shirt, and every *pugree* made from the fabrics of Indian cotton manufactured by Indian mill-owners. The present Hindoo is a mere tiller of the soil . . . but the increased knowledge, energy, and wealth of the Indians of the twentieth or twenty-first century, would enable them to follow both agriculture and manufactures, to develop the subterranean resources, to open mines and set up mills, to launch ships upon the ocean, and carry goods to the doors of the consumers in England and America. (168–69)

The "officialization" of a statist political-economic grammar underwrote the formation of critical evaluations of colonial state practices from the collective standpoint of an imagined domestic space, one that corresponded to an all-India scale. Colonial practices did not merely transform economic conditions but helped forge the normative and conceptual vocabulary of popular imaginings of political-economic space.

THE HOMOGENIZATION OF FINANCIAL SPACE

The centralization of taxation systems, the imposition of a unified temporal regime across colonial India, and the standardization of weights and measures were all, in varying registers, crucial means for securing an increasingly uniform and homogenous state space. Until the last third of the nineteenth century, for instance, there were vast differences not only in the linear weights and measures used in different localities and regions but also in measures of capacity. Weights were based largely on a linear scale that corresponded to different bodily parts and physical/natural phenomenon. These measures were not, however, uniform with respect to either administrative or cultural-linguistic boundaries. In the United Provinces, for instance, there were broad intraregional disparities in linear measures of length. These ranged, for instance, from the length of the foot, a finger-breadth *(angul)*, the span of the hand *(hath)* in eastern UP, the length of two barley corns *(angusht)* in western UP, the distance along which a cow's bellow could be heard *(guakos)* in northern UP, received imperial Mughal measures of forty-one fingers, the length of which was fixed at thirty-three inches (the *Ilahi gaz*), and the like.[36] These diverse standards for measures were commodity specific, based on the weight of the measure (seed, rice, horse-gram, mixed seeds) rather than the determination of capacities. The common standard for measuring gold and jewels in the United Provinces, for instance, were particular seeds *(ghungchi)*, whose weight was fixed at 1.933 grains (171). The fragmented and localized character of weights and measures posed severe problems for the state's attempt to translate locally specific economic transactions (e.g., food prices and quantities) into abstract, transregional aggregates. It was virtually impossible before the 1870s to compile time-series data on agricultural prices because the locally embedded measures and scales were not mutually intelligible. Colonial representational practices, which were rooted within the increasing sway of the commodity form, established an order of equivalence between concretely unequal and incommensurable objects and transactions.

This process was starkly evident in the introduction of a novel financial and monetary framework. It was during the post-1857 period that an increasingly uniform financial space emerged, based on the generalization of modern accounting and statistical procedures, the assimilation of British company law, and, above all, the extension and consolidation of state money. This new monetary and financial regime brought into being through the regulation of money by the state and a series of social and technological innovations caused a radical shift in the time-space coordinates of the financial system, in the trajectories of received forms of credit money, and in everyday imaginaries of space and time. A key aspect of the process of financial homogenization was the extension of state money into spaces previously dominated by exchange based on multiple, specialized, and regionally specific currencies.

As the Ur-commodity that condenses the attributes of all other commodities, money represents the ultimate power of transposability. As the measure of value, it enables the unconditional convertibility of the elements of daily life (land, labor, nature) into commodities. It embodies par excellence the leveling effect of commodification that transforms qualitative differences into quantitative equivalents. Its use-value as the medium of exchange, the "perpetuum mobile of circulation," entails the continual bursting through of "all the temporal, spatial and personal barriers imposed by the direct exchange of products."[37] Yet, at the same moment, it embodies without resolving a structural contradiction between its status as a measure of value and as a medium of exchange. In the context of colonial India, this structural contradiction assumed a highly particular and particularizing form.

Studies of the historical geography of monetary systems in the late Mughal and early colonial periods indicate that although monetary exchange was extensive, its workings were highly specific and localized.[38] The ways and means of daily life had by the late eighteenth and early nineteenth centuries long been cast into the expanding net of the commodity form — relations and transactions involving money were well entrenched in everyday processes of production and consumption — but there were multiple monetary forms in circulation. Official colonial accounts from the early and mid-nineteenth century represented inherited monetary networks and systems as paradigmatic of a "riotous, anarchic" proliferation.[39] A focus on the geography of money during the early colonial period, however, indicates a patchwork of discrete currency systems and geographically extensive credit networks scattered widely over space and through time, each reflective of specific concepts, texts, and negotiable instruments, and bound together by localized knowledge structures, expert systems, and relations of trust rooted in kinship and caste affiliations.[40] The proliferation of multiple currency systems was not just a legacy of the historical fragmentation of space into competing polities and patterns of layered sovereignty; it also expressed the absence of an exclusive, institutionalized tie between territory and sovereignty. Consequently, not only was the minting of money farmed out to local contractors rather than regulated or monopolized by state agencies, but indigenous merchants, bankers *(shroffs)*, and money changers occupied the central institutional and regulatory nodes of late Mughal and early colonial financial systems.[41] They were, as various studies have shown, central to the expansion of both intensive and extensive credit markets over local, regional, and interregional scales, the generation of new financial instruments, and the institutional pivot of the expansive trade networks of the Indian Ocean economy over several centuries.[42]

Until the 1830s and the beginning of a uniform silver standard, there were more than "1139 kinds of gold *mohurs* [mohurs were employed for

ritual purposes], 61 kinds of gold *huns* or south Indian pagodas, 556 kinds
of silver rupees, besides 214 kinds of other coins." Not only were different
monetary forms current in particular regions but they were symbolically
and functionally specific. Silver rupees, which were employed for long-
distance trade in bulk commodities, circulated in northern India (which had
been the center of the late Mughal regime), gold *pagodas* in southern
provinces, Chandore rupees in the western Deccan, and Varanasi, Mirzapore, and Farukhabad coins in the northern Gangetic plain, and so on. Furthermore, currencies were "classified according to the place of fabrication,
the persons issuing them, and the distinguishing symbol impressed on them,
such as the *Trishuli* [the trident of Shiva] on the Benares rupee, the figure
of a sword on the Hyderabad coin, the fish and tiger on the Lucknow rupee,
and the like."[43]

The movement toward a generalized and abstract money form, which literally gained a wider currency beyond specific provinces, was brought
about through direct force, as the colonial state imposed its monetary regime on existing transactional networks and practices. The homogenization of financial space was predicated on two successive movements. First,
colonial India was subordinated, during the East India Company regime, to
the silver rupee under Act XVII of 1835, and a network of government-
regulated banking institutions was established to issue rupees of a standardized value. The act of 1835 established "the silver rupee" as "the
standard coin of the whole of British India" and stipulated that "no gold coin
shall henceforth be a legal tender of payment in any of the territories of the
EIC."[44] Second, the homogenization of financial space was extended and
consolidated under Act XIX of 1861 through the introduction and circulation of state paper currency or fiduciary money. The chief architect of the
latter initiative was James Wilson, the secretary for finance and a leading
member of the Banking school of monetary thought in Britain. His minute
of December 25, 1859, articulated the animating rationale for a state-issued
paper currency in the language of contemporary political economy and
within the Ricardian framework of the Banking school:

> The only object of a currency is to facilitate the exchange of commodi-
> ties, by representing some common standard of value to which that of
> all other commodities is made referable, and in which it is expressed. . . .
> Inasmuch, then, as the coin required for circulation is a real abstraction
> from the available active capital of the country, it follows that any
> method that can be adopted by which the quantity of coin required for

the transactions of the country may be reduced . . . to that extent so much capital will be released from an unprofitable employment, and returned into the channel of reproductive use.[45]

The explicit rationale for pure paper currency (that is inconvertible to commodity money) included the complete severing of the connection between money and the process of production of any money commodity (gold or silver), thereby liberating the money supply from physical production constraints, imparting greater economy of circulation, and ensuring the flexibility of money supply.

With specific reference to the role of the colonial state, Wilson argued that "there are very special grounds which point to the facility which the Government of India possesses more than any other government in the world, for such a duty" (7). The "government alone . . . has agencies established in every part of India, however remote" and "therefore . . . the only means by which a paper note circulation can be extensively applied to India" and rendered "universally current" is "through the agency of the government" (11). The circulation of a pure paper currency was to be secured, then, through direct state issue rather than the previous East India Company system of bank-issued silver rupee coins or the contemporary system in Britain based on Bank of England (central bank)–issued notes. The 1861 introduction of state money (paper currency, silver coins, and smaller-denomination coins) followed the broad contours of Wilson's plan and remained unaltered until 1920. Under Act XIX, the colonial state monopolized the right of note issue within "British India," prohibiting both private and presidency banks from issuing notes.[46] Further, following the charter of the Bank of England enacted by the British Parliament in 1844, the Indian currency system remained strictly bound to the bullion in state coffers. This fiduciary reserve against total note issue was fixed initially at rupees 4 crore (40 million) but raised to rupees 6 crore in 1871, rupees 8 crore in 1890, rupees 10 crore in 1896, and rupees 14 crore in 1911.[47]

State-issued paper money, unlike commodity money, has no inherent value in itself. Its value, or more precisely "its objective social validity," remains contingent on the state's supervision and regulation of the financial system.[48] The introduction of the even-more-reified form of inconvertible paper currency in colonial India, which became dominant on a global scale only in the twentieth century, expressed, at one level, a modernist political imaginary oriented toward the authorization of the state's mastery of financial space in and through routine everyday economic transactions. More crucially, it was rooted within the specific relationship between colonial state space and the imperial economy as concretized in the annual sterling obligations or "Home Charges" from the colonial to the British imperial state. The paper currency system and the policy of rendering currency notes inconvertible between distinct currency circles in colonial India sought to ensure that this annual remittance could be met without interruption. In seeking to maintain the value of state money, the colonial state disciplined and sanctioned through various means transactional networks and received forms of credit money that were seen as undermining faith in fiduciary money as the medium of exchange and the measure of value. Through a range of regulatory practices, the colonial state consolidated its domination over the financial system, instituting and normalizing certain practices, while at the same time coercively stamping out alternatives to state commodity money and state-issued paper currency within the territorial boundaries of colonial India.

This state-directed process eased the economic integration of localities and provinces within the larger territorial whole of colonial India, secured the unification of conditions of circulation, and eliminated the uncertainties associated with previous forms of monetary exchange. The regulation of monetary instruments and units of value made possible the record and representation of the total currency in circulation, which, in turn, facilitated the possibility of envisioning individual and apparently separate exchanges as interlinked moments in a dynamic economy. The annual fixing, by the secretary of state for India in Britain, of the exchange rate of the silver rupee against the pound sterling rendered palpable the articulation of the colonial Indian financial system and the wider imperial space economy.

The circulation of state money was a crucial means of aligning everyday practices and imaginings with the territorial-institutional framework of the colonial state. More than the aggressive policing of external physical-territorial boundaries, the formation of a state-regulated financial and transaction space helped naturalize conceptions of colonial India as a territorially bounded and singular entity. The emergence and consolidation of new economic categories and representational schemas allowed both emergent nationalists and colonial officials to engage in a struggle over not only statistical representations of the economy but the institutional, ideological, and spatial coordinates of the economy of colonial India.

However, the ascendancy of state paper currency—that "would be known and pass everywhere" and was intended to transform colonial India "for commercial purposes into one great dominion"—was a highly uneven and contested process.[49] Colonial financial and monetary practices were confronted with a range of received forms of credit money or negotiable instruments ranging from promissory notes, bills of exchange, bills of lading, and interest-bearing certificates of deposit that represented long-established means of distanciating credit. The most common and enduring forms of received credit money were *hundis or suftajas* (bills of exchange that were also called *path* or *tip* in the United Provinces) and *chittis* (documents in epistolary form that either extended credit or registered debt to named persons). A complex range of customary practices and linguistic signifiers grounded in relations of trust and kinship networks defined the trajectory of *hundis* or bills of exchange. For instance, bills payable on sight to named bearers were termed *darshani* (from the word *darshan* or sight), those payable to an established financier mutually recognized by both parties were called *shajog*, those payable to specifically named individuals and accountable by at least two other traders were called *namjog*, and those payable at a future date, closely calibrated with physical distance, were named *miadi*. Once a bill was redeemed it was called *khokha* (empty, hollow), but bills were pervasively re-endorsed several times over, containing thereby a flexibility and negotiability absent in state-backed credit instruments.[50] Carried on the backs, as it were, of community-based networks of credit, trust, and trade, *hundis* and more generally indigenous financial instruments seemingly traversed colonial state space and the wider field of the Indian Ocean economy without leaving a trace. *Hundis*, and by extension indigenous bankers and money changers, became key figures of anxiety in the official financial imaginary of the post-1857 era. They recurrently figured in official debates on monetary policy as a key source for the lack of trust in state paper currency and increased speculation on state money. Yet despite this recurrent haunting, the actual scale and scope of transactions between private joint-stock banks (almost entirely British run) and indigenous merchants rapidly expanded during the last third of the nineteenth century.[51]

Resistance to state money was especially fierce in regional centers such as Mirzapore and Farukhabad in the United Provinces, because they had long been central nodes of the indigenous banking and credit network with its specific mediating relations of kinship and caste-based relations of trust. An official survey of the operations of the state currency system held up the "great commercial *entreport*" of Mirzapore as exemplary of the resistance to state monetary forms and institutions. It had been thought that given its long history as a sophisticated center of regional and interregional finance, Mirzapore would be a test case for the forced circulation of government paper currency. However, the report elaborated the errors of this presumption:

> No place perhaps in India presents a more interesting field for studying the subject of the currency than Mirzapore. It is a great commercial *entreport*, where the necessity of having some fixed circulating medium to represent large amounts of coin had led to the rude devise, as noticed by Wilson, of sealed bags supposed to contain rupees 1000 each, which, to the extent of six lakh rupees constituted the circulating medium of the merchant community. Nowhere, it was argued . . . would a paper currency of assured credit be so readily introduced and take root. But what has been the result? On inquiry during a recent visit, the Governor found the self-same system of sealed bags containing 1000 rupees each still in use, uninfluenced by the actions of the government paper currency; and his honor was assured by the leading native bankers that so strong was the force of *dustoor* [custom, established practice] and the attachment to prior systems, that unless all such bags of rupees were bought up by the government at a suitable rate, they would not be displaced or removed from circulation![52]

Hundis and other financial instruments were embedded within and reflective of a complex, internally segmented, and parallel transactional network of indigenous merchants, financiers, money changers, and bankers. The latter had long engaged in various forms of arbitrage, which provided, for instance, a centralized discounting function for the innumerable bills of exchange that originated and circulated among merchants, traders, and commodity producers, thereby working as important regulatory nodes within the multiple and overlapping currency systems of the early and mid-nineteenth century. Although *hundis* remained a central instrument for various discounting and arbitrage practices, the imposition of a uniform currency and monetary framework negated its earlier uses for coin changing and insurance, rendering it, thereby, a pure trade bill.[53] What is more, during the post-1857 era, the various practices and institutions that helped produce colonial state space — financial and monetary regulation, the formation of a vast grid of state works, especially railways — realigned the received cartography of the *hundi*-mediated *bazaar* economy. Whereas the *hundi*-propelled "*bazaar* economy," as Rajat Kanta Ray shows, had previously been centered in such commercial and trading cities as Surat (Gujarat), Benares (United Provinces), and Patna and Murshidabad (Bengal), the indigenous banking network of the post-1857 era increasingly coalesced in Bombay and Calcutta, following the spatiotemporal grid of state works and the new imperial economy.[54]

The 1899 report of the Fowler Committee on Finance (of which Alfred Marshall was a member as an employee of the India Office) underscored both the continued density of indigenous financial practices and networks and the gap between state-regulated versus received financial instruments. Much of the evidence summoned concerned the ways in which local financiers, by substituting their own bills of exchange for those of individual traders and producers, functioned as a parallel banking network, one defined by greater elasticity than the state-codified banking regime. J. H. Sleigh, treasurer of the Bank of Bombay, elaborated the complex relation between the official bank rate and bazaar rate, that is, the rate at which the majority of the inland wholesale trade was financed:

> The *shroffs* [native bankers] who finance nearly the whole of the internal trade of India, rarely, if ever discount European paper and never purchase foreign or sterling bills. Neither do they lend money on Government paper or similar securities but confined their advances to the discount of *hoondees*, to loans to cultivators and against gold and silver bullion. The *hoondees* they purchase are, for the most part, those of traders, small and large, at rates of discount ranging from 9 to 25 per cent per annum but the *hoondees* they buy from and sell to each other, which are chiefly the traders *hoondees* bearing the *shroffs* own endorsement, rule the rates in the native *bazaar* and are generally negotiated, during the busy season at from 5 to 8 per cent discount. They also discount their endorsements pretty largely with the Presidency Banks when rates are low and discontinue doing so when they rise above 6 per cent. They also speculate largely at times in Government Paper, especially during the off-season, but rarely or ever hold it or lend on it. . . . aggregate financial resources are very great, which, with their high credit and elasticity of their system, enables them in times of severe stringency not only to continue but increase their support to the internal trade of the whole country without the assistance of the Banks or any necessity to materially raise their rates of interest. They possess great facilities too for laying down funds in the Presidency towns by calling for remittances from their numerous agencies established in every exchange center in India, and are able to do so at rates much more favorable than at the same time obtain in Calcutta, Bombay, and Madras [referring to presidency banks].[55]

The relative autonomy of the bazaar rate—the fact that it was calibrated with but was largely autonomous from the bank rate—attested to the vast stores of money capital held by *shroffs*, who were able to under-quote the bank rate. The differential structure of rates of interest and credit policies expressed both the complex interdependence and the highly segmented character of the colonial money market. The calibration between bazaar and official bank rates—bazaar rates tended to increase above the bank rate in periods of monetary stringency and lower in comparison during periods of slackness—expresses the ways in which the spatiotemporal coordinates of official financial and banking practices framed a range of indigenous banking practices from various hedging operations to practices of price discrimination. The segmentation of the colonial money market, as Amiya Bagchi has shown, defined the hierarchical relations between the "apex banking system" (comprising the presidency banks and private, largely British-held joint-stock banks) and indigenous bankers and financiers, and those between different communities of indigenous bankers and financiers.[56] The differentiation within the indigenous money market was marked, for instance, by the operation of a distinct and relatively steady *sahukari* or *shroff* rate (the rate of interest charged by indigenous financiers in transactions among themselves) and the consistently higher bazaar rates charged by *shroffs* for discounting the bills of those outside specific kinship networks, such as smaller traders, artisans, and peasants.[57]

Although official discourse anxiously documented indigenous financial flows and circuits, they were in practice rapidly assimilated into the codified precincts of British-colonial commercial and banking practice. The debates leading to the passage of the Negotiable Instruments Act of 1881 index the broad acknowledgment of the practical congruence between indigenous and British banking and merchant practices apparent in the growing transactions between indigenous financiers and bankers and British-run joint-stock banks. The Bank of Bengal provided evidence, for instance, that "the native usages as to negotiable paper have of recent years been greatly changing, and the tendency is to assimilate them more and more to the European custom."[58] Through various measures—including the Negotiable Instruments Act—indigenous financial and credit practices were increasingly brought into the fold of the universal principles mandated for negotiable instruments throughout colonial state space.[59] The "time-space compression" wrought by the infrastructural grid of state works and cognate colonial financial and monetary networks transformed the temporality of *darshani hundis* (bills of exchange drawn on sight).[60] By the last decades of the nineteenth century, the previously dominant form of *darshani hundis*, which had been drawn at 111 day's sight, could now be drawn at 45 to 63 days, with 51 days emerging as the mean average.[61] The hierarchical incorporation of indigenous financial and banking networks and practices into the representational and material structure of colonial state space was nowhere more apparent than in the official annual publications of the bazaar rate by the controller of currency from 1921 onward.

The interdependent yet hierarchically organized structure of imperial finance and currency shaped the spatial delimitation of the activities of different financial agencies and the operative monetary standard. From the late 1850s, London-chartered banks—such as the Chartered Bank of India, Australia and China, Mercantile Bank of India, Lloyds Bank, and Hong Kong and Shanghai Bank—held absolute monopoly over the exchange system.[62] These banks were granted exclusive rights by the India Office in London to transfer money to and from colonial India and control external trade. The transactions of chartered banks were not confined to exchange dealings and foreign trade. From the 1870s onward, a period of intensified challenges to Britain's global hegemony, they were authorized to use local capital, especially the funds of the presidency banks that had liberal access to government balances. And by legislative fiat, all official (presidency banks), private (joint-stock banks), and indigenous banks were confined to the money market within the territorial boundaries of colonial India. Although the colonial state instituted an increasingly uniform monetary system within state-territorial boundaries, it also ensured the worth and stability of the pound sterling, the uncontested universal equivalent on a global scale.

Because the state did not give gold or pound sterling in exchange for silver rupees or paper currency, it institutionalized a differential capacity of circulation for what was an essentially regionally locked silver rupee versus the globally articulated and transposable pound sterling. There were, in effect, two currencies that coalesced on different spatial scales of the imperial economy: the silver rupee, employed for local, regional, and India-wide trade; and the gold pound, employed for intraregional and global trade. Act XXII of 1899 partially modified this system by rendering the sovereign and half-sovereign legal tender at fifteen rupees to the pound. However, as a result of high exchange rates, gold coins remained an insignificant proportion of the total circulation. As a consequence, indigenous bankers and money changers were able, for instance, to fix high *batta* (discount rates) for the conversion of state money in local and provincial bazaar (markets) into gold bars and pound sterling required for international transactions and the like.

Even within the state-demarcated scale of exchange, colonial policies impeded the mobility of money on regional scales, undermining thereby its use-vale as a medium of exchange. For although the uniform state paper currency was legal tender throughout colonial India, the institution of circles of issue effectively restricted interprovincial and interregional exchange. Colonial India was divided into a number of circles of issue, which were self-contained currency districts insofar as notes issued from particular circles were only payable within them. The only exceptions to this system — and this bears centrally on the state's monopolization of sociospatial relations — concerned the payment of government land revenue, taxation, court fees, railway travel, and other state-related transactions. This system, which departed from the original plan envisioned by James Wilson, impeded non-state-related economic transactions. It was justified on various grounds, including the nonhomogeneity of trade flows within colonial India as evinced, for instance, in the "difference of exchange between Calcutta and the upper provinces" (which a central bank could have monitored), and, above all, the perceived efficacy of this system in "protecting the government from endeavors to shake its credit for political reasons."[63] The latter concern had heightened during the initial sharp resistance to state-issued paper currency. The policy of rendering currency notes inconvertible between circles of issue for non-state-related economic transactions also generated high profits for the state financial agencies in the form of fees for remittance of money to treasuries scattered across colonial India and carried on railways that were characterized by high carriage rates. Although there were only three circles of issue in 1861 (Calcutta, Bombay, and Madras), the total number of circles of issue between 1864 and 1920 ranged from ten to seven. In 1865, for instance, there were ten circles of issue: (1) the Calcutta Circle, which covered the Bengal Presidency; (2) the Allahabad Circle, which encompassed the United Provinces; (3) the Lahore Circle, which covered the province of Punjab; (4) the Nagpur Circle, which covered areas under the Central Provinces; (5) the Madras Circle, which consisted of the district of Madras, North and South Arcot, and Salem; (6) the Tricnopoly Circle, which consisted of the districts of Tanjore, Tricnopoly, Madurai, and Tinevelly; (8) the Vizagapatam Circle, which extended to the districts of Ganjam, Godavery, and Kistna; (9) the Bombay Circle, which covered the Bombay Presidency; and (10) the Karachi Circle, which embraced the province of Sindh. In 1887, there were seven circles of issue. In 1921 there were seven circles as follows: Calcutta, Kanpur, Lahore, Bombay, Karachi, Madras, and Rangoon (by Act XX of 1882, Burma was brought within the scope of the Paper Currency Act, although a circle office was not established until 1893).[64]

Beyond particular spatially delimited circles of issue, paper currency was rendered into the very form that official discourse remained haunted by and that the Currency Act was intended to overcome, namely, bills of exchange. The fragmentation of financial space—that proceeded in tandem with the unification of the monetary standard and banking regulations—had ensured that "the note that a man can present at Buxar in payment of his debt is valueless to him for a similar purpose at Ghazepore, 20 miles further west."[65] The assistant collector of the treasury in Futtehpore, North-Western Provinces, enumerated the ways in which this system of currency circles facilitated the persistence of various indigenous financial instruments that the state had sought to overcome:

> In case of pilgrimages, of which the people are very fond, even if *hoondees* are lost they are duplicable by going to a native banker, whereas, if a man loses state notes he has to go to the *Kutchery* [court], where he is closely and formally interrogated, kept waiting, and perhaps told the note belongs to a different circle and cannot be cashed . . . the printing of these notes in English adds to their lack of popularity. . . . In this district we have had special opportunities of seeing how unfavorably the present system works. The inhabitants of these districts are extremely fond of service, and will take service anywhere; we have sepoys in almost every regiment in the country; we have men serving under every government in India as *chuprassies* [guards], clerks, private servants etc. Since the currency notes have been in circulation, these men have begun to remit their usual payment to their families in currency notes, but some are in the Punjab, some in Bombay, some in Madras, and some in Bengal, and they each have a different note, and not one of these notes is cashable at the treasury. I have had instances where the whole amount on which a family has been dependent for subsistence for half a year remitted in a note of another circle. . . . I have received numerous complaints from natives expressing their lack of confidence in these notes due to their limited cashability . . . they ask me "If India is one country, and we are under one *amaldari* [dominion], we do not understand why a Bengal or Punjab or Nagpur note is not cashable here"?[66]

The uneven reach of paper currency outside specific market nodes stemmed less from the continued traversal of received financial and credit instruments than from the multiple contradictions within state monetary and financial practices. These included, as detailed earlier, the workings of the sterling exchange standard; a system of currency circles that imposed limits on the mobility of money; and the absence until 1921 of a central bank that could guarantee the creditworthiness of private bank money, temper speculative activity, and prevent the devaluation of commodities. The circulation of paper currency was thus largely restricted to particular market nodes, usually port cities and provincial urban centers, producing thereby an extremely compressed financial space. The infilling of paper currency into the spaces that surrounded these nodal centers did not occur until the turn of the century. This was effected through the universalization of lower denominational notes across colonial India, excluding Burma (five rupees in 1903, ten and fifty rupees in 1910, and a hundred rupees in 1911), the construction of an extensive network of official mints and branch offices of presidency banks, the spread of transportation and communication infrastructures, and the growing use of telegraphic transfers across currency circles. This process was aided as well by the assimilation of indigenous financial practices and instruments, expressed in the Negotiable Instruments Act of 1881, into the officially regulated traded bills generated by the branch offices of chartered banks in colonial India.[67]

The consolidation of a novel monetary framework in the form of nonconvertible paper currency also generated a powerful movement for a gold currency that was remarkable for the unprecedented, if short-lived, convergence between local elite interests and those of the colonial state against the India Office in London during the late 1860s. There were numerous representations and memorials sent to the colonial state, by indigenous *shroffs* and merchants from Calcutta, Bombay, and Madras as well as provincial centers, on this issue. The memorial sent by the Bombay Association represented one modality through which local merchants and bankers sought to gain mastery over an increasingly abstract and refracted financial space. The concrete demand articulated in an era of rampant inflation and financial crisis was the restoration of a less-reified form of commodity money, namely, gold currency. The memorial argued that "from time immemorial until recent times," gold had been the dominant currency and that despite recent efforts by the state to impose silver and paper currency, gold "continued to be highly prized." In fact, not only did the "few gold coins remaining in circulation command a considerable premium in *bazaars*" but there had been recurrent attempts to "circulate gold bars authenticated by forging the stamp of Bombay banks."[68] Anticipating a central theme of later nationalist critiques of colonial financial policies, the memorial emphasized the anomalous status of the dominant monetary standard in relation to prevalent monetary policies on a global scale. Composed during the speculative cotton boom of the 1860s, the memorial emphasized internal transformations that had "enormously" expanded the domain of "commerce" and which rendered the coercively maintained difference between the monetary standard of colonial India and elsewhere impossible from the standpoint of everyday monetary and commercial transactions (6–7). India was "compelled to purchase silver, the dearer and scarcer of the precious metals, and prevented from taking gold, which is cheaper and more abundant" (8). Not only was there "no justification for the exclusion of gold from our currency," but an inconvertible paper currency unmoored from commodity money was deemed "barbarous, irrational and unnatural" (9).

Another memorial by merchants and financiers self-consciously deployed key tenets of colonial ideology—which maintained that colonial subjects were resistant to change, enslaved by custom, and suspicious of all innovation—to assert new political demands. It observed that "the uneducated and timid natives" had confidence only in "gold" rather than state-issued paper currency not out of irrational attachment but "because as yet it is the only thing that has been known by which value could be recognized, and the only thing which has been proved by the experience of ages to be durable and recoverable, when all other produced things might be swept away." Building on this argument for a less reified money form, one able to represent "real" commodity values, the petition observed that "Mr. Wilson thought, and acted on the thought, that through the order of government, the people must at once be induced to participate and use a paper currency, which was dropped on them as a novelty to be understood and fed on, as manna was by the Israelites in the wilderness." Reproducing the widespread figuration of India as the fabulous paradigmatic sink of metals, the memorial observed that colonial policies ignored "our craving for precious metals combined with the new activity of modern commerce and industry" (48). In an era of heightened global competition, anything other than a gold currency, the memorial intimated, was an impediment to the realization of the official promise of material progress.

From the 1870s onward, the demand for gold currency assumed a specifically nationalist and neomercantilist cast. The issue of gold currency was represented as the "restoration of a national currency" and as a crucial means for liberating India from what Dadabhai Naoroji called "foreign financial domination," encoded, above all, in the sterling exchange standard and the annual sterling obligations, the so-called Home Charges, of the colonial state.[69] The vexed issues regarding the sterling exchange standard—which John Maynard Keynes fiercely defended in his first work, *Indian Currency and Finance*, and upheld as a member of the 1913–14 Royal Commission on Indian Currency and Finance—became a central site for the articulation of economic nationalist critiques of colonial rule. More often than not, colonial officials and architects of financial and monetary policy understood demands for the abrogation of the sterling exchange standard and for a "true" gold standard in terms of the transhistorical image of India as a sink of metals (repeated from Jevons to Marx to Keynes), and its peoples as inveterate hoarders of precious metals. Official discourse understood these recurrent demands in ontological terms that denied the concrete historicity and lived experience of unevenness that rendered them intelligible. Written during his tenure at the India Office, Keynes's first work characterized demands for a gold currency and a gold standard in colonial India as indexical of the "vague stirrings of the original sin of mercantilism always inherent in the mind of the natural man" (as opposed to civilized and rational political-economic subjects) that authorized a misrecognition of gold as "beyond everything essential wealth." He categorically dismissed "incitements against malevolent financiers who would seek to deprive India of her 'fair-share' of the world's new gold" as "unfounded prejudice." The nationalist motif of the drain of wealth, of colonial financial domination, and the creation of a dependent colonial economy—explored at length in later chapters—was for Keynes merely a sign of the *ressentiment* of uncomprehending subjects. It expressed, he observed, "jealously of the powerful magnates of the London Money Market obtaining what should belong to India's Market for their own purposes . . . jealousy of Great Britain, who might use or regard India's earmarked gold as her own war-chest."[70]

Keynes explicitly acknowledged and analyzed at length the official institution of a nonconvertible currency in colonial India. But he obsessively returned to the spectral image of the nonproductive accumulation of gold and silver hoards in colonial India, of the "ingrained fondness of handing hard gold," the "uncivilized and wasteful" monetary habits of the populace, and the "ruinous" and supposedly pervasive phenomenon of "India's love of the precious metals" (99). And what is more, in the context of increasingly frequent financial crises, he nonetheless hoped that the paper currency system, a central prop of the sterling exchange standard, would become the object of the intrinsic "native" drive toward hoarding. He observed that "assuming a sharp financial crisis to be accompanied by increased hoarding it would plainly be better if it were a hoarding of rupees and notes rather than of gold" and offered the following account:

I know, for example, a very conservative Brahmin family, small landowners in Eastern Bengal, where this is the case. Once a week the head of the family will retire privately to a corner of the roof of the house, take out the little hoard of notes with ritual care, count and check them, dust each with a feather brush, and lay them out in the sun to air and to recover from any trace of damp. If a note shows signs of age or wear, it is taken to the nearest currency office and changed for a new one. This, however, is no more than an illustration of the point I have already dwelt on and emphasized — the manner in which any increase in the popularity of gold diminishes the stability of the currency. (165–66)

Shifting abruptly from this colonial ethnographic register, Keynes mounted a sustained defense of the sterling exchange standard as the most appropriate monetary framework for the specific political-economic configuration of colonial India as an agricultural country (the colonial historicity of which nationalists would passionately underscore) embedded within a wider globally organized British economy. He noted that "speaking as a theorist," the sterling exchange standard "contains one essential element — the use of a cheap local currency artificially maintained at par with the international currency or standard of value" that rendered it "the ideal currency of the future" (36). He upheld the adoption of this specifically imperial monetary framework, first forged in colonial India, by the British colonial office in strait settlements and West African colonies, and by the United States in the Philippines in 1903, and later in Mexico and Panama as suggestive of its promise as the "ideal currency of the future" (35). Keynes's preferred outcome of the hoarding of state paper currency in periods of financial crisis and the global acceptance of a sterling exchange standard as the "ideal currency of the future" did not quite materialize.

Colonial monetary and financial practices, especially from the 1870s onward as explored in chapters 7 and 8, both enabled and fueled the consolidation of an insurgent nationalist political economy framework. Figures such as Dadabhai Naoroji, Mahadev Ranade, G. V. Joshi, V. G. Kale, B. R. Ambedkar, G. Findlay Shiras, L. C. Jain, and C. N. Vakil elaborated, at varying conjunctures, an impassioned critique of official practices grounded in a productivist nationalist framework that insisted on a territorial correspondence between money, state, and political power.[71] These middle-class colonial subjects, many of whom either were professors of economics or had extensive experience in colonial merchant and banking institutions, critically evaluated official policies from the standpoint of contemporaneous global developments and elaborated what they called an "Indian" nationalist position on finance and currency. The growing consolidation of nationally organized financial spaces on a global scale, the increasingly apparent effects of colonial monetary and financial policies in an era of high inflation and devaluation, and the progressive diffusion of categories such as internal-domestic and external-foreign as salient "principles of vision and division" enabled the counterhegemonic envisioning of colonial state practices as specifically nonnational.[72] Although the emergent nationalist political economy was initially spawned within a resolutely middle-class and urban milieu, the lived contradictions of colonial state space suffused everyday life. This was especially apparent, as argued in the next chapter, on the colonial railway line.

CHAPTER THREE

MOBILE INCARCERATION:
TRAVELS IN COLONIAL STATE SPACE

Railways may do for India what dynasties have never done—what the genius of Akbar the Magnificent could not effect by government, nor the cruelty of Tippoo Saheb by violence; they may make India a nation.

> —Edwin Arnold, *The Marquis of Dalhousie's Administration*
> *of British India,* 1865

Traveling by the Rail very much resembles migrating in one vast colony, or setting out together in a whole moving town or caravan. Nothing under this enormous load is ever tagged to the back of a locomotive, and yet we were no sooner in motion than Calcutta, and the Hooghly, and Howrah, all began to recede away like the scenes in a Dissolving View. The first sight of the steamer no less amazed than alarmed the Burmese, who had a tradition that the capital of their empire would be safe, until a vessel should advance up the Irrawady without *oars* and *sails*! Similarly does the Hindoo look upon the Railways as a marvel and miracle—a novel incarnation for the regeneration of *Bharat-versh.*

> —Bholanauth Chunder, *Travels of a Hindoo to Various Parts*
> *of Bengal and Upper India,* 1869

It would hardly be an exaggeration to say that railways came closest of any state work to distilling and communicating the ideology of colonial state space. The late-nineteenth-century colonial imagination figured railways as the universal vehicle for its self-proclaimed program of "moral and material progress." The rhetorical excess that marked official discourse on railways serviced the ideological encoding of India as colonial state space. Although railways were overdetermined symbols of modernity and economic exploitation in colonial and nationalist discourse, respectively, they have not occasioned extensive study in the literature on late colonial India. This gap between the rhetorical inflation and the historiographical underdevelopment of railways is a consequence, in part, of the highly particular and particularizing optic through which the railway question has long been viewed. The postcolonial scholarship on railways has almost exclusively focused on the economic impact of railways. This organizing focus owes its origins to the long shadow cast by the nationalist thesis of the deindustrialization and denationalization of the economy within which railways acted as chief agents of colonial economic exploitation. Railways figured centrally in the emergent nationalist imagination, especially the economic critique of colonial capitalism that crystallized in the 1870s and 1880s. Nationalists such as Dadabhai Naoroji, Mahadev Ranade, and Romesh Dutt reversed the logic of colonial discourse that presented railways as a universal magical agency for development by recasting them as particular vehicles for intensified imperial exploitation. Railways had, in their view, directly serviced the British imperial economy and impeded the formation of a coherent, autonomous, and homogenous national economy.

The postcolonial scholarship on railways has largely focused on such questions as the impact of railways on peasant rationality, the reordering of trade routes, the de-segmentation of markets, interregional price differentials in agricultural commodities, the dynamics of economic imperialism, and the economic impact of railways on specific regional economies.[1] Although this literature has yielded insights, it has been highly particularizing, oriented to the details of one particular sector, region, or community. The near absolute focus, with some notable exceptions,[2] on the economic consequences of railways has obscured from view their wider political and social significance.

Chapter 1 placed railways (and other "state works") within a broader investigation of the transformation of colonial state power and the relationship between state and space. Here I chart the complex itinerary of railways as metonyms of a colonial modernizing project, as mediums for the reconfiguration of social space, and as producers of a hierarchical, fragmented, and contradictory topography of social encounter and exclusion. As a privileged vector of colonial state space, railways not only enabled the massive and unprecedented circulation of peoples and commodities within the boundaries of colonial India. They were also key sites for the institution of the colonial political economy of difference, the refashioning of everyday experiences and collective self-understandings, and the shaping of a range of categories of practice.

My general argument is that railways, which were paradigmatic state works, materialized at the everyday level the tension between the simultaneous homogenization and differentiation of social relations. To make this case, I explore the dynamic interplay between official discourses on railways, colonial policies toward railway workers, and the everyday experience of railway travel. Although official discourse presented railways as the bearers of even development, an abstract space of exchange and circulation, and modern subjects rid of particularistic attachments, colonial practices continually produced the very particularities and forms of unevenness they proclaimed to transcend. The tension between the homogenizing and particularizing orientation of colonial practices fashioned the lived experience of colonial space.

A MAGICAL AGENCY: RAILWAYS IN THE COLONIAL IMAGINATION

Within official discourse, railways were conceived as a magical agency that would promote and secure the material welfare of the people, tame entrenched prejudices, and enable the production of an industrious and disciplined social body. The following account, written by George Macgeorge, the chief consulting engineer for railways, is exemplary:

> A land where the very names of innovation, progress, energy and the practical arts of life were unknown, or were abhorred, and which appeared sunk in a lethargic sleep . . . under the guiding direction of Providence it is from the British nation that the vast continent of India has received the leaven of a new moral and material regeneration, which can now never cease to operate until it has raised the country to a high level of power and civilization. The most potent factor in this truly wonderful resurrection of a whole people, so visibly taking place before the eyes of the present generation, is unquestionably the railway system of the country; and there is little reason to doubt that the powerful onward impetus already imparted by railway communication . . . will continue to prevail . . . and will ever remain as a lasting memorial of the influence of Great Britain on the destinies of India.[3]

According to this account, the "mighty agency of steam" had brought methodical, step-by-step enlightenment to the uncivilized, disciplined the "usually lethargic Eastern," and taught the "virtue of punctuality under the uncompromising tuition of the locomotive whistle" (220). It was widely claimed that railway space-time had at once uplifted and contained colonial subjects.

In the colonial context, however, the orderly progression of such narratives required the continual orchestration and staging of a fetishized differ-

ence. A key focus of the official discourse on railways was the imagined encounter between two reified social forms: the social morphology of caste and
civilizing technology. It was widely held that under the impact of railways,
deep forms of social regimentation would simply wither away. As Macgeorge observed:

> The strong barriers of one of the most rigid and exclusive caste systems
> in the world have been penetrated on every side by the power of steam.
> In India for many years past, caste prejudices have been practically ex-
> tinguished within the fences of a line of railway, and the most sacred
> Brahmin will now contentedly ignore them rather than forego the lux-
> ury and economy of a journey by rail. (230)

As pedagogical and disciplinary nodes of colonial governance, railways
were figured as the progenitors of an abstract, homogenous space of production and circulation, and as the incubators of modern subjects liberated
from entrenched prejudices and customs. In an influential work, Edward
Davidson, a central figure in the Public Works Department, claimed a
determinate temporal coincidence between improvements in locomotion
and "moral" progress. Reiterating the almost obligatory juxtaposition between a reified understanding of both caste and civilizing technology, he observed that

> a sacred Brahmin now sits in a third class carriage in contact with a
> Dome (the lowest caste, employed in burying the dead), and . . . pre-
> ferring a saving to his caste exclusiveness, drops his prejudices. . . . I
> saw an instance of this one day at a station on the East India Railway.
> The horror of the high caste Baboo when, entering the carriage, he saw
> the sweeper, and yet perceived, from a hasty exclamation of the guard,
> that he had the alternative of sitting with a Dome, or of being left be-
> hind, was most evident. He however went. . . . And while locomotion
> has thus improved, India has passed from prevailing sutteeism, gross
> ignorance and torpor, to a remarkable degree of civilization, intellectual
> advancement, and activity.[4]

Railways were understood, then, as potent caste-dissolving forces that
would progressively attenuate the "pathology of difference" that constituted
the indigenous social body.[5] Such narratives and their rhetorical excess
were crucial components of the attempted legitimization of colonial rule.
For it was one of the grand clichés of nineteenth-century Orientalism that

South Asia was a vast, vegetative space, a timeless space of ceaseless reiteration. History began, in this account, with British colonial rule.

The narrativization of state works as agencies of uniform progress also spoke volubly of attempts to normalize, domesticate, and efface the unevenness engendered by colonial policies. Consider, in this regard, Bipin Pal's (a radical *swadeshi* nationalist) recollection of his first journey on the recently inaugurated steam-powered ship from Sylhet to Narayanganj (Bengal) in the early 1870s:

> The people of the villages on the banks of the river along its route had not as yet become sufficiently familiar with it to treat the sight of these huge things, moving on the water without human hands, with indifference. As soon as we passed close to a village, the whole population . . . came out in full force to the river-side, and literally rendered *puja* or worship to the boat. The women cried out *ulu, ulu,* the cry, which is made by them on all auspicious occasions, and prostrated themselves devoutly on the ground, taking the apparently self-moving boat to be some manifestation of the Deity. Sometimes they would bring flowers and vermilion and other materials of worship and throw these in the direction of the boat to the immense amusement of the European captain and his crew.[6]

Pal's narrative bears no trace of the objectifying logic of official discourses on "native" responses to technology nor does it make grand teleological claims on behalf of state works. His attempt to render intelligible the subaltern responses to novel technologies suggests more than the familiar workings of colonial middle-class habitus primed to render the unfamiliar familiar for both a British colonial audience and colonized elites. It gives expression rather to the lived unevenness of colonial space, the everyday visual spectacles it afforded, and the particular burden assumed by middle-class colonial subjects in rendering visible the complexity of colonial space-time.

It is important to note here that official narratives on the universalizing force of railways only gathered force from the late 1860s onward. Locked within the terms of a colonial sociology of knowledge that rendered the social body as an immutable assemblage of agonistic interests and groups, railway authorities had initially rejected the possibility of passenger traffic. Promoters of railways and railway officials assumed that within the boundaries of colonial India, the circulation of commodities, not people, would constitute the principal source of revenue because the supposed "prejudice, timid-ity, and stationary character of natives" would deter them from travel. It was pervasively taken for granted that the "remuneration for railroads within India would be drawn from the conveyance of merchandise, and not from passengers."[7] Official discourse in this period envisioned colonial subjects as producers of raw materials, as consumers of British manufactured products, as unskilled laborers in state works, and as potentially disciplined loyal subjects but not quite as mobile passengers.

The exponential and sustained growth in passenger revenues challenged the vision of stationary masses fixed in villages and rendered immobile by religious prohibitions. More than 96 percent of Indian passengers traveled third class, and the bulk of passenger revenues derived from third- and fourth-class fares. The number of annual passengers rose from 80 million in 1880 to 200 million in 1904, and to more than 500 million by 1920–21. During the last quarter of the century, the number of passengers equaled that of France, and the passenger–miles ratio (the number of miles traveled per passenger) was higher than that of continental Europe.[8] Until the early 1870s, railway travel in Britain was largely restricted to the middle and upper classes, and the proportion of third-class travelers (which ranged over time from 17.5 to 59 percent) was higher in the north than in the south. It was not until 1911 that third-class travelers accounted for 96 percent of the total passengers carried by the various railway companies in Britain.[9] In colonial India, the predominance of third-class passengers across regional divides was an early and enduring element of railway space.

Official reports from the early 1860s expressed astonishment at the rapid increase in railway travel and the enthusiasm generated by the opening of railway lines and stations. The following report describes the "unexpected" scene at the opening of the East India Railway line at Delhi in 1865:

> The native population of Delhi poured to the event in a remarkable and unexpected manner . . . the people of the city had of their own accord applied to the local authorities for permission to pass over the bridge of boats on the Jumna free of toll, in order to see the opening of the EIR and had made it a holiday. Looking from the railway platform on the top of the high embankment . . . I saw at one time a continuous stream of natives emerging from the fort of Selimgurh on the other side of the Jumna, passing over the bridge of boats and extending past the Railways station along the railway embankment and the grand trunk road parallel to it for about two miles down the line. The crowd at the railway station and along the two platforms was great. There were men of all classes there . . . and the general excitement among them rendered

this unusual scene animated and gay. . . . The spontaneous manifestation of the people is very gratifying . . . and all the more striking as being wholly unexpected, and is a good sign of railways finding favor
among the people of the country.[10]

In a related account, John Brunton, the resident engineer of the Scinde
Railway, observed:

> It was at first thought that it would be difficult to get natives to travel
> together in the same carriages on account of caste prejudices, but this
> proved a delusion. An hour before the time of a train starting, vast
> crowds of natives surrounded the booking offices clamoring for tickets,
> and at first there was no keeping them to the inside of the carriages.
> They clambered up on the roofs of the carriages and I have been
> obliged to get up on the roofs and whip them off.[11]

Official surprise at the unexpected presence of passenger traffic within the
abstract space of production and circulation envisioned for railways was
matched by increasing anxiety about policing and disciplining these "vast
crowds." Railways not only enabled the circulation of vast numbers of passengers but also became a key locus for new forms of colonial domination,
political anxiety, and social struggle.

THE HOMOGENIZATION AND DIFFERENTIATION OF LABOR

Speaking at the opening of the Bhore Ghat incline in 1862, Bartle Frere, the
governor of the Bombay Presidency, articulated official interpretations of
railways as securing a unitary space-time in colonial India.

> I can safely say that . . . before the commencement of what I may call
> the *Railway Period* . . . not only were the wages in most parts of the coun-
> try fixed by usage and authority, rather than by the natural laws of sup-
> ply and demand, but the privilege of labour was in general restricted to
> particular spots . . . for the first time in history the Indian coolie finds
> that he has in his power of labour a valuable possession which, if he uses
> it right, will give to him and to his family something much better than
> mere subsistence. . . . Follow him to his own home, in some remote Dec-
> can or Concan village, and you will find that the railway labourer has
> carried to his own village not only new modes of working, new wants,
> and a new feeling of self-respect and independence, but new ideas of

what government and laws intend to secure to him; and he is, I believe, a better and more loyal subject, as he is certainly a more useful labourer.[12]

The narrative rendering of railways as the carriers of a uniform modernity that would spawn universal economic subjects, generalize instrumental rationality, and install the apparently natural harmonies of the laws of "supply and demand" expressed the modernizing ideology that shaped the making of a distinctive colonial state space. The implicit identification of capitalism with homogeneity repressed the on-going production of difference and unevenness that was the very condition of the expansion of capitalism and the reproduction of colonial rule. Such official claims about the universalizing powers of railways were concurrent with the differentiation and fragmentation of the labor force employed in state works.

The production of a massive network of state works necessitated a massive labor force. Most of the labor force was drawn from landless peasants who were the unacknowledged product of colonial spatial-economic restructuring. The labor employed in the construction and operation of railways was actively recruited, organized, and divided in accordance with colonial classificatory frameworks. Official records of railway construction attest to the way popular colonial and state epistemologies framed the differential placement of workers at work sites by various agents — contractors, engineers, jobbers, and the like. Chief engineer of the Scinde Railway John Brunton's ethnographic register of laborers at a construction site illustrates the everydayness of such categorizations:

> The Scindee . . .is naturally indolent and devoid of muscular power; at the same time he is not deficient in talent, easily acquiring a knowledge of account-keeping and writing. The natives of the neighbouring state of Cutch are a much superior race. Cutch sends carpenters, masons, smiths, and skilled handicraftsmen. . . . From the hill tribes of Beloochistan and Afghanistan [*sic*] were obtained a hardy race of labourers; men of great stature and personal strength, but wholly ignorant of the use of other tools than the *powrah* [hoe] and a basket in which to carry loosened earth.[13]

The hierarchy of unskilled versus skilled labor-power was overdetermined, in colonial India, by the language of caste distinctions: "For operations requiring physical force, the low-caste natives who eat flesh and drink spirits, are the best; but for all the better kinds of workmanship, masonry, brick-

laying, carpentry, for instance, the higher castes surpass them."[14] A specifically "colonial sociology of knowledge" thus directed the classification
of specific subaltern communities as paradigmatic railway construction
workers.

In a recent history of railway contract management in colonial India, Ian
Kerr notes the ubiquitous presence throughout work sites of the so-called
tribe of Wudders or Uddars.[15] Following the classificatory logic of the
colonial archive itself, he describes the shifting use of the term in order to
show that

> speculations aside, what is known is that *Wudders* were . . . an important
> component of the railway construction workforce throughout south,
> central and western India. . . . [They] were a significant component
> of . . . the navies of India . . . who migrated over long distances to work-
> sites, who moved earth more effectively than any other group and who
> helped to free the railway companies from labour obtained from village
> populations whose presence at work-sites at certain times of the year
> could not be counted on. (110)

I want to suggest here that the transformations in the categorical fortunes
of this specific group illustrate a broader process of the simultaneous homogenization and differentiation of the colonial body politic. Early census
classifications and official records classified this group as an "aboriginal
tribe" engaged in various forms of earthwork, including constructing tank-
bunds, sinking wells and the like, and identified their regional provenance
as the Deccan, especially Tamil-, Telegu-, and Kannada-speaking areas
(105). By the late 1860s, however, the distinguishing feature of this so-
called tribe, as recorded in official documents, was their employment in the
construction of state works. Census and railway labor records classified
them as "professional navies," "the most useful and efficient class of labourers in public works who have a hereditary aptitude for such work," and
"who always work on contract" (110). The displacement of subaltern
groups from the localized agrarian landscapes in which they had previously
been embedded was registered in official accounts as unchanging, hereditary characteristics. In fact, the term *Wudder*, which had initially signified a
specific regional community, came to refer generically to circulating labor
employed as excavators on state works. Diverse and territorially specific
subaltern groups (e.g., Nuniyas or Luniyas) from the United Provinces,
Bengal, Bombay Presidency, and so forth, were subsumed under the putative all-India category of Wudders, and defined as groups with an appar-

ently hereditary calling for employment in state works. The shifting representational fortunes of the category Wudder reveals the intimate interlock between the de-historicizing operations of colonial classifications and the production of difference that reached a critical conjuncture in the last decades of the nineteenth century.

The extension of the railway system was crucial to the formation of a transregional labor market and a mobile labor force. However, it did not imply the creation of a unified and homogenous labor force. Railway labor in both state-owned and privately run enterprises was organized and divided into discrete, bounded groups of "European, Eurasian, West Indian of Negro descent pure or mixed, non-Indian Asiatic or Indian."[16] Such abstractions were rendered socially effective by requiring workers to provide medical certification and documentary proof of their racial and caste identities because these determined the very condition of work for remuneration, location within the railway hierarchy, promotions, leave, education, and housing. The proliferation of distinctions based on caste, race, lineage, and region of origin represented at once the state's monopoly on forms of symbolic violence and its apparently paradoxical investment in particularistic attachments.

The colonial political economy of difference directed the absolute closure of upper-level positions (not merely engineering and managerial positions) in the railway bureaucracy to "Indians" and the privileging of resident Europeans and Eurasians (or Anglo-Indians) in the railway hierarchy from 1870 until 1930. In 1923, the railways employed approximately half of the Anglo-Indian community, and until the early 1930s, Europeans and Anglo-Indians occupied all of the upper-level positions on state-managed railways.[17] The absolute closure of upper-level positions in railways from "Indians" was justified on the basis of their supposed constitutional inadequacies. The exclusive demarcation of such posts as engine drivers, guards, stationmasters, and shunters to either Europeans or Eurasians — despite the higher costs of imported labor in the case of the former and inflated pay scales in the case of latter — exemplifies how colonial practices created and helped sustain an isomorphism between particular skills and communities. Edward Davidson, a chief architect of railway policies in the 1860s and 1870s, provided an authoritative justification of the near absolute exclusion of "natives" as engine drivers and shunters. He observed:

> The natives of India cannot be depended on for any occupation in which punctuality, forethought, and presence of mind are eminently needed. While numbers of them have been employed as engine fitters,

cleaners, and stokers, they have not been found fit to be trusted as drivers. . . . Natives are wanting in presence of mind, courage to deal with emergencies, forethought and caution which a good driver of engines must have before he can be competent to manage and engine the train. But on the other hand, natives of India have a fineness of touch and quickness of apprehension, which soon enables them to handle lathes or any steam driven machinery, and to acquire the skill needed to manage a steam engine or drive a locomotive; but they are wanting the nerve, the punctuality, and constant attention to cleanliness, which even this charge requires.[18]

Colonial stereotyping had a self-referential quality. Davidson's simultaneous acknowledgment and disavowal of the possibility of "Indian" drivers exemplify the co-production of the colonial sociology of knowledge and labor practices. The gesture toward the potential employability of "natives"— their apparent "fineness of touch and quickness of apprehension" itself based on colonial stereotypes—was quickly disavowed in the repetition of the codified regime of deficits seen as intrinsic to colonized bodies. The few "Indians" who were trained as engine drivers and shunters in the late 1870s were restricted to low-speed goods trains and level branch lines, for they were deemed incapable of safely conveying passenger traffic.

A comprehensive report on railway administration from the early 1880s reiterated the fiction of natural competencies. In a section titled "Employment of Natives as Engine Drivers and Shunters," the report acknowledged that the handful of Indians employed in such positions had performed "impressively," but they were characterized as "exceptional" cases. Instead, the standardized objections to the employment of "native" drivers were reproduced: "deficiency in intelligence, want of judgment, want of promptitude in case of emergencies, low physical power, deficiency in stamina and presence of mind." This list was supplemented with such apparently intrinsic failings as "want of sufficient technical knowledge to adjust the mechanism of an engine."[19] According to this logic, because "natives" were constitutionally unable to transcend caste as well as physical and mental deficiencies, any training or education would be necessarily wasted.

The privilege accorded to Europeans and Anglo-Indians (an emergent category during this period) was part of an anxious attempt to maintain the reified binarism between colonizer and colonized, European and native. Anglo-Indians inhabited a liminal space within the racialized colonial (and subsequently national) social landscape. This liminality threatened to disrupt, yet in effect reinforced, the continual staging of the reified binarisms constitutive of colonial racialization.[20] It was therefore imperative to contain their potentially transgressive circulation and make them fit within the binary structure of the colonial political economy of race. The report observed that direct state assistance to this group as a whole, and to indigent children in particular, who were "either orphans, deserted by their fathers, or illegitimate, or the children of men out of work," was "absolutely necessary." Failure to provide for their employment in railways would have been a "lamentable and glaring reproach on the character of government." It was argued that an Anglo-Indian

> [c]ould not support himself in this country by working as a day-labourer, or by adopting the avocation of a native peasant. An uneducated Eurasian almost necessarily becomes idle and profitless, and a dangerous member of the community. . . . It must be remembered that he (or his English ancestor) was brought out to India originally to do work that could only be done by a European . . . a fact, which in itself gives him claim to careful consideration.[21]

Not only did state practices continually generate shifting sociologies of knowledge, but state-generated classificatory schemes were institutionalized in a range of quotidian policies. These included the caste-based recruitment of construction workers, the privilege accorded to Europeans and Anglo-Indians in upper-level and middle-level positions, the classification of locals "from Bengal" as the most "adequate station masters," and the proliferation of particularizing discourses about the suitability of Sikhs, Parsees, Madrasis, and the like for specific lower-level positions.[22] Although official discourses presented railways as potent universalizing and civilizing forces, colonial labor policies reified the salience of identities based on caste, race, and religion.

Colonial policies generated intense debate. The numerous petitions sent to the railway department and the proliferation of newspaper articles demanding greater "native" employment in railways illustrate the ways in which the increasingly apparent contradictions of colonial practices became the template for new claims and demands. An article published in 1871 in the United Provinces, in the prominent Hindi newspaper *Sadadarsha*, articulated the constitutive hierarchies that characterized the organization and experience of state space. Its immediate context was the declaration by the state-owned East India Railway that it intended to hire more "natives" as engine drivers and shunters. It observed that

[t]he EIR has earned the thanks of the unprejudiced portion of the community by introducing a bold measure of economy. We cannot sufficiently admire the courage it has shown in its stated decision to hire native drivers and guards. It is not at all surprising, however, that its actions in this manner were condemned with one unanimous voice by the European press. They have all come forward to repeat without hesitation that natives lack the moral qualities which are so essential to railway drivers and guards — that their employment will increase the dangers of railway travelling; and that the proposed system is a piece of false economy. . . . For some time to come, the European press, with that remarkable love for impartiality and fair play which distinguishes them in this country, will be only too ready to attribute every accident which may happen to native negligence and want of pluck. A native guard was lately convicted of being asleep in the train, and the case is held up as a typical one, as if no European guard has ever been convicted of a similar offence. An unfortunate accident took place the other day at Vidaywati near Serampore, and European journalists, without waiting for particulars, at once jumped to the conclusion that it was attributable to the stupid system of employing native drivers and guards. Can race antagonism and race prejudice go further?[23]

The inclusion of greater numbers of "Indians" as engine drivers, shunters, stationmasters, and engineers in public works in the last decades of the nineteenth century was a product as much of economic considerations (e.g., the greater expense of imported English labor) as of the force of collective protest. From the 1890s onward, the Indian National congress maintained a sustained campaign demanding greater "Indian" employment in state works. More dramatically, the foundation of the first trade union in 1897 and a series of strikes by Indian rail workers in 1906, 1908, 1909, 1917–18, and 1921–22 undermined the economic and military network of railways and forced the state to revise race-based privileges and pay scales. However, the middle and upper echelons of the vast railway bureaucracy remained closed to "Indians" until the late 1930s.[24] The formation of an increasingly homogenous and uniform communication and transaction space was coeval with the intensification of various forms of exclusion and differentiation. The contradictory character of colonial practices, together with the force of official representations of railways as the very motor of modernity, also spurred critical understandings of colonial domination.

Colonial practices of spatial-economic restructuring did not establish an

interchangeable, freely circulating labor force liberated from the nightmarish burdens of a deadening tradition. Rather it produced a hierarchically organized, fragmented labor force wherein both skilled and unskilled workers
were differentiated along the very particularistic lines that the magical
agency of railways was supposed to overcome. Although local social groups
were increasingly incorporated as a mobile labor force into the universalized social relations entailed in commodified wage labor, they were actively
marked as particularized bodies differentiated by race, caste, religion, lineage, and region of origin. The antinomy between practices of homogenization and differentiation was not an aberration of the natural laws of political economy as envisioned by classical political economists. It was rather
an everyday expression of the doubled and uneven character of colonial
space-time.

MOBILE INCARCERATION

The microspatial elements and practices that defined railway travel illustrate how millions of passengers shared a formally similar structure of experience of mobile incarceration wherein the internal divisions and distinctions within communities were rendered less salient than that between
colonizer and colonized, European and native. The spatial organization of
railway travel along particularized lines at once homogenized and bound
colonial subjects within the hierarchical and fragmented grid of state space.
Yet the everyday experience of state space, as forged along the railway lines,
spurred the articulation of new forms of social struggle and collective self-
understandings.

The internal hierarchies that structured colonial relations were etched
into the spatial ordering of railway stations, platforms, and the interior of
rail carriages. Railway stations were located with reference to the classic
spatialized racial grid that prevailed throughout the towns and urban centers of colonial India. Colonial racial ideologies were inscribed in the formation of separate spaces for European (civil lines, military cantonments,
and railway colonies) and "native" residents. In accord with this spatial ordering, railway stations were located near civilian and military areas, away
from the "diseased and malarious native quarters."[25] The placement of railway stations along this grid was driven as much by military as sanitary concerns. It was argued that "railway stations should be located at a convenient
distance from cantonments of European troops, and should not be placed
too close to native areas." This was considered necessary to ensure the status of stations as "places of security and a last resort for troops." Moreover,

it would serve as a protective "health measure for European residents and travelers" (August 1859, 7).

The constitution of a "proper" sanitary and military distance between railway stations and native quarters was expressed in the "clear space" that surrounded railway stations. Both legislative fiat and overt force effected these measures. The Public Works Department was authorized, for instance, to "undertake the summary removal of all houses and building" if native quarters were considered perilously close to station yards and grounds (July 1865, 39–40). Such practices were generalized throughout colonial India. In 1859, colonial railway authorities enshrined the principle of defensibility as the template for the architectural form of railway stations. Although the first railway stations such as the one at Lahore were built as formidable fortresses, in later decades the degree and extent of fortifications at railway stations hinged on perceived local particularities. In the United Provinces, for instance, which was the major site for the rebellion of 1857–58, stations were built in accordance with the strictest military standards of defensibility. Consequently, the railway station in Kanpur, a key locus of the 1857–58 rebellion and deemed awash still in "revolutionary tendencies," had higher enclosures, a greater number of flanking towers, and deeper and higher ditch fences (May 1865, 6–8). Although the architectural form of railway stations varied — from Norman to the neo-Gothic domed clock towers, cathedral-like arches, soaring spires, and stone animals springing from the walls like gargoyles in the Victoria Station in Bombay — the internal spaces of platforms and waiting sheds were ordered in a regularized fashion throughout colonial India. There was a deliberate attempt, through various means, to regulate and contain the movement of what were seen as unruly, disease-ridden bodies and to minimize the possibility of encounters between them and European passengers.

A look at the microgeography of railway travel illustrates the structuring of colonial space by the hierarchical and entwined economies of race, class, gender, and religion. The attempt to regulate the movement of colonial subjects was variously concretized. A number of regulations were put into place from the 1860s onward in response to the perceived dangerous transformation of railway stations into "spaces of gossip and general assembly for natives." A key target of the various attempts to police the mobility of bodies concerned the proliferation of "native idlers" who had made "it a practice of coming down to meet the trains for the purpose of inspecting the passengers, meeting their friends, and having a gossip" (August 1865, 39). Not only was entry into railway stations regulated through a system of special passes, but third-class passengers were only allowed into railway stations forty-five minutes before the distribution of tickets. They were then "marshaled" into third-class coaches (less than 4 percent of "Indians" traveled second class) by the ubiquitous railway police. Such practices "would ensure that the platform will be left clear for the service of first and second class passengers." Railway platforms in colonial India, unlike those in Britain during this period, were owned by the state yet seen as the private property of the railways. Consequently, there were strict legal prohibitions against trespassing on station platforms. Until allowed entry into the station, third-class passengers were sequestered in "waiting sheds" marked in vernacular languages and English and located outside the railway stations (October 3, 1859, 65). These provided a striking contrast to the "Gentleman waiting rooms" that were located within railway stations. Ironically, many of the "native waiting sheds" at principal stations were located in close proximity to the railway compounds set up for European railway employees. These presented a striking and visible contrast. The surrounding railway compounds for European and Eurasian railway employees, privileged subjects of colonial state space, were constructed in accord with the standardized regulations for state buildings. The railway compound was provided with a "vegetable garden adequate to the wants of its European residents, with well raised tanks, edged with trees, and furnished with benches . . . well kept cricket and rifle grounds, alleys for bowls, skittles, and quoits, . . . a well constructed library and coffee room in a raised situation, with benches for smokers in the verandahs and on the roof" (July 1865, 24).

The racialized parcelization of railway space materialized the hierarchical ordering of subjecthood in relation to colonial state space. The production of differentiated spaces and subjects was expressed in the separate "privy and urinal accommodations" constructed for Europeans and "Indians" at railway stations. Such accommodations for the latter were placed "outside the main building of the station, but which communicated with the platform by a covered passage" (July 1869, 8–10). Moreover, third-class carriages did not contain lavatories until sustained agitation during the 1870s when such facilities were provided on some lines, yet many railway lines continued to have no such station facilities until the late 1930s. As one official report from the United Provinces observed, "it was not desirable to give the water closet accommodations called for [the reference is to numerous petitions and protests] considering the dirty, careless habits of even the most respectable natives." And, not surprisingly, the usual suspects of "native caste and religious prejudices" were summoned to justify the absence of refreshment rooms on third-class carriages and trains.[26]

The hierarchy and differentiation of colonial state space reached an absurd level in the proliferating forms of rolling stock. There were, for instance, discrete, enclosed carriages classified as first-class European, second-class European and Eurasian, third-class Indian (reclassified in 1885 as inter class), and fourth or so-called coolie class (introduced in 1874). The obsessive concern to calibrate the movements of differentiated bodies, and reproduce the reified binarism of colonizer and colonized, underlay the endurance of these multiple divisions, despite the fact that railway companies only made profits on third- and fourth-class traffic. The attempt to contain the accelerated circulation engendered by railways fashioned even the internal partitions of third-class carriages. These were organized spatially to enable quick and efficient counts of "Indian" passengers.[27] Despite the greater numbers of third-class passengers in relation to first-, second-, and inter-class travelers, third-class carriages were remarkably compressed spaces. It was argued, in this regard, that "a native does not want cubic, but superficial space whereupon to dispose his bundle, his brass pots, and other property" (August 1865, 12). In fact, third-class carriages did not contain any seats until 1885, following sustained agitation and protests by nationalist organizations, at which point the third class was renamed inter class and the fourth reclassified as third.[28] In Britain, third- and fourth-class passengers traveled in open boxcars until the passage of the Gladstone Act in 1844.[29] In colonial India, until the early 1870s, mobility within the train was effectively circumscribed, because the doors of third-class coaches were kept locked for the duration of the journey. As a result, passengers had to struggle to get the attention of railway police guards in order to signal stops.

Unlike the multiple divisions generalized across state space in colonial India, the category *class* in British railway space—first employed on the Liverpool and Manchester Railway in 1830 and codified in 1844 with Gladstone's Railway Regulation Act—represented the central vector of differentiation (110). What is more, the provision of separate entrances, booking stations, and waiting rooms along class lines at British railway stations was restricted to particular railway companies; it was not a generalized feature of railway space (111). In contrast, colonial railway space was marked by a remarkable coherence between microspatial elements (coaches, division of platforms, waiting sheds) and macroconstructions (location and placement of railway stations, the classic racial grid of urban spaces, the ideological form of state space). These various practices and spaces were expressive of, and embedded within, the hierarchically structured field of colonial social relations. Colonial practices at once differentiated between putative racial types and classes and placed Indian bodies into the homogenized category of third- and fourth-class passengers. By creating and policing discrete boundaries between the raced and classed subjects of colonial state space, such practices tended toward the flattening of the internal divisions within "communities."

The generalization of the intricate microgeography of railway travel was increasingly translated into sharp political commentaries that took as their central focus the internal divisions of state space. Exemplary of such protests was a petition authored by the recently established British-Indian Association of the United Provinces (established by local elites) and signed by 3,251 people. This petition was sent in 1867 to the governor-general with suggestions for the reform of "existing railway arrangements."[30] It began by locating itself within the official script on railways: "we approach your majesty with the liveliest appreciation of the numerous material and moral benefits conferred on the country by the introduction and progress of railways, and with the deepest gratitude to those great and good men to whom we are indebted for it." It abruptly shifted, however, to a more contentious register. It observed: "the government is fully aware that railway traveling in regard to natives has for a long time been full of the most bitter and serious grievances . . . the entire number of poor, native passengers are groaning and suffering from what cannot but be termed as a dire evil and slavery. . . . the miseries suffered equal the horrors of the 'middle passage'" (10). The petition made clear that these "grievances" did not refer to railways as such, that is, they were not a function of the encounter between the novelty of railways and supposed native prejudice. Instead, it stressed that the "dire evil and slavery" was "not inherent to railways" but contingent on "particular railway arrangements," and hence "open to reform." Building on this claim, it urged the state to consider the proposed reforms in the system of "public works" as not only an "act of State Charity" but also "a case of simple justice" (2–3).

Among the "points of issue" raised by the petition were the inadequacies of the "open and unsheltered waiting sheds," where "crowds of hundred [have to wait], for several hours at a time, before they can purchase tickets." The petition stressed the privileged accommodations provided for the "very few wealthy" Europeans, who had recourse to enclosed waiting rooms within the station. In contrast, the "vast masses of the poor, weak, sick, infirm and feeble have practically no shelter at all" (4). The petition claimed that the differentiations made between various groups were exacerbated by the gaps between the linearity of railway space-time and the competing times that marked the every day of the "masses":

It cannot be expected from them that they come in only at the proper time. Most of them have only an indefinite idea of time, knowing little beyond *purhurs* of three hours each. A large number, too, come in from surrounding villages and rural districts where no time is kept. . . . Still more, over and above and beyond all, trains with third-class coaches arrive habitually irregularly and behind the time, that even without any fault of the passengers . . . they are compelled to wait for long hours. (4)

The petition suggests how emergent middle-class engagements with the colonial state grounded their legitimacy on both an assertion of difference (differing conceptions of time) and the reproach of an incomplete universality (the delays specific to trains with third- and fourth-class carriages, for first- and second-class coaches alone were run through in long-distance trains).

It also expressed the competitive, if unequal, struggle between an increasingly assertive colonial middle class and state agencies over the self-assigned task of representing subaltern communities. In this regard, both local middle classes and the colonial state constructed subaltern communities (the "masses") as the legitimating ground for competing articulations and assertions of sociopolitical power. Yet the task of representing subaltern communities carried internal ideological limits. For a key "point of issue" was the ways colonial practices tended to homogenize not only "peculiar feelings and customs" but differential locations in "rank and social scale":

We would beg to draw attention to some other evils . . . which are felt very seriously and grievously . . . to the unfailing bad treatment of native passengers of all classes and grades, no distinctions being made between them. . . . they have to suffer the greatest insolence, impudence, hard language, contempt, and ill usage, from the menials of the railway police and lower level railway officials . . . this Indiscriminate abuse is lavished freely without regard to differences in rank and social scale. . . . Passengers have often been struck and otherwise treated with great indignity. . . . Those like the intending second class passengers are not allowed to get in even to the platform, but made to herd with the masses outside. . . . In connection with what may be termed railway licenses or official outrages, we have to set forth the painful fact that the most respectable natives are liable to personal ill-treatment and loss of honor from their European fellow passengers in the second-class carriages. The evil is of such magnitude that we would humbly beg the most serious attention given it. Native gentlemen of birth and respectability, in striving to avoid the large crowds and company to be found in third-class carriages find themselves even worse off in a second class seat. In a variety of ways attempts are incessantly made to degrade and insult native second-class passengers. (6)

The perceived loss of "honor" for those of "birth and respectability" was a consequence, in this view, of the official flattening of the dynamic social hierarchies that fissured colonized communities. This elite male discourse on "honor" found its sharpest and most persistent articulation in the anxiety spawned by the presence of women in the public spaces of the colonial modern.

A central focus of early petitions concerned the ways in which existing practices rendered railway travel "impossible" for "respectable women":

> it is most desirable to bring native ladies to travel by the rail; but as long as the evils as we have shown above continue, this very desirable consummation will be an impossibility. . . . we want to draw attention here to the present impossibility of native ladies of respectable birth and breeding taking advantage of railways. . . . the mode of allotting a separate carriage for females, as in some trains in the Punjab and Bombay presidency, does not meet the wants we complain of . . . respectable native gentleman will not tolerate a separation from their wives, specially in such public places as the railway line. . . . some special provision is required for respectable [*purdah nasheen*] ladies including the possibility of mounting platforms from their palanquins and the provision of separate retiring rooms . . . the lower classes hardly require any special provision to meet their case, as these women are always visible to every one. . . . the honour of our wives and families is very dear and sacred to us, and the advent of the railway has cut off old modes of transit without providing adequate ones for respectable women. (6–7)

This protectionist discourse sought to ensure that middle-class women of "birth and breeding" remain folded within a domestic, private space. They were to remain rooted, even while mobile, in proximate kin networks and familial surroundings. What provoked particular anxiety was not only the circulation and visibility of "respectable" women in "such public places as the railway line." It was the absence of precise distinctions between the always already "visible" subaltern female body and those marked by birth and respectability. In his remarkable travelogue, Bholanauth Chunder observed the practice of peering through *ekkas* (buggies) stationed outside the Delhi railway station in the late 1860s to catch a glimpse of "faces of females whom the rash innovator, Rail, had drawn out from the seclusion of their zenanas, to throw them unto the rude gaze of the public."[31]

In 1871, Raja Shiva Prasad, the author of the first systematic history of India in Hindi (1864), designed a carriage for upper-caste "*purdah* ladies." His accompanying memorandum addressed to the Railway Department was a potent mixture of a critique of colonial racialization and an elite paternalism:

> The liability of compartments — occupied by ladies who live habitually in absolute seclusion — to be entered suddenly by railway guards and ticket collectors renders traveling by railway prohibitory to them. . . . it proves a bar against traveling by railway for '*purdah nasheen*' women. . . . All native ladies of rank will prefer to travel in bullock carts from one corner of India to the other, than expose themselves to the gaze of European ticket-collectors. . . . If it is urged that persons who wish to travel by the railway must conform to the usages of railway traveling everywhere observed (I have already pointed out the difference in first-class compartments reserved for European women), it must be replied that, from the particular customs of this country, women of rank cannot appear in public. Sooner than be exposed to the gaze of a stranger of the opposite sex, they will certainly forgo the advantages of railway travel. If such traveling is to become popular, or even possible, for women of rank, some concessions must be made. Railway traveling itself, if in the first instance rendered practical and convenient to them, may in the end lend most powerfully to modify this habit [*purdah nasheen*], but it must be first made possible.[32]

His design for a carriage reserved for "*purdah* ladies" was not accepted. It was argued that "the Lieutenant Governor considers that the accommodation provided for native third class females is sufficient, and that the better class of native females can always secure seclusion and private bathroom accommodation by traveling second class as befits their rank and position."[33]

Scores of petitions sent to railway authorities and numerous newspaper articles, during the 1860s and beyond, elaborated various modes of regulating the mobility of "respectable" women and secluding them from the public gaze. The various proposals advanced to ensure the enclosure of the female body with such means as curtains, folding portable doors, palanquins, obscured windows, and so forth transposed familiar features from the everyday built environment of the patriarchal home onto the terrain of railway space. These proposals were part of an attempt by middle-class male colonial subjects to contain the reach and scope of the colonial appropriation of space by marking the middle-class female body as inalienable, domestic (national) property precisely as it became potentially more mobile. An article published in 1869 in the *Ukbhar Alum* expressed the painstaking detail of the remarkable numbers of proposals sent to railway authorities:

> The coaches in which women travel should be of three grades, as they are now for men or first, second and third class; they should be nicely enclosed on all sides, the venetians to be so contrived that nothing can be seen through them, which is not the case with those in use; that the glass windows should, in addition, have a plank to be pulled up or down by a screw at will; the carriages inside should have different spaces, screened off with cloth, so that although they may all sit in the same carriage, there will be different compartments for them. . . . there should be a bath-room in each carriage; and in order that they should not be inconvenienced at stations, the station-master's wife should be appointed to see that a room properly screened is ready for women travelers, so that they may be able to go in and out of carriages without being exposed. . . . further, that in each carriage an *ayah* [female maid] be kept to attend upon native ladies, and convey messages between the ladies and their husbands during the journey; and that at both small and large stations, palanquins, doolies, bearers etc be provided at a cost. . . . the present system jumbles all classes together. . . . respectable women are placed in indiscriminate association with common women . . . and are subjected to the degradation of sitting with women of lower ranks, who often are doubtful characters . . . and such doubtful, public women are, according to the custom of this country, regarded and looked upon the same as men.[34]

Such proposals echoed, if in a different key, not only official anxieties about the regulation of particularized bodies in public spaces but the practice of mobile incarceration constitutive of colonial railway travel. The increased presence and mobility of undesirable gendered and classed bodies was a common theme of middle-class vernacular newspaper accounts across regional contexts.

The sustained mobilization around the mobility of female bodies spawned a protracted official debate. Colonial railway authorities acknowledged the volumes of petitions and letters received from "reliable native sources which indicated the prevalent feelings amongst natives of the better classes that it is not desirable that females while traveling should be separated from their male relatives or protectors . . . and that special provisions are necessary for women from the upper grades of society."[35] Railway authorities introduced separate, reserved compartments on second- and third-class carriages for "native women of rank" at extra cost on many lines in the early 1870s. Both colonial state agencies and elite male subjects conjured female bodies as the repository of a reified tradition along discrete class lines. Middle-class female bodies were sequestered outside the public gaze but within the protective sphere of the colonial state. In contrast, subaltern female bodies, categorized as "public property," were literally and symbolically externalized.

Although gender anxieties about railway space were articulated by middle-class male subjects, there was a stunning convergence in narratives of railway travel across class lines. The characterization of railway travel as a form of "slavery" was a recurrent motif. The following account published in 1869 in the *Najmool Akhbar* is exemplary:

> The railway department is insufficiently appreciative of the value of their third class passengers from which a large amount of passenger revenues is derived. . . . consider the practice of locking the doors of third class carriages, so that if anyone wants to get out at any station, and asks the peon to open the door, it depends entirely upon the temper of the peon whether he will do so or not. . . . In England and other European countries, it is not the custom, why, then, should a difference be made between other countries and here? There is no justification for this whatsoever, except that the people of this country are mild and humble, and whether you bind us with ropes, or lock us up, we are silent.

A letter to the editor published in the *Rohilkhand Akhbar* observed:

> The natives of this country are treated worse than beasts in a cage. . . . Is it not incumbent upon the government to protect the poor from the oppression of the powerful? . . . the European employees consider themselves proprietors of the train and carriages, and never do anything without abuse. It is with abuse that they lock up passengers into carriages, and it is with abuse that they open the doors for them to get out.[36]

Such narratives underscored the distance between official narratives on railways as the carriers of the dreamworld of a uniform modernity and popular perceptions of them as the prison house of colonial rule. Railways, a state work unlike any other, took center stage in popular debates. They became the vehicle for systematic critiques of colonial domination. The experience of railway space was increasingly presented as exemplary of the constitutive hierarchies of colonial rule as such. An article in the *Rahbar-I-Hind* of Lahore observed:

> Any one traveling by railways in India will be struck with the invidious distinctions made between Europeans and native passengers. . . . this is the case even in the signboards placed for wash rooms . . . those intended for Europeans are classed "Gentleman's waiting rooms" whilst those for Natives are styled 'natives'. We do not feel the least mortified at being called thus, but the term gentlemen is used for Europeans only, in contradistinction to the natives of this country. . . . the wide gulf that separates the two classes, that is, the European subjects of Her Imperial Majesty and native subjects . . . is part of the discrimination between England and India. . . . this is as follows a) there is a parliament in England, but not in India b) In England laws are made with the consent of the people, but here new laws are forced upon the people against their will c) Englishmen are eligible for the highest offices in England, but here a native cannot obtain even a deputy commissionership d) The home government assists English merchants and traders in carrying on trade, but the natives receive no aid from the government of India. (1870, 220–23)

Although railway travel reinforced and made visible internal differentiations along class, gender, and "respectability" lines, it also enabled the translation, over time, of these different perspectives into systematic and comprehensive visions of the political and social world. The consolidation of notions of colonial space as a contradictory whole, and its subsequent recasting in popular discourse as an organic national space, was enabled by and expressed the lived unevenness of colonial space. The growing currency of claims, during the 1870s and 1880s, of an organic tie between individuals and national space, of an isomorphic relationship between history, territory, and identity, attests to the profound dislocations wrought by colonial space-time.

In their railway journeys, late-nineteenth-century colonial subjects both encountered and challenged the visible hierarchies and divisions that structured the new spaces of colonial modernity. The colonial project of regulating and containing local bodies was not completely effective, especially in regard to the colonization of consciousness. During the last quarter of the nineteenth century, the constitutive hierarchies of railway space-time were contested in various forms and registers and not only by the delegates of the Indian National Congress, who traveled to the annual meetings from 1885 onward by rail. These included the proliferation of critical petitions, debates within vernacular public spheres, the deliberate courting of arrest by entering first-class European railway compartments, the stoppage of trains, wide-spread pilfering of railway stock, the rapid growth of groups classified as "railway criminal tribes" that resisted the disciplinary practices of the ubiquitous railway police, and the like.[37] By the turn of the century, the experience of railway travel became a central leitmotif in collective and individual narratives of radicalization in colonial India and the wider imperial field as suggested, for instance, by Gandhi's iconic experience of racialization on the South African railway lines. Indeed, Gandhi devoted an entire chapter of his autobiography to the "Woes of Third Class passengers" and denounced railways as the embodiment of the interlock between capitalism and colonial rule.[38] By the 1920s, the revolt of colonized bodies gathered fury and force in the staging of mass protests, demonstrations, and violence directed against railway stations, lines, and rolling stock.[39] Out of the experience of state space were forged increasingly systemic understandings of colonial space-time, forms of domination, and social hierarchies.

CONCLUSION

Railways have now linked up different parts of the country and have constituted India into, as it were, one market. The deficiency in one part of India now makes itself felt all over the country within a very short space of time and is made good at once, the rise in the price-level being comparatively small. Every village and every district which is connected by rail are no longer self-supporting units. The powerful and ubiquitous agency of organized commerce has taken the place of the former system, the isolated and self-sufficing village.

                    —K. L. Dutta, "Report on High Prices," 1912

    Reader: Be that as it may, all the disadvantages of railways are more than counterbalanced by the fact that it is due to them that we see in India the new spirit of nationalism. . . .
    Editor: I hold this to be a mistake. The English have taught us that we were not one nation before, and that it will require centuries before we make one nation. This is

without foundation. We were one nation before they came to India. . . . Only you and
I and others who consider ourselves civilized and superior persons imagine that we are
many nations. It was after the advent of railways that we began to believe in distinctions, and you are at liberty now to say that it is through the railways that we are
beginning to abolish these distinctions. An opium-eater may argue the advantage of
opium-eating from the fact that he began to understand the evil of the opium habit
after having eaten it. I would ask you to understand well what I have said on the
railways.

—M. K. Gandhi, *Hind Swaraj and Other Writings*, 1910

During the last third of the nineteenth century, the consolidation of colonial
state space spawned the formation of an insurgent grammar of political
economy that assumed nationalist shape in the 1870s and 1880s. It was
within this context that sections of an ascendant colonial middle class began
to reflect on the transformations wrought by colonial practices. Writing
at the turn of the century from this national developmentalist perspective,
K. L. Dutta emphasized the homogenizing function of railways, especially
their significance in producing a single market by integrating local economies into an overarching dynamic and complex economic grid.[40] As mediums of massive spatial and social restructuring, railways in the nineteenth
century, wherever installed, at once "diminished and expanded space," that
is, they simultaneously opened up new spaces not previously accessible
while stripping them of their spatial presence or unique character by destroying the space between them.[41] For Dutta, unlike Gandhi, the fact that
one of the casualties of railways was the "isolated and self-sufficing village"
inspired neither nostalgia nor moral outrage. Such casualties merely punctuated the perceived inexorable path toward the universal goal of development that the fantastic spectacle of colonial space promised yet failed to deliver and which a postcolonial national state would ultimately make good
on. However, if one strand of nationalist responses to colonial domination
thematized its homogenizing function, another more prevalent and politically potent response bemoaned its particularizing and differentiating effects. These seemingly opposed responses derived from shared everyday experiences of a colonial state space that was at once homogenizing and
fragmenting.

The contradictory texture of colonial state space—the proliferating economic and cultural distinctions together with various effects of homogenization—engendered longings for a transcendent organic space-time.
Among the most passionately felt responses to colonial unevenness was
Gandhi's articulation of eternal, organic, self-enclosed forms of community.

In 1909, while returning to South Africa from Britain by ship, Gandhi wrote in ten days, in Gujarati and on ship stationary, what would become a foundational nationalist text titled *Hind Swaraj*. In this work he identified railways not only as "having impoverished" the country, echoing the ideas of Romesh Dutt and Dadabhai Naoroji, but as being a constitutive "disease" of modern industrial civilization (the two terms *industrialization* and *civilization* were, for Gandhi, interchangeable).[42] Railways had, he argued, generated a space riven by "distinctions" and peopled by alienated subjects whose internal relations were defined by a new "aloofness."[43] The violence of the "life-corroding competition" generalized by modern civilization had erased the earlier knowledge that "India was one undivided land so made by nature" (68, 49). Gandhi articulated his critique of "cursed modern civilization" from the normative and literal ground of an "India" that had remained supposedly exempt from the "*kudharo*" or barbarism of capitalism and colonialism (70, 34).[44] He implored the subjects of the differentiated space of colonial India to discard the alien and alienating space of colonial rule by inhabiting instead this pure, inviolate place:

> The inhabitants of that part of India will very properly laugh at your new-fangled notions. The English do not rule over them, nor will you ever rule over them. Those in whose name we speak we do not know, nor do they know us. I would certainly advise you and others like you who love the motherland to go into the interior that has not yet been polluted by the railways, and to live there for six months, you might then be patriotic and speak of home rule. (34)

This posited place-time, the unpolluted "interior," was literally and figuratively placed beyond the railway line. The assumed alterity of the "interior" had ensured the retention of its auratic character, its spatiotemporal uniqueness and presence. This imagined "interior," composed of village communities pursuing an authentic mode of existence, was conjured by Gandhi both as the original inside of the nation and its normative future. The interior was by this reckoning a pure space of authentic immediacy unpolluted by the abstraction and fragmentation that defined colonial space. Although this strand of nationalist discourse appeared to recognize the coexistence of economic and cultural unevenness, it repressed the historicity of its own vision of a timeless national locale whether located in the present or in a normative future. For the expressed longing for an organic national interior was rooted within, even as it sought to overcome, the internal contradictions of colonial state space.

It is one of the deepest ironies of postcolonial India that the more radical strains of Gandhianism, especially its radical communitarian impulse, have more often than not been domesticated as the legitimating ground for the modernizing imperatives that the postcolonial state embraced as its own. This vexed fate has been especially apparent in the status of Indian railways — which, with 1.6 million employees, is the largest employer in the world — as an institutional and symbolic node for concretizing the project of national developmentalism and cultural homogenization.

In the contemporary era, railways are a chief leitmotif in the ongoing practices and rituals of Indian nationhood. Following the lineaments of the nationalist critique of colonial rule, the postcolonial developmentalist regime, particularly in its Nehruvian avatar, sought to overcome the inherited colonial geography of uneven development by extending infrastructures and capital investments to so-called backward regions understood to have temporally lagged behind the nation as a whole. Contemporary popular culture and official discourse have long presented railways — which carry more than eleven million passengers daily in contemporary India — as collective national property, as engines of national development, and as a literal portal for national pilgrimages undertaken by secular citizens. These representations carry the imprint of the nationalist critique of colonial capitalism and the mass mobilization campaigns of the early twentieth century. Following Gandhi's injunction and during the noncooperation movement of the 1920s, many self-understood nationalists spent extended time in rural areas in order both to mobilize and discipline the masses in "whose name" they spoke. This practice, with its ritualistic and pedagogical overtones of cultural purification, was institutionalized in the Nehruvian era in the form of mandatory all-India rail journeys for covenanted government officials (the postcolonial "competition wallahs" of the Indian Foreign Service, Indian Administrative Service, Indian Railway Service, and the like) as part of their training for public service. The accompanying motif of rail travel as sacred national duty imbues as well English-language and vernacular slogans of the Department of Tourism that proclaim "Discover India, Discover yourself." Such slogans, which gained broad currency in the transnational marketing circuits of the 1970s and 1980s in India as well as the United States and Japan, instructed Indians to undertake rail journeys as part of a collective national pilgrimage with formally equivalent secular citizens.[45] Whereas colonial discourse privileged railways as a central vector for the expansion of colonial capitalism, the railways are for the postcolonial state a literal and symbolic carrier of both an iconic Indianness and the attempted formation, at least during the preliberalization era, of an economically homogenous national space.

Railways remain central to the avowed postcolonial nationalist project — besieged as it is by its own spectacular tensions — of suturing the uneven space-time of contemporary India. Given the pivotal place railways occupy in the nationalist imaginary, it is not surprising that they were prominent in the festivities marking the fiftieth anniversary of India's independence. On August 15, 1997, an "exhibition" train consisting of carriages named after the principal mountains and rivers of India embarked from the central station in New Delhi to traverse the main trunk lines of India.[46] The train's passage symbolically reenacted the appropriation of colonial space as national space and the isomorphism of state, nation, and space. By invoking the ancient Vedic ritual of a horse sacrifice whereby a *chakravartin* (universal monarch) would perform his sovereignty through the *vahan* (vehicle) of a horse sent across the kingdom, the "national exhibition" train reiterated constructions of India as a transhistorical national entity. Emptied of people yet replete with models, dioramas, photographs of nationalist leaders, historical charts depicting "the country's march into the 21st century," and scenes from national history, the carriages of the train embodied the doubled image of railways as containers of both the future and the past of India. Conceived in accord with the linear, teleological framework of nationalist historiography, the exhibits threaded together such disparate events as the establishment of the East India Company, the 1857 rebellion, the achievement of independence in 1947, the 1971 war between India and Pakistan, and the like as part of a continuous national space-time. This staged display, which closely cleaved to the generic conventions of statist and nationalist aesthetics, charted the predictable coordinates of national history for citizen-spectators. If the choreographed movements of the "exhibition" train concretized the imagined linearity of national time, it did so through the flattening of history into ordered spatial bits enclosed within one of the paradigmatic spaces of the national popular in India — the railway carriage. What is more, the exhibition train could not quite excise the specter of 1947. For the ghostly train unwittingly summoned what, for millions of people in northern India, remains one of the most pressing collective memories of 1947: the horror of trains arriving at stations, carrying the bodies of slaughtered Muslims and Hindus across the newly nationalized territory of the emergent nation-states of Pakistan and India.

CHAPTER FOUR

COLONIAL PEDAGOGICAL CONSOLIDATION

Each new form of state, each new form of political power, introduces its own particular way of partitioning space, its own particular administrative classification of discourses about space and about things and people in space. Each such form commands space, as it were, to serve its purposes; and the fact that space should thus become classificatory makes it possible for a certain type of non-critical thought simply to register the resultant "reality" and accept it at face value.

—Henri Lefebvre, *The Production of Space*, 1978

T he territorialization of colonial state power was coincident with the codification of an array of spatial categories, practices, and discourses that sought to naturalize state space. The constitution of colonial state space referred not only to a process whereby state agencies sought to appropriate and monopolize the organization of space but denoted the reconstitution of everyday practices and categories of understanding. The material production and attempted naturalization of state space were dual aspects of a single process of the remaking of colonial spatiality.

The materialization of state space as at once abstract and concrete, homogenous and differentiated, was coeval with the proliferation of various pedagogical practices from the spread of vocational training in land measurement and registration, to the retraining of local functionaries of the land revenue establishment, to the dissemination of official maps to the teaching of the modern discipline of geography. This chapter explores the active, deliberative, and productive character of state pedagogical practices. These practices helped localize and socialize aspects of colonial state space in everyday practices, interpretative frames, and educational institutions. Although historians have documented many of these practices, they have understood them as ends in themselves and as separate and autonomous. The meaning and significance of these interlinked practices reside in the broader reconstitution of the institutional and spatiotemporal form of colonial state power. Part of the incessant, mundane activities of colonial bureaucracies at the local and regional level, these practices expressed and directed the everyday production of locality and local subjects. The attempt to render state space as a taken-for-granted, habituated, and uncontested reality was a regular and regulated aspect of official pedagogical labor.

THE COLONIAL EDUCATIONAL FIELD

The educational apparatus of the United Provinces in the second half of the nineteenth century was defined by the long shadow cast by Anglicist educational visions, the inordinate weight accorded to institutions of higher education over primary and secondary education, and the privileging of a humanistic curriculum.[1] The crucial moments of the state's crafting of the educational field include the debates between Orientalists and Anglicists in the early nineteenth century; the acceptance by the East India Company of Macaulay's infamous minute of 1835 that enshrined English as the principle medium for effecting the progressive "westernization" of "Indian" cultures and subjectivities; and Charles Wood's dispatch of 1854. Wood's dispatch represented the inaugural gesture toward the institution of a comprehensive educational scheme. Aptly described by Gauri Viswanathan as "functionalist," it envisioned colonial political economy as both the model and the means for creating industrious subjects.[2] The dissemination of "European knowledge" would

> [t]each the natives the marvelous results of the employment of labour and capital, rouse them to emulate us in the development of the vast resources of the country . . . and gradually . . . confer upon them all the advantages which accompany the healthy increase of wealth and commerce; and, at the same time, secure to us a large and more certain supply of many articles necessary for our manufactures and extensively consumed by all classes of our population, as well as an almost inexhaustible demand for the products of British labour.[3]

Wood's dispatch and subsequent state directives on educational policy urged the restriction of state investment to higher education and the upper classes, for they would purportedly disseminate "European knowledge" to the masses. English-medium instruction was the exclusive provenance of the first universities established in 1857. The overwhelmingly classical, humanistic focus of higher education was oriented toward the creation of a colonial middle class whose habitus would, it was hoped, be avidly consumerist and loyal. What this ensured, in a tangible measure, was the regularized production of an efficient and inexpensive labor pool of local administrative and juridical functionaries.

Studies of colonial educational institutions have long stressed the privileging of liberal arts, especially literary and aesthetic disciplines in higher education, over advanced scientific and technical training. A central focus of colonial education research has been on the role of English-language education at the university level in the constitution of a bilingual elite intelligentsia, the formation of national consciousness, and the forging of colonial hegemony.[4] The educational curriculum of secondary schools, however, especially that of vernacular-medium schools, has been virtually ignored. The hierarchical structure of the colonial educational field informed the differential constitution of curriculum at the school and university level. The education of the "masses," secured through vernacular education at the primary and secondary school level, was oriented toward "useful," practical knowledge. The mechanical arts, arithmetic, rudimentary science, geography, and agricultural practice, especially such skills as land registration and measurement, comprised the primary emphasis.

The extraordinary place of such apparently prosaic knowledge cannot be understood apart from broader processes of colonial sociospatial restructuring. The expansion of cadastral survey operations, the rationalization of administrative boundaries, and the formulation of ever more abstract measures for calculating the value of land and the revenue claimed by the state necessitated trained surveyors and the retraining and disciplining of a veritable army of local revenue functionaries. Such practical knowledge would "enable each man to look after his own interests" and navigate what had become routine bureaucratic encounters with colonial revenue officials and official transactions.[5]

The project of pedagogical consolidation was concretized in the institution of novel disciplines in schools during the post-1857 period. A crucial element of the restructuring of the educational curriculum was the centrality accorded to a vocational variant of "European" sciences. An official directive from the mid-1850s, titled "Reports on Educational Books in the Vernacular," laid out the broad pattern of the educational curriculum of vernacular-medium schools, especially with regard to the "communication of European knowledge and science." In accord with the broader ideological framework of the colonial educational field, it set particular selection criteria for the massive program of translations of English works into vernacular languages. Such works had to be "universal, not local, those which speak to all time and to all peoples" (examples of such works deemed "universal" included *Pilgrim's Progress, Gulliver's Travels,* and *Robinson Crusoe*!). Yet at the same time it was also declared necessary to "induce educated native men to write original works" connected with the "country, its history, productions, resources, and geography." This was the case because "the natives can only be reached through their own countrymen, and works of indigenous growth, even if they contain errors and prejudices, will circulate far more widely . . . than any translations from foreign tongues." Although the post-1857 colonial regime retained the broad contours of this framework, it reversed the earlier latitude toward "indigenously" produced works. The new colonial educational field was now premised on the assumption that "the thinking native public are a small minority, but they are a most potent minority, and a minority, for the most part, essentially hostile to European science and literature, as well to Europeans and their government."[6] The previous call for indigenously produced works was now tempered with more direct monitoring through officially commissioned and subsidized works, financial grants to presses, and the incorporation of select local officials on the schoolbook committees that were formally instituted in the late 1860s.[7] The generalization of "useful" knowledge as authored and directed by state agencies heralded the reorientation of colonial pedagogical labors.[8]

RECONSTITUTING "LOCAL" KNOWLEDGE

The honored place of land measurement and registration in the new educational curriculum was partly impelled by the skilled labor requirements of an expanding colonial revenue bureaucracy. The 1870 establishment of a department of Revenue, Agriculture, and Commerce at regional levels signaled the restructuring of land revenue bureaucracies and marked the beginning of an accelerated round of the rationalization of systems of revenue settlement. The department established in the United Provinces had an ambitious brief encompassing the collection and organization of "agricultural and commercial statistics," the supervision of agricultural experiments, the monitoring of "the progress of trade," and the investigation of "facts connected with the condition of agricultural classes."[9] The accurate valuation of land, considered state property, concerned the fiscal heart of colonial state space. The new sciences of statistics, land measurement, cartography, meteorology, fisheries, and geography were pervasively mobilized to secure the state's monopoly over sociospatial relations. The recently instituted department of Revenue, Agriculture, and Commerce, emboldened with new techniques for the rationalized mapping of land and revenue assessments, spawned a "revolution" in the everyday operations of land surveys and settlement.[10] Earlier field maps and records called the *khasra* and compiled by *patwaris* (revenue officials located at the bottom rung of the revenue bureaucracy and deemed keepers of village records) were considered inadequate as sources for "accurate statistics of assets."[11] Constructed in the received genre of a "genealogical tree," these field maps commonly spanned out from a central place, usually provincial headquarters, noting distances and recording watering places, fortified places, and the like.[12] The "recorded rentals" found in existing village records were not only declared archaic but "more or less fictitious."[13] Dubbed as outcrops of the constitutional mendacity of native revenue functionaries, such received practices of mapping and record as *hudbusts* (maps of village boundaries), *thakbusts* (settlement boundary maps), and *quiblanumahas* (a rough compass) were abandoned in 1863, giving way to abstract, functional representations of space in the form of cadastral survey maps and plane tables.[14]

From the early 1860s onward, revenue maps were modeled on cadastral surveys that meticulously recorded areas of "cultivated land, culturable waste or jungle land, limits of forest reserve roads, drainage in all its ramifications, tanks, village sites, temples, embankments" and the like (18). The generalization of scientific techniques of mapping land and property rights was concomitant with the institutionalization of new modes of assessment. The revisions of modalities of assessment were linked not only to the shifting fortunes of particular theories of rent and land revenue assessment. They were a direct response to the intensified commodification of the ways and means of daily life. During the course of the nineteenth century, localities and subjects were firmly drawn into the rapidly expanding orbit of the colonial economy and the commodity form whether as wage earners, taxpayers, consumers, or sellers of agricultural produce. From 1833 onward, assessments had been based not on valuations of the gross produce of estates but on the direct monetary valuation of individual estates with reference to the rental value. This modality of assessment, named the "aggregate to detail" method, entailed rough calculations of the gross rental of each estate, with the state appropriating two-thirds of it in revenue payment. Under the post-1857 colonial regime, the central organizing principle of revenue assessment came to rest, as Elizabeth Whitcombe observes, on a mathematically derived "average rental rate" based on determinations of soil types.[15] Colonial officials divided cadastral and topographical survey maps into *hars* (tracts), filling in rental rates based on the character of soils. This system displaced previous methods of ascertaining the actual rental on the basis of the village returns as recorded by the *patwari;* it especially displaced the *nikasi,* or roll of cultivators. The *nikasi,* embedded within complex local social structures and agrarian practices, reflected the reciprocal structure of dues and claims that defined the locally specific relations between landlords and peasants (129). Yet it was precisely this fidelity to local particularities that undermined the use-value of such records for the project of constituting an abstract, homogenous state space.

Even the best-trained British revenue "settlement officers" had been, it was claimed, ensnared by the particularistic and irreducibly local tangle of agrarian relations. A former British settlement officer and a principal author of the revised settlement procedures noted the skill and labor of British settlement officers under the old regime, but argued that

> [t]he circumstances on which the value of land depends are so numerous, so diverse, and often so occult, that, however great be the talents or energy of the Settlement officer, it is impossible that he should not occasionally slip into error: and a single error on a point of detail may vitiate a whole assessment. It is notorious that past assessments have from the outset pressed unequally on the people. No sooner has a Settlement been completed than it has become a matter of common record that such and such a village has fared badly, whilst others have got off very lightly — the all sufficient explanation to native minds lying in the temper of the Settlement officer *(hakim ki mizaj)*.[16]

The new settlement schema was actively committed, then, to the taming of the "occult" forces that shaped the valuation of land. It was accordingly now grounded on the apparently "scientific and natural order of soil rates," and in anticipation of a higher volume of collection, the state demand was reduced to 50 percent of the average or so-called natural rent.[17] This revised settlement regime established a logic of quantitative equivalence between qualitatively different local relations and dependencies. Complex localized relations were homogenized in the arithmetical standard of the rent rate. The fetishized notion of a "natural average rate" that would vary "only with the quality of the soil or the position of the land in the village" acquired a self-evident status (13–14). The determination of the rental rate inscribed within revenue maps functioned as the "central index to the village" and, more generally, local agrarian relations.[18] Whereas earlier field records expressed the diversity of local agrarian relations, the revised revenue maps were uniform and abstract. The local particularities of agrarian relations were thus increasingly erased or read off from an abstract and homogenous frame of reference.

The codification of the new regime of land survey and settlement was

shot through with a triumphal discourse. Baden-Powell unequivocally declared that the overhaul of the "entire land administration" in the 1860s and
1870s had resulted in the achievement of nothing less than the "perfection
of the *local* official machinery."[19] By most official accounts, the long-waged
battle against local duplicity had been won. As H. H. Butts, a senior revenue
official in the United Provinces, observed

> [t]he native little knows, or fails to grasp, the means at our disposal. He
> has not the powerful weapons of our system to fight with. He does not
> comprehend that you have mapped out, and classified all his village;
> that you know the exact area of manured lands near the homestead and
> the dry *bars* [tracts] unapproachable by water on the outskirts, and that
> your statistics show you whether labour and skill are amply or only
> poorly applied. He does not know, in a word, that you can measure out
> the amount of money that a village can produce, or he might try and
> practice a better and more systematic course of deception, but the odds
> are now against him.[20]

This triumphal discourse proceeded apace with the deepening of the colonial state's reach into society. As Charles Crosthwaite, the lieutenant governor of the United Provinces, declared: "the structure of the revenue administration and the organization at the disposal of the Government of these
provinces is such as to enable them to reach the very lowest strata of which
society is composed."[21] A glance at the hierarchical structure of the bureaucracy at subprovincial or district levels (which remain largely intact in the
contemporary period) attests to a constitutive paradox: the reproduction of
the revenue apparatus hinged on the much-denigrated order of lower-level
revenue functionaries.[22]

   At the top of the revenue bureaucracy and situated in the central station
of the district was the district collector entrusted with, as the title suggests,
the collection of the rents. He was also responsible for the supervision of
revenue accounts, the administration of criminal and civil justice, and the
construction and maintenance of roads, bridges, and official buildings, or
other state works not subsumed under the centralized Public Works Department. The degree of subordination of each lower-order district official
literally corresponded to his territorial distance from the office of the collectorate where the collector and assistant collector were stationed. Beyond
the office of the collectorate, in the district itself, the deputy collectors or
tehsildars performed the function of the collector in their subdivision
(tehsils), under his absolute authority. Beneath the *tehsildars* came the vast

establishment of functionaries located at sub-*tehsil* levels. Among these were the *mokudams* (village headmen), *lambardars* (tax collectors), *kanungos* (accountants and field inspectors), and, most crucially, the *patwaris*. Although located at the bottom rung of the revenue hierarchy, *patwaris*, as recorders of village maps and keepers of field records, were in charge of those local records that were the master key for the everyday workings of a behemoth revenue bureaucracy.

Although the collector officially dominated local administration, the increasing demands placed by expanding state functions along with the system of regularized circulation of British officials in various districts, meant that everyday activities of land settlement devolved on local functionaries. The non-British establishment were the bulwarks of the colonial revenue bureaucracy. There was recurring anxiety that the "central matter" of land revenue settlements "could not be confided with safety to native officials."[23] Thus from the early 1860s onward, elaborate measures were crafted to discipline and retrain *kanungos* and *patwaris* by introducing an "enlightened professionalism" among them.[24]

Local revenue functionaries were the sustained targets of colonial pedagogical practices precisely because they possessed "minute and extended knowledge of the people and the land beyond the reach of their European superiors."[25] Under the new system, *patwaris*, *kanungos*, and *amins* (field clerks) were placed on regular salaries instead of receiving a percentage of the revenue collected, as they had in the earlier system. What is more, they underwent an intensive process of retraining, and a system of periodic checks of their records and practices was instituted. The directive of instructions to British covenanted officers and district commissioners for use when performing periodic checks on the accuracy of *patwari* records observed that

> [c]ultivators should be examined on the field as to the correctness of entries of occupancy and rent. . . . in testing the *khasra*, it should be specially noted 1) whether the *patwari* has entered all the crops on the field at the time of his drawing up the record; 2) whether he has entered the details of irrigation fully and correctly; 3) that all changes in occupancy, area, and rent are recorded. The map must be examined, and it should be seen whether the rules for survey and keeping the map up to date are observed. The *patwaris* private records i.e., the *siaha*, the *roznamcha* [periodic miscellaneous record], and *bahikhata* [account book] should be inspected, and it should be seen that they are kept up to date and according to the new rules laid down for *patwaris*.[26]

The institutionalization of measures of surveillance over local officials rein-forced the intensely hierarchical character of the revenue establishment. At the most proximate or close-to-the-ground level, the so-called registrar *ka-nungos* (that is, accountants at the headquarters of the local subdivision or *tahsil*) and lower-level *kanungos* were given the role of inspection officers over *patwaris* responsible for the survey and record keeping of the land of three to four villages. In 1890, there were more than 20,000 *patwaris* in the United Provinces and approximately 450 *kanungos* working as field inspec-tors, or one *kanungo* to every 45 *patwaris*. The average area under a single *patwari* was approximately 1,130 acres of cultivated land, so the local in-specting officer was directly entrusted with about 50,000 cultivated acres.[27]

Writing some twenty years after the reworking of land revenue settle-ment and survey, Baden-Powell identified its "chief feature" as the "utiliza-tion, under efficient control, of the local agency in each village, for the pur-pose of maintaining maps, statistics, and records, correct and up to date year" (353–54). The economy effected by the reconfiguration of local prac-tices and the deployment of retrained and disciplined "local agencies" was projected on an annual basis as between 12 to 16 *lakh* (354).[28] The new sys-tem had, as Baden-Powell, announced "put us in possession of what I may call the *analytical knowledge of the districts;* the knowledge, as regards each estate and groups of lands, whether it is fully developed, well cultivated, and secure from famine, or only partially so, and what estates must be treated as precarious" (359; emphasis in original). The vast, complex apparatus of land revenue settlement and survey procedures was a crucial conduit for the generalization of the categories and practices of the colonial state as com-mon sense. The various documents, systems of record, and practices of mea-surement that comprised the activities of the revenue bureaucracy were part of the complex system of the disciplining and surveillance of lower-level functionaries. The collection of statistics, the detailed record of proprietary rights, the rational measurement and parcelization of space, and the intri-cate routines and rules that accompanied these practices helped localize state categories and practices.

The construction of a vocational school curriculum was calibrated with the restructuring of revenue settlement and survey procedures. A report from 1864 argued that in those districts in which the periodic revenue set-tlement was not imminent, the "government and the revenue board have ample time for preparing for the settlement by a systematic education of the *patwaris* at their own expense; and . . . that all extra costs for special settle-ments operations will be saved to the state by judicious previous arrange-ments, including the internal measurement of villages."[29] In effect, the colonial state sought to procure a trained class of lower revenue officials who would subsidize their own retraining. During the 1860s and 1870s, more than two hundred technical handbooks for *patwaris* were published and a number of special schools for their retraining established.[30]

The attempt to seed the persuasive hegemony of colonial state space in local consciousness was not restricted to revenue functionaries. It was enshrined in the curriculum of vernacular *tehselee, halkabandi, patwaree,* and village schools (often the terminus rather than the entrée into the promised portal of material success), which were the "mass" arenas for the reconstitution of local schemas. In fact, such schools were construed as directly productive from the standpoint of state space. In his authoritative manual for colonial officials, Baden-Powell observed that "village schools and the dissemination of agricultural knowledge are matters which . . . directly affect the welfare of the villages, and thus affect their power to bear up against calamity and pay with ease instead of with pressure the demands of the state."[31] Official reports from this period approvingly recount the efficacy of the educational department in bringing about a class of lower revenue officials. The "enlightened and zealous" efforts of M. Kempson (director of public instruction during the 1860s and 1870s) were lauded, as was the "progress observable in the *Tehseelee* and *Hulkabandee* schools in creating a class of youths who will be of the greatest assistance at the next revision of settlement in these Provinces."[32] The reworking of local conceptions of land mapping and recording was integral for securing subaltern communities more firmly in the sanctioned boundaries of the colonial economy while protecting them from the presumed predatory designs of native officials. It was argued that

> [t]he sooner the people can be taught that the internal economy of their villages is a matter for their own earnest consideration — involving surveys, records, registration to save them from the fraudulent dealing of native officials on the one hand, and from the cost of litigation between themselves on the other — the sooner will they be fit for a permanent settlement of the fiscal relations with the state. (28)

The transformation of sociospatial relations proceeded in tandem with the reconstitution of habitual frameworks and classificatory schemas. The resolute stress on such skills as land measurement and property registration, together with the new educational curriculum, helped fix subaltern communities more firmly within the material and conceptual coordinates of colonial state space. State space was literally taught on the ground.

The ideology of colonial state space hinged on the false transparency of a modernist logic of visualization, that is, of making public the promise of "moral and material progress." A dramatic illustration of this specular logic is seen in the first royal tour of Prince Alfred to colonial India in 1870. Set in the period of aggressive consolidation that followed the repression of the 1857 rebellion, the royal tour was punctuated by finely choreographed events, including Prince Alfred's "inspection" of vernacular-medium schools in the Benares district of the United Provinces. Presented in the hyperbolic language of royal tours, reports of the educational department pronounced the royal inspection as the "most important event in the history" of the school system. The Royal Prince, the governor-general, and local colonial officials gathered at a meeting of more than fifteen hundred schoolchildren drawn from neighboring *tehselee, halkabandi,* and village schools. The prince "examined the boys and expressed great pleasure in witnessing their readiness in geography and geometry." The following question was dictated to the crowd of students in the presence of the visitors: "See, his Royal Highness Prince Alfred, son of our queen, and his excellent governor-general, have come to see you. How affable they are, and yet so illustrious! What have you to say about it?" Scores of students wrote the prescribed responses on their slates and the best responses were read out aloud. The governor-general then addressed the students on the wondrous pedagogical benefits enabled by "enlightened rule." He observed that "schools in which the two higher forms are put through a course comprising, among other things, the elements of grammar, the geography of the four continents and the world, the whole of arithmetic, two books of Euclid, algebra up to simple equations, with practical lessons in field measuring . . . is not found even in English towns."[33]

The recasting of the material and conceptual coordinates of local space was part and parcel of the creation of loyal colonial functionaries. The reconfigured educational field was widely perceived as the principal motor behind the transformation of an alleged duplicitous revenue establishment into exemplary subjects of colonial state space. Census Commissioner J. A. Baines observed: "Without the co-operation of the village accountant, I must admit that our statistics about India would be grievously circumscribed. Births, deaths and the census are all within his province in addition to his more specialized functions in connection with the record of cultivation, assessments and transfers of land." Yet the annexation of *patwaris* and other local officials into the epistemic framework of colonial state space occasioned expressions of regret at the disappearance of earlier methods and records. Baines, for instance, observed "with regret" that the revised system of settlements had resulted in the "loss" of the "picturesqueness and originality" of the "former records" of village accountants.[34] Such expressions of official nostalgia only underlined the apparent triumph of the colonial reconstitution of local space and knowledge.

TEACHING STATE SPACE

The new science of geography, grounded in the empiricist framework of British geography, was at the core of the colonial pedagogical order.[35] British colonial geography had at once a pedagogical and disciplining function, for it was widely held that the diffusion of modern geographical knowledge would spawn rational colonial subjects liberated from the fictions of received cosmological schemas. Not surprisingly, a central target of colonial geographical texts was the systematic critique of received Puranic schemas of space-time. The refutation of Puranic categories acquired an almost obligatory status, for not only were they held responsible for popular conceptions of the civilizational centrality of Hinduism but they were considered the very antithesis of enlightened rationality. The high gloss of colonial state space demanded instead the inculcation of geographical and historical knowledge rooted in exactitude, reason, functional utility, and, above all, the demonstration of pervasive state mastery over the space-time of its subjects.

Consider, for instance, the standardized schedule of instruction in vernacular schools in the United Provinces in the post-1857 period. The typical educational curriculum in vernacular-medium schools laid out a graduated system of instruction in both history and colonial state space:

Class Three: Map of the district.

Class Four: Map of the province.

Class Five: Map of India and definitions, history of Hindu and Muhammadan period (from Mill's History of India), grammar of the vernacular noun.

Class Six: Map of Asia, history of Hindu and Muhammadan periods concluded, grammar of the vernacular (verb and participle), algebra.

Class Seven: Map of the World, history of the English period, grammar revised, algebra up to simple equations, books one and two of mensuration, and Pritchard's and Blandford's rudiments of physical geography and natural science.[36]

Although this curriculum served as a template for vernacular-medium schools, the emphasis on land mensuration and surveying was a central strand of English-language schools as well. In his memoirs, the radical *swadeshi* nationalist leader Bipin Pal recounted the contents of the curriculum during the last two years of his schooling in eastern Bengal in the late 1860s as encompassing "Clarke's Physical Geography, Todhunter's Arithmetic, Euclid's Geometry, Barnard Smith's Algebra, Mensuration and Surveying with Field Exercises . . . English History (Collier's) . . . Goldsmith's Vicar of Wakefield, Addison's *Spectator*, Johnson's *Rasselas* . . . and Gulliver's Travels."[37] The specific pedagogical instructions that accompanied the curriculum from the United Provinces demonstrates the categorical kinship between the empiricist framework of British colonial geography and the attempt to naturalize colonial state space. With specific reference, for instance, to the teaching of history and geography, teachers were urged that

> [c]haracteristics of race, climate and character, should be studied as a distinct lesson apart from the sequence of events. The geography and map teaching should be a central focus, and it should be the business of the teacher to construct extra maps to illustrate the government partition of provinces . . . the subject of physical geography is one which it is specially necessary for the pupils to be encouraged to ask questions. . . . it should be remembered that the introduction of physical sciences into the course of study is intended to promote the spirit of inquiry and observation in which the ordinary native is deficient.[38]

The injunction to separate categories of self-understanding and identity ("characteristics of race and character") from history and the teaching of geography bears an elective affinity with the attempt to naturalize colonial state space. Colonial pedagogical practices attempted to institute a "legitimate vision of division" and render self-evident both the fact of colonial rule and its partitioning and ordering of space.[39] The official textbooks, which circulated in educational institutions, were purveyors of a unified common sense of what territory and history were, and why they were ordered in a particular way.

Of particular importance here is the unprecedented circulation of official maps in schools in the post-1857 period. During the 1860s and 1870s, thousands of district, provincial, and all-India maps were published for use in vernacular schools.[40] The diffusion of cartographic knowledge was grounded within the creation of increasingly uniform, abstract, and generalized practices of spatial restructuring on a local, regional, and all-India scale. The expansion of mathematically rigorous representations of space was coeval with colonial practices oriented toward determining property rights, the delimitation of territorial boundaries of villages and cities for purposes of taxation, and the location and planning of state works. Colonial state maps were abstract and strictly functional systems for the factual ordering of phenomena in space. They bore no affinities, as discussed in later chapters, with Puranic schemas that were suffused with sacral and metaphysical content. The dissemination of colonial geographical knowledge in vernacular-medium schools — through textbooks, maps, and globes — represented one mode of induction by which colonial state space framed everyday horizons of understandings.

The dissemination of geographical knowledge, especially official maps of colonial India, also enabled local subjects, for the first time, to assume effective visual and conceptual possession of the territorial unit in which they lived and the larger territorial-political whole of which it was a part. The visual device of the map that represents the world as a "discrete spatial partitioning of territory" with "no bleeding boundaries" also helped establish an identity between people, territory, and state.[41] Scholars have long emphasized the circulation of the "logo-map" and other cartographic artifacts as central elements in the nationalization of consciousness during the late nineteenth century in diverse regional locales.[42] Yet their emergence and diffusion must also be seen as signs of wider sociospatial processes, from the intensified commodification of space to the growing institutionalization of the space-time matrices of the nation form and the wider consolidation of an interstate system.

During the last third of the nineteenth century, emergent nationalist discourse transfigured the geographical determinism of official discourse toward a stress on rational, willed agency. Appropriating the cognitive logic of modern maps, especially the unambiguous fixing of people and territory, nationalists forged a practical and visual revaluation of colonial state space as specifically nonnational. Baptized with a proper name, *Bharat,* colonial space was reconfigured as national property.

TRANSPOSING COLONIAL SCHEMAS

The proximate linkages between the dissemination of a vocational variant of scientific knowledge, the restructuring of property relations, and land revenue structures were the subject of a number of critical discussions in the vernacular press during the late 1860s and 1870s. Among the sharpest of these was the following allegorical tale from the popular Lucknow newspaper *Oudh Punch* from September 1877:

> To spread civilization is not the mission of Europeans alone. Every man, who can, has the right to essay it. Since I had mastered the new sciences and acquired civilization I decided to go forth myself and instruct the people of the other countries. So I took a few friends with me, and set out in my ship of courage on the sea. . . . On my way I visited many cities, but I was filled with great wonder to find that the people of those cities were already civilized. Wherever I went, the people said they did not need my help, and I should go elsewhere in quest of my object. At last I reached a village hard by the sea coast. The land was very fertile and men rich and happy. The master of the village gave hearty greetings, and I was of good cheer to find that I had great scope for the discharging of my duty. The dwellers of this place, like a barbarous folk, deemed their world to have been made in the fashion of a flattened square that was fixed and immobile . . . and the sky therefore a solid body. . . . And they had a great fear too of fact, which is historical destiny. . . . The owners of this village took revenues of 4,000 from the villagers, which he spent on the observance of annual rites and ceremonies. In kindness to him and with honest intention I ousted him from his lands, and taking 3,000 for my own charges, I made over to him 600 for himself and set apart 400 for the instruction of the people in the new sciences. He, being but an ignorant fellow, was wrath with me for my action, and far from showing gratitude made war upon me. By help of my companions and our better equipment I was able to without much ado to overpower him. Thereupon he resorted to a legal complaint against me in the civil court of Europabad, from the issue of which suit the manner of foul favor which befell my honesty of purpose and zeal for the betterment of the world, is discernible to all men. For the aforesaid complaint ran this way—"Be it known to the court that a fierce beast, in the shape of an ape, has come from the shores of the green sea and by force has taken possession of our lands. Whereby having brought us to grievous straits, he lives in ease and comfort on the income of our estates, while he pretends that he has come to teach us civilization." I did believe that the judge would be versed in the modes by which the civilizing arts are taught to ruder people and doubted not that he would summarily dismiss the complaint. But his judgement proved his ignorance of the principle of civilization. For he chided me

for having gotten possession of the lands of the complainant, and affirmed that in place of bettering the state of the aforesaid, I had been bent on the betterment of my own. And he told me withal, that though I was free to teach civilization, and even to receive wages in requital of my labour, the law by no means allowed me to usurp the complainant's estates. . . . Thereon I made an application and appeal to the higher courts in Europabad but of no avail. For though they admitted the justice of my doctrines, they affirmed that it was lawful for Europeans alone to put them into practice. True, it was not forbidden to natives to teach civilization to others, yet the law allowed them not to benefit themselves thereby. Thus, it will be apparent that I was put to a great loss by misconception of the law. Notwithstanding this I comfort myself with the thought that my actions were founded on the best motives.[43]

It is tempting to read the allusion to the "village hard by the sea coast" and the subsequent conflicts as a direct reference to the inaugural institution of the colonial "rule of property" in Bengal in the late eighteenth century. Less ambiguous, however, was the reference to the British colonial denigration of Puranic conceptions of space (the globe as "flattened square that was fixed and immobile") and history (the "fear of facts, which is historical destiny"). What is especially notable about this desperately satirical allegory is its resolute stress on the linkages between the "new sciences" and concrete forms of colonial sociospatial domination, especially the restructuring of property relations, land assessment, and the reconfiguration of previous networks of social relations. By directing attention to the ossified binarisms (native and European; civilized and barbarian) that informed official self-representations, the author excoriates conceptions of the "new sciences" as the expression of an enlightened civilizing mission and directs attention instead to the colonial politics of space. By gesturing toward the racialized limits of self-understood liberal juridical and pedagogical practice, the essay highlights the internal fissures of colonial practices. The concluding satire on the rhetoric of intentionality—"I comfort myself with the thought that my actions were founded on the best motives"—assails the self-presentation of British colonial discourse as forever torn between the legitimating idea versus degraded practice of colonial rule. For although colonial state space conjured the promise of material progress ("the bettering of their state"), its actual practices were widely perceived as producing inequalities and differences.

An 1869 petition sent to the colonial Education Department underlines the internal relation between the efforts of colonial subjects to refashion educational production and the contradictory character of colonial practices. The petition was sent by members of local elites who were part of the British-Indian Association, an organization active in the cause of vernacular education, to the colonial Education Department of the United Provinces.[44] The petition opened with a sharp critique of the privileging of English as the vehicle for "higher sciences" and the vocational-driven orientation of vernacular schools (1–3). This was followed by an attempt to reconcile between the received oppositional stances of "Anglicanism" and "Orientalism" that had beset the colonial educational field, especially during the early colonial period. The petition argued that

> We do not wish to enter into this very grave and important subject with any spirit of Orientalism, nor with any spirit of Anglicanism, nor indeed with any spirit which identifies itself with the surfaces of things leaving their essence untouched. The spirit of Orientalism is useful and good in its way, the study of Sanskrit and Arabic as languages is as valuable as that of Greek of Latin is in Europe. . . . We do not wish, however, to see Orientalism over-rated as it was during the early part of this century. Neither do we wish to see the spirit of Anglicanism riding rough shod over it, as it has done since Lord William Bentick's time. This Anglomania was, as might have been expected, an extreme rebound from the previous absurd lengths to which the Oriental mania was carried. (4–5)

Both stances were deemed inadequate from the explicit standpoint of the "growth of national life and prosperity," which was the "root of the question," the very "essence" of the proposed reform (5).

The authors of the petition effected a double move that foreshadowed the ideological form of later nationalist discourse. While they grounded the legitimacy of their demands by evoking the universal goals of enlightenment and scientific development, they simultaneously framed this goal in terms of a particularistic understanding of national development. The principle of nationality, conceived in terms of a fundamental difference, was presented as an immutable fact:

> No effort at effacing nationality even among the feeblest race or nation has yet been known to succeed, and probably never will a nation become an inanimate tree which may be pruned and lopped to any required shape. . . . it is not a political assertion therefore, to state that Indian nationality will always remain its own, it is a fundamental

maxim of the science of being. We state this in order that we may not be misconstrued. (5)

Yet the boldly stated goal of the proposed reform was "the universal spread of European enlightenment among the large mass of people and throughout all of India" (7). The tension between the universal and the particular, in this reckoning, could only be overcome through the progressive national-ization and vernacularization of the educational system, especially with ref-erence to the teaching of "scientific" disciplines. The concluding statement made this endeavor clear:

> What is it then that we want? We want an educational system that will not touch the few but the many . . . it is unjust that the vast majority of the nation should have higher science closed to them unless they con-sent to go through a difficult language like that of English. . . . We want [an educational system] that will bring western learning and science face to face, as it were, with the nation. We want it to be one that will not be foreign, but native. We want [an educational system] that will not ignore the existence of nationality. We want a system that will be permanent and abiding in it effects and progressive in its nature. . . . this can only be done by the vernaculars — the language of the people them-selves. . . . the task of acquiring a foreign language like the English is really a very difficult one. . . . it is but a veneer, and is further most in-jurious in its tendency of keeping scientific knowledge in an artificial soil, and preventing its fruition. The vernaculars of the country are not a coating of foreign polish, but are a national growth. (10–11)

The problem with the colonial educational curriculum was not, then, the universal forms of rationality associated with European science as such but rather its uneven actualization along these lines. Such an advancement could only be made through a grounding of the universal within the partic-ular or, more specifically, through the mobilization of vernaculars, which, being of "national growth," could alone carry the burden of such a task.

The petition foreshadows by several decades the *swadeshi*-era nationalist critique of the alienating effects of colonial educational schemas as marked and made by a radical severing from the lived actualities of an imagined in-digenous present. In 1907, Bipin Chandra Pal, a central *swadeshi* nationalist leader, argued:

> We have grown like orchids . . . on the verandah of a European Gov-ernment. . . . This is what our education has been . . . and the greatest

pity of it is that it has divorced our mind, our heart, our spirit, our character and our manhood from our national life. We have been taught to
botanise the oak, to botanise the elm, to botanise the beech to the neglect of our Banyan, our Mango grove, our Champak tree . . . our birds
that resound in the morning in Mango groves with their thousand
notes, do not form any part of our intellectual or emotional life.[45]

Colonial subjects, as Bipin Pal suggested, had been instructed how to
"botanise the oak . . . [and] the elm" but not the indigenous "Banyan" tree
(257). At issue were the ways in which state-mediated intellectual and affective horizons were inadequate to the task of either grasping or preserving the perceived indigenous and organic constituents of the lived everyday.
Both the petition and Pal's lament shared an understanding of the indigenous and the received not only as persistent elements of the everyday but as
the potential fatalities of colonial pedagogical labors. Only an autonomous
nationalized vernacular curriculum could overcome, in this view, the es-
trangements wrought by colonial state space. Although the petition left
open the question of the specific content of the nationhood it claimed as axiomatic in terms of such vexed questions as language, community, region,
religion, and the like, it prefigured later nationalist appropriations that presented the nation as the universal form of cultural particularity. It was a por-
tent of the undermining of the hegemony of colonial state space.

CONCLUSION

The history of space does not have to choose between processes and structures, change
and invariability, events and institutions. Its periodizations, moreover, will differ from
generally accepted ones.

— Henri Lefebvre, *The Production of Space*, 1978

Some key issues — conceptual and historiographical — have yet to be addressed. They also serve as a conceptual bridge to the chapters that follow.
The preceding chapters elaborated the production of an internally contradictory colonial state space in a range of social and institutional fields. The
chapters that follow explore the multiple concrete responses, in different
registers and fields, to the internal contradictions of colonial state space. As
such, they imply a correspondingly deeper focus on the reconstitution of
spatiotemporal imaginings as figured in vernacular historical and geographical works.

My analysis of vernacular geohistorical discourse in the next two chapters at once builds on and departs from the work of subalternist historians. It is hard to exaggerate the historiographical and political significance of the turn to vernacular historical works inaugurated by Ranajit Guha and the subaltern school.[46] It signaled a decisive departure from the near absolute dominance of official English-language state archives and the sanctioned erasure of vernacular historical archives and sources in the historiography on modern colonial India. From the perspective of the early subaltern project, the turn to vernacular records carried the promise of grasping that elusive phantom — the self-expression of the colonized subaltern. Following Guha, with his pioneering analysis of Bengali historical works, a number of historians have identified the constitution of a nationalist historiography in different regional languages as a formative moment of anticolonial nationalism. They have also emphasized key differences between early-nineteenth-century vernacular works and the modern historiographical form associated with nationalist discourse.[47] Yet there has been no account of the sociohistorical transformations that made possible the distinctive field of late-nineteenth-century geohistorical discourse. What is more, the analysis of vernacular historical works has, more often than not, been oriented by a central measuring index — the presence of a national consciousness explicitly defined as a "critique of . . . the constitutive power relationships of colonialism."[48] In this view, the formation of a nationalist historiography, which Guha locates in the "first decade of the twentieth century," marked the *realization* rather than the *constitution* of nationhood (211).

Consider, in this regard, Guha's indictment of the first wave of vernacular historians for remaining hostage to a "colonialist education" that severed them "from their own tradition," made "their own past inaccessible to them as history," and ensured that they "did not know how to think it in any way other than did their rulers" (211, 175). These vernacular histories were symptomatic of the fact that it is not possible, as Guha observes, "to appropriate a people's past without imposing the appropriator's will on their will, without ousting them from the site of an autochthonous occupancy, without violating the traditions of a pre-existing right of use" (195). This line of critique implies, without providing an adequate basis for, the existence of an objectively discernable "Indian" people who bore a collective national relationship to a distinct "Indian" history to which nineteenth-century colonial subjects (and contemporary postcolonial scholars) were privy but ultimately blocked from recovering by the mystifying veils of English education and British colonial historiography. This historicist assumption rests on a teleological model of sociohistorical change, wherein the progressive emergence of categories and practices is presumed to be intrinsic to an already given national/social formation. To pursue the lineaments of an autonomous nationalist discourse in early-nineteenth-century works, and then bemoan their absence, only makes sense within a framework that takes for granted precisely what requires explanation. That is to say, such a perspective brackets the wider sociohistorical processes that engendered the production of a historically novel field of spatial and temporal imaginings. In so doing, it leaves unexamined the historicity of spatiotemporal matrices and brackets their entwinement with specific sociospatial formations.

If we take seriously the proposition that conceptions of history and territory are expressive of and embedded within specific sociospatial formations, then we cannot explain discontinuities by considering a discursive realm alone. Such an approach would place categories of thought and cultural schemes on one side and the social organization of space and time on the other, thus not only neglecting their internal relations but reproducing the divide between objectivist and subjectivist approaches. For, as Nicos Poulantzas, following Henri Lefebvre, observes, "the genealogy of the production of space" bears a dialectical relationship to the "the history of its appropriation."[49] The reconstitution of spatiotemporal matrices in late colonial India was rooted within and expressive of transformations in the social organization of space and time. History and territory acquired a novel, mutually negotiated meaning because they were inscribed within a radically distinct social field.

To assert a historically specific rather than merely contingent relationship between spatiotemporal conceptions and the sociohistorical field of their production need not entail a structuralist bias. Such a perspective accords with a conception of agency as the creative transposition and remobilization of dynamic and contradictory structures.[50] Nationalist agency, as I elaborate in the following chapters, rested on the way it transposed categories and practices initially formulated within the internally contradictory field of colonial state practices onto new terrains. By doing so, it affected a broader change in the initial fields of their constitution such that the meaning of original categories of understanding no longer resided wholly within them. There is (then as now) a deeply "recursive" relationship between spatiotemporal imaginings and the sociohistorical fields of their emergence, constitution, and transposition. In colonial India, where the articulation of received and transposed categories resulted in particular enrichments of meaning and signification, this relationship between categories of understanding and sociohistorical forms was especially overdetermined. An analytical focus on spatiotemporal imaginings can help unravel, then, the dynamic intercontextuality between received schemas of space and time, the contradictory effects of colonial practices, and the emergence of novel categories of space and time between 1860 and 1880.

CHAPTER FIVE

SPACE, TIME, AND SOVEREIGNTY IN *PURANIC-ITIHAS*

F ollowing Ranajit Guha's pioneering analysis of forms of temporal consciousness and memory encoded in nineteenth-century Bengali historical texts, historians have elaborated the ways in which history, as universal narrative, became a complex site and register for the problem of subjectivity in late colonial India.[1] Yet more often than not, this scholarship has articulated a fundamentally historicist transition narrative of a rupture between an ideal-typical construct of *Puranic-itihas* (historical chronicles), a placeholder for the precolonial/premodern, and late-nineteenth and early-twentieth-century modalities of historical writing that we have come to associate with modernist nationalist historiography.[2] Dominant analyses of received forms of temporal consciousness and historical memory have failed to adequately situate them, as suggested previously, in relation to sociohistorical transformations beyond the mediation of colonial education and the positivist evidentiary protocols that organized British colonial historiography. Without a sustained engagement with the sociohistorical transformations that conditioned the reworking (rather than either the simple transplantation or erasure) of historical narratives and forms of temporal consciousness, the intimations of an epistemological break suggested by various scholars remain a provocative but ultimately ungrounded assertion.

My foray into early-nineteenth-century imaginings of territory and history contests both historicist transition narratives that posit an ungrounded rupture from an undifferentiated Puranic modality and apparently opposed, but fundamentally complementary, accounts that posit a continuist "civilizational" narrative, thereby eliding the historicity of spatiotemporal schemas.[3] I turn to early-nineteenth-century Puranic-inflected chronicles here neither to rehearse dominant historicist narratives nor to elaborate the local and regional heterogeneity and complexity of Puranic schemas for itself. I seek rather to lay the ground for the exploration, in the next chapter, of the complex re-articulation and re-signification of specific Puranic spatiotemporal schemas and categories of understanding in geohistorical imag-

inaries of the 1860s and 1870s and, more crucially, the formation of historicist and modernist conceptions of India as *Bharat*.

The dominant form of upper-caste, Hindu vernacular historical writings
in northern colonial India in the early and mid-nineteenth century was
Puranic-itihas or Puranic chronicles. The word *purana* literally means old or
ancient. The body of literature called Puranas was a central repository for
the circulation, affirmation, and renewal of various Brahminical schemas
about the origins of the world, its topographical ordering, sacred geography,
and genealogies of gods, sages, and kings.[4] As a distinctive class of sacred
and political literature, the Puranas exhibit certain fundamental spatiotemporal assumptions that constituted the unquestioned and unmarked frame
of reference of early- and mid-nineteenth-century historical works. Among
the most influential of early-nineteenth-century historical accounts, organized in accord with Puranic modalities and schemas, are Ramram Basu's
Raja pratapkitya charitra (1801), Rajbolachan Mukhopadhyay's *Majaraj
krishanachandra rayaysa chairtram* (1805), and Mritunjoy Bidyalankar's
Rajabali (1808). In its attempt to incorporate the entire span of dynastic suc-
cessions from mythical pasts to the contemporary colonial period, *Rajabali*
has been regarded as among the most comprehensive in scope of existing accounts from the early colonial period. As such, it serves as a useful point of
entry for the excavation of the broader contours of Puranic spatiotemporal
schemas. It also affords an entry into the larger task of delineating the limits of historicist transition narratives from an undifferentiated and transhistorical precolonial Puranic to a modern nationalist register. My reading of
Rajabali attempts to locate its spatiotemporal conceptions within a broader
exploration of Puranic imaginaries that selectively entered historical-
geographical works of the 1860s and 1870s under the historicizing sign of
tradition and with a novel ideological content.

Widely conceived as exemplary of *Puranic-itihas*,[5] *Rajabali* was officially
commissioned by Fort William College, Calcutta (the major center for early
colonial orientalist scholarship), as a Bengali-language textbook for East India Company officials. Despite the immediate context of its production, and
unlike later nineteenth-century historical accounts that self-consciously
grounded their legitimacy on modern research protocols, it reproduces, as
various scholars have noted, the dominant Puranic inflected mode of historical memory specific to north Indian Brahmin literati. It is precisely what
various scholars have characterized as the resolutely "pre-colonial historiographical allegiances" of works like *Rajabali* that render them significant.[6]

Written as a commemorative chronicle of the unfolding of successive
genealogies of divinities, heroes, and dynasties, *Rajabali* resonates with the

broader framework of Puranic imaginings in its organizational and thematic form. It opens with a rehearsal of Puranic cosmological imaginings of space:

> There are seven islands *(dvipas)* on earth of which ours is called *Jam-budvipa*. *Jambudvipa* is divided into nine varsa of which *Bharatvarsa* is one. *Bharatvarsa* in turn is divided into nine parts *(khanda)* which are called *Aindra, Kaseru, Tampraparna, Gavastimata, Naga, Saumya, Varuna, Gandharva* and *Kumarika*. Of these, the part in which the *varnasrama* [loosely, caste] system exists is the *Kumarikakhanda*. The other parts are inhabited by the *antyaja* people [those outside *jati*/caste].[7]

Reiterated here is the received Puranic cosmological imaginary of the world as consisting of seven (and in some instances nine) concentric islands, each of which was encircled by a sea. The central island within this schema, Jambudvipa, was in turn divided into nine parts or *kshetras* of which Bharatavarsha was the southernmost, which was, in turn, further divided into more (usually nine) sections. In Puranic schemas there was no single, comprehensive, or fixed geographical designation attributed to either Jambudvipa or Bharat. Considered as absolute in itself, the space of the whole could not be given a fixed territorial designation, for it embodied all spaces.

Of particular importance here is the Puranic term *Bharat* or *Bharatavar-sha*, for it acquired, as discussed in the next chapter, a novel political signification in later geohistorical discourse, underscoring the highly selective appropriation of received categories (such notions as Meru or Jambudvipa, for instance, remained merely of antiquarian interest). According to various Puranic sources, the term derived either from the mythical King Bharata, who was a descendant of the first Manu (the androgynous first being of Puranic myths), or from the "tribe" of Bharata, which figures centrally in Vedic and epic traditions. For late-nineteenth-century nationalists as well as the intensely nationalist industry of postcolonial Puranic geographical studies, the very existence of the term *Bharat* has been read as proof positive, as irrefutable evidence, of an ancient, historically continuous, and geographically stable nation.[8] This doxic understanding of the supposedly transhistorical national signification of the category *Bharat* animated, for instance, the constituent assembly's decision in September 1949 to adopt it as the official name for India as expressed in the first article of the Indian constitution, which states, "India, that is *Bharat,* shall be a union of states."[9] However, the conception of *Bharat* as a national-territorial entity, and the identification of its territorial and cartographic coordinates as roughly analogous to those of the colonial state, only emerged during the

1860s and 1870s. This term, which was to assume an inflated ideological significance in later works, had multiple, shifting geographical referents. Within Puranic-inspired accounts, such as *Rajabali*, there were divergent representations of both the spatial configuration of the earth and Bharat. Puranic representations of the earth had a metaphysical meaning rather than an abstract, modern geographic reference. Certain Puranic texts, for instance, conceived the world as a flat disk divided into four islands that were shaped as four petals of a lotus, at the center of which was Mount Meru.[10] Similarly, the shape of Bharat was variously described as a half-moon, a triangle, a rhomboid or unequal quadrilateral, a drawn bow, and as a floating tortoise *(kurma)* facing east.[11]

The metaphysical rather than strictly geographical register of Puranic spatial categories was expressed in the fact that there is no word in Sanskrit that corresponds to *map* as such. The word *naksha*, conventionally used as the closest approximation, was adapted from the Arabic *naqshah* and adopted in modern South Asian languages around the late seventeenth century.[12] Even the word-concept *naqshah*, as well as such related Sanskrit words as *chitra* and *alekhya*, signifies "a picture, a plan, a general description, an official report"; it does not carry the semantic load of a map as an abstract representation of territory.[13] Surviving maps, or more aptly, Puranic-inspired cosmographies and visual diagrams or *mana-chitras*, were mostly painted on cloth and metal and served as wall hangings in shrines and sacred spaces.[14] Along with map-like representations, there were also globes of the world called *bhugola* (literally, earth-ball), which date from the sixteenth century onward. These globes departed from Puranic spatial schemas in that they figured the world as a spherical whole, in contrast to the flat disk of Puranic textual representations (much reviled in official colonial textbooks on geography). However, they conformed to the broader topography of Puranic imaginings. They were inscribed with religious deities and human figures — malevolent and benevolent, male and female — that were all inseparably bound within a spherical whole. The *bhugolas* from the early-nineteenth-century period were organized in accordance with Puranic conceptions — with Jambudvipa on the north and the bands of continents and seas in the lower half.[15]

Although Puranic map-like representations and *bhugolas* (globes) had dimensions, they did not correspond to the mathematical dimensions of modern geographic space. None of the extant Puranic-inspired maps or globes was based on coordinate cartography, nor do any of them carry a scale in the modern sense of the term as a quantitative measure of distance. There was no standard measurement of distance until the late-nineteenth-century constitution of a colonial state space.[16] Insofar as these maps accord divergent scalar features to sites, the underlying notion of scale was qualitative rather than quantitative. Conceived in qualitative terms, scale was an index of the relative social and religious importance of particular places and areas such that particular sites were accorded exaggerated scalar feature. Similarly, directions in Puranic spatial representations had symbolic meaning rather than a strictly geographical referent. The majority of surviving maps, for instance, marked east at the top, unlike the more familiar placing of north at the top.[17]

Susan Gole has provided a detailed description of the few surviving maps dating from the early nineteenth century. One of them represents a pilgrimage undertaken in the valley of what is now Katmandu, Nepal. It charts the spatial itinerary of a man called Chikidhi, his wife, two children, and several other pilgrims through various sites that differ in size according to a scale of sacral importance. Another map of the sacred pilgrimage site of Varanasi or Benares, from the same period, shows sacred sites crowded with pilgrims completing the seven circular routes in accordance with ritual practices.[18] These maps include, through pictorial figuration, the ritual and spatial practices that enabled them. These representational strategies fundamentally differ from modern mapping techniques that homogenize heterogeneous territories and represent the totality of space within a single, Cartesian grid. Modern maps allow for no distinction between places on a qualitative and symbolic scale of importance; rather, spaces are defined by the erasure of the tactile, particularistic qualities of places and the spatial journeys that shaped them.[19]

The space of the world as envisioned in Puranic schemas was sacral, concentric, infinite, and fundamentally open, for as an absolute space it had no demarcated or fixed limit. Although the spatial matrices of Puranic cosmology were oriented around a center (Mount Meru or Kailas), there was no frontier in the specifically modern sense of a bounded space or enclosure that demarcates an inside and outside.[20] Territorial zones or *khandas*, although separated from each other, were not externally bounded but rather intersecting and overlapping spaces. According to this topographical ordering, the various *khandas* were concentrically superimposed such that each particular space derived its internal unity from its orientation to the center. The topographical ordering of Puranic schemas was based, as Ronald Inden suggests, on homology: "The Ganga was taken to be the ultimate source of all rivers . . . and each region was constituted of features held to resemble those that constituted the others. The Vindhyas, the mountains that divided the *Uttarpatha* (northern region) from the *Dakshinapatha* (southern region), were, for example, considered homologous with the Himalayas, and several rivers of the later region were taken as equivalent to the Ganga."[21] The center was located, then, in a spatial matrix that was ordered through symmetry and similarity rather than differentiation and hierarchy. The multiple spaces that comprise Puranic sacred space are best understood, in this regard, as dispersions within a single absolute space. In this schema, each *khanda* or *kshetra* (part, region) was a replication of the previous space and of the whole. Later nineteenth-century geohistorical works attributed an exceptional significance to the northern region. In this north Indian, upper-caste, and Arya-centric geohistorical discourse, the Gangetic basin, commonly designated as Aryavarta (land of the Aryans), was hierarchically privileged as the paradigmatic space of the imagined nation.

Although Puranic mappings of space do not contain a notion of a determinate territorial frontier, they do contain a notion of sociocultural alterity embodied in the conception of *antayaja,* or more commonly, *mlecchas.* This distinction, however, is not so much a function of territorial delimitation as one of socioreligious mapping. Bidyalankar, for instance, echoes this formulation in the passage quoted earlier by referring to the part of Bharat "inhabited by *antayaja.*"[22] This notion of fundamental alterity assumed a specific political-ideological valence in later nineteenth-century nationalist writings. These later writings reworked this distinction within a territorially grounded vision of original nationals versus belated nationals. This territorially grounded distinction, which marked a profound departure from received Puranic spatial imaginings, presupposed a notion of Bharat as a spatially determinate and externally distinctive national space. It encoded a specifically historicist understanding of the interrelations between territory and history that framed the criterion of territorial origin as indexical of purity and authenticity.

Later works express as well a specifically historicist conception of the interlinkages between territory, people, and sovereignty. Bidyalankar's account replicates the distinctively Puranic configuration of sovereignty and political power. *Rajabali,* as a genealogy of the rulers of the earth, opens with the divine installation of the first mythical ruler:

> In the *Satyayuga,* the Supreme lord *(parameswara)* had planted in the form of an Asvahva tree a king called Iksaku to rule over the earth *(prithvi).* The two main branches of this tree became the *Surya* [solar] and *Chandra* [lunar] dynasties *(vamsa).* The kings born in these two lineages have ruled the earth in the four yugas [temporal ages]. Of these, some *chakravartin* were able to acquire the greatest powers of *dharma*

(righteousness) and thus ruled over the entire earth consisting of seven
islands. . . . If a King from one lineage became the emperor *(samrata)*,
then the king of the other lineage world become the lord of a *mandala*
[circle of kings]. The accounts of these kings are recorded in the
branches of knowledge *(sashtras)* called the *Purana*. (79)

Bidyalankar's text yokes together a conception of *dharma* (righteousness) as
the transcendent, unifying, and legitimating principle of political formations
with notions of divine kingship as embodied in the figure of a universal
monarch. The latter schema pivots on the notion of a *chakravartin* (lord
of the entire earth or *sarvabhauma*) whose overlordship was constituted
in and through a relational network of alliances with concentric, multiple
dominions.[23]

The notion of sovereignty that organized many Puranic accounts was
neither exclusive nor tied to territory. Sovereignty was embodied in the
figurative ideal of a universal monarch or exceptional man *(mahapurusha)*,
who constituted his overlordship by forging successive alliances and rivalries in the name of the overlord of the cosmos. The domain of the
chakravartin was not delimited with reference to territory but through a
dense, intricate nexus of political alliances (with allies or *mitras*) and rivalries (with enemies or *amitras*). This conception imbued the figuration of a
non-spatially bound circle of kings *(mandala)*. The scheme of this *mandala*
referred to a political realm defined by the structuring distinction between
mitra and *amitra*.

The operative conception of sovereignty reproduced in Bidyalankar's
work differed from modernist conceptions of the territory-sovereignty
nexus specific to the spatiotemporal matrices of the interstate system and
the nation form.[24] Integral to the notion of the indefinitely expansible circle
of kings was the non-isomorphism between people, territory, and dominion
and the absence of demands for exclusive attachment from subjects. As an
important work on late-eighteenth-century conceptions of sovereignty suggests, "since the *janapada* [literally, abode of people] is shared with the enemy," all dominions are said to consist of those "who are likely to be won
over by the enemy" and "those who are not likely to be won over by the enemy." The posited paradigm of conquest or expansion of sovereignty was
not grounded on territorial and military conquest but the forging of alliances through a complex of means, including conciliation *(santva)*, gift giving *(dana)*, inciting revolt and the winning over *(bheda)* of constituents, and
only lastly, physical force *(danda)*.[25] This notion of a non-territorially bound
sovereignty hinged on a radically distinct conception of space and sover-

eignty. The domain of the universal monarch did not extend outward by territorial expansion and the internalization of frontiers, because what was at stake was not the forging of a unified political space through the coercive assimilation or erasure of heterogeneous dominions and *janapadas*. Rather, the expansion of dominion occurred in a continuous and dynamic field of alliances and rivalries, which, although premised on a historically specific notion of *mitras* and *amitras* or friends and enemies, did not contain a modern capitalist understanding of either physical territorial or sociopolitical closure.

Puranic representations of space as absolute, concentric, and open bear an elective affinity with the conception of time as concrete, divinely ordained, and fundamentally qualitative. The conception of temporality in Puranic chronicles can be understood as concrete insofar as it is a "dependent variable," grounded in events, and qualitatively configured, unlike the abstract, empty, homogenous temporality specific to modern capitalism that underwrote nationalist historiography and spatiotemporal imaginaries.[26] Bidyalankar, for instance, locates his work with reference to this divinely ordained concrete temporal structure:

> In course of the circular motion of time . . . passing through the thirty *kalpas* such as Pitrakalpa . . . etc., we are now situated in the *Svetavaraha* [white boar] *kalpa*. Each *kalpa* consists of fourteen manu; accordingly, we are now in the seventh manu of *Svetavaraha* kalpa called *Vaivasvata*. Each manu consists of 248 yuga [ages or epochs]; we are now passing through the one hundred and twelfth yuga of *Vaivasvata* manu called *Kaliyuga*. This *yuga* consists of 432,000 years. Of these, up to the present year 1726 of the Saka era, 4,905 years have passed, 427,095 years are left.[27]

In this account, time is structured according to divinely ordained ages (the four *yugas*) that signified distinct substantive moral conditions largely articulated from the specific standpoint of Brahminical schemas and hegemonic projects. The *yuga* cycle, from "the Mahabharats down to Mrityunjoy [Bidyalankar]," as Sumit Sarkar argues, reiterated "the indispensability of right caste and gender hierarchy . . . the recurrent criteria for immoral behavior are *strayinata* (subordination to women) and *nimakharami* (being 'untrue to one's self,' i.e., violating obligation of loyalty and obedience and thus implicitly weakening proper hierarchical relationships)."[28] Although there were specific time sequences (e.g., past, present, and future ages) within this temporal order, they were enveloped within an overarching concrete con-

ception of time wherein events occurred not so much in time but were constitutive of it.[29] Despite the specific datings of various rulers and their
chronologies, the eras of different kings do not approximate a notion of temporal periods that are at once irreversible and divisible into quantitatively
homogenous segments. In Bidyalankar's account, the various chronologies
are enfolded in a continuous, sacral temporal order distinguished only by
the absence and presence of divinely sanctioned moral orders. Temporality
in these works is the absolute, qualitative time of patterned recurrence. Embedded within a concrete conception of time as a dependent variable and as
cyclical return with linear sequential reckonings rather than a historically
determinate and irreversible linear progression, Bidyalankar's recounting of
different eras does not entail a fundamental departure from the present that
is constitutive of modern historical thought. Rather the past is placed in the
midst of current time and regarded as an integral part of the present. In this
modality of historical writing, the before and after do not exist in a relation
of fundamental opposition with one another but are rather fully co-present.

Puranic imaginings of time, as instantiated by *Rajabali*, thus exist in a
concrete and sacral continuum. In later geohistorical discourse, temporality,
or more specifically, historical time, was figured as a cumulative, irreversible
series that marked the progression toward the present. The succession of
sovereigns in Bidyalankar's account, for instance, does not correspond to an
overarching, abstract progression of events, a process of historical sedi-
mentation, or the blank chronology of "homogenous, empty time" particular to the closed and evolutionary self-presentation of capital and an uncritical modern historiography.[30] It is rather the circulation of a divinely
sanctioned transcendent power defined in substantive moral rather than
quantitative temporal terms. In this schema, political fortunes reflect divine
will and hinge on the ability to retain *dharma*. Bidyalankar's text follows
such Puranic spatiotemporal schemas from the first mythical ruler, Iksaku,
down to the installation of British rule; the entire series of dynastic succession, including the British regime, was regarded as instances of divine installation such that, as Partha Chatterjee observes, the "the passage from
one to another . . . is entirely unproblematical."[31] Unlike later texts,
Bidyalankar's text represents the succession of kings and dynasties as neither a fraught process of political struggle that requires positivist causal explanation nor the historicist figuration of a progressive working-out of an
implicit national consciousness, much less an inner dialectic.

Grounded on a notion of a continuous transference of divine power,
Puranic-itihas at once presupposed and expressed a historically specific form
of subjectivity and temporal consciousness. Absent from such Puranic

-inspired accounts as Bidyalankar's was precisely the reflexive operation particular to modern historicity and historical thought that renders them more concerned with the commemoration rather than the making of history as such. Bidyalankar, unlike later historians and writers of textbooks, does not assume a position with reference to the various pasts he recounts. Nor does he claim or attempt to forge an identification with past or contemporary *prajas* (subjects) or hold up particular social groups or figures as exemplary of a larger sociocultural and spatial whole. There is no attempt here to trace in the record of dynastic succession the lineaments of a continuous solidarity, a unified people, or a singular collective self.

It is the very givenness of Puranic schemas of thought and appraisal, their status as belonging to a realm of facticity beyond and outside historical process, that distinguishes early-and mid-nineteenth-century Puranic -inflected works from the selective reworking of Puranic categories in works from the 1860s and 1870s. Ranajit Guha's reproach against the "mythic drift" of early-nineteenth-century narratives and his reading of it as a sign of a "failure" to realign received forms of historical writing and memory in the linear, homogenous temporality of modern historiography ignore the dialectic between social forms and forms of thought.[32] The presence of "mythic genealogies, sacred geographies, and divine interventions" in such works cannot be understood in narrow teleological terms that represent their relationship to later modalities of historical consciousness (whether nationalist or not) and sociospatial formations as one of either sharp rupture or straightforward transplantation (181). For although later discourses historicized key Puranic spatial categories as received tradition, they also encoded them as active elements of the past in the present, in the specific form of received tradition. Puranic categories continued to inform popular temporal consciousness, but did so in ways that were self-conscious through the reflexive appropriation of specific categories and their investment with novel ideological meanings. In the last two decades of the nineteenth century, for instance, as Sumit Sarkar observes, the novel experience of the disciplinary time of *chakri* (wage labor) in colonial bureaucracies, mercantile offices, and shop floors in Calcutta was figured in urban, male lower-middle-class narratives in the dystopic idiom of received Puranic *kali-yuga* narratives.[33] During the 1920s, as Rosalind O'Hanlon shows, oral Marathi historical ballads or *powadas* were deployed by *dalits* (i.e., scheduled castes in Indian constitutional parlance) as part of an oppositional anti-Brahminical project and were invested with a specifically anticolonial nationalist content during the civil disobedience campaigns of the 1930s.[34] The very understanding of *Puranic-itihas* as received tradition in emergent geohistorical discourse of the 1860s and 1870s, as elaborated in the next chapter, hinged on the formation of a historicist and modernist episteme that posited them as its own prehistory and within the framework of which terms such as *Bharat* acquired a novel ideological meaning. Within the framework of this later discourse, tradition was no longer the remembrance and commemoration of a past that was fully coeval with the present. By figuring and claiming Puranic modalities as received tradition, emergent geohistorical discourse at once objectified and historicized the past in a paradigmatically modern historiographical operation. This signaled not the definitive erasure of Puranic categories but rather the reflexive and radically novel re-signification of select categories in popular affective and nationalist imaginaries.

CHAPTER SIX

INDIA AS *BHARAT:* A TERRITORIAL NATIVIST VISION OF NATIONHOOD, 1860–1880

Those who so persistently deny any fundamental historic unity or any real national individuality to our land and to our people, either do not know, or they do not remember the fact that we never called our country by the alien name of India or even that of Hindoostan. Our own name was, and is still today, among the Aryan population of the country, Bharatvarsha.

—Bipin Chandra Pal, *The Soul of India,* 1923

Bipin Pal's denunciation of the colonial thesis that India was a "mere geographical expression" was written some decades after the heady maelstrom of the *swadeshi* movement.[1] A radical nationalist and self-understood secularist, Pal combined a strongly autarkic vision of India's political-economic future with an idealist understanding of the imminent universalism of Hinduism. What evoked particular rancor was the colonial state's contention that there "never was such an animal as Indian, until the British rulers of the country commenced so generously to manufacture him with the help of their schools and colleges, their courts and their camps, their law and their administration, and their free press and open platform" (47). The colonial state's attempted negation of "any real national individuality to our land and to our people" was more than a routine instance of its ideologically motivated particularization of India (49). It expressed, Pal claimed, the subject position of the "stranger" who could not "grasp the nature and reality of the fundamental unity" signaled by the "native name of the land" given by "her own children" and which was proof positive of a "distinct historic" and "national consciousness" (48, 49). Pal's identification of India as Bharat was beholden to a *swadeshi*-era project that sought to establish the autonomy of indigenous institutions and practices. Yet the ideological and utopian energy that animated imaginings of Bharat as a distinct national space had permeated popular geohistorical discourse in northern colonial India from the last third of the nineteenth century. By the turn of

the century, the conception of Bharat as a territorially bounded and historically singular national entity had acquired a self-evident givenness, especially among the upper-caste, middle-class Hindu constituency glossed by
Pal in unabashedly normative terms as the "Aryan population." Indeed, the
unremarked status of key spatiotemporal categories — especially of Bharat —
in the historiography of late colonial India attests to the force of nationalist
narratives in rendering the historically produced as historically received.

Through a close reading of a range of popular histories, geography texts,
newspaper accounts, and pamphlets produced between 1860 and 1880, this
chapter outlines a critical genealogy of the notion of India as Bharat. I locate its emergence in the specific regional context of the North-Western
Provinces and Awadh (later designated United Provinces) — the birthplace
of the so-called two-nation theory deployed in the partition of India in 1947
and which retains today the dubious status of the heartland of Hindutva.
The works examined include the first systematic history of India written in
Hindi by Raja Shiva Prasad (1864), the writings of provincial elites and social reformers, as well as an unexplored archive of vernacular textbooks of
history and geography produced for secondary schools. Although most of
the works drawn upon are from this period and region, I also explore works
from other regional contexts to underscore the remarkable convergence and
robustness of emergent discourse on history, territory, and nation.

This neglected terrain of historical-geographical imaginings invites our
attention not only for its intrinsic interest, and not only because the themes
and methodological protocols of the works examined prefigure later nationalist historiography, but also because they initiated, in all senses of the word,
a conception of Bharat as a real, enduring, spatially bounded national entity.
These works were not uniformly oppositional in relation to the colonial
state, nor were they necessarily anticolonial in the narrow political sense
of demanding sovereign statehood. Their historical significance lies in the
way the conceptions and categories that underlay them marked a socioepistemological break from received conceptions of space and time and
prefigured central assumptions and ideological tensions that informed later
institutional nationalism associated with the Indian National Congress. The
discursive elaboration of India as a spatially bounded and historically determinate national entity marked the constitution of a novel understanding
of the liaison between history, territory, and identity. The specifically modernist provenance of this formation resided in the privilege accorded to the
criterion of territorial origin in delimiting the organic core of the nation, an
ideological operation that effected a hierarchical positioning of extant social
groups within the imagined national space.

The reflective demarcation of a distinct national space was the very condition of possibility for the linear periodization of a singular nationalist history. During this period, making history became coterminous with establishing a national space, that is, a historically continuous national territory, and reciprocally implied the creation of a novel subjectivity—a national people. The construction of colonial India as a national space was predicated on a double movement of the territorialization of history and collective identity and the delimitation of an organic core nation from the standpoint of a fictive continuity between the past and present. On the one hand, the emergent popular discourse of India as Bharat sought to inscribe the imagined nation within a potentially universalistic framework of an idealized space-time that was understood as outside of and temporally prior to colonial space. Yet, at the same moment, it defined, along lines of spatiotemporal and cultural purity, what the imagined core of the nation was (the *Arya* or Hindu as the true national) in order to preserve it against contamination from both the colonial present and the particularistic foreign body of the Muslim. This territorial nativist understanding of nationhood — rooted in the historically specific reworking of conceptions of space and time wrought by the contradictory experience of colonial space — empowered the hierarchical and relational elaboration of the interlinked categories of Hindu, Muslim, and India as Bharat.

Certain themes predominate in the following analysis: the re-signification of the Puranic category *Bharat* and its foundational status in popular geohistorical discourse; the appropriation of Puranic schemas as received tradition; the pedagogical project of teaching the nation; and the complex signification of nation-as-mother or *Bharat Mata* (mother India).

THE CONSTITUTION OF THE NATION
AS A GEOHISTORICAL CATEGORY

A Novel Arena

During the 1860s and 1870s, colonial pedagogical consolidation was paralleled by the exponential growth of new institutional spheres of publicity in regional vernaculars concretized in educational institutions, public media, and historical archives. The emergence of a vernacular institutional field — made and marked by new forms of communication media, the proliferation of vernacular presses and newspapers, the generalization of distinct regional print cultures and idioms — signaled a wider transformation of "prior communities of embodied knowledge" toward "more routinized, abstract" forms of publicity."[2]

The institutionalization of this new vernacular field was both an expression and a vehicle for the making of an ascendant, if internally differentiated, colonial middle class. The colonial middle class forged in this field encompassed not only the usual suspects of upper-caste Hindus and the land-owning Muslim gentry or *ashraf* classes of the United Provinces but also incorporated Persian- and Sanskrit-trained literati, schoolteachers, amateur writers, and salaried government officials. There was a reciprocal relationship between the ascendancy of the new colonial middle classes understood in this broad sense and the consolidation of a vernacular field of publicity.[3] Bholanauth Chunder's remarkable two-volume travelogue, published in 1869, details the specificity of the Hindu middle-class habitus in the United Provinces from its increased investment in emergent public arenas to the regulated distinctions of the interior furnishing of their homes, replete with the new artifacts and signs of colonial space-time from wall clocks to maps of the world and colonial India. His host at Agra, a certain "Lallah," exemplified this formation: "The Lallah, our host is an Income-Tax Assessor. He has a press and edits an Oordoo paper. He also maintains a school at his own private expense."[4] It was, Chunder observes, at the "house of our host," that

> we happened after many days [of traveling by rail] to take up the latest number of the *Delhi Gazette*, and read the latest telegram from England. The newspaper-reading public of Agra is daily increasing in number. The native press already counts four papers in Oordoo—all weeklys. . . . In time they are expected to become powerful organs—heard across the ocean. The *press* and the *platform* are that for which England is the great benefactress of India. It is to be hoped that the *elite* of Hindoostan should be wisely engaged more in defending the true interests of their country. . . . The parlour of our host is by itself a sufficient commentary on the taste and habits of *Young Hindoostan*. It looks out upon a little plot, laid out in flower-beds. The walls of the room are not hung with miniatures of the sensualist Jehangeer or the *Nemazee* Aurungzebe, but pictures of an "English Cottage Scene" and "Fox Hunting Race." There are, too, an English map of the world, and an Ordoo map of India. Upon a bracket against the wall ticked away the huge pendulum of a Sam Slick. Facing it stood a cast of Sir Walter Scott. The book-shelf made a choice little library, to which our lawyer

[a Bengali fellow traveler of Chunder's] added a copy of "Thornton's Gazetteer." (391–92; emphasis in original)

As early as 1865, an official report observed, "rich natives now make handsome presents to the editors of Native papers, as well as subscribe for their publications, and the sense of their editorial power is growing."[5] George Grierson, the famous scholar of linguistics, remarked that there "is scarcely a town of importance which does not possess its own printing presses. Every scribbler can now see his writings in type or lithographed for a few rupees, and too often he avails himself of the power and opportunity."[6] In 1848, for instance, there were 32 vernacular presses in the provinces, and in 1851 only 42.[7] However, by 1876 there were more than 300 presses located in key urban centers and provincial towns in the United Provinces. There were, for instance, 82 presses in Kanpur, 74 in Benares, 62 in Meerut, 58 in Aligarh, and 44 in Allahabad.[8] By 1869 more than 358 vernacular works were published by local presses; in 1876 this figure had increased to 564 and in 1882 to 1,029.[9]

The expansion of this new arena was concomitant with the deepening of the "archival depth of indigenous society."[10] This process was concretized in the growing fashion among local and regional elites to construct clock towers, educational institutes, and other works of public utility, especially public libraries. Chief among them was Bharat Bhawan (India House) in Allahabad, which was closely associated with Madan Mohan Malaviya (who later became a central figure in the Indian National Congress). Bharat Bhawan collected state papers, records, and treatises on social subjects as well as early Hindi prose literature. Conceived as a counterpedagogical site, the library attracted numbers of "educated native youth in the old city, who were repelled by the costs of access and racial exclusiveness of the Thornhill-Mayne Library in the European Civil lines." By the late 1870s, the cities of Allahabad and Lucknow alone possessed over twenty archival collections and libraries and more than fifty private ones associated with local elites (chiefly lawyers and journalists) (349).

The latitude toward the few vernacular newspapers and presses that existed in the pre-1858 period gave way to increasingly authoritarian and stringent measures of surveillance. Colonial state agencies had the power to orient, regulate, and monitor the field of cultural and intellectual production through a variety of means. These included subsidies to schools not directly under the control of the state, the endowment of financial grants to vernacular presses, the enforced seizure and closure of presses deemed subversive, and regularized surveillance measures through various agencies of the Department of Public Instruction, which produced quarterly reports on vernacular school curricula, on all vernacular publications, as well as periodic surveys of vernacular newspapers and magazines that were circulated to the police and civil officials. In fact, by the late 1860s, the surveillance of vernacular publications was withdrawn from the Department of Public Instruction and made the exclusive provenance of the various state agencies in charge of political surveillance and counterintelligence (341).

The most significant decrees regarding the control of vernacular publications were instituted during the 1860s and 1870s, especially Act XXV of 1867, which mandated the recording and scrutiny of all vernacular publications. This was followed by a series of stringent and repressive censorship acts against the vernacular press, especially the all-India Vernacular Press Act of 1878. The justification for the latter was based on the perceived threat posed by the formation and dissemination of an oppositional discourse among a hitherto unimagined diversity of social groups and classes. W. B. Jones, a chief advocate of this intensely repressive act, observed that

> [w]ithin the last twenty years of my own recollection, a feeling of nationality, which formerly had no existence, or was but faintly felt, has grown up. . . . Now . . . we . . . are beginning to find ourselves face to face, not with the population of individual provinces, but with 200 millions of people united by sympathies and intercourse which we have ourselves created and fostered. This seems to be the great and most dangerous political fact of the day.[11]

The specific social composition of readership for vernacular works included students in vernacular schools, urban middle classes, and—via daily bazaar iterations—a wider subaltern audience. What especially troubled the colonial state was precisely the potential of new technologies of print to elicit and forge a counterpublic. Alexander Arbuthnot, the architect of the act, observed:

> It is supposed that because we have a population of 200 million, while the circulation of the vernacular newspapers does not amount to more than 500,000, or so, therefore that circulation must be regarded as insignificant. But the fact is that the circulation of Vernacular newspapers and works is in no way limited by the number of copies actually struck off. The great majority of those who become acquainted with the contents of vernacular publications do so, not by reading them, but by

hearing them read aloud in *bazaars* and public spaces. The mischief that is done by a single seditious article cannot be measured then by the number of copies of it which has been printed. . . . the vernacular papers constantly treat the persons and things they denounce as the types and necessary results of a foreign rule, of the British Raj, and assail our system as a whole. (68–69)

A panoply of legislative acts, practices, and institutions controlled what could be said and how, what could not be said, and which and whose representations were considered relevant and representative. The mediation of intellectual production by the colonial state thus entailed the continual delimitation of the legitimate field of discourse.

However, the expansive network of newspapers, magazines, journals, and published works in numerous regional contexts both expressed and enabled a novel field of discursive interchange. The expansion of this field meant that colonial state institutions as well as British colonial historiography and geographical discourse no longer had exclusive monopoly over the constitution and dissemination of regimes of publicity. The Hindi- and Urdu-speaking professionals and intellectuals of the United Provinces — teachers, lower-level officials, writers, journalists — eagerly embraced the task of forging a geohistorical discourse, with all the renewed prestige that attended their status as cultural brokers imbued with the mission of both demonstrating and forging the unity of an imagined nation adequate to the modern era. The formation of an institutionalized vernacular field represented a central arena for the articulation and generalization of key categorical conceptions, collective identities, and political projects. Central among these was the notion of colonial India as a singular geographical and historical entity, namely, India as Bharat.

The Constitution of Bharat as a Chronotope

Every entry into the sphere of meaning is accomplished only through the gates of the Chronotope. . . . the study of temporal and spatial relationships . . . has only recently begun, and it has been temporal relationships by and large that have been studied — and these in isolation from the spatial relationships indissolubly tied up with them.

—M. M. Bakhtin, *The Dialogic Imagination,* 1937

The category *chronotope* — which literally means time-space — refers to the dialectical co-constitution of spatial and temporal categories. Chronotopes are historically constituted and socially embedded space-time categories that have an exemplary, normative status. The doubled character of chrono-topes as both social and normative and their representational importance for "materializing time in space" provide a useful optic for understanding the emergent conception of India as Bharat (250). The notion of Bharat was at once a historically specific formation and the locus of a normatively satu-rated emergent nationalist discourse. It was discursively forged by the self-conscious appropriation and transposition of at once British-colonial his-torical, geographical, and ethnological discourse as well as received Puranic chronotopes.

Raja Shiva Prasad's three-volume work titled *Itihas timirnasak* (the En-glish title was *A History of India*) serves as a point of entry into the broader consolidation of notions of India as Bharat.[12] Initially published in 1864, it was subsequently translated into Urdu and other regional languages, and remained the standard history textbook in vernacular schools in the United Provinces until the turn of the century. Raja Shiva Prasad's exceptional ca-reer was a product of the expansion of the colonial educational field and the growing institutional thickness of the post-1858 colonial state. Despite be-ing a direct descendant of the famous banker Jagat Seth (the principal financier of the late Mughal state who allied with the East India Company) and a member of the branch of the Seth family that had moved to Benares in the mid-eighteenth century, Prasad forged his career as a public official and an intellectual.[13] Following his education at Benares College, he took on an impressive range of positions that included ambassador *(vakil)* of the raja of Bharatpur, an intelligence officer for the colonial state in the North-Western Provinces and Punjab, the *mir munshi* (chief clerk) of the Simla Agency, the founder of the first Hindi newspaper, *Benares Akhbar* (est. 1845), and the first non-British inspector of schools in the United Provinces (then called North-Western Provinces and Oudh) directly responsible for the supervision and regulation of a large staff of subinspectors, textbook au-thors, and teachers. His career linked, as Chris Bayly notes, the "age of the last late-Mughal *munshis* with the public arenas of the Indian National Con-gress."[14] As the first non-British inspector of schools in colonial India, he was among the first non-British officials (the others were Bapudeva Sastri and Lakshmi Shankar Misra) appointed as advisers to the textbook com-mittees of the Education Department set up in 1873–74, and later was ap-pointed a fellow of both Allahabad and Calcutta Universities.[15] He worked as well as an adviser to the census commission in 1881, elaborating cate-gories for caste and religious divisions, and in 1882 he was appointed to the newly established legislative council.[16]

A controversial figure, Shiva Prasad was a central participant in the highly contentious Hindi–Urdu debate.[17] In an influential 1868 memorandum on the language question titled "Memorandum: Court Characters in the Upper Provinces of India," Prasad contested British language policy and grounded his defense of Hindi on its status as an "organic" formation. He declared that the existing practice of employing Urdu in official correspondence "thrusts a Semitic element into the bosoms of Hindus and alienates them from their Aryan speech [i.e., Hindi]"; also, he claimed that the policy of discouraging Hindi for official purposes amounted to an attempt to "turn all the Hindus into semi-Muhammadans" and thereby destroy "our Hindu nationality."[18] He engaged in many public and rancorous exchanges with Sayyid Ahmad (the founder of Muslim nationalism and the famous Muhammadan Anglo-Oriental college in Aligarh) on the language question and was a critical interlocutor of Dayanand (the founder of the highly influential social reformist organization called Arya Samaj) over the social trajectory of Hinduism.[19]

Prasad remained deeply ambivalent about the formation of the Indian National Congress, although he made a controversial appearance at its Allahabad session in 1888. Bipin Chandra Pal noted that Prasad had "made himself unpopular with Congressmen by joining hands with Sir Syed Ahmad in trying to oppose" the Congress.[20] Prasad's speech at the 1888 Allahabad session of the Congress had, Pal notes, invoked much concern:

> it was feared that the presence of the Rajah Shiva Prasad in the Congress pandal might provoke serious unpleasantness. . . . When Prasad entered the pandal there were some hissing from the back benches which were almost immediately suppressed by the leaders . . . he had brought a speech written out for him. He went up to the platform, read it without any serious interruption and having finished what he had to say he rapidly made his exit like an actor on the stage. (442–43)

Yet despite a formal loyalist posture toward the colonial state, Prasad publicly assailed key aspects of colonial policy. In 1876, for instance, at a public meeting held at the town hall in Calcutta, he protested recent orders to resurvey land holdings in the North-Western Provinces:

> You, Gentlemen, do not know what a survey of this kind means in the North West Provinces; the people call it *"chotti kayamat"* [a small day of

judgment] . . . they know very well that these districts [eastern districts of the province] have already been scientifically surveyed, and so they at once attributed the motive to something else. They met, raised funds, and protested; but the survey was commenced. . . . Government land revenue must have elasticity; nature itself is elastic. . . . If one throws a *bandh* [dam] across a torrent, the banks are sure to outburst, sooner or later . . . I am certainly not a friend to the periodical settlement of the north-west provinces, which the people call *"bari kayamat"* [a great day of judgment].[21]

The director of public instruction was quickly ordered to

rebuke Raja Shiva Prasad for the impropriety of his conduct . . . the language was plainly intended to create a belief that the government was seeking under the cover of a scientific survey to disturb the permanent settlement of the eastern districts. . . . you will give him clearly to understand that he will not be allowed with impunity to publish reckless and unwarrantable imputations against the government by which he is employed, and that a repetition of such an offence will result in his immediate dismissal from its service.[22]

Along with an official rebuke, the state rescinded a free land grant previously conferred on Prasad.

Between the late 1840s and late 1870s, Prasad wrote and translated more than thirty works on such wide-ranging subjects as history, geography, the lives of exemplary women, and social reform.[23] His numerous textbooks on history and geography, especially *Itihas timirnasak* (1864) and *Bhugola hastamalaka* (Geography of the World: Crystal Clear), were the most influential and widely read history and geography textbooks in northern colonial India during the second half of the nineteenth century. Prasad's work *Itihas timirnasak* has been identified as the "first original work in Hindi historiography"[24] and was hailed by Harischandra, the leading Hindi litterateur of the period, as the "first of its kind ever written in our language."[25] Yet there has been no sustained engagement with the content of his work, much less an appreciation of the works' significance for their articulation of a historically novel understanding of territory and history. His historical and geographical works mark the self-conscious historicization of Puranic spatiotemporal imaginings within a modality of historical writing that we now recognize as characteristic of late-nineteenth and early-twentieth-century nationalist discourse. What is more, his works prefigure the broad lineaments of what became, by the turn of the century, a distinctively nationalist geohistorical episteme.

The 1864 preface (written in English) of Prasad's first volume of *Itihas timirnasak* began with a striking claim:

> I was not fully aware of the difficulty of my task when I undertook to prepare a work on the History of India in Hindi and Urdu, for the use of our schools. I knew how imperfect and full of errors the so-called histories are which have hitherto been written in the vernacular, but I had not imagined for a moment that these errors were also committed by British writers . . . indeed, by such writers as James Mill, Monstuart Elphinstone, John Marshman, Alexander Dow.

The preface also tells us that although the first two volumes on the "Hindu and Muslim periods" and the "Rise of the British Empire from 1775–1858" followed the canonical form of British colonial historiography, the third volume departed from this established genre to discuss the "changes in the manners, customs and thought from the earliest ages, when our ancestors were drinking the exhilarating *soma* juice on the banks of the Sarasvati to the historical revolution in law, religion and commerce over the ages." Prasad's remarkable innovation lay in the sociological and cultural themes taken up in the third volume and the decisive departure from previous forms of historical memory that had taken the form of genealogies and lists of kings. His work exemplifies the broader reconstitution of notions of history and territory that organized historical works from this period—works that were self-conscious histories of the country *(des)* and the ordinary people *(janata)*. With characteristic irony, he observed in his 1864 preface that his project was driven by an

> [e]ndeavor . . . to prove to my countrymen that, notwithstanding their strong antipathy to "change," they have in fact changed, and will change; that notwithstanding the many heroic actions ascribed to our ancient Hindu *rajas* [kings], there was no such thing as an empire in existence; that the country was divided between numerous chiefs always fighting with each other for temporary superiority; that notwithstanding the splendour attributed to Muhammadan dynasties, the country was sadly misgoverned, even during the reigns of the most powerful emperors; and that, although the diamonds and pearls were weighed in maunds in the royal treasures the people in general were very poor and utterly miserable.[26]

Prasad's revised 1873 preface (written in English) presented an even sharper and bolder formulation of his project. The 1873 preface stated:

> No sober man is expected to go through these pages and again believe in the absurdities of the *Puranas* or long for one of the old regimes. This of course will be very hard for those who always tune their pipes with the praises of the Muhammadan Empire. . . . Writing history is, I have learned, a most thankless business. But a historian has no choice to please this or that party. He has a day in judgement in miniature before him. The greatest men of the world have to rise before him from their peaceful graves and stand up before him to give an account of their doing, he can spare neither high nor low, he must deal with facts and facts alone.[27]

Shiva Prasad's commitment to fashion—what he called a "modern [*adhunik*] synthetic history" based on objective research protocols—was as controversial as his stated refusal to valorize the precolonial past (6). Indeed, his revised 1873 preface and the third volume of his work led to his dismissal from the editorial board of *Harischandra's Magazine,* following a scathing review by Harischandra for expressing "views offensive to the orthodox Hindus."[28] Yet despite his stated aim of demystification, he nonetheless projects a notion of a distinct national space or Bharat onto the so-called Vedic period, asserting thereby a temporal continuity between an indeterminate past and the present. This proleptic move informs Prasad's delineation of an organic, national space and undercuts his stated attempt to focus on historical transformations, in favor of an abstract continuity tied to the notion of Bharat as a bounded geographical and historical entity.

Building on his opening assertion of the difficulty of writing a history of India, Prasad stated that although Bharat has an ancient history, comparable to that of China and Persia, there were few reliable historical accounts. He noted:

> Before the Mughal period it is difficult to accurately ascertain the history of our country [*des*]. No one, for instance, can claim to definitely establish the numerous kingdoms and kings found in the Ramayana and Mahabharata. Not only is it difficult to ascertain the activities of these kings and construct their royal genealogies[,] even the names of the regions, rivers, and mountains found in these works are open to dis-

pute. Perhaps these rivers, mountains and regions are still present but the historical changes in their names render them unrecognizable to us. . . . From the six hundred or so years of Mughal rule there are hundreds of historical works from which some important political information can be gleaned. . . . As for the time before this, if we exclude the Vedas and Puranas and related works according to which time is divided into *Satyayuga*, *Thretha*, and *Dvapar* . . . , there are very few works which can be classified as properly historical.[29]

Such an assertion rehearsed the claims of British colonial historiography that there was, before British colonial scholarship, no rationally defensible and true historical account in existence. In fact, Prasad mocks the "grief" that the imagined loss of historical works under the Mughal regime inspires (2–3). Even if there had been properly historical works during this period, they would have been, he argued, written under Brahminical prescription. And as such they would have been fanciful fabrications.

Having refuted the assimilation of Puranic-inspired histories into the category of modern historical accounts, he made two further crucial moves. First, extending his defense of a positivist historical method oriented by "facts and facts alone," he distinguished between what he called "general [*prasid*], modern [*adhunik*] historical accounts [*itihas vritanth*]" and forms of historical narrative grounded on "opinion [*nischay*], oral narratives, and religious faith [*shraddha*]" (5–6). Second, he claimed that previous chronicles, produced under the Mughal regime, lacked the necessary objectivity required in a modern historical account, and although he singled out Kalhana's *Rajatrangani* as exceptional, he relegated it to the category of a "regional" work (that is, a history of Kashmir). For without an expansive geographical scale and comprehensive historical reach, such works did not constitute an "integrated, comprehensive, and true" history *(itihas)* of the nation *(des)* (9). He thus explicitly identified a comprehensive geographical scale as an essential component of a modern historical account of the *des*.

Prasad broadened the theme of the difficulty of his project by asserting that there was no accurate indigenous mode of historical periodization. Unambiguously scornful of the organizing temporal schemas of Puranic and popular Hindu astrological systems, he presents an anecdote of a recent visit to the "rustic" region of Uttarakhand (in northern United Provinces). The "rural, mountainous people" of this region are identified as the last surviving constituency for unquestioned faith in Puranic temporal schemas.

Saturated with an elite paternalism that marked many of the defenders of scientific rationalism, Prasad remarks:

> When I asked these people of events that had occurred three hundred years ago they would say that it occurred during the *satyayuga*. On further prodding they would assert that it occurred during the time of the Kauravas and Pandavas [the protagonists of the classical epic Mahabharata]. And when I pushed them to measure [*hisab*] temporal periods [*yuga*] they would throw up measurements of lakhs and lakhs of years. (8–9)

This anecdote was followed with a more studious attempt to distinguish between what he termed the aesthetic splendor and "pleasures" *(athi manohar)* of "poetical and mytho-religious" time and the objective, universal time of modern world history (11–13). The underlying temporal schemas of the classical Vedas, Puranas, and epics should, he argued, be placed in the former category and the temporal organization of historical works of the post-Mughal period should be classified in the latter. Acutely conscious of the politics of this categorical opposition, he defended this schema by asserting that it organized "modern world history" *(adhunik jagadh itihas)*, and as such it constituted the basis for adjudicating between historical evidence and religious faith. Addressing the "Hindu" section of his imagined national audience, he remarked:

> I know that many Hindus will not concede to a classification of the Shastras [religious and philosophical texts] as existing in a poetic time, and will consider such a claim as against *dharma* [religious sanction or law]. . . . Against people who would assert such a claim, I can only reiterate and plead that I am not concerned with the construction or destruction of any particular doctrine or sect. Rather I am only interested in writing a history of our nation [*des*], that is, I seek to make visible [*prakashit*] only those matters that are universally held and recognized among all faiths. . . . In order to substantiate my differentiation between religious opinion and historical fact I shall offer further examples. (14)

He was painfully aware of the politics of such a methodological protocol, for it had inspired a heated debate during the 1860s and 1870s. An annual report from the director of public instruction noted that native outspokenness on matters of Indian history or creed is apparently much more irritating than similar criticism by Europeans. . . . Raja Shiva Prasad's Hindi History of India, Part III, is a case in point. His account of Brahminism, and his attempt to apply the principles of historical criticism to the bases of the creed, excited wrath among the Hindu community, especially in his native Benares. Instead of proving him to be incorrect, they attempted to borrow point to their virtuous indignation by asserting that the book had been published by the government. This is not the case. The author has published his work at his own expense though the work is used in both government and private vernacular schools as a class-book. The Urdu version of part 1 was found fault with by Muhammadan critics, because in some instances the Emperors of Delhi were judged by their actions, and because some of the allusion to Muhammadan rule were seen as intentionally aggressive.[30]

Prasad's work was assailed by conservative Brahmins and Hindu social reformers (including Harischandra) outraged by his rationalistic critique of Puranic schemas and his rendering of the Shastras as articles of faith, and by Muslim scholars for his denigration of the Mughal period. The attempted distinction between poetic-religious and modern historical time was animated by an acute recognition of the difficulty of securing an adequate ground for adjudicating between competing collective memories. His self-conscious commitment to positivist methodological protocols—what one contemporary British-colonial admirer called the "appeal to reason and reality which is the peculiarity of the Rajah's work"—that organized world history was symptomatic of the radically relational character of the conception of India as a spatially bounded, historically singular national entity.[31] The intelligibility of Bharat as a distinct national space was coeval with its placement within a world historical-geographical framework wherein it could be read as a particular instantiation of a universal sociospatial form.

In a specifically modern dialogic construction, Prasad continually interrupted his historical narrative by staging debates between himself, as the historian, and his imagined audience, the larger arena of fellow nationals. One such staging was the following:

> Many of my fellow nationals will ask on what basis I characterize as false matters written in ancient texts and transmitted in oral narratives that Hindus have held sacred since time immemorial? In response to them I shall confine myself to the following line of questions. Is not the

Jain religion as illustrious as the Vedic? Don't the Jains have their own oral narratives from time immemorial and moreover, have written texts deposited in ancient libraries such as Vaisali, libraries whose traces are not even discernible during the Vedic age? So I ask you what manner of tradition organizes your beliefs that you selectively conceive some of our common ancestors as true and others as false? To this question of mine you shall assuredly reply that such a distinction is a matter of individual religious faith. Should you reply thus, I have no interest in refuting your claim. For I seek only to write a modern and universal historical account of our nation, I have no interest in attacking or supporting anyone's individual opinion and religious belief.[32]

Having established an apparently objective and secular framework of reasoning, Prasad turned to the ancient "Hindu" age. If this move followed the linear, homogenous time of British colonial historiography, it also departed from it in several respects. Whereas British colonial accounts conceived the "ancient" Hindu age as a dead relic, Prasad stressed the contemporary significance of analyzing this era. In fact, the "Vedic civilization" was rendered the classical heritage of the "nation," its civilizational glory and learning constituted, we are told, at once a normative and social "exemplar" and, most crucially, represented the origins of "our nation," namely, "Bharat" (20).

Yet the turn to an indeterminate past as the exemplar for the present invoked an anxious series of specifications regarding the vexed category *Hindu*. Prasad observes that the original referent of the word *Hindu* was geographical rather than religious. The term *Hindu* was first employed, he duly acknowledges, by Arabic travelers to designate the people who lived east of the river Sindhu or Indus. That the most interior sign of belonging—that is, the category *Hindu* —was, from the standpoint of his own narrative, foreign invoked a profound anxiety about the essential alienation of the national core. The alien interiority of the category *Hindu* required the positing of a supranational category that exceeded historical space-time. For Prasad, and many later nationalists, the category *Arya* signified the transcendental ground of collective identity, and it signaled a self-same original and pure originary space. The term *Arya*, according to Prasad, constituted the self-description of "our ancient ancestors" and referred to an affective relationship with place whose trace was discernible in contemporary sacred geographical conceptions of the northwest region. There was, for Prasad, no "doubt" that for the *Aryas*, like "ourselves," the northwestern region was the most "central, sacred space." The northwest region of Aryavarta was, he

notes, "universally praised" in all the ancient Shastras and marked the spatial core of the imagined nation (24). Building on this theme, Prasad notes
that although the term *Hindu* referred to the inhabitants east of the river
Sindhu, this boundary was not historically fixed because the entire north-
west region during the Vedic era was considered Aryavarta. The isomorphism between people, culture, and territory on both sides of the river
Sindhu was, we are told, comparable to the contemporary match between
regions north and south of the Ganges. It was only with the establishment
of "Muslim" rule in the western region that the river Sindhu came to mark
a constitutive limit, and from that point onward this region was no longer
understood as part of "our Bharat" (26–27). The identification of the category *Arya* as the proper substitute for the originary lack signaled by the term
Hindu and the emphasis on the continuities of a sacred geography sought to
smooth over historical dislocations.

Prasad's delineation of the historical geography of the Vedic era was interspersed with long polemics against Puranic geographical imaginings. Toward this end, he attached a Puranic map-like representation and observed:
"The fanciful sketch [*naksha*] of this country according to the Puranas,
copied in the next page, is worth observing. According to this schema the
country was divided into nine sections [*khandas*] in the shape of a lotus. If
this was the state of knowledge of our country then one can only speculate
what the rest of geographical knowledge [*bughol vidya*] consisted in!"
(22–23). At issue for Prasad was not only the geographically nondetermi-
nate character of Puranic schemas but their unintelligibility from the standpoint of the procedures and protocols of "modern world history" *(adhunik
jagadh itihas)*. Following such positivist protocols, he attached a map of colonial India as the accurate representation of the geographical contours of
Bharat.

What is significant here is the way the contemporary territorial boundaries of the colonial state constituted the approximate spatial scale of the
imagined nation of Bharat. Only at the time in which Prasad was writing did
a notion of Bharat as a unified national entity roughly coextensive with the
boundaries of the colonial state emerge. Although Prasad appropriated the
category *Bharat* from Puranic sacred geography, he profoundly reworked
its meaning by assigning it determinate geographical and historical contours. This central geohistorical category constituted the taken-for-granted
frame of reference of Prasad's history of India.

Despite the initial stress placed on the difficulty of reconstructing the
pre-Mughal period and the fragmentary character of the historical sources,
Prasad details the social, philosophical, economic, and literary accomplish-

ments that distinguished the so-called Vedic age. The record of these achievements culled from late-eighteenth and early-nineteenth-century Orientalist discourse and positioned against the utilitarian thrust of James Mill and later British colonial historiography became an almost obligatory inventory in later nationalist works,[33] because such an inventory was part of the appropriation of a classical civilization as the basis for the imagined nation's autonomous future. Prasad's work prefigures at once the retrospective projection of a unified nation, namely, Bharat, onto the absolute space-time of the so-called Vedic era, the increasing racialization of the category *Arya* in nationalist discourse,[34] and the obsessive archaism of later nationalist historiography.

Fragmentary Histories and Nostalgic Narratives of Origin

A constitutive aspect of nationalist historiography was the inversion of the enlightenment theme of progress into a narrative of decline from the pure wonders of an ancient space-time to the degradation and fragmentation constitutive of the present. In Prasad's work, this takes the form of a persistent equivocation between a narrative of origins and the recognition of a fragmentary history. On the one hand, Prasad exhorts his readers to eschew uncritical narratives of the precolonial and emphasizes historical ruptures that suggested a fragmented history. On the other hand, he posits the Vedic era as the original space-time of Bharat and as the privileged source to which one must turn to capture the authentic meaning of nationhood. Situated across these two registers, emergent nationalist historiography looked both forward and back, signifying a gathering of struggle to overcome the fragmentation of the present by realizing an organic space-time grounded in an indeterminate past.

Exemplary, in this regard, was Prasad's elaboration of the imagined egalitarian character of gender practices and forms in the ancient "Hindu period." The idealized description of the status of ancient "Hindu women" summoned against colonial discourse served, as various historians have shown, to bolster claims about the superiority of an ancient Hindu civilization.[35] However, such an excessive construction of "ancient Hindu women" only accentuated the problem of accounting for the discontinuity between this idealized era and the present. In a move that would assume a self-evident status in later nationalist works, Prasad identified the origins of the patriarchal relations constitutive of the present as inseparably linked to the "arrival of the Muslims":

The expansion of the Muslim religion and rule did not just inaugurate an unprecedented era of massacres, robberies, the razing of temples and new forms of slavery [*gulami*], but led to a profound transformation of the customs and way of life of Hindus. The cruelty, coercive force, and decadence of Muslims drowned us. It marked the beginning of such practices as female infanticide, the imprisonment of young girls within their homes, and the use of *purdah* [veil] among women. In an attempt to protect them from Muslim onslaught, Hindus began to draw sharper boundaries around their internal communities [*jatis*] and such practices as segregated eating and living became increasingly prevalent. As a consequence the very religion of Hindus was transformed. The first sign of the fall of our nation was the excessive absorption in particularistic communities [*jati ka bachav*]. This blocked progress [*tarakki*] within and did not allow for progressive practices from the outside [*bahar*] to filter in. . . . Those people, in the present period, who willingly place their live mother on the funeral pyre of their father's corpse and ignite the fire themselves, those who murder their girl-child at the moment of birth, those who marry multiple women and keep all of them imprisoned within the home, those who place their girl-children in store fronts and sell them like cattle . . . I cannot consider such people true Hindus, descendants of the Aryans. I do not even know to what community such people correspond.[36]

The displacement of the degradation of women to the Mughal Empire and the "arrival" of Islam prepared the metaphorical ground for constructions of Bharat Mata, of the nation-as-mother and mother-as-nation, in later nationalist discourse.

Within the terms of nostalgic narratives of origin and decline, the term *Arya* was the fetishized guarantor of national continuity, homogeneity, and solidarity. The categorical ideal of the Arya as the true Hindu connects both the first assumed national and the projected national of the future (the recuperated, reformed male Hindu). The term *Arya* came to represent a renascent Hinduism, a reformed Hinduism excised of corrupting external currents, and the traumatic imprimatur of what were seen as successive colonial intrusions that were imaged, more often than not, as instances of collective symbolic castration. Prasad held up the imaginary Aryan community that existed in the absolute space-time of Bharat as the originary, organic nationals. The contemporary nation was urged to contemplate its own identity in its pure, unspoiled state by looking at the so-called Arya community in the Vedic civilization. In short, the imagined nation was urged to recognize as its own the normative, historical, and spatial ideal signaled in the term *Bharat*. This assumed national inheritance was to be preserved from all further degradation and dispersal.

The equivocation between a nostalgic recovery of origins and the recognition of fragmentary histories assumed multiple narrative forms, especially the growing prevalence of binarist conceptions of the categorical identities of Hindu and Muslim. Prasad cited with approval, for instance, Henry Elliot's influential work, *The History of India as Told by Its Own Historians*. This eight-volume work, edited and published by John Dowson between 1867 and 1877, was a select translation of extracts from more than 150, mostly Persian, historical accounts dating from the ninth to the eighteenth centuries.[37] Prasad argued that even a cursory glance at this work demonstrated that "under the sway of Muslims the nation [*des*] could not rise in the scale of civilizations." The writings of Muslim chroniclers were, he stated, "actuated by motives of either ambition or fear. They have concealed blemishes and exaggerated good qualities to such an extent that it is impossible to believe even what may be fact."[38]

It is instructive, in this respect, to examine Elliot's opening claim:

> It must be understood, then, that this Index has not been constructed on account of any intrinsic value in the histories themselves. Indeed, it is almost a misnomer to style them histories. They can scarcely claim to rank higher than Annals. . . . If the definition of Dionysious be correct, that "History is Philosophy teaching by examples," then there is no Native Historian.[39]

This grand dismissal was, of course, a central motif of late colonial ideology about the Mughal Empire. The principal political purpose of Elliot's extensive compilation, especially for the inhabitants of the North-Western Provinces, is made clear:

> Though the intrinsic value of these works may be small . . . they will make our native subjects more sensible to the immense advantages accruing to them under the mildness and equity of our rule. . . . we should no longer hear bombastic Babus, enjoying under our Government the highest degree of personal liberty, and many more political privileges that were ever conceded to a conquered people, rant about patriotism, and the degradation of their present position. . . . I speak here with particular reference to my own Presidency, the North-Western

Provinces . . . the very seat of Muhammadan supremacy. . . . The scientific survey alone of the North-Western Provinces is sufficient to proclaim our superiority; in which every field throughout an area of 52,000 square miles is mapped, and every man's possession recorded. It altogether eclipses the boasted measurements of Akhbar and is as magnificent a monument of civilization as any country in the world can produce. (xxvi–vii)

Prasad's account of the "Muslim Period" resounds with such interlinked themes as the collective oppression, political apathy, and fragmentation of Hindus. The self-sameness of the category *Hindu* hinged on the denial of the numerous sectarian and doctrinal differences within the imagined core national *jati* (community) through the construction of a monolithic "long suffering, oppressed Indian nation [*Bharat des*]." For Prasad, a central consequence of Mughal rule was the progressive depoliticization of the "ordinary [Hindu] populace."[40] The rise and fall of successive "foreign" regimes took on a specular quality for "us, the ordinary populace":

Over a thousand years or so there was a rapid succession of various Muslim regimes in *Bharat des*. Gradually, this long period of living unfree [*adheen*] and of being enslaved [*gulam*] became second nature. It became an integral part of our character and disposition [*swabhav*]. The rise and demise of various kings became a mere spectacle or theatrical performance [*tamasha*]. As a consequence, there was no notion of collective rights [*hak*] that animated the popular English uprising against King Charles. We lost that quest for independence [*aazadi*] that led the French people in battle against King Louis. . . . there was, in this country during the Muslim regime, no possibility for the formation of that unity and courage that gave birth to these struggles. . . . Even our language lacks a word for that "Patriotism" [Prasad uses the English word in his Hindi text to underscore this point] which, in contemporary Europe, people are willing to die and kill for. Instead, we remain content as slaves [*gulam*] of whoever captures power. There is little more to say on this theme when we consider the fact that we did not resist such kings as the mad Mahmud Tughlak and the cruel and fanatic Nadir Shah. Our poverty and unfreedom are, then, the fruit of our loss of unity. (97)

The figure of the Muslim was symbolically overdetermined: the internal antagonisms within the categorical identity marked *Hindu* were displaced in a mythic struggle between an imagined organic national collective and the Muslim as the paradigmatic alien force.

By the 1870s, the interpretation that national decline had followed the establishment of so-called Muslim rule had become doxic, especially among upper-caste colonial middle classes.[41] The effort to overcome the perceived ravages of colonial and Mughal rule was undertaken through the attempted resacralization and nationalization of space through such self-understood Hindu categories as *Aryavarta* and *Bharat.* The instituted equivalence between British colonial and Mughal rule, and the racialized construction of the category of *Arya* — which followed late-eighteenth-century Orientalist scholarship and nineteenth-century romantic discourse — were part of what can be understood as a transvaluation of colonial racism. This transvaluation, condensed in the doubled character of Bharat as both a sociohistorical and a utopian category, became a central motif of upper-caste Hindu historical imaginings.

British colonial historiographical constructions of India as a subsidiary segment of British history comprised a productive axis in the reinforcement of historical consciousness and categorical solidarity. Consider, in this respect, Henry Maine's famous convocation address to Calcutta University on March 17, 1866. A central administrative figure and prominent legal and historical scholar (the architect of the notion of "village republics"), Maine was the vice-chancellor of Calcutta University and law member of the viceroy's council from 1862 to 1869.[42] In his convocation address, he rebuked "the most highly educated class of natives who had broken for ever with much in their history, much in their customs, much in their creeds" for attempting to weave apparently diverse and discordant elements and narratives toward an autonomous and celebratory historiography. At issue was the way colonized elites were conducting

> [e]laborate attempts to persuade themselves and others, that there is a sense in which these rejected portions of Native history, and usage, and belief are perfectly in harmony with the modern knowledges, which the educated class has acquired, and with the modern civilization to which it aspires. . . . I myself believe that European influences are, in great measure, the source of these delusions. The value attached in Europe to ancient Hindoo literature, and deservedly attached for its poetical and philological interest, has very naturally caused natives to look back with pride and fondness on the era when the great Sanskrit poems were composed and great philosophical systems evolved. But unquestion-

ably this tendency has its chief root in this—that the natives have caught from us Europeans our modern trick of constructing by means of works of fictions, an imaginary past out of the present, taking from the past its externals, its outward furniture, but building in the sympathies, the susceptibilities and even the knowledge of the present time . . . on the educated natives the past presses with too awful and terrible a power for it to be safe for him to play or palter with it. . . . the Past cannot be colored by him in this way, without his misreading the Present and endangering the Future . . . the natives must realize that their real affinities are with Europe and the Future, not with India and its Past.[43]

Maine was acutely aware of the way the so-called native preoccupation with the past signaled a displaced critique of the colonized present. The dangers of "misreading the Present" stemmed from the concrete political signification of an obsession with the past that was irreducibly bound to the present. Although Maine identified the practice of constructing an "imaginary past out of the present" as a specifically "modern trick," he remained anxious about its improvisational deployment in the refracted form of a nationalist historiography driven by an impulse toward a different, specifically noncolonial, future. Thus, in a subtle move, Maine attempted to realign the colonial present as the determinate future of India and render the precolonial past as dead, unrecoverable time. His speech resounds with a deep anxiety about the political enrichment of sense that accompanies the transposition of categories from their imagined "original" locale and their articulation with the extended range of experiences of unevenness and nonsynchronicity constitutive of colonial societies.

The denial of the temporal and spatial coevalness of nationalist discourse was part of the larger refusal to admit the possibility of willed, rational agency of colonial subjects independent of British colonial tutelage. However, the very denial of coevalness reinforced already-vital mythico-historical themes within nationalist discourse. The construction of the nation as the site of collective political agency sought to undercut the geohistorical determinism of colonial discourse. At the same time, the construction of a transcendental nationness concretized in such terms as *Aryavarta* and *Bharat* conjured away the awkward historical complexity of internal dissensions and fractures within the so-called Hindu community. *Bharat* came to represent at once a geohistorically delimited national entity, a utopia realized in the ancient past, the exemplar for present political and social projects, and the object of nationalist desire. Prasad's work, among others during this period, expresses this palimpsestic imaging of the chronotope *Bharat*. The very capacity of the notion of *Bharat* to shuttle between a utopian and sociohistorical register endowed it with a robust and troubling endurance.

The lived experience of colonial unevenness and the challenges posed to received practices and categories of envisioning time and space shaped the lineaments of popular geohistorical imaginings. It is not surprising that popular geohistorical discourse focused on the issues that it did: the articulation between history, territory, and collective identity; the presumed existence of a concrete social body in an ancient past; and the fictive unity between an ancient past and a noncolonial future. This constellation of themes underwrote a historicist conceptualization of the relationship between history and territory on a collective scale. The rendering of Mughal and British rule as homologous "colonial" structures, and the identification of the former as an external, extraterritorial imposition only becomes intelligible with reference to the organizing assumption of an already existent, organically constituted national entity, *Bharat*. Works that regarded the Mughal Empire and by extension Muslims as foreign were formally similar to those that argued that long-run inhabitation had naturalized their status as fellow nationals. Both positions shared in common a historicist understanding of the liaison between territory and identity that rendered Hindus as the original, organic, core nationals. Within this schema, Muslims were regarded as the foreign body, an external element within the corporatist vision of an organic national whole, or, at best, as belated nationals whose relationship to the imagined nation could only be figured as a problem. This territorial nativist vision of nationhood enabled a dual obscuring of history and geography. The "territorialization of history" condensed in the central category of *Bharat* pushed aside and severed historical interrelations among various social groups. And the progressive "historicization of territory" secured a conception of territory as the organic and natural ground for the excavation and forging of collective identities.[44]

THE NATURALIZATION OF BHARAT

Teaching the Nation

During the 1860s and 1870s there was an astonishing proliferation of vernacular geography and historical works, authored by teachers, journalists, and local and provincial officials, that were principally circulated in vernacular schools. A synthetic reading of the spatial and temporal categories of more than forty such texts illustrates the naturalization and nationalization of a specifically modern understanding of history and territory.[45]

The pedagogical project of teaching the nation from its historical geography and demographic composition to the embodied disposition of its people imbued works from this period. An early textbook of geography from the late 1850s, titled, *Bhugol varnan* (Description of Geography), and written by Bapudeva Sastri (who, along with Raja Shiva Prasad, was among the three non-British inspectors of schools), observes:

> It is remarkable that the people of Bharat know very little about their own country, its history, geographical features, and people. When this is the state of knowledge about their own country, it follows that their knowledge about England, France, America etc., which are outside Bharat is even less precise. In fact, a lot of people consider Calcutta as a foreign capital; indeed, they assume that it is a part of England! The people of *Bharat* are largely ignorant of their own nation, its geographical extent and features, its languages, customs, religions, and people. It is for this reason that I consider it necessary to detail the geographical extent and features of Bharat as well as its people and their way of life [*chal challan*].[46]

Many works explicitly justified such an endeavor as integral for broadening and deepening knowledge about the nation, and thereby about the self. A textbook on the historical geography of Lalitpur, titled *Bhugol o itihas Lalitpur* and written by Pandit Sitarama in 1869, foregrounds the association between knowledge of the self and that of the nation. It identified its broad aim as the following:

> By reading this book students will learn about *Bharat des* in a comprehensive manner. They will discover, for instance, the various regions, towns, villages etc., that are part of this *des*, about the various products that are found here, about the languages and customs of our people and the like. By reading this book students will also learn about their failings, our decline, and the desperate [*durdasha*] condition of our *des*.[47]

The project of teaching the nation was positioned not only against official claims of moral and material progress but against the teaching of colonial state space. Vernacular historical geography consequently stressed the apparently arbitrary nature of colonial administrative territorial boundaries and crafted linear, continuist histories of varied spatial units—localities, cities, regions, and Bharat. The simultaneous focus on multiple spatial scales and the larger territorial whole of colonial India underscore the ways in which the relationship between emergent local-regional and national histories is best understood as a process of dialectical co-constitution. The histories produced of Awadh, Indore, Bengal, Meerut, Madhya Pradesh, Benares, Lucknow, and the like express the ways in which the meaning and evaluation of particular places came to be understood as instances of the larger imagined nation of Bharat.[48]

The common prefatory section of historical geographies of particular regions and towns was variously titled the "ancient history of Hindustan" or the "ancient history of Bharat." This section was generally followed by a delimitation of the contemporary administrative boundaries of the colonial state, an account of the chief agricultural products of particular regions, and the demographic composition (caste, religion, population) of various localities, against which the particularity of the place examined was situated. Most works explicitly compared and contrasted areas under direct colonial rule with the juridical and political space of princely states. However, the histories of both were narrated as inseparably tied up with an older, historically continuous, spatially determinate form, namely, Bharat. The organization of these accounts reinforced a conception of the intrinsic organic links between particular places and the larger territorial whole. Raja Shiva Prasad's historical geography titled *Bhugola hastamalaka* compared the various regions that comprise Bharat to "rooms within a large house." In this view, the knowledge of particular "rooms" (or regions) was inextricably linked to a broader understanding of the historical and geographical foundation of the "larger house" (or nation).[49]

The particularity of regional communities was directly positioned in terms of a larger national whole. This construction paralleled the ways the specificity of the local and regional became unthinkable outside its relationship to the spatial scale and temporality of the imagined nation. Vernacular histories and geography texts detailed traits (including enumerations and classifications based on religious and caste divides) common to the people of Bharat as well as of particular regions and localities. A historical geography of Lucknow from 1872, written by Pandit Mulacanda, notes:

> The people of Bharat are renowned for their generosity, compassion and non-violence. . . . However, because of the hot climate they have become lazy and lack the desire for active pursuits found in other nations [*desaon*]. . . . This trait has been exacerbated by widespread feel-

ings of exclusive loyalty to one's own *jati* [community]. I am not suggesting that people contrary to this general trait are not found; only that this has become increasingly prevalent and has hindered the progress of *Bharat.*[50]

A geography textbook used in primary schools during the late 1870s, written by Vishnu Shrikhande, contained various songs to be learnt for recitation. Among them was the following song: "the people of *Bharat* are compassionate but lazy. . . . Those in the north are fair and tall. . . . Those of the south are dark and short . . . Rajputs and Mahrattas are very brave. . . . Bengalis are physically weak and cowardly but have sharp intellects."[51] In sharp contrast, a geography textbook from the early 1840s that circulated within vernacular schools classified together Chinese, Sikhs, Japanese, Kashmiris, Bengalis, and the like as formally similar *jatis*. It observed:

> The Arab *jati* is brave and resourceful but are also known for being tricksters. The Chinese are hardworking and clever but are vain and duplicitous. . . . The Bengali *jati* is soft-hearted, intelligent and obedient, but are lazy, physically weak and greedy. The people of Japan are learned and intelligent. The Sikh *jati* is proud and brave. Kashmiris and Nepalis are known for their beauty.[52]

Specific communities (e.g., Sikhs, Bengalis, Kashmiris) were not seen as part of a larger whole; they were not regarded as internally related or embedded within a single territorially defined national whole of Bharat. The notion of the "people of Bharat" had yet to assume shape.

Prasad's *Bhugola hastamalaka* devoted an entire chapter to the dispositional specificity of regional social groups:

> The people of Uttarakhand, especially those that live between the Ganga and the Indus rivers, are fair, handsome and noted for their honesty and simple mindedness. The women of this area are so beautiful that they seem like fairies brought to earth. . . . But the practice of polyandry in certain parts of the region is deplorable. . . . it is in this respect that the women of this region are like bills of exchange [*darsani hundi*]. . . . the people of Lucknow and Awadh are extremely effeminate in their manner and clothes. . . . the flares of their pajamas are excessively long and if picked up would reach their heads. . . . they are known for their decadence, exaggerated courtly manners and untrustworthy characters. . . . .the Bengalis lack courage [*kam himmat*], are exception

ally timid [*asahassi*], and cowardly [*darpok*]. They are known for their
indulgence of sweets [*sandesh*]. Bengalis by the time of middle-age are
remarkably portly. . . . like the English they generally do not cover their
heads and leave them bare. . . . the women of this region wrap only a
very small cloth around their chests and thereby negate the difference
between nude and clothed women . . . they have very little modesty [*la-
jja*]. . . . The men and women of this area [Bengal] have, however, sharp
intellects and are thus commonly found in government services and
learned professions. . . . the people of *dakshin* (southern India) demonstrate a way of life and ethos that is distinctively and authentically [*asli*]
Hindu . . . this has to do with the minimal Muslim presence in this area,
both historically and at present.[53]

Such cataloging of regional stereotypes appears, at first blush, to mime the
objectifying and normalizing procedures of British colonial ethnological discourse. These were generalized by such midcentury British colonial works
as James Duff (1826) on the Marathas, James Tod (1829–30) on the Rajputs, Joseph Cunnigham (1849) on the Sikhs (all quickly translated in various vernaculars), and the Borgesian eight-volume state-sponsored ethnographic project titled *The Peoples of India* — all of which secured India as a
vast ethnographic storehouse.[54] However, popular vernacular discourse on
internal differentiations (regional, caste, religious) owed less to the objectifying procedures of colonial historiography and ethnology as such than to
the pervasive institutionalization of colonial categories of caste and religion
in mundane bureaucratic encounters,[55] and the more intimate, proximate
(and indeed affective) medium of stereotypes, exaggerations, and prejudices
enshrined and circulated in gossip, rumor, oral narratives, folktales, and
songs. Bholanauth Chunder's narrative of his journey to the upper
provinces (United Provinces) from Bengal, undertaken from 1860 to 1866,
was punctuated, for instance, by distinctions between the "Young Hindoostan" and the "Young Bengal" in the minutiae of everyday life, from devotional practices, physiognomy, habits of betel-nut chewing, clothing,
"oil-rubbing," interior furnishing of homes, and the like. A characteristic
cataloging of the differences between rural Hindoostan and Bengal is as
follows:

> As we proceed everything about us bespoke Hindoostan — the stalwart
> and muscular men, the turbaned heads, and tucked-up *dhooties*, their
> Hindu colloquy, the fields of *jowara*, the dry soil and air, the superior
> cattle, the camels, the absence of the bamboos and cocoa, and the wells

in place of tanks. . . . From Allahabad to Shecoabad there are four large cities, and villages at frequent intervals. A similar distance in Bengal is no doubt dotted with the same number of villages, but not one town equal to Futtehpore, Cawnpore, or Mynporee. . . . The ryot in Hindoostan is no less a bondsman to the *mahajun* [moneylender] than the ryot in Jessore or Dacca; but he is more independent-minded, and would not tamely put up with the outrages that are inflicted by a Bengali Zemindar or Indigo-planter. . . . In Calcutta, the Baboos who talk big of politics and reformations, do not know what it is to ride. In Hindoostan, rural women perform journeys on horsebacks.[56]

On the habitus of middle-class, urban Bengalis versus that of the residents of Agra, Chunder observed:

Not alone in point of eating, but also in dressing and in politeness, do the North-westerns beat us. As far as the outward air of good breeding goes, almost every Agra-wallah is well bred. The decorum of his appearance, and the propriety of his speech, indicate the civilized life that is spent in a metropolis. The local dialect is the polished Oordoo, in which one can hardly detect a vulgarism. Not a little do the Agra-wallahs pride themselves in their refinements of an ancient metropolitan citizenship. (1:390)

Yet he also emphasized the overcoming of distinctions in an imagined north India–centric national whole:

Between the public mind of Hindoostan and the public mind of Bengal, there has existed for several centuries a great gulf. To bridge that gulf the epoch has arrived. Under the auspices of a liberal education, and the growth of enlightened sentiments, races of one parentage, but separated from each other by hereditary prejudices of fifty or more generations, and forming an ill-cemented mass of petty nationalities, are to acknowledge one common brotherhood, and form one great welded nation. (1:388)

The possibility of this imagined national whole rested for many upper-caste, self-identified Hindus on an expansive ideological understanding of Hinduism closely bound up with the notion of hierarchically organized nationals wherein the Muslim, as Chunder observed, "has always been" an "alien" and was "now moreover a non-entity" (1:432).

The overdetermined figure of the Muslim as an irreducible alterity underwrote the pervasive reading of the Mughal Empire and colonial rule as homologous structures and the history of the former as part of an external, supraterritorial history of Islam as such. Chunder, for instance, enunciated a genocidal fantasy that more than rivaled Orientalist prejudices against Islam contained in British colonial discourse:

> The Moslem has left indelible traces of his presence everywhere in the ruin of countries, and in the slavery of nations. He was born not for the progress, but the retrogression of mankind — not for amelioration, but for the perpetuation of evil. . . . Under the progress which the world has made now, the Mahomedan has become an absoletism, — and to tolerate his existence is to tolerate an anomaly — a diseased limb endangering the soundness of the whole system. If it were possible to destroy all Mahomedan institutions, and to eradicate all Mahomedan traditions, by one vigorous and simultaneous effort, and if all that is Mahomedan in name or spirit were to become extinct by a combination of circumstances, it would be well. . . . The Mahomedan sits as an oppressive incubus upon society, hindering the onward progression of some three hundred millions of men. (2:356–57)

Official representation of the fragmented montage of the "Peoples of India" as expressive of an irreducible "pathology of difference" underwent a significant transformation in popular discourse.[57] For the latter represented the "People of Bharat" (rather than Peoples) as a corporate singularity within which particular social groups, with their multiple distinctions, were lodged. The notion of a singular national people, territory, and history was the constitutive difference, the foundational fiction, of national imaginings. Insofar as this categorization remained grounded in a historicist and territorial nativist episteme, its internal fractures and potential for violence continued to haunt both popular imaginaries and later institutional nationalism.

The Reconstitution of Spatial Categories

The discursive constitution of India as Bharat was concurrent with the reconfiguration of such received categories as *Hindustan* and *des* that acquired a spatially expansive meaning. During the second half of the nineteenth century, the term *Hindustan* lost its particularized reference to the Indo-Gangetic plain and came to figure the area encompassed by the colonial state. In fact, during the 1870s the dominant terms for the territorial whole of colonial India became *Bharat* and *Hindustan* (in its expanded geographical meaning), eclipsing and reworking such received terms as *mulk* (imperial possession), *kishwar* (region, continent), and *vatan* (homeland), which had multiple, shifting spatial referents and did not signify the modern link between territory and sovereignty. The modern territory-oriented conception of sovereignty inscribed in the revaluation of the term *Hindustan* represented a break from Mughal administrative and cartographic traditions.

The Mughal cartographic repertoire consisted of two key forms: medieval guides and route maps derived from the descriptions of travelers, and a coordinate-based cartography. As Irfan Habib observes: "The former suited a flat surface framed by grids; and the latter, a sphere encompassed by meridians and parallels."[58] Even the latter form of cartography based on coordinates was not strictly geographical in the modern sense but rather rooted in astrological and religious determinations (128–29). More crucially, the division of space into seven latitudinal climes *(iqlim)* militated against representations of contiguous territories. In the 1644–65 encyclopedia compiled by Mirza Muhammad Sadiq Isfahani, titled *Shahid-i sadiq*, for instance, the Mughal Empire is not represented as a spatially bounded, singular whole but as a plurality or network of places (128–29). Such a construction underlies as well the most famous Mughal work, *Ain-i akhbari*, compiled by Abul Fazl (1556–1605). This work, completed in 1589, contains an extensive section titled "The Area of Twelve Subhas," which includes tables on the rivers, mountains, mines, craft production, chiefs, and revenues of various administrative divisions.[59] And although large route-maps were common, Mughal maps did not display "scalar fidelity in a geometric sense" precisely because the modern territory–sovereignty nexus was not operative.[60] There are no atlases of the entire territory of the Mughal dominion, no maps that depict it as a singular, spatially bounded whole.[61]

Mughal accounts from the late-eighteenth and early-nineteenth centuries represented the sociogeographic landscape as a hierarchically organized order. At the base there was "distance, climate, and physical effects," the second level comprised the domain of human communities embedded within the physical environment, and the apex was composed of testimonies to the influence of divinity and great men. The late-eighteenth-century work *Waqyai-i azfari*, which recounts the journey of an exiled Mughal prince through various regions of colonial India, suggests how geographical descriptions approached, as Chris Bayly observes, a "kind of itinerant threnody for the relics of the great and learned." Works from the mid-nineteenth-century period, conceived in the context of a territorially expansive colonial regime, configured previous charismatic landscapes as a site of despoliation, redolent of the failure of spiritual conquest, and as *dar-ul harb*, a terrain of legitimate war.[62]

Mughal administrative practice was based on a multiform and intricate geometry of plural polities that were interconnected to each other in and through the mediation of the singular sovereign. Imperial rule was exercised over particular peoples (Afghans, Iranis, Rajputs, Marathas, and the like), not over territory. Space was not neutral or politically insignificant but jurisdiction hinged on the personal status of the agent rather than the spatial coordinates distinctive to the modern territorial state, the commodified form of abstract space, and conceptions of absolute property right. The late-nineteenth-century figuration of *Hindustan* as spatially coextensive with the boundaries of colonial India thus bears, at best, a tenuous relationship to received meanings of the term.

A similar transformation occurred with regard to the term *des* or *desiya*, which had been employed to refer to spatial units of varying scales. By the late 1860s the term *des* assumed the meaning of national territory, starkly simplifying the received multivalent and multiscalar meanings of the term. This usage informed numerous world geographies. In a textbook titled *Jagadh bhugol candrika* (The Geography of the World), published in 1865 and written by Pandit Ramajasana, the term *des* refers to a singular, spatially bounded national space:

> The globe is divided, as noted earlier, into many distinct *deshaon* [nations]. There are many kinds of distinctions [*bhed*] between the people of these distinct nations. Between one nation [*des*] and the next there are strong divides between culture, history, language, race and customs.[63]

Another work from this period opened by remarking, "The earth is divided into many *deshaon* [nations]. The nation [*des*] in which you live is called Bharat."[64] The nationalization of the term *des* was most obviously expressed in the increasing use of *Bharat Des* or *Bharatvarsha* to designate an Indian nation. Prasad's *Bhugola hastamalaka* opened with the following claim:

> It should be noted that within Asia, *Bharat des* was the most advanced in ancient times. At one time this nation [*des*] was with respect to matters of knowledge and wealth considered foremost. This nation [*des*] constituted the object of universal desire [*abhilasha*] among all the nations [*deshaon*] of the world [*jagadh*]. . . . But observe how today these

foreigners [*phirangistaniyaon*] now teach knowledge to the original holders of knowledge. For they first acquired knowledge and civilization from the Romans, who acquired it from the Greeks, and who, in turn, had come to study with Brahmin priests. . . . There was a time when this nation's [*des*] wealth was the most desired and envied object in the world. Consider how a struggle ensued across the earth [*prithvi*] to find a route to *Bharat.* However, the people of our nation [*des*] held all other places with contempt and did not seek to extend their dominion in the world. Since at that time every material object was found here in abundance there was no need to search for other territories.[65]

The novel meaning of *des* as national territory was consolidated in later decades with the spread of *swadeshi* movement practices. The very term *swadeshi* embodies this novel usage. It is a literal welding of *swa* or self and *des* as national space.

Integral to the reworking of spatial categories was the hierarchical delimitation of categorical identities on the basis of territorial origin. The following introduction from a work titled *Awadh ka bhugol* (The Geography of Avadh), written in 1876 by Pandit Mohan Lal, is exemplary of this broader practice:

> The nation [*des*] in which we live extends from the Himalayas in the north to the Indian Ocean [*Bharat ka samudra*] in the south and from Afghanistan and the Arabian Sea in the west to Burma in the east. The English, following ancient Greek practice, have given this land the name of India. The names *Hind* and *Hindustan* were given by Muslims to this country. The terms *India, Hind,* and *Hindustan* are derived from a geographical demarcation of the country [*des*] based on the river Indus [*Sindhu*]. However, the most ancient name for our nation, as evinced in Sanskrit texts and Puranas, is *Bharatvarsha* or *Bharat,* named after the ancient Hindu king Bharat. As the oldest inhabitants of this country used this term it is the most appropriate.[66]

The importance attached to self-assigned categories only makes sense with reference to the formation of a territorial nativist conception of nationhood. For the boundaries of the organic, core national self were increasingly rendered coterminous with those of a historically continuous and singular "Hindu" community. Another work from 1870, written by Ishwar Prasad, explicitly justifies its use of the term *Bharat* by stating that "Hindus are the oldest inhabitants of this nation [*des*]; therefore it is most appropriate to follow the ancient Sanskrit name of *Bharat.*"⁶⁷ The nationalization of such categories as *Bharat, des,* and *Hindustan* was intimately bound up with their Hinduization.

The nationalization of conceptions of *Bharat* was elaborated in an arena of popular intellectual and cultural production constituted by its own self-reference. Consider, in this respect, the titles of leading newspapers, journals, and novels — *Bharat Bandhu* (newspaper), *Bharat Jiwan* (newspaper*),* *Arya Darpan* (newspaper), *Bharat-Dipak* (newspaper), *Arya Patrika* (newspaper), *Bharat durdarsa, Bharat janani* (Harischandra's famous Hindi novels from 1880), and *Arya kritti* (Rajani Kanta Gupta's widely influential account of "Hindu India," written in Bengali in 1879, and in its fifteenth edition in 1882). Such categories imbued, as well, folk songs from this period. The following popular folk song from Bengal in the 1870s illustrates the generalization of this notion:

> How long will it take, you, Oh *Bharat,*
> to swim across this ocean of misery?
> Or, sinking and sinking in despair
> will you enter the nether regions for ever?
> Having gladly offered your jewels to the strangers, you
> carry now only an iron chain on your breast
> There are rows of lights in your cities, owned by the stranger
> But you are in darkness all the same.⁶⁸

Hem Chandra Banerjee's "Bharat-sangeet" or "Song of India," composed in the 1870s, explicitly thematized the notion of Bharat as a singular national entity situated within a broader partitioning of global space into mutually exclusive national spaces:

> Sing, O my clarionet! Sing to these words:
> Every one is free [*swadhin*] in this wide wide world,
> Everyone is awake in the glory of science, India alone lies asleep!
>
> China [*Chin*] and Burma [*Brahmadesh*] and barbarous Japan [*asavya Japan*],
> Even they are independent, they have become superior [*pradhan*],
> Bharat alone knows no awakening. (207)

A popular Hindi poem written in the 1870s by Harischandra juxtaposed Bharat and the consolidation of other nationalist movements and nation-states.

Rome and Greece have recovered their ancient might
Only Bharat remains prostrate in every respect.
Alas! Bharat (today) cannot claim equivalence
even with the once exceptionally weak Siam and Japan.[69]

Other popular Bengali songs, including "Bharat parajaya" (The Defeat of
Bharat), as well as folks songs from the United Provinces underscore the
transposability of the notion of colonial India as a national space, one imbued with a resolutely territorial nativist and historicist signification.

THE GENDERING OF NATIONAL SPACE-TIME: ENVISIONING BHARAT MATA

Motherness — excuse me if I underline the point — is a big idea in India, maybe our
biggest: the land as mother, the mother as land, as the firm ground beneath our feet.

— Salman Rushdie, *The Moor's Last Sigh*, 1995

Our history is the sacred biography of the Mother. Our philosophies are the revela-
tions of the Mother's mind. Our arts — our poetry and our paintings, our music and our
drama, our architecture and our scripture, all these — are the outflow of the Mother's
diverse Emotional Moods and Experiences. Our religion is the organized expression
of the Soul of the Mother. The outsider knows her as India. The outsider sees only her
outer and lifeless physical frame. The outsider sees her as a mere bit of earth, and looks
upon her as only a geographical expression or entity. But we, her children, know her
even today as our father and their fathers had done before, for countless generations,
as a Being, as manifestation of Prakriti, as Our Mother and the Mother of our Race.

— Bipan Chandra Pal, *The Soul of India*, 1923

A constitutive aspect of the modernity of the nation form lies precisely in its
self-presentation as an organic, traditional order. The figure of Bharat Mata
(Mother India) embodied par excellence the organicist self-understanding
of popular nationalism. Bharat Mata worked as an enduring matrix of nationalist identification and desire; it enabled and rendered plausible constructions of the nation as an organic formation rooted in an ancient past.

The search for autonomy and authenticity was concretely figured in the
representational form of a gendered body politic. Bharat Mata was conceived as at once a place of originary plenitude, an object of affective
identification and collective desire, as well as the territorial-economic whole
within which nationals were organically bound. This central icon offered —
in the general idiom of biological reproduction and in the specific perfor-

mative logic of upper-caste, north Indian Hindu devotional practices — a potent origin myth for national history and territory.[70] The gendering of national space-time expressed the reworking of a perceived alien and alienating colonial space-time in the affectively resonant image of the self and world-constituting universal power of a Hindu mother-goddess, the very embodiment and preserver of an enduring national patrimony.

Exemplary of this representational schema was a Hindi play from 1876 titled *The Fall of Bharat,* which was published in the leading newspapers *Kavi Vachan Sudha* (one of the oldest vernacular newspapers in the United Provinces) and *Arya Darpan.*[71] In this play, written as a popular dancing opera or *natak* but self-described as a "tragedy," the principal dramatis personae embody the historical destiny of Bharat Mata. This work, along with others like it, testifies to constructions of Bharat as existing apart from individual and collective agency, that is, as a fundamental reality sui generis. In this particular play, the various characters are respectively Bharat, the ill destiny of Bharat, and the good destiny of Bharat (315–16). The fall of Bharat is attributed to the lack of internal unity and successive "invasions" that reiterate the slippage between British colonial and Mughal rule. The play concludes with an enumeration of various strategies necessary for restoring the disrupted "good destiny of Bharat" (321–25). These included social-cultural reform, economic independence, and transcending caste divisions. Clearly addressed to a "Hindu" audience, as the injunction to overcome caste divides makes clear, the play depicts Bharat as having "been sucked dry" by the cumulative force of "invasions, famines, taxes and octroi duties" (323). Indeed, there were recurrent depictions of the rape and assault of a predatory economic imperialism on the gendered space of Bharat.

The gendered figuration of Bharat in the form of the mother-goddess common to Hindu Shakta traditions underlies the play's depiction of colonial assault:

> She is now quite prostrate, unable even to stir. All her body is covered with wounds inflicted by the European lion. It is the loss of unity among us that is the cause of her current condition. Wherever we turn, we see the rampant European standing like a terrifying Shiva [in the Hindu pantheon, Shiva represents the figure of the destroyer who is organically entwined with the mother-goddess] with a bow in hand taking aim at us. (325)

This scene works a menacing transformation of familiar visual representation of the mother-goddess astride a lion (the symbol of sophisticated brute force) and suggests instead the dematerialization of the mother-goddess as the very embodiment of the universal power *(shakti)* constitutive of the phenomenal world. It also explicitly rewrites, in a concretely political register, a well-known mythological tale about the mother-goddess Kali, who in a moment of uncontained murderous rage threatens an indiscriminate campaign of universal ruin. She is stopped only by the arrival of Shiva, who prostrates himself before her and, as an organic principle of *shakti* itself, is able to restore the mother-goddess to her true self. In the play's concluding scene, Shiva represents a fundamentally alien force who seeks the outright destruction of the physical and spiritual power of Bharat Mata. The expressed yearning for an originary organic unity, of a holistic vision of the nation, and the acute sense of a collective loss of inner and social power were constituted against the perceived everyday violence of colonial social relations.

The image of Bharat as a transcendental mother-goddess represented nationalist desire in general. Yet as an embodied space whose successive history of violation so preoccupied nationalist thought, the nature of this desire was fraught with tensions. How could an absolute value be placed on the despoiled, multiply-violated national space of Bharat Mata? It was precisely the rhetoric of the despoliation of Bharat Mata by the predatory figure of British colonial capital and Muslim assault that discursively summoned a novel sense of collective political agency.[72] In popular corporatist and gendered visions of national space-time, the figure of the Muslim designated an internal negativity that had to be overcome and subsumed in order to establish a stable collective national identity. Bharat Mata, as figured in numerous popular plays, folk songs, and stories, worked as a symbolic gatekeeper and protector of the ethical substance and collective virility of the national community, which, in turn, was constituted by a specifically masculine and upper-caste Hindu political agency. It is in this sense, then, that Bharat Mata served as a boundary marker upholding the territorial and spiritual inviolability of the organic (Hindu) core of the nation, visibly embodying national-cultural purity and endowing upper-caste Hindu males with the patrimony of territory and history.

In Bengal, the generalization of discourses about Bharat Mata was roughly concurrent with a wider shift in upper-caste Hindu debates about the ethical substance of patriarchal family structures. The debate in the 1860s and 1870s, as Tanika Sarkar suggests, between advocates of a reactionary familialism and Hindu social reformers had principally centered on conjugality as "a site of willed surrender" propelled by colonial legislation on the age of consent.[73] This gave way in the last decade of the nineteenth

century to a new emphasis on the imminent divinity of mother–child relations and the construction of a normative national subject centered not in
the Hindu home but in the abstract sphere of a Hindu community. What
cemented this ideological formation was the construction of an idealized
spiritual womanhood in the form of the "pure Hindu wife," who, purged of
all alien elements, represented the "last unconquered space" in what was increasingly perceived as an abstract colonial space-time.[74] This idealized image of woman-as-nation and women-as-mother triumphed over competing
visions about the unruly modern wife whose wanton consumption of British colonial commodities tightened the skein of disciplinary time and wage-
labor bondage for indigenous males (206). During the *swadeshi* movement,
the image of an ascetic Hindu woman was yoked to an anticonsumption,
productivist ethic of indigeneity that preserved both the form of patrilineage
and the patriarchal structure of a labor market constituted by the severing
of domestic from value-producing labor.

The durability and symbolic power of Bharat Mata hinged on its doubled
character, for this figural representation of national space traded on its status as at once real and transcendent, human and divine, universal and particular. At one level, this doubled character expressed the imminent contradiction between the modernity of the nation form and nationalist
representations of the nation as an organic, natural order. However, this
contradiction was refracted through a specific constellation of upper-caste
Hindu philosophical concepts and a quotidian field of devotional practices.
The relationship between Bharat Mata and her progeny mimed upper-caste
Shakta or Shaivite devotional practices wherein *santan-bhava* (the relation
between mother and child or divine mother and human devotee) represented a privileged medium for realizing divine consciousness from within
the phenomenal world. Unlike Vaishnavite doctrines and the austere
monism of Sankarite traditions that construed the phenomenal world as a
misrecognition of the undifferentiated substance of the absolute Godhead,
popular Shakta practices regarded everyday relations in all their phenomenal diversity as concretizations of a simultaneously unitary and differentiated Godhead. The reconfiguration of colonial state space as Bharat Mata,
of nation-as-mother, drew on the constitutive slippage in mother–child relations and that between devotee and godhead in popular Hindu devotional
practices. It was this constellation of concepts and practices — animated in
the embodied, taken-for-granted practice of visualization or *darshan* (auspi-
cious sight) in the presence of divinity — that informed the affective force of
Bharat Mata.[75] The transposition of Hindu practices of *darshan* onto novel
terrains and its interlacing with modern technologies of reproduction (nov-

els, newspapers, popular songs, maps, coins, and the like) expressed the superimposition of ideologies, practices, and artifacts that defined the relationship between colonial state space and emergent nationalism.

Although such received devotional practices and concepts as *santan-bhava* and *darshan* shaped the affective power of Bharat Mata, it is important to emphasize the qualitatively novel character of the cultural and political subjectivities that were written into this figuration of national space. During the last decades of the nineteenth century, the emergent national icon of Bharat Mata worked as the ground for the enactment of nationalist fantasies of the territorial displacement of colonial rule. The seizure, repossession, and taking hold of Bharat Mata in a myriad of popular songs, plays, novels, cartographic representation, historical works, and the like were presented as an act of legitimate expropriation.

Nationalist imaginings of colonial India as Bharat Mata were anchored within the broader reconstitution of relationships to land—from that of lived simultaneity to a possession in need of expropriation. Although popular Hindu devotional practices and aesthetics shaped the reception of the cartographic and iconic form of Bharat Mata, they were not the autonomous incubus of its production, nor did they herald the presence, as Dipesh Chakrabarty argues, of an "age-old," "subjectless" religious modality exempt from historical transformation.[76] The language of displacement and territorial repossession employed in popular figurations of Bharat Mata was a product of the contradictions of colonial state space. Bharat Mata powerfully expressed the nationalist fantasy of the territorial displacement of colonial rule in favor of a presumed organic national community. The resolutely "subject-centered" language of possession was transposed from individuals (upper-caste, Hindu, male) in relation to land to Bharat as a national territorial possession (178). Bharat Mata marked the historically significant reconstitution of colonial spatiality into national property.

The Co-Construction of a National People and Space

The constitution of Bharat as a national space reciprocally implied the creation of a novel subjectivity—a national people. The discursive co-constitution of the notion of Bharat and that of a socioculturally and territorially delimited national people informs the novel *Duradarsi yogi: Bharat ka saccha swapna* (the English title of the work was recorded as "A brief account of the state of Bharat, past and present, written in the form of a true dream").[77] The novel was written by Sitalaprasada Upadhyaya, an assistant editor of the journal *Hindustan*, published from Ghazipur in the United

Provinces. An acutely critical work, it exemplifies, in a fictional register, how the affective resonance of the idea of Bharat Mata was secured through the territorialization of history.

Rather than a linear historical narrative, the temporal structure of *Duradarśi yogi* forms a triptych that somersaults back and then forward though time, evoking mythical space-times for an anticipated national future. It begins with a description of a denuded and despoiled landscape that is compared to a vast "cremation ground" *(śhamśhan ghat)* (2). Situated within this colonial landscape the narrator, a disembodied voice that floats from the top of a mountain called Meru (the sacred center of Puranic spatial schemes), attempts to exhume the past of the land. In a series of vignettes, the history of the denuded landscape is recounted. Time in this work is not memorialized as flow but as the memory of experienced spaces, such that history gives way to allegory, and time to space.

Chief among the interspersed vignettes that organizes this work is the memory of an ancient nation *(deś)* that is deemed the *matri bhumi* (motherland) and *punya bhumi* (sacred or consecrated land). The narrator details a vast geographical panorama that extends from a northern range of mountains to a "large sea in the south." In the middle of this landscape, a mountain range separated two distinct terrains. The northern half of this land was inhabited by a "fair-skinned race," which was juxtaposed against a "darker-skinned race" that lived farther south (5). This reference to the imagined historical geography of the Vedic civilization was followed by an account of the splendors and wonders of the people and land.

Endowed with a prophetic vision, the all-seeing narrator discerns two invasions that transform the *matri bhumi*. The accounts of "invasions" closely follow the generic racialized lines of colonial and nationalist historiography: the Muslim period and the British colonial present. In the first such vignette, the narrator describes the invaders as men with "long hair and flowing beards," as "meat eaters" with astonishingly "cruel and fanatical visages" (10). The word *Muslim* is never explicitly employed, an absence that attests to the accumulation of stereotypes and negative signifiers that stood in for an explicit naming. The narrator details the "cruelty" of the "invaders" and the successive transformation of the "pure [*pavan*] motherland [*matri bhumi*] into an impure [*apavan*] land." The *matri bhumi* becomes, we are told, "stained red with the bloody bodies of injured men" as the invading "enemies" *(śhatru)* yell "*Kafir* [infidel], *kafir* do not leave a single temple standing, smash them, smash them, smash them" (10). The narrative of the second invasion differs from the first account insofar as there is an attempt to account for the rationale of colonial conquest. The typicality of the earlier account of invasion lies precisely in the absence of such an attempt, for the signifiers that designated "Muslim rule" (despite the absence of an explicit naming) as an absolute difference were deemed sufficient in themselves. As a particular historical event and as a general dispositional trait, the trope of invasion was inscribed as the second nature of the category *Muslim*, thus obviating a historical accounting of specific political formations.

In contrast, the account of the colonial invasion opens with a record of the investment in local knowledge, crafts, and commodities by European traders: "these highly influential [*prabhavshali*] people can be seen recording the motherland's [*matri bhumi*] products, its natural resources, its crafts, and agricultural produce with wondrous enthusiasm and interest" (20). The narrator alternately "marvels at the courage and cunning of these people" and despairs at the "fallen state of the *matri bhumi*" (18). Unable to "comprehend" the complex intrigues and political protocols of the "invaders," the inhabitants of the "motherland" fragmented into dissonant groups (23–25). They could, therefore, only passively observe the "produce and wealth" of the "motherland being shipped to the invader's island-nation" (24).

Colonial domination in this work is explicitly linked to the emergence of a spectacular field of educational, juridical, and bureaucratic institutions and infrastructural and communication technologies. The fact that the materialized apparatus of rule was presented as the sign of the superiority and beneficence of an alien state only demonstrated the colonial state's "hold on the mind" *(man par prabhav)* of the populace (27–28). Embedded within colonial state space, the people of Bharat Mata misrecognized the logic of its particular production of value and thus regarded the proliferations of such "novel [*navin*] developments [*parivardhan*]" as schools, railways, electric telegraphs, and the like as a straightforward "boon" *(dakshina)* (27–28). What the narrator urges his readership to consider are the ways "Europeans have enslaved [*adhin*] the mind of the people. It resembles the way a sorcerer [*jadugar*] transforms his audience into passive puppets [*katputhlis*] that merely applaud the spectacle [*tamasha*]" (29). With the hollowing out of a critical consciousness under the sway of colonial hegemony, the precise geography of colonial economic flows remained hidden from view, especially the fact that

> [t]he European government extracts from the inhabitants of Bharat Mata lakhs and lakhs of rupees, that it pilfers their homes and lands and transports vast stores of agricultural produce unto their own nation

[*des*], which is an island in a distant sea. The establishment of schools, hospitals, railways, roads and the like are based on the appropriation of the wealth of the people. But the inhabitants of the land are unable to fathom this. Such is the extent of their mental enslavement [*man ki gu-lami*] that instead of recognizing the abstruse [*goorh*] secrets [*bedh*] and intrigues of the government, they sing the praises of the efficiency and organization of the government. In fact, they have developed an absolute [*purnn*] faith [*vishvas*] in the egalitarian [*samdarshitha*] character of European rule. (29)

In an effort to counter the opacity of colonial economic flows, the narrator turns toward the organizational structure of the colonial government. The ultimate source of power lies, he notes, in the British Parliament *(pradhan sabha)* that was spatially exterior to the "motherland." The policies of the British Parliament were exclusively oriented to the profit of two constituencies, namely, "the king and people of England and the English who now reside in our motherland" (31). Thus within this spatial and political structure, the "motherland" could only exist as a sign of its despoliation. The quarrel with colonial rule lies, in this view, with the constitutive non-isomorphism between people, nation, territory, and state.

The narration of Bharat's past as a dreamworld was a common trope in late-nineteenth-century accounts. The colonial present was in these works the nightmare that impinged on the present as long as its spell was not broken. In a vivid futuristic account, the narrator observed the emergence of a new class of "courageous, enthusiastic, and educated men" who, emboldened with the memory of the "ancient motherland" *(matri bhumi ka purana swapan)*, commit themselves to the restoration of her former glory (45). This "dream-like vision" was quickly offset by a cry emanating from a "massive" crowd of "semi-naked, hungry peasants" who had lost their rights to the land and were migrating from villages into towns (46). In a dramatic concluding scene, the growing numbers of landless peasants conceived as a collective, corporate body attempt to confront the island-nation of England. However, colonial officials stopped short the progress and movement of this surging crowd toward the island-nation. Although this collective peasant-body recited tales of utter poverty and destitution, it was of no avail. The narrator helplessly observes the irrevocable "cruelty" *(krurtha)* of the colonial officials, who continue to subjugate the inhabitants of the motherland (46). The image of a homogenous collective body that confronts the island-nation of England powerfully expresses the discursive co-constitution of a bounded and singular national space and people. It also anticipates the centrality of corporate images of peasants as a communal body with an organic connection to the nation that fueled the imagination of later nationalists such as Radhakamal Mukherjee and Gandhi. The work concludes with the cries of this national peasant-body shouting *"Insaf* [justice], *insaf, insaf"* (50). This dystopic conclusion critically pointed toward the limits of reformist attempts that defined the first decades of the Indian National Congress as it sought to work within the political structure of the colonial state. By stressing the disjuncture between the motherland and the metropolitan locus of power (identified as the British Parliament), this work exemplifies the mobilizing rhetorical force of an imagined, territorially delimited, and organically linked national community.

CONCLUSION

For many nationalists such as Bipan Pal, the very existence of *Bharat* as a "common name" for the country "conclusively proved the presence of some undeniable principle of historic and national unity in the consciousness of the people."[78] What was the content of this national unity? What were the ethical and regulatory moorings of this supposedly archaic national consciousness? Pal's answer was, as should be clear, hardly singular:

> India had ceased to be a mere geographical expression long long before
> the advent of the British EIC. . . . It had been a social unit long before
> the Mahomedans came to her. . . . The old Indian unity, in spite of local
> and communal and denominational differences . . . was not in its details,
> but in its general outline and outlook, more or less homogenous. It was
> what may be called a Hindu unity. (70)

Conceptions of India as Bharat carried a resolutely historicist signification: the claim that its fundamental unity was bound up with Hinduism and with the status of upper-caste Hindus as the organic, originary nationals. The generalization of this territorial nativist vision anchored nationalist narratives of history as the moment of a becoming designated by itself, that is, of the continuity even in decline of a distinct and singular national space-time and people. It underlay the continual references to a singular national heritage, a common Arya ancestry, and a rootedness in an ancient sacral terrain—all terms that evoked an organic, original, and historically received rather than historically produced national community. It drove the obsessional search for authenticity, purity, and homogeneity that took the form of notions of an organic national space-time. This quixotic quest shaped as well the marginalization of particular social groups whose alleged foreignness was set up as a sign of impurity and exteriority. These tensions, and their potential for violence, inhered in the very imagining of colonial India as Bharat.

CHAPTER SEVEN

THE POLITICAL ECONOMY OF NATIONHOOD

The ideal of the national economy arises with the idea of nations.

— Friedrich List, "Outlines of American Political Economy," 1827

Their economic and historical studies, have strongly impressed Indian thinkers with the beneficent efficacy of the measures which foreign nations have taken during the last two generations to promote their industrial development, and they have been convinced that the reasoning and conclusions of the National School of Political Economy, are applicable to the conditions of India rather than the theories of natural law of the Orthodox school.

—Vaman Govind Kale, *Introduction to the Study of Indian Economics*, 1918

The first sustained articulations of nationalism crystallized around the notion of a territorially delimited economic collective, a national economy, during the 1870s and 1880s. The conception of a national economy, welded to popular affective imaginings of India as a bounded national space, represented the point of departure for nationalist critiques of colonialism. The economic critique of colonialism constituted the normative content of institutional nationalism (associated with the Indian National Congress established in 1885) and laid the foundation for the nationalist project of development.

The nationalist movement did not contain within itself the principle of its emergence and organization. The category of a national economy was a historically specific formation embedded within a particular transnational field and historical conjuncture. Like the historically specific category of *labor*, the concept of a national economy was a "concrete abstraction" that only became thinkable and achieved "practical truth" within and against a concrete multiplicity of developments.[1] The transnational circulation of this concept did not rest, as recent observers of contemporary neoliberal global restructuring aver, on the apparently frictionless mobility of commodity flows, migrant labor, ideologies, aesthetics, and technologies in the modern global era as such. Rather, the transposability of the idea of a national economy hinged on the relational dynamic between processes of global restructuring and nationalization in a particular historical-geographical field.

It was during the last third of the nineteenth century that the contradictions of colonial versus national space became increasingly evident on a global scale. This historical moment and transnational field were marked by two interrelated processes: first, the unprecedented challenge posed to Britain's global hegemony by the rise of nationally regulated capitalism in Germany, France, Russia, the United States, and Japan; and second, the corresponding intensification of the financial domination of colonial South Asia by the British imperial regime. The emergence of autocentric developmentalist models across regional contexts, the generalization of the doctrine of self-determination that closely followed the period of German and Italian nationalism, and the progressive naturalization of the tie between nation and state dynamically reconfigured the discursive terrain of national imaginings. The historicity of the conception of India as a bounded national economic space cannot be understood apart from, or outside of, the coeval formation of the concept of a national economy in the late-nineteenth-century transnational field. More proximately, the nationalist critique of colonialism had its experiential basis in the lived contradictions of colonial socioeconomic practices. With the convergence of these processes in the 1870s and 1880s, the problem of the articulation between state, economy, and territory presented itself with particular force. Through a detailed analysis of the nationalist argument against both colonialism and classical political economy, this chapter explores the progressive naturalization of the interlinked categories of nation, economy, and territory.

A POLITICAL ECONOMY OF NATIONHOOD

The broad contours of what was to remain the dominant nationalist argument against colonialism emerged during the 1870s and 1880s. Within institutional nationalism, the canonical bearers of the emergent political economy of nationhood were middle-class intelligentsia, most notably Dadabhai Naoroji (1825–1917), Romesh Chunder Dutt (1848–1909), and Mahadev Govind Ranade (1842–1901).[2] Employing the language of nationalist debates of the time, received historiographical debates have gathered these figures under the rubric of "moderates," against the "extremists" who rose to prominence in the late 1890s and were associated with the *swadeshi* movement.[3] What this entrenched distinction occludes is that although there were divisions among nationalists about political strategies for overcoming colonial rule, both so-called moderates and extremists had a shared economic critique of colonial rule.

Despite differences in conceptual orientations and analytical emphases, these early nationalists shared a common object of analysis. They focused on the accelerated "impoverishment" of the nation and its territorial integration within a global world-system dominated by British capital, and they sought to specify analytically and to historicize the production of a "dependent colonial economy."[4] This phrase, first employed by Ranade, referred to the structural location of colonial India in the global division of labor. By directing attention to the historical production of a colonial economy, Ranade denaturalized the notion of a territorial division of labor as resting on a naturally given comparative advantage. With characteristic sharpness he argued: "The orthodox economists assign to the backward torrid regions of Asia the duty of producing raw materials and claim, for the advanced European temperate zone countries, the work of transport and manufactures, as a division of labour in production, which is fraught with the highest advantage to all and is, we are told, a providential dispensation against which it would be foolish to rebel."[5] What was remarkable about the attempt to historicize the production of a "dependent colonial economy"—beyond its anticipation of dependency frameworks associated with Latin American intellectuals in the twentieth century—was the recognition that colonial state practices were expressive of global processes of integration and differentiation. While tracing dependent colonial economies to eighteenth-century colonial formations such as colonial America—that is, the production of colonies growing "raw produce . . . to be manufactured and exported again to the colonies and to the rest of the world"—Ranade emphasized the unique configuration of a global present. The "great tendency of the time" was marked by the unprecedented expansion of Britain's empire on a global scale during the nineteenth century and the sharpening differentiations between metropolitan states (the centers of manufacturing and industry), settler colonies (which were granted fiscal autonomy), and those, like colonial India, that had come to "supply the place of the old [eighteenth-century] colonies" tout court (411). India, as Ranade argued, had been actively transformed into a

> [p]lantation, growing raw produce to be shipped by British Agents in British ships, to be worked into Fabrics by British skill and capital, and to be re-exported to the Dependency by British merchants to their corresponding British firms in India and elsewhere. The development of steam power and mechanical skill, joined with increased facilities of

communication, have lent strength to this tendency of the times, and as one result of the change, the gradual ruralization of this great dependency, and the rapid decadence of native manufacture and trade, has become distinctly marked. (411)

Nationalists raged against the economic "drain" on the nation (as elaborated by Naoroji) and colonial economic practices of "ruralization," "deindustrialization," and "denationalization" (as analyzed by Ranade). Yet they were also convinced of the universalistic promise of development, and thus began the quest for a historical and comparative framework adequate to the current predicament.

Common to the work of these nationalists was a critique of the abstraction and transhistorical presuppositions of classical economic theory. Ranade excoriated the scientific pretensions of classical political economy as condensed in its litany of a priori assumptions (identifying eleven such axioms), its false "Universalism and Perpetualism," and its self-understanding as a deductive science whose axioms were equivalent to the "first law of Mechanics . . . or the First Law of Physics" (336, 327). Economic theory was properly understood, according to him, as a "Political and Social science" necessarily based on a "Historical line of thought" and the principle of "Relativity and Correspondence" in relation to actually existing sociohistorical formations (322).

An especially recurrent refrain was the incommensurability of extant classical economic theories and the socioeconomic condition of India. As a colonial economy, India was a historically unique configuration where, as Dadabhai Naoroji argued, the "natural laws of economy" were not operative. Naoroji, unlike Ranade, did not seek to repudiate the organizing principles of classical political economy. At issue for him were the ways in which India embodied the "pitiless perversion of economic laws by the bleeding to which it is subjected."[6] With particular reference to the institution of a massive network of railways, for instance, Naoroji stressed the difference between the United States and colonial India. He argued that in the United States, the capital invested in infrastructure technologies had generated a massive increase in employment and spawned a range of related industrial enterprises. In contrast, railways in colonial India had generated widening poverty. Even such apparently "universal" tools of national development as railways were necessarily "distorted and perverted" in a colonial context (48). In a direct inversion of official discourse that presented railways as the privileged vector of economic growth, Naoroji suggested that state works were part of a fetishized colonial economy of appearances. He observed:

So our condition is a very anomalous one — like that of a child to which
a fond parent gives a sweet, but to which, in its exhausted condition, the
very sweet acts like poison, and, as a foreign substance, by irritating the
weak stomach makes it throw out more and causes greater exhaustion.
In India's present condition, the very sweets of every other nation appear to act on it as a poison. (48)

Colonial state works were, in this view, particularized instruments for the
reproduction of a globally organized British imperial economy. They were
part of an imperial scale-making project.

Evaluating the postulates of classical economic theory with reference to
actual colonial state practices, nationalists stressed the gap between theory
and practice. Consider Ranade's searing critique of one of the fundamental
ideological constituents of colonial state space — the self-understanding of
the state as universal, ideal landlord.

Men, who come from a Country where private property in land is most
absolute, develop on their arrival here a taste for Socialistic doctrines.
The state aspires to relegate all Private Property in land into mere superior and inferior holdings. A love for Capitalist farming on a large
scale gives way to a taste for *petit culture* by poor Tenants. In England the
Landlords as such pay no special Tax to the State, but here Land is taxed
on the ground that there is an unearned increment based on the Theory
of Economic Rent, and that this unearned increment belongs of special
right to the State. While the nationalization of land is but a Socialist
dream in England and Europe, it is in full swing here, and furnishes a
scientific justification for periodical Revisions and Enhancements.[7]

Beyond colonial India, the example of contemporary "American, Australian
and Continental Political Economy, as applied in practice" entailed, Ranade
observed, a practical repudiation of the "hypothetical" and "a priori positions of the abstract Science" of classical political economy (297). The
"dreams of Cobden and Bright, Ricardo and Mill" that the "world would . . .
embrace their principles" lay shattered against the hardening shell of an increasingly global protectionist political economy that reproduced economic
and racial differentiations. For "Americans dispute the rights of Chinese to
settle in their Country, the Australians fear the same . . . and even in England, legislation was contemplated against the immigration of alien Jews,
on the ground that they were likely to under-bid the indigenous labourer"
(325). This disjuncture of theory and practice obtained, as Ranade ob-

served, "not in one, but all points, not in one place or country, but all over the world, . . .[it] distinguishes contemporary history" (326).

The doctrine of free trade was widely identified as a self-serving modality of British imperial domination. It not only glossed over the steeply hierarchical structure of the world system but also served as an intellectual justification for colonial practices that reproduced unequal social relations. Ganesh Joshi, closely allied with Ranade, emphasized the tightly knotted interweave between colonial spatial-economic practices and the legitimating ideology of free trade. He observed:

> It was Lord Dalhousie's dream to strengthen the domination not only of English rule, but also of English trade and commerce in India and the permanent interests of this country were subordinated to this all-engrossing ambition. The contemporaneous rise of the school of Free Trade in England and the great reputation which its apostles enjoyed, furnished the metaphysical groundwork for this essentially selfish and grasping policy. The value of India to the British nation was measured by the quantity of raw material which the resources of Indian agriculture enabled it to export for the feeding and maintenance of the Lancashire manufactories. India was to devote all its energies to raise the raw exports, and canals, railroads and improved communications were to be pushed on at any cost to facilitate the export of raw materials and the import of English manufactures.[8]

Lala Murlidhar captured the tenor of this nationalist critique in his 1891 address to the Indian National Congress:

> I know that it was pure philanthropy which flooded India with English-made goods, and surely, if slowly, killed out every indigenous industry—pure philanthropy which, to facilitate this, repealed the import duties and flung away three crores of revenue which the rich paid, and to balance this wicked sacrifice raised the Salt tax, which the poor pay. . . . the phantasm of free trade drains us. . . . Free Trade, fair play between nations, how I hate the sham! What fair play in trade can there be between impoverished India and the bloated capitalist England? . . . No doubt it is all in accordance with high economic science, but, my friends, remember this—this, too, is starving your brethren.[9]

Nationalists recast both the rhetoric and practice of laissez-faire economics as the coalition partner of Britain's global economic hegemony. Against the abstractions of classical economic theory, they sought to develop a conceptual framework that was at once explicitly historicist and nationalist. They were, in this regard, part of a broader transnational transformation.

A Concrete Abstraction: The Notion of a National Economy

The conceptual elaboration of the economy as a distinct sphere of social relations had begun during the eighteenth-century Enlightenment. As Susan Buck-Morss argues, this endeavor was inseparable from the emergence of capitalism: "The economy, when it was discovered, was already capitalist, so the description of one entailed the description of the other."[10] The conception of the economy as an autonomous, self-contained, and objective realm imbued classical economic theory. Through an imminent critique of classical political economy, Marx had sought to show that the notion of the economy as a self-contained, distinct sphere was among the most spectacular instances of the reification of social categories and forms under capitalist modernity. From this perspective, the burden of a critique of political economy (rather than the forging of a critical political economy) was the analysis of the social processes that engendered the violence of abstraction and the appearance of an external, objective, self-contained economic sphere.[11]

Here I direct attention to one crucial shift in the history of the conceptual category of the economy. During the late nineteenth century, the conception of the economy acquired a highly specific spatial referent. The economy was deemed coincident with the spatial boundaries of the modern territorial state. Friedrich List's work *Das Nationale System der Politischen Oekonomie* (1841) exemplified the rise of historicist and nationalist schools of political economy during the late nineteenth century.[12] Although List's status as the totemic ancestor of the idea of a national economy has received acknowledgment, the sociohistorical conditions that made a "national economy" thinkable have not been fully explored. Furthermore, the significance of his work in shaping the contours of the anticolonial nationalist critique has been virtually ignored within the field of South Asian historiography.[13] List's work became a foundational text for anticolonial nationalists in South Asia. It shaped the insurgent idiom of nationalist political economy developed in works by Mahadev Govind Ranade, Gopal Krishna Gokhale (1866–1915), Ganesh Vyankatesh Joshi (1851–1911), Subramania Aiyer, Kashinath Trimbak Telang, and Vaman Govind Kale, as well as later works by the prominent *swadeshi* leaders Benoy Kumar Sarkar (1887–1949) and Radhakamal Mukherjee (1889–1968). List's reformulation of classical political economy was rooted in the problematic of German national unification and industrial development in the context of Britain's world hegemony. Its location in political concerns and structural conditions formally similar to those of Indian nationalists underpinned its profound resonance in a colonial context that had, it should be noted, been explicitly excised from List's delineation of his imagined audience. Indeed, List explicitly delimited the constituency of his work to "civilized" sovereign nations suffering under the dual yoke of Smithian economics and British economic dominance. The rapid economic ascendancy of Germany and the United States only confirmed the value of his work for Indian nationalists.[14]

List's work marked a radical departure from the spatial assumptions of classical economic paradigms. Classical political economy conceived the division of labor and markets as abstract configurations with no specific spatial extension. In contrast, the central organizing category of List's framework was the self-enclosed nation, signaling a shift from an abstract spatial reference to a place-bound focus. The place-bound nation was regarded as the territorial unit or container of economic development. List indicted classical economic theory for its "rootless [*bodenlosem*] cosmopolitanism" and its exclusive focus on denationalized, profit-maximizing individuals.[15] List's analytical strategy was one of unmasking: the regime of free trade was dismissed as a direct expression of British national economic interest, and classical economic theory's stress on cosmopolitanism was regarded as a ploy to retain Britain's economic and imperial hegemony. Classical economic theory, in List's view, ignored the fact that "between each individual and entire humanity stands the Nation [*Nation*] (174). According to List, the "economy of the people [*Volksoekonomie*]" developed into the national economy *(Nationaloekonomie)* under specific historical-geographical conditions (196). At a certain historical threshold, which is conceived in both descriptive and normative terms, the *Nationaloekonomie* becomes spatially isomorphic with the *Volksoekonomie* (196). This "true conception and real character of national economy [*Nationaloekonomie*]" had, he argued, eluded theorists because "for the distinct and definite term Nation [*Nation*] men had everywhere substituted the general and vague term society [*Gesellschaft*]" (195).[16] According to this formulation, the specificity of the nation lay in the spatial isomorphism between the nation and national economy, in a place-bound welding of a national people and economy. The nation was a concrete historical-geographical form of the abstract category society. The posited territorial isomorphism of economy and nation, the fusion of the territorial state with capital, and the productivist critique of the realm of exchange became defining themes of anticolonial nationalism.

Among the historically significant precursors of List's framework was Johann Fichte's *Der geschlossne Handelsstaat* (The Closed Commercial State), which first appeared in 1800.[17] It conjoined mercantilist ideologies in its demand for the closing of borders to the circulation of goods and commodities with an egalitarian call for the abrogation of the right of landed property in favor of the right to work and an outright rejection of colonization. In contrast, List's developmental schema held up as a normative exemplar a vision of a self-sufficient national economy protected by tariffs and custom barriers from the world market even as it endorsed not only the regime of private property but the colonization of "barbarous" nations as a legitimate strategy of national economy making. He defended the institution of protective tariffs from the standpoint of the long-run development of what he termed "national productive powers." The category "productive powers," as employed by List, encompassed at once nature or natural capital, material capital, and what he called "human capital" or capital of the mind. Against Ricardian conceptions that expanding trade resulted in equal benefit, List stressed the unequal exchange of human capital. He defended the system of protective tariffs as a national "educational tax" against the domination of "British manufactures." He observed:

> A nation which has an agrarian economy and is dependent upon foreign countries (for its manufacturing goods) can . . . stimulate the establishment of industries by means of a protective tariff. Such a nation may well sacrifice much "exchange value" [i.e., material capital] for the moment, if its new workshops produce expensive goods of poor quality. But it will greatly increase its productive powers of the future.[18]

In this view, the confederation of national productive powers constituted the repository of ultimate value.

In a trenchant, if unfinished, analysis of List's schema, Marx argued that this would-be total critique of classical political economy relied on the same idealized presuppositions that it sought to undercut. According to Marx, List left unexamined the intrinsic connections, within classical political economy, between the "social state" and its "corresponding theoretical expression."[19] In this view, the German historical school's departure from classical political economy was restricted to the "theoretical expression of this [capitalist] society," not the "present organization of society" (277, 276). For although Adam Smith represented only "the theoretical starting-point of political economy," its "real point of departure, its real school was civil society [*die burgerliche Gessellschaft*]" (273). In a polemical formulation, Marx identified List as a "true German" who "wants to leave this reality (i.e., cap-italist society) everywhere just as it is and only change the expression of it" (277). Marx argued that Listian developmentalism was a particular form of a revamped nationalist mercantilism that desired the "laws of commerce, of exchange value, of huckstering, to lose their power at the frontier territory of his country" (280). Yet it actively sought the continued operation of the law of value within a delimited political-economic space such that the "ma-jority of the nation should remain a mere exchange value, a 'commodity,' one which must finds its own buyer, one which is not sold, but which sells itself'" (279). The authoritarian closing of borders called for by List, a means of doing away with the intrinsically globalizing thrust of capital, sought the territorialization of capitalism within a national-territorial domain.[20] It rep-resented not a critique of political economy but the inauguration of modern economic nationalism.

National developmentalist frameworks as elaborated by List in Ger-many, Henry Carey (the son of Mathew Carey, List's close associate in the late 1820s) in America, John Rae in Scotland, and Arthur Griffiths in Ire-land assumed that the nationalization of capital, with the aid of an interven-tionist state, would restore the presumed laws of harmony that governed economic relations against their distortion by Britain's economic hegemony on a global scale.[21] In a powerful analysis of the burgeoning school of na-tional political economy, Marx identified Henry Carey as an innovative thinker in light of the increasingly formalistic character of post-Ricardian political economy. Political-economic literature after Ricardo and Sismondi was, Marx argued, "altogether a literature of epigones; reproduction, greater elaboration of form, wider appropriation of material, exaggeration, popularization, synopsis, elaboration of details."[22] In this context, the emer-gent school of national political economy, as instantiated by Carey and List, highlighted the contradictions of capitalism. However, it did so only on the scale of the world economy and only as the expression of Britain's economic domination. Marx observed:

> All over the world, the harmony of economic laws appears as dishar-mony, and even Carey himself is struck by the beginnings of dishar-mony in the United States. What is the source of this strange phenom-enon? Carey explains it with the destructive influence of England, with its striving for industrial monopoly, upon the world market. Originally [for Carey], the English relations were distorted by the false theories of her economists, internally. Now, externally, as the commanding power

of the world market, England distorts the harmony of economic relations in all the countries of the world. This disharmony is a real one, not
one merely based on the subjective conceptions of the economists. . . .
The harmony of economic relations rests, according to Carey, on the
harmonious cooperation of town and countryside, industry and agriculture. Having dissolved this fundamental harmony in its own interior,
England, by its competition, proceeds to destroy it throughout the
world market, and is thus the destructive element of the general harmony. The only defense lies in protective tariffs — the forcible, national
barricade against the destructive power of large-scale European industry. Hence, the state, which was at first branded the sole disturber of
these "harmonies economiques," is now these harmonies' last refuge.
On the one side, Carey here again articulates the specific national development of the United States, their antithesis to and competition with
England. . . . with Carey the harmony of the bourgeois relations of production ends with the most complete disharmony of these relations on
the grandest terrain where they appear, the world market, and in their
grandest development, as the relations of producing nations. (886)

National developmental paradigms, which emerged as a counterhegemonic
response to Britain's economic dominance on a world scale, assumed that
the "concentration of capital within a country" would resolve the disharmonies of capitalism as such (887). What the advocates of a national political economy failed to grasp was the multiscalar and multitemporal dynamic
of capitalism. In mid-nineteenth-century British political economy, as previously explored, the chimera of a resolution to the inner contradictions of
capitalism had taken the form of the privileging of colonial territories as
a potential "spatial fix."[23] This promise was now relocated on a national-
territorial scale, yet one within which colonial territories were lodged as
internal rather than external components. What the political economists of
nationhood effectively bracketed, according to Marx, was the fact that
"world-market disharmonies are merely the ultimate expressions of the
disharmonies which have become fixed as abstract relations within the economic categories" and which have "a local existence on the smallest scale."[24]
   The emergent national developmental paradigm ran up against a seemingly intransigent paradox. For the national developmental trajectory it
pursued had to navigate the radically dynamic historical geography of capital and its worldwide space of accumulation. Capitalism necessarily accel-
erates spatial integration within the world market by means of the continual
annihilation and conquest of space by time. What national developmental-

ism attempted was a calibrated process of temporal displacement (protection of infant industries, long-term state investments in infrastructure) and spatial expansion (the production of a national economic space as well as an argument for colonization). Such a developmental schema assumed the possibility of a national "spatial fix" to the unstable contradictions of capitalism.[25] This framework assumed a linear and abstract logic of development, which not only erased the geopolitical specificity of particular forms of economic dominance (i.e., British economic hegemony) but rendered universal development a secular dogma. In a striking critique of what would become a persistent claim of developmentalist paradigms as well as orthodox Marxism, Marx argued that "to hold that every nation goes through development internally would be as absurd as the claim that every nation is bound to go through the political development of France or the philosophical development of Germany."[26] Yet it was precisely the promise of formally replicable, self-engendered, and territorially delimited economic development, which underwrote Listian national developmentalism, that helped propel its increasing popularity.

Of particular importance here is the way List's reformulation of the core spatial assumptions of classical economic theory powerfully expressed the naturalization of the modern territorial state. The idea that society was spatially bounded within particular state structures assumed a self-evident status in late-nineteenth-century sociological and philosophical paradigms as well as in emergent nationalist discourse.[27] In the late nineteenth century, the modern vision of the social world as constituted by differentiated spheres (culture/economy/politics) underwent a novel process of spatialization. This imagination of the social world was increasingly naturalized and nationalized. Individual nations akin to modern individuals were understood as possessing a particular culture, economy, territory, and history.

The constitution of a territorial state-centered conception of society/economy was grounded historically in the dialectical tension between the territorialization of social relations within sharply delineated, mutually exclusive spatial units and the deterritorializing thrust of capital and colonial expansion. The constitution of a profoundly uneven global space found concrete expression in the formation of a world market, the consolidation of an interstate system through interimperial rivalry, the reconstitution of conceptions of space and time along supralocal and national lines, the interlocking network of socioeconomic and cultural interconnectedness and competitive interactions, and the dialectical interweaving of particular histories within a global interactive terrain. Processes of global restructuring were matched by the interregional proliferation of struggles to constitute an autonomous national economic space. The profound resonance of Listian developmentalism in a range of peripheral (China, Turkey, Hungary) and colonial (South Asia) configurations, as well as in emergent dominant industrial powers (United States, Germany, Japan), needs to be situated within this global force field of sociospatial, economic, and interstate transformations. The subsequent economic ascendancy of Germany, Japan, and the United States reinforced the strength of Listian developmentalism for anticolonial nationalists.

Nationalists in colonial India attempted to find a space between what they indicted as the excessive abstraction of classical political economy and the "self-serving materialism" of colonial economic policies. Ranade, the chief exponent of List, announced this broad problematic in his influential essay titled "Indian Political Economy," first delivered as an address in 1892.[28] The task of establishing an Indian political economy, which was enthusiastically taken up by G. V. Joshi, V. G. Kale, and G. Subrahmanya Aiyar, among others, necessitated a framework that at once grasped the particularity of Indian socioeconomic conditions and inscribed at its conceptual core the universal principle of nationality. Classical economic theory had, Ranade argued, systematically privileged "individual interests"; it was too economistic (337). Its central assumption of self-interested, disembodied monads "ought to give way or at least be subordinated to the higher interests and aspirations [of a people] if political economy is to be anything more than schoolmen's metaphysics (149–50). How, according to Ranade, was the individualism of classical economic theory to be breached? Particularistic, individual interests had to be subsumed and rationalized with reference to the larger national whole or the nation as general interest. The project of bringing back the excised normative dimension within classical economic theory took the form of an idealizing, nationalist political economy. Akin to List, Ranade absolutized the nation as the singular subject-object of political economy: "Individual interests are not the center round which the Theory should revolve. . . . . the true center is the Body Politic of which that Individual is a member, and that Collective Defense and Well-Being, Social Education and Discipline . . . must be the center, if the Theory is not to be merely Utopian" (336). Within this schema, the principle of territorial nationality ("the Body-Politic of which that Individual is a member") was welded to a practical reformulation of the objectives of political economy. According to this formulation, political economy should be rendered pragmatic. It ought to explicitly enable the universal function of the development of "national productive powers" (336). The "mischievous error" of a "divorce between Theory and Practice" enshrined in classical political econ-

omy demanded not only the adoption of a historicist framework but a recognition of the "predominant claim of Collective Welfare over Individual Interest" (336, 337).

Following List's emphasis on the multiple forms of capital (natural, material, and mental) as intrinsic to national productive power, Ranade advanced a non-economistic yet nonetheless state-centered understanding of
development. He argued that

> National well-being does not consist only in the creation of the highest
> quantity of wealth measured in exchange value, independently of all va-
> riety of quality in that wealth, but in the full and many-sided develop-
> ment of national productive powers. The nation's economic education is
> of far more importance than the present gain of its individual members,
> as represented by the quantity of wealth measured by its value in ex-
> change. . . . The function of the state is to help those influences which
> secure national progress through the several stages of growth. (336)

Invoking List as the "fullest expression" of the "rebellion against the Orthodox creed," Ranade argued that a conception of the state as the "National
Organ for taking care of National needs" was increasingly recognized, in
theory and practice, across diverse regional contexts (335, 344). The "province of State Interference and Control," the "true functions" of a national
state, included infrastructural investments in

> Education, both liberal and technical, Post and Telegraphs, Railway
> and Canal Communications, the pioneering of new enterprise, the in-
> surance of risky undertakings, . . . subsidizing private cooperative ef-
> fort . . . building up . . . Credit on broad foundations by helping people
> to acquire confidence in a free and largely ramified Banking system . . .
> utilizing indigenous resources, and organizing them in a way to pro-
> duce . . . in State factories all products of skill. (344–45)

A central element of the nationalist thesis against colonialism was that it
had systematically distorted, fragmented, and disrupted a previously
unified, internally coherent, autonomous, and diversified economic space.
G. V. Joshi, a contemporary and close collaborator of Ranade's, provided a
succinct account of the nationalist indictment of colonial rule. Following
Ranade's emphasis on a long-term developmental strategy based on the reciprocal calibration of multiple forms of national capital (i.e., human, material, and natural), he braided together the themes of deindustrialization and

deskilling that have cast a long shadow on subsequent (especially Marxist and nationalist) economic historiography. His analysis prefigured what postcolonial Marxists such as Hamza Alavi identified as the "internal disarticulation and external articulation" of colonial economies.[29] Joshi argued:

> We are often told that one of the advantages of the expansion of our import trade is that we get our supply of manufactured articles much cheaper and better than we can have ourselves with our present means and appliances. This is true enough and is no doubt our gain as *consumers* but what a price are we paying for this gain, as *producers* and *labourers?* Our home manufactures are almost now gone and this collapse means to us much more than is commonly supposed. Firstly, it means to us to the disruption of our industrial organization and a change from a many-sided system to one resting on the basis of a single industry; Secondly, it means to us the transfer, the enforced, compulsory transfer of one half of our industrial population from fields of skilled labour to fields of unskilled labour, involving as its necessary consequence a distinct deterioration in their standard of life and comfort; Thirdly, it means to us a fearful falling off in the condition and resources of the middle classes, who are the backbone of every progressive community; Fourthly, it means to us a dangerous contraction of the total national provision for a growing population: changes all of a grave and wide-reaching character, amounting to a most disastrous economic revolution highly detrimental to the moral, social and intellectual well-being of the entire nation.[30]

Such analyses implicitly revealed the social origins of the nationalist critique of colonialism, that is, its roots within an emergent professional, urban middle class. They also expressed the increasingly taken-for-granted status of the project of national developmentalism that was being instituted in a number of regional contexts across the globe. A proclamation of the Indian National Congress reiterated the developmentalist and statist vision of the political economy of nationhood: "The industrial movement is flowing deep; fraught with national ideals. . . . Our industries need protection. But this government will not grant them protection . . . the time has come when the scattered national impulses may be focused into an organic and organized whole for a supreme effort for the promotion of our industries."[31] The nationalist critique of classical political economy was animated by the structuring motif of collective national ownership, of the nation as collective sacred property. Nationalists mobilized a Listian notion of a national econ-

omy, with its related connotations of autocentric development, as a normative ideal and an institutional counterfactual against the limits of a colonial
state space oriented toward the reproduction of the imperial economy.

The Drain of the Nation

Emblematic of the conception of a national economic space and a common
economic collective was Dadabhai Naoroji's neomercantilist formulation of
the drain of the nation. Naoroji's long and extraordinary career began with
his appointment as the first non-British professor of mathematics and philosophy at Elphinstone College, Bombay. In 1855, he established the first
Indian trading firm in London and became a professor of Gujarati at University College, London, in 1856. Initially committed to working for political and economic reform within the framework of the British Empire, he became the first nonwhite member of the British Parliament as a Gladstonian
liberal elected from Central Finsbury (London). He understood his role, at
this particular juncture, as representing India's interests in the British Parliament. It was during his tenure as a parliamentary liberal that he acquired
the infamous epithet "Black Man" proffered by the Tory leader Lord Salisbury, which embodied the wider imperial political economy of race that
many colonial subjects in Metropolitan Britain would intimately experience.[32] Steadily disillusioned by the prospect of reform from within the
imperial-national framework of Britain, he returned to colonial India and
became a founding member of the Indian National Congress in 1885, serving as its president in 1886, 1893, and 1906.

In July 1870, Naoroji provided the first estimates of India's national and
per capita income, along with figures that indicated the widening of regional
disparities within colonial India, in an address titled "The Wants and Means
of India" to the East Indian Association in Bombay.[33] His calculations were
based on an extended critique of official statistical and economic records
that had, as argued earlier, been a central focus of the discursive representation of colonial state space (particularly the annual *Moral and Material
Progress Report*). His figures tore apart official claims of material progress in
an era beset with recurrent, devastating famines, an exponential rise in
peasant indebtedness, widening regional disparities, and "deepening impoverishment" (190). Naoroji's protracted quarrel with the colonial regime
over the accuracy of official statistics led him to further develop and empir-
ically research his theory of the annual "bleeding drain" of the nation. He estimated that the per capita income of colonial India in 1871 was 20 rupees

against 450 rupees for England and that the annual drain of the national income approximated 200 million pounds sterling. According to Naoroji, the drain of wealth to Britain included remittances of colonial official salaries to England; the cost of the military establishment, which was greater than the cost of the entire imperial army outside of colonial India; the debt incurred on capital investments in public works; and the purchase of manufactures in Britain.[34] In other words, Naoroji's work sought to establish the complex structure of imperial financial domination and the relations of unequal exchange that were pivotal to the reproduction of Britain's financial and military hegemony.

Naoroji's demand for the incorporation of per capita income and costs of subsistence figures in official economic reports sought to overcome the spectral logic of colonial statistics that claimed to represent the everyday conditions of colonial subjects by fashioning instead a positivist national register of political economy. Spurred by the political controversy unleashed by his work, the colonial state adopted per capita income figures in annual colonial economic reports from the 1890s onward, even though the colonial state persistently provided much higher figures for per capita income (ranging from 30 to 47 rupees) than did the economic nationalists of the period. In an effort to counter Naoroji's figures of per capita income, Lord Curzon provided the competing calculation of per capita income as 30 rupees in 1901. Other colonial officials and economic reports provided figures ranging from 37 to 45 rupees.[35] For the next several decades, the accurate determination of per capita income became a sub-industry of its own. There developed a highly choreographed challenge and riposte relationship between calculations provided by colonial officials and those provided by nationalist economists and British socialists that followed Naoroji's analysis.[36]

I do not intend here to summarize Naoroji's analysis of the drain. The point here concerns the way his analysis of it presupposed the existence of a spatially delimited national economy. His representations of a national economy took the form of an elaborate statistical and historical analysis of the drain during the years 1787–1865, and this analysis underpinned the collective-origin myth of nationalism. In his most famous work, *Poverty and Un-British Rule in India*, Naoroji argued:

> English capitalists do not merely lend, but with their capital they themselves invade the country. The produce of the capital is mostly eaten up by their own countrymen, and, after that, they carry away the rest in the shape of profits and dividends. The people of India do not derive the

same benefit. . . . The guaranteed railways not only ate up everything in this manner, but compelled India to make up the guaranteed interest also from her produce.[37]

More crucially, he distinguished colonial and national India along distinct political-economic lines:

> In reality there are two Indias—the one prosperous, the other poverty-stricken. The prosperous India is the India of the British and other foreigners. They exploit India as officials, non-officials, capitalists, in a variety of ways, and carry away enormous wealth to their own country. . . . The second India is the India of the Indians—the poverty-stricken India. This India, "bled" and exploited in every way of their wealth, of their services, of their land, labour and all resources by the foreigners, helpless and voiceless—this India of the Indians becomes the poorest nation in the world. (338)

The rhetorical force of Naoroji's analysis derived, in part, from the mobilization of neomercantilist metaphors of economic vampirism as signaled in the juxtaposition of a "bleeding India" against a triumphal and cannibalistic imperial economy. Naoroji argued that "It is at India's cost and blood that this Empire has been formed and maintained up to the present day. . . . It is no wonder that the time has come when India is bleeding to death" (645). Nationalists articulated colonialism's threat from the perspective of a territorially delimited economic collective. The deterritorialization of the national economy was seen as the product of a foreign, colonial rule that had drained, looted, and pillaged the presumed national wealth beyond national territorial boundaries. The nationalist remedy, in the main, concerned the reterritorialization of the economy. In other words, the economy had exceeded its proper national-spatial boundaries and had to be reterritorialized.

The drain theory was popularized in vernacular texts and newspapers, circulated by British and Continental socialists (especially Henry Hyndman and Karl Kautsky), and soon became one of the most famous indictments of colonialism of the late nineteenth century.[38] Naroji's drain theory found a prominent place in the influential work of William Digby, former editor of *Madras Times* and an outspoken critic of colonialism, who was widely read in colonial India. In Digby's monumental treatise titled *"Prosperous" British India: A Revelation from Official Research*, the per capita income of India (which he calculated as 17.2 rupees, or even lower than Naoroji's reckoning) was inscribed in gold on the spine of his book.[39] Marx deployed Naoroji's drain theory to posit the category of "unrequited exports" in volume 3 of *Capital* and observed elsewhere that

> [w]hat they [the British] take from them [Indians] annually in the form of rents, dividends for railways, pensions of military and civil service men . . . without any equivalent return and quite apart from what they appropriate to themselves annually within India—speaking only of the value of commodities the Indians have gratuitously and annually to send over to England—amounts to more than the total sum of the income of 60 million agricultural and industrial labourers of India. This is a bleeding process with a vengeance![40]

Vernacular press reports from this period index the ways the notion of an economic drain acquired a commonsense status. An article from the late 1870s identified the "chief cause of the poverty of India" as the "annual, economic drain" that enriched "foreign traders and artisans. . . . The only way of improving our condition is to establish all kinds of mills and factories in the country, so that we may not have to depend upon England for the supply of necessary articles of consumption."[41]

The notion of India as a national economic space, condensed in the drain theory, informed as well the growing protests against a range of the economic policies of the colonial state. Central among these was the repeal of import duties in 1879. The financial crisis of the late 1850s that followed the 1857 rebellion had led the colonial state (under the leadership of the first financial minister of colonial India, James Wilson), against the tenets of free trade, to impose a 10 percent tariff on English manufactured goods and a 5 percent tariff on yarn. By the 1870s, in the context of the intensified challenge posed to Britain by rising industrial powers, these relatively low tariffs became the center of a sharp controversy as an increasingly politically powerful Manchester chamber of commerce allied with the Metropolitan wing of the colonial government.[42] The demand for the abolition of import duties, despite the financial privations this would pose for the colonial state, given the proliferation of famines and the depreciation in silver, was made on a number of grounds. Among these was the increased importance of colonial India as a captive source of raw material and a market for manufactures against growing competition from the United States, France, and Germany, and the phenomenal growth of a largely indigenously owned textile industry in colonial India.

The tenor of the arguments for the repeal of the tariff duties, within the

India Council in London, indicates the issues at stake. Sir Henry Maine (law member of the India Council) argued that

> [t]he one solid, tangible, material interest which Great Britain has in India is its interest in Indian trade. The importance of the trade has greatly increased as market after market is blocked or closed by the rising protectionism of the world. . . . The maintenance and development of British and Foreign cotton manufactures, which are directly dependent on the maintenance and development of the sale of the manufactured goods imported into India, are essential to the existence of the export trade of Indian raw cotton, and the revival of this trade. . . . India should be restored to her natural productive vocation i.e., as a primary commodity producer.[43]

In an impassioned speech, John Strachey, the finance member of the India Council, reiterated in stridently imperial-nationalistic terms the conception of colonial India as a necessarily subordinate economic space:

> I have not ceased to be an Englishman because I have passed the greater part of my life in India, and have become a member of the Indian government. The interests of Manchester, at which foolish people sneer, are the interests not only of the great and intelligent population engaged directly in the trade in cotton, but of millions of Englishmen. I am not ashamed to say that, while I hope that I feel as strongly as any man the duties which I owe to our Indian subjects, there is no higher duty in my estimation than that which I owe to my own country.[44]

Such economic nationalist proclamations were countered in vernacular press reports that held up the abolition of tariff duties as part of the perceived colonial policy of deindustrialization. Given the institution of a repressive vernacular press act during the late 1870s, the critique of colonial policies often took the form of innuendo and allegory. The following quotation from the *Nasimi Agra* (an Urdu newspaper from the city of Agra, United Provinces, which was the northern center for the indigenous cotton textile industry) from 1879 is exemplary of popular perceptions that colonial rule had rendered "India" as the countryside of Britain:

> There is an old story that is handed down to us by tradition. A greedy gardener got hold of an excellent garden in a foreign country. He was so delighted with his good fortune that he became indifferent to its

preservation and improvement. His countrymen appealed to his patriotism, and induced him to transplant all the flowers and fruit trees to their own country, and the few trees and plants that still remained in the garden withered through his carelessness. When his garden was absolutely ruined in this way, he was suddenly exposed to a number of calamities, namely, famines, boundary disputes with his neighbors, and the growth of competing gardens, and so forth. He went into the garden to see if he could find anything there to gratify his hunger, but the garden was absolutely ruined. A nightingale, which was in the garden at the time, rebuked him for his folly in neglecting the garden. He remained obstinate, however, and eventually he had to abandon the garden and return to his own country. . . . There is as great a difference between England and India in point of wealth as there is between sovereign and farthing. In spite of this, poor India gives twenty million sterling every year to England. This drain has soaked India dry.[45]

Less allusive was an analysis in the *Hindi Pradip* of 1879 of the repeal of the cotton duties.[46] The article opens by posing a rhetorical question: What is the difference between a national and foreign government? The repeal of the tariff duties was offered as the most recent instance of the contrast between a national versus a colonial state:

It will not be out of place here to refer to the specific causes which led the government to this act. . . . At first Manchester supplied Europe and India with cloth. However, the cotton industry of Manchester induced the French, Germans, and Americans to establish cotton mills in their own countries, and the Manchester trade suffered greatly from the competition that grew up. Some cotton mills were lately established in India, and the coarse goods manufactured at the Indian mills lessened the demands for Manchester coarse goods. Another cause which seriously affected the Manchester trade was the high rate of exchange between England and India and the result was that the Manchester trade was paralyzed, and the mill owners of Lancashire responded by reducing the wages of the operatives. This led to a general strike and all production came to a stand still. The mill owners of Lancashire were thus forced to conciliate the labourers. They then tried to find some other remedy for the paralysis of their trade. Since Manchester could do nothing in France, Germany, or the US, it turned towards where it was possible to intervene — India and the abolition of the duties. . . . We do not mean to say that the old form of native industry should have been

kept intact, but that a non-foreign government would have provided
the means of improving the industrial arts and trades and thus improved the material condition of the people. In that case the people
would have identified their own interests with that of the state. . . . In
our present distressed condition, which borders on starvation, we cannot appreciate the blessings of foreign rule.[47]

The politically radical implications of the drain theory were not lost on
the colonial regime. Nationalists were chided, in officially commissioned re-
buttals, for attempting to deploy universalistic frameworks inadequate to
what they deemed as the specificity of India. A turn-of-the-century official
memorandum addressed to the provincial heads of the colonial territorial
state registers the continued anxiety over the nationalist analysis of the
drain (long after its initial formulation) and the colonial regime's investment
in nativist particularization. Directed against the "literate middle classes engaged in seditiously propagating nationalist views," the memorandum opens
with a reference to their "intellectual activities in the domain of history and
economics." It claimed that

> lessons drawn from the history of the West are misapplied to the pres-
> ent circumstances of India; the broad generalizations of European writ-
> ers on political science are stated without mention of their important
> reservations; and natives, left without proper guidance, are led to be-
> lieve that what is appropriate in the case of Switzerland and Italy must
> necessarily be good for India. In the region of economics the most mis-
> chievous doctrine is that which is based on the theory that India is
> drained of her wealth by her connexion with Great Britain. This belief
> is honestly held by growing numbers. . . . The Governor General in
> Council believes that the prevalence of this idea has done incalculable
> mischief, and it behooves every officer of Government, and in particu-
> lar those connected with education, to study the arguments put forward
> in support of it and to seize upon every opportunity of exposing their
> fallacy.[48]

Four years later, the Finance Department proposed the publication of an
authoritative and comprehensive repudiation on the subject of the theory of
the drain. After considerable debate, it was decided that the current political situation demanded that a reputable and "reliable native" undertake
such an enterprise. The Minto Professor of Economics at Calcutta University, Babu Manohar Lal, was selected (with a "handsome honorarium") to

prepare such a work. For given the "nationalization" of the issue and the "high emotional current," only a native would be "able to make the case in a way which would carry conviction among the ordinary thinking native than if government were to issue a formal and dry pronouncement."[49]

Against the particularization of colonial India within colonial discourse, Romesh Chunder Dutt stressed in 1902 that the economic critique of colonialism was grounded on "plain, self-evident laws which operate in every other country."[50] He observed, "place any other country under the same conditions, with crippled industries, with agriculture subject to a heavy and uncertain Land-Tax, and with financial arrangements requiring one-half of its revenues to be annually remitted out of the country, and the most prosperous nation of the earth will soon know the horrors of famine."[51] A central leitmotif of nationalist thought was the objective intelligibility of its economic critique of colonialism, especially against the magical illusion of progress conjured by colonial development. Writing some decades after the consolidation of a nationalist political economy, Bipin Pal noted that the "increased use of shoes and umbrellas by our rural population" was "proof" not, as colonial ideology maintained, of "advancing economic progress" but rather a material sign of the "perpetuation of our economic serfdom." For the "shirts and coats . . . which are seen on the person of our poorer classes are made of imported stuff, and the value of all of these articles less the wages of the local tailors and the profits of the middleman who trade in these stuffs, goes to foreign manufacturers and alien merchants engaged in our import trade."[52] The critique of colonial relations of unequal exchange was articulated from the standpoint of a productivist and nationalist political economy.

THE TENSIONS OF INSTITUTIONAL NATIONALISM

For institutional nationalism, the problem with the colonial state resided in its systematic obstruction of the universal trajectory of national development. Almost singularly wedded to this diagnosis of colonial domination, elite nationalism privileged economic and political issues at the same time as it sought to repress the internal tensions that clung to territorial nativist visions of India. The explicit privileging of economic and political concerns was powerfully expressed in the Indian National Congress's (INC) historic decision of 1888 barring the discussion of any subject, subsumed under the category *social*, that was defined as a field constituted by particular interests and identities. All discussions, for instance, to which Hindu or Muslim delegates as a "body . . . unanimously or nearly unanimously objected" were banned.[53] The decision to restrict potentially controversial issues to internal deliberation within discretely conceived social groups (Hindus, Muslims, Parsis, Christians) was justified on pragmatic grounds. W. C. Bonnerjee (the INC president in 1887) argued that delegates belonging to different religious groups should "discuss their respective social matters in a friendly spirit among themselves. . . . Social questions are to be left out of the Congress programme . . . the Congress commenced and has since remained, and will, I sincerely trust, always remain a purely political organization devoting its energies to political matters and political matters only."[54]

In the context of bourgeois nationalism in colonial India, social questions were figured as belonging to a negative domain against the legitimate field of politics that had the nation as its sovereign subject. Questions about the relational dynamic and hierarchical positioning of religious, caste, class, and gender identities within the imagined community of the nation were therefore confined to corresponding subcommittees of the separate institution of the Indian National Social Conference, which was held concurrent with the annual INC proceedings. In 1895, the Social Conference was excluded from the venue of the INC all together. Such policies reinforced an economic critique of colonialism. Although the spheres of economy and politics were linked, the links between social and economic domains were severed. Within this schema, the crucial issue for nationalists was the territorial disjuncture between the imagined nation's political and economic structure. This framing of nationalism's critique of colonialism exemplified the naturalization of the territorial-institutional structure of the colonial state. Colonial space was appropriated as national space.

The conception of the nation as a territorial-economic collective implied an immediate, direct relationship between individual members and the sovereign national whole. Thus, appeals to the sovereign national collective were deployed against other competing loyalties and against critiques based in the internal differences within the imagined national community. To bring forward a claim on behalf of a subsidiary category of the nation—workers, religious minorities, peasants, "tribal" groups, women—was implicitly to challenge the presumptive normative sway of the nation. Institutional nationalists sought, in this regard, the monopolization of the field of practices designated as political and the corresponding particularization of the social. Only properly national concerns (economic, political, territorial) could be legitimate and authoritative in the newly constituted public realm. Identities deemed particularistic—those based, for example, on religion, gender, and caste—were coercively relegated to a private ahistorical ream of preferences. The internal tensions of institutional nationalism became increasingly visible during the period of mass mobilization for the *swadeshi* (indigenous manufactures) movement. It was precisely when nationalism redirected its attention from forging an oppositional critique of colonialism toward the project of mobilizing the population as a national community that its internal fissures became ever-more-apparent nodes for violent conflict.

The nationalist decision to ban discussion of potentially conflictual social issues was also a self-conscious challenge to the colonial thesis of the impossibility of India. This thesis maintained that the heterogeneity of indigenous society was nontranscendable; it could not be translated into the abstract rational form of the nation. A succinct formulation of this thesis was John Strachey's claim:

> This is the first and most essential thing to learn about India — that there is no, and never was an India, or even any country of India, possessing, according to European ideas, any sort of unity, physical, political, social or religious. . . . That men of the Punjab, Bengal, the United Provinces, and Madras, should ever feel they belong to one nation, is impossible.[55]

The nationalist counterresponse informed debates, during the late 1880s, within the INC. In 1890, two years after the decision to ban discussions of cultural and religious issues, Pherozeshah Mehta exclaimed:

> Indeed, so far as the historical argument is concerned, we [the INC] have been successful in turning the tables upon our adversaries. We have shown that it is they who defy the lessons of history and modernity when they talk of waiting to make a beginning till the masses of the people are fully equipped with all the virtues and all the qualifications which adorn the citizens of Utopia, in fact till a millennium has set in, when we should hardly require such institutions at all.[56]

It is important to recall that the INC was a product of the tentative and limited experiments with self-government from the late 1870s onward. The dominant addressee of institutional nationalism was the colonial state, and this profoundly conditioned its self-understanding and presentation. The very particularities, for instance, that rendered colonial subjects incapable of representing themselves had to be formulated within the terms of the denied universality of nationhood. In an address to the INC, M. V. Bhide (a former railway switchman) noted:

> I know that there are among our critics . . . who proclaim with an air of superior wisdom that India is but a geographical expression and that there is no Indian nation as such, but only a congerie of races and creeds, who have no cohesion in them. . . . here in this gathering we have representatives from the most distant provinces, Bengal, Assam, Punjab, North Western provinces, Rajputana, Sind, Gujarat, Maharashtra. . . . but the watchword of these congressman is India, Indians first, Hindus, Muhammadans, Parsees, Christian, Punjabees, Bengali . . . afterwards . . . the aggregate of those that are residents of one territory . . . urged by like impulses to secure like rights and to be relieved of like burdens.[57]

Notions such as an Indian history, an Indian economy, and the like were intelligible only with reference to a spatially fixed, singular national entity of India.

Nationalist discourse was shot through with "arborescent root metaphors" that at once suggested temporal continuity and spatial fixity.[58] Consider, in this regard, the following address to INC by P. Ananda Charlu, a prominent swadeshist, in 1895:

> In the first place it [nationality] has for its central stock like the trunk of a tree, the people who have for ages and generations settled and domiciled in a country with more or less ethnic identity at bottom, and more or less unified by being continually subject to identical environments and to the inevitable process of assimilation. In the next place it gets added to from time to time, by the accession of other peoples, like scions engrafted on the central stem or like creepers attaching thereto, who settle in the country in a like manner and come under the many unifying impulses already referred to, though still exhibiting marks of separation and distinctness. Affirm this standard, and you have an Indian nation. Deny it, and you have a nation nowhere on the face of the earth.[59]

The particularistic and organicist strain of popular visions of nationhood was increasingly sublimated within the terms of a self-understood universalistic conception of national territorial-economic belonging. However, the intrinsically violent kernel of territorial nativism continued to haunt institutional nationalism. Before exploring this tension in the context of the *swadeshi* movement, I revisit the emergent late-nineteenth and early-twentieth-century field of Indian economics, because it presaged issues and themes central to ongoing debates about the specificity of colonial and postcolonial formations.

"PROVINCIALIZING POLITICAL ECONOMY": THE BURDEN OF INDIAN ECONOMICS

Oriented toward the pragmatic goal of securing national development, the emergent literature on Indian economics did not self-consciously proclaim that it was an autonomous field of enquiry. In fact, Indian economics located its standpoint of critique within and against the structural and experiential contradictions of colonial state space. In his influential 1918 work, *Introduction to the Study of Indian Economics*, Vaman Kale restated the broad aims that informed Ranade's programmatic statement about the task of "Indian Political Economy."[60] Formulated within a colonized context, "Indian Economics" did not, Kale argued, represent a "separate science or a branch of the science of Economics," nor did it necessarily signify a new economic theory. Rather the commitment to undertake a "scientific investigation" of the "peculiar political, social, intellectual and economic conditions" of India expressed a "general agreement" that the ultimate goal of such "research and study" was "the progress of the country and the promotion of the welfare of its people."[61]

More than twenty years after the publication of Ranade's programmatic 1893 essay titled "Indian Political Economy," Kale reiterated the influence of List on the nationalist critique of colonialism. Nationalists in colonial India had, he observed, exulted in the rude shock delivered to "advocates of free trade" by List's system of "National Political Economy." The publication of List's work was "as great a land-mark in the development of economic thought as the appearance of *Wealth of Nations* had been two generations ago. . . . He introduced two ideas that were new to current theory namely, the idea of nationality as contrasted with that of cosmopolitanism, and the idea of productive power as contrasted with that of exchange values." Kale argued that the "awakening of national consciousness in countries which were economically backward" and the growing "desire among them for many-sided national development" put paid to the British-imperial "dream" of the universal acceptance of the doctrine of free trade (211). From this perspective, the realignment of political economy along nationalist lines was both a product of and helped to reinforce the "ideal of independent nationality" in an era of intensified global economic competition. The concrete realization of this universal ideal entailed "each nation devoting itself to all branches of economic activity, and thus evolving its own individuality" (212).

The project of Indian economics was not a passively received copy of Listian developmentalist frameworks. Nor was it a unified monolith along lines of regional origin, research focus, and ideological inflection. Kale, for instance, belonged to what can be called the Bombay school of Indian political economy (composed of, among others, Ranade, Joshi, Aiyar, Naoroji, Ambedkar), which focused on colonial finance, banking, and the sphere of exchange.[62] In contrast, what can be called the Bengal school (e.g., Romesh Chunder Dutt, Bipin Chandra Pal, Radhakamal Mukherjee), which rose to prominence in the *swadeshi* era, principally concerned itself with issues of land-revenue restructuring, agrarian relations, and peasant indebtedness, and more crucially, emphasized the particularity of "indigenous" institutions and practices.

In a chapter titled "The Indian Outlook," Kale mounted a searing critique of perspectives that rendered "indigenous" society as essentially stagnant, bound to a world-renouncing spirituality, and incompatible with modern economic institutions. Rather than embracing an avowed "spiritualism" in the manner of many *swadeshi* nationalists in Bengal, Kale saw such constructions as not only "superficial" attempts to suggest a "fundamental difference" but as ideological tools of colonial economic policy. It was, he noted, "usual to contrast the materialism of the West . . . with the spiritualism of India, and this contrast is sometimes cherished by Indians as a compliment and often made by outsiders through a feeling of contempt mingled with pity" (22). What such perspectives ignored was the historicity and politics of this opposition. He observed:

> In the words of the late Mr. Ranade, India has been ruralized and at the present moment, stands upon the threshold of the capitalistic and factory regime. Because India is poor . . . it does not follow that she is more spiritual and dreamy than the West or that she is of a weaker mould. There is abundant evidence to prove that India was once rich in the goods of this world as well as in spiritual and cultural wealth; and that her people desired and enjoyed material pleasures. (22)

In a trenchant critique of sociological master narratives that presented capitalist development as an outgrowth of a uniquely Western cultural habitus, Kale argued that the alignment of the West with modernity derived not from some intrinsic essence or unique cultural logic but from the generalization of capitalism. It was, he argued, "the modern methods of production, exchange and distribution of wealth that have imposed on the West a peculiar stamp of modern civilization" (34). To suggest otherwise would entail ignoring a central fact, namely, that the most successful "Indian capitalists, mill-owners, and traders," those in the "front ranks of commerce, banking, and manufactures carried on Western lines, quite out of harmony with supposed Hindu or Muslim ideals," belonged to groups whose members were "little tinctured with Western civilization" (22, 34). Citing the example of such merchant communities as the Khojas, Marwaris, and Memens, Kale argued that it was "the unwesternized, unenlightened, and uncultured classes, fully under the influence of old religious ideas, social customs and prejudices," who occupied the very apex of indigenous capitalist banking and industry (22, 34). Although Kale's formulations are subject to critique on different registers, the larger point here concerns the way the specificity of Indian economics — as an object of study and a lived experience — stemmed for Kale, following Ranade, from its status as a historically produced "dependent colonial economy."

One of the self-assigned burdens of Indian economics, and one taken up with particular fervor in Bengal during the *swadeshi* era, was the formulation of a framework adequate to the perceived inner dynamic of indigenous social institutions and practices. The *swadeshi* intellectual and activist Radhakamal Mukherjee (professor of economics at Krishnath College, Berhampur, and the founder of cooperative societies in Murshidabad) provided one of the strongest articulations of this project in his magisterial 1916 volume titled *The Foundations of Indian Economics*.[63] His analysis — from the violence intrinsic to exchange relations, the envisioning of village communities as the normative exemplar for a national economic space, and the emphasis on decentralized institutions of political and economic governance — anticipated the conceptual armature of Gandhi's critique of modernity. Taking as his point of departure the attempt to constitute a properly national economy in accord with the "regulative social and ethical ideas of India," he elaborated an influential vision of a nationalist political economy (xix).

Drawing on the work of the German sociologist Werner Sombart, Mukherjee advocated a model of industrial and agricultural production based on cottage industries, handicrafts, cooperative banks, and credit societies.[64] Mukherjee mobilized the methodological protocols of emergent economic sociology — from Frederick Engels to Werner Sombart — in order to make an impassioned case for grounding national economic institutions on the model of actually existing village communities. With specific reference to his ethnographic and sociological methods, Mukherjee noted that for

> some of these data I am indebted to artisans and laborers who are taught in my night schools, rural and urban, and also to agriculturalists and traders who are members of the Co-operative Credit Societies in villages established by me as Honorary Organizer of Co-operative Societies in the district of Murshidabad. I have been able to collect, after Engel's method, the statistics of consumption partly through them as well as through friends and pupils of Krishnath College, Behrampore, who took the trouble of filling up the tables I prepared for this purpose. (xxii)

His innovative welding of economic sociological models and ethnographic techniques in this work and elsewhere helped establish key socioeconomic categories (village, working class) as a central preoccupation of "Indian" socioscientific and economic research in subsequent decades.[65] The specific burden of Indian economics — articulated in the idealist inflection of the *swadeshi* era — resided in the selective appropriation of modern economic institutions toward the "expression of the Indian genius, of the particular phase of universal humanity which the Indian people are unfolding."[66]

Writing with a profound sense of urgency, Mukherjee held up contemporary village communities as the archetypal casualty of colonial development. The "great economic revolution" wrought by colonial spatial-economic restructuring was nowhere more apparent than in the intensified differentiation, the spectacular "contrast between city life and village life" (3). Although it was "still almost self-sufficing . . . as an economic unit," the village was rapidly assuming its assigned status in the dominant "system of production" as merely a "field of exploitation" with no "separate existence of its own" (3, 402). The fate of the village community was for Mukherjee, as it was for Gandhi, exemplary of the constitutive inequalities intrinsic to "a system of production [in which] the worker is a mere servant to machinery" such that in the corresponding "system of social organization the village" could only exist as "a slave of the city" (402). His account of the rapid evisceration of the autonomy of village communities, their formal subsumption within the urban-centered logic of colonial state space, resonates with theories of uneven development developed during the 1930s and 1940s from outside "Euro-America" — from the Japanese Marxist Kozo Uno to the more well-known tradition of Chinese Maoism.[67] The profound resonance of the problematic of urban-rural differentiation expressed the historical and experiential specificity of colonized, semicolonial, and so-called late-industrializing social formations.

Whereas Naoroji's neomercantilist drain thesis focused on modalities of financial domination in the sphere of circulation and between Britain and "India," Mukherjee broadened the drain thesis to emphasize the "drain from the village to the city" of "all skill, enterprise, knowledge and wealth" in the sphere of production and within the imagined national economic space. This intra-national drain was producing a highly differentiated economic and social space evinced in intensified rural migration, the exponential growth of landless classes, and the flight of the "natural guardians, the [rural] middle class" from villages to cities in order to find employment in an "unfruitful" and unproductive colonial sphere.[68] For Mukherjee the internal drain was part of the social process of reification constitutive of modernity itself, that is, the "separation between village and city, the labourer and the employer, the specialist and layman, the multitude and the genius, the brain worker and the manual labourer" (449). Although such differentiations were intrinsic to the dominant "system of production," the violent agency of colonialism had ensured an especially painful articulation of village communities bathed, in Mukherjee's figuration, in an eternal present of custom and endogenous reproduction with the concentrated and accelerated time of the world market. Under the sway of colonial development, "villages that for centuries followed customary practices are brought into contact with the world market all of a sudden. For steamship and railways which have established the connection have been built in so short an interval as hardly to allow for breathing time to the village . . . the sudden introduction of competition into an economic unit which had from time immemorial followed custom has wrought a mighty change" (5).

Although Mukherjee's analysis emphasized the historical production of forms of unevenness on multiple scales (urban–rural; metropole–colony) and spheres (intellectual versus manual labor), it also simultaneously sought to recover a self-sufficient, self-moving village economy based on cooperative principles and a regulated hierarchy of social differences based on caste, *jati* (464). His emphasis on the village as the model for a properly Indian national economy prefigured Gandhi's anxiety that under the sway of modern national developmentalism, the imagined village economy and community would become a permanent subaltern remainder in the anticipated national space. Both Mukherjee and Gandhi regarded village communities as the principal fatalities of colonial development and rejected urban-centered national industrialization on that basis. They profoundly differed, in this regard, from Ranade and later Nehruvian formulations. Yet the precise spatiotemporal referent and meaning of villages was, then as now, a contested question. There was a decided oscillation in this strand of nationalist economic thought and practice between a vision of village communities as a reservoir of indigenous institutions that had to be restored and/or preserved wholesale and a more utopian, radically futurist attempt that sought their transformation, that imagined villages of the future in the present. Mukherjee, like many other swadeshists, established a range of cooperative enterprises in rural Bengal. These enterprises sought to foster autonomous village economies and were oriented toward an anticipated national space devoid of internal differentiations and inequalities. Yet the futurity of such projects coexisted with practices that reactivated the disciplinary and scopic regime that marked and made the everyday experience of caste-as-lived. Mukherjee insisted that the "joint-Hindu family and caste or *jati*" were and should remain the "ethical and social basal factors" of an Indian economy and society and characterized his own institutional experiments as exemplary in this regard (464). The deeply troubled implications of this vision lay not only in its transformation, to borrow a phrase from Theodore Adorno, of a "bad empirical reality into transcendence" but in its endorsement of an upper-caste Hindu ideology as the normative content of an imagined Indian national space and economy.[69]

Yet, at the same moment, the attempt to fashion a nationalist political economy attentive to "indigenous" institutions represented a sharp riposte to authors of Eurocentric frameworks who homogenized and repressed forms of historical difference. Mukherjee unequivocally characterized dominant theories of "social evolution," as elaborated by "Western sociologists," as "essentially false." At issue for him was not only the deployment of an "abstract and arbitrary standard deduced from the evolution of Western civilization" in order "to judge the progress of different peoples." The problem concerned the ideological origin and function of theories of social evolution. For Mukherjee there was little doubt that social evolutionary perspectives were direct expressions, the normative ballast, of European colonialism. He specifically identified theories that "regarded the Hebraic-Graeco-Romano-Gothic civilization as representing the culmination of cultural progress" and construed "the eastern types of culture as if they were either monstrous or defective forms of life, or only primitive ancestral forms, the earlier steps of the series that have found their completion in European society and civilization" as the ideological scaffolding of colonial domination.[70] Drawing on the work of the Hegelian philosopher and *swadeshi* activist Brajendranath Seal, Mukherjee prefigured key themes of contemporary colonial historiog-

raphy and postcolonial theory—the intimacy between colonial power/
knowledge, the socioideological moorings and functions of teleological assumptions, the denial of coevalness and the like—by more than a half century. It was, he proclaimed, a "gross and stupid blunder" to

> link Chinese, Hindu, Semitic, Greek, Roman, Gothic, Teutonic in one
> line of filiation, in one logical (if not chronological) series . . . to conceive
> these statically, to reduce each living procession to a punctual moment
> in a single line is to miss their meaning and purpose. . . . Universal
> humanity is not to be figured as the crest of an advancing wave, occu-
> pying but one place at any moment and leaving all behind at a dead
> level. For universal humanity is immanent everywhere and at every mo-
> ment. (329)

The insurgent field of Indian economics rejected the territorialization of
modernity in specific regions by directing attention instead to what
Mukherjee called the "multiform geographical and historical conditions"
that underwrote a singular yet internally differentiated global formation
(329). The critique of dominant evolutionary frameworks stemmed, in part,
from recognition of the concrete multiplicity of differential and contending
times and spaces (e.g., urban–rural divides) that coexisted and constituted
a global space-time. Yet rather than simply affirming or celebrating a particularistic difference, anticolonial nationalists sought the actualization of
the universalistic promise of development and the realization of forms of
universality rooted in the particularity of indigenous institutions.

Grounded in social categories of the universal (capital, economy, state),
institutional nationalism couched its very claims to singularity and autonomy in a recognizably modernist idiom. Even as nationalists attempted to
reconstitute an organicist, particularist community, they worked within
and through modern social categories. The basic premise was that the elim-
ination of an alien colonial state would enable the realization of a stable
national-organic whole.

CHAPTER EIGHT

TERRITORIAL NATIVISM: *SWADESHI* AND *SWARAJ*

In the name of India we loved Europe, and therefore, we fed our fancy not upon Indian but European ideals, European arts, European thought, European culture. We loved the abstraction we called India, but, yes we hated the thing it actually was. . . . The one great good that the social and religious reactions of the last twenty years have done is to cure us . . . of this old, this unreal, this imaginary and abstract patriotism. Love of India now means a loving regard for the very configuration of this continent — a love for its rivers and mountains, for its paddy fields and its arid sandy plains, its towns and villages however uncouth or unsanitary these might be . . . a love, as Rabindranath Tagore put it the other day at the Classic Theatre, for the muddy weed-entangled village lands, the moss-covered stinky village ponds, and for the poor, the starved, the malaria-stricken peasant populations of the country, a love for its languages, its literatures, its philosophies, its religions.

—Bipin Chandra Pal, *Swadeshi and Swaraj*, 1907

The nationalist critique of colonialism shaped, in a relation of reciprocal determination, the *swadeshi* (home manufactures) movement. The latter represented the first systematic campaign to incorporate and mobilize the "masses" within the elite structure of institutional nationalism. The movement assumed its radical mass form in 1905, after the highly contested spatial partitioning of Bengal into two separate provinces in the name of administrative efficiency.[1] For nationalists, the partition scheme was a transparent strategy of pitting the large and predominantly peasant Muslim population of eastern Bengal against the middle-class, land-owning Bengali Hindu professionals of western Bengal, whose political radicalism had become increasingly marked in the late colonial political field. The *swadeshi* movement—which authored techniques of passive resistance that formed the basis of subsequent nationalist mass mobilizations—sought to overhaul collective and individual practices of consumption and production, transform entrenched structures and habits of feeling and perception, and create an autonomous national space and economy. The broad socio-aesthetic

242

complex of its repertoire included the reconstitution of social taste from Manchester cloth to coarse handloom; the boycott of foreign commodities and consumers of foreign goods; the social scrutiny of consumption practices as indicators of authenticity and patriotism; the valorization of indigenous handicrafts and enterprises as the material symbol of historical continuity and the concrete embodiment of the imagined singularity of an Indian nation; and the proliferation of novel philosophical, aesthetic, and cultural projects that self-consciously aimed to overcome the lengthening shadow of "European" epistemologies and disciplines. In 1880 Naoroji had observed, in response to official reports about the proliferation of popular songs bemoaning "the destruction of Indian industry and arts," that

> [w]e may laugh at this attempt as a futile attempt to shut out English machine made, cheaper goods against handmade dearer ones. But little do we think what this movement is likely to grow into, and what new phases it may take in time. . . . The songs are at present directed against English wares, but they are also a natural and effective preparation against other English things when the time comes. . . . if the present downward course continues, if the mass of the people at last begin to despair of any amelioration . . . it will be but a *very, very* short step . . . to turn the course of indignation from English wares to English rule.[2]

In 1906, *swadeshi*—which is a literal welding of the words *swa* (self) and *desh* (national territory in its reconstituted late-nineteenth-century meaning)— was officially endorsed by the Indian National Congress in the avowed objective of a *swadeshi swaraj* (national self-government).[3]

The authors of Indian economics had elaborated a powerful critique of colonial domination grounded in a normative vision of an autonomous, self-moving, and autarkic national economy. By the turn of the century, the notion of a spatially discrete national economy had the status of a rational transparency within elite nationalist discourse. *Swadeshi* radicalized and generalized the nationalist critique of colonialism on multiple, overlapping sociocultural terrains and in a deeply passionate idiom of autonomy, self-reliance, and sacrifice. The conception of India or, more specifically, Bharat Mata as a bounded organic national space was the template on which popular *swadeshi* repertoires were forged. The *swadeshi* movement fused together the abstract and universalistic notion of a common economic collective with a particularized idealist vision of the social body as specifically Hindu. *Swadeshi* practices indicate how persuasively the conception of a national economic collective and an organically constituted national society was popularized. Nationalists yoked together the demand for *swaraj* (in its varied meanings of self-rule, autonomy, and independence) with the developmentalist and productivist ideology of *swadeshi* (indigenous manufactures). This welding of *swaraj* and *swadeshi*, underwritten by a territorial nativist conception of nationhood, embodied the contradictory character of institutional nationalism.

NATIONAL PEDAGOGICAL CONSOLIDATION

Although the response to the 1905 partition spurred mass mobilization on an unprecedented basis, the first *swadeshi* associations, journals, industrial *melas* (festivals), and key features of the movement's repertoire were forged during the late nineteenth century. The first exhibition-festivals of indigenous arts and manufactures were held in 1867 in Calcutta and by 1870 spread to Lahore (Punjab), Lucknow (United Provinces), and Poona (Bombay Presidency); from 1901 such exhibitions were a regular feature of annual Congress sessions. Poona, in particular, became a key center for the self-conscious elaboration of both the economic critique of colonialism and the forging of *swadeshi* practices. Under the leadership of G. V. Joshi, M. G. Ranade, and G. K. Gokhale, societies for the "revival and encouragement of native arts and industries" proliferated during the 1870s and 1880s. Members of such associations took oaths never to consume British products when the corresponding indigenous products could be procured, and a number of shops and cottage industries were set up on cooperative principles. Ranade, in particular, sponsored, directed, and established a range of economic enterprises and sociocultural institutions from a cotton and silk-spinning and weaving company, a paper mill, an industrial association, a girls' school, a library, a museum, an arbitration court for the settlement of civil disputes, and organizations that sought to promote Marathi literature.[4]

Among the most striking elements of the early *swadeshi* repertoire was the establishment of a range of parallel, competing institutions: shops, cottage industries, secondary schools, colleges, newspapers, and presses, as well as parallel juridical arbitration courts *(nyaya sabhas)* for the settlement of civil disputes against colonial courts and counterfamine relief associations in 1872 and 1876–78. Such practices were accompanied by systematic scholarly and research efforts to analyze the problem of recurrent famines and increasing peasant indebtedness from the perspective of a nationalist political economy. The institutional nucleus of this project in the Bombay Presidency was the Poona Sarvajanayak Sabha (PSS), established in Poona on April 2, 1870—the Hindu New Year's Day. The ninety-five founding members of the PSS, elected by six thousand people from different localities of the Bombay Presidency, fashioned themselves as representative delegates (40). The constitution of the organization—whose membership rapidly rose to 132 by 1875—deliberately excluded from its purview religious issues and focused on an ambitious range of research projects and socioeconomic initiatives. In 1872, for instance, the PSS appointed various subcommittees to conduct an elaborate sociological investigation into the condition of the peasantry. The agents of the PSS traveled extensively into the rural interiors, interviewing peasants about prices, wages, indebtedness, the pressure of land revenue, local and central taxation, and the appropriation of customary rights to forest lands under the colonial regime. They recorded and disseminated their findings in numerous volumes, including the *Quarterly Journal.* Among the most influential works were Ranade's volumes titled *Material Conditions in Maharasthra District* (1872), *Famine Administration in the Bombay Presidency* (1872), and the massive *Revenue Manual of the British Empire in India* (1877). The colonial regime responded by disciplining key leaders of the PSS: Ranade was denied the post of joint judge of Thana in 1880 and was transferred from Poona to Nasik to Dhulia in rapid succession. Colonial authorities regarded him as equivalent to "what Mr Parnell is in Ireland, an ardent home ruler."[5] However, the project of instituting a nationalist sociology of knowledge against the abstractions of colonial state space—inaugurated with the doubled critique of colonial economic policies and classical political economy—expanded and deepened at the turn of the century. The *swadeshi* repertoire, as forged in the late nineteenth century and consolidated at the turn of the century, entailed the establishment of parallel authorities, institutions, and subject-positions that were privileged on the grounds of their affective liaisons with an imagined, organically constituted national collectivity.

As institutional nationalism sought to construct its sovereignty over ever-widening arenas of cultural, social, and economic hegemony, the project of producing disciplined nationals became increasingly rooted in the reconfigured content of various institutional sites, especially schools and colleges. British colonial ideology maintained that nationalism was the outcome of a premature encounter between deracinated, Westernized colonial subjects and liberal political theory. The nationalist counterresponse to the permanent ideological structure of temporal deferral and the charge of bad mimesis animated the counterpedagogical consolidation of *swadeshi* ideologies in the educational curriculum of vernacular schools and privately run secondary schools. The post-1900 revamping of the education apparatus, initiated by Lord Curzon, the governor-general and viceroy, had been driven by the perceived threat posed by the expansion of indigenously run educational institutions.[6] Focusing largely on works of history, politics, and economics, the official Text-Book Committee banned various works on nineteenth-century European history (the curriculum in *swadeshi*-inspired vernacular schools, for instance, contained liberal doses of works by Mazzini), especially those on the French revolution (for example, Burke's and Carlyle's works on the subject) and those dealing with Ireland (a principal target was William Butler's *Gordon*). This was justified on the basis that the "oriental mind cannot grasp the true significance of these events and ideas and a false idea of patriotism is the only result."[7] The selective focus of the Text-Book Committee on historical, geographical, and economic textbooks ironically enabled, until 1916, the unchecked circulation of a popular Marathi textbook in Algebra that ingeniously incorporated the broad tenets of *swadeshi* discourse. The following example from this work is typical: "A man takes a *Swadeshi* vow and in a month he persuades two others to do the same, the next month two others and so on; if the population of *Bharat* is seventy million how long will it take the entire country to be converted to *Swadeshi?*"[8]

Among the most popular and influential *swadeshi* texts was Sakharam Ganesh Deuskar's (1869–1912) Bengali work *Desher katha* (Story of the Country). First published in 1904, *Desher katha* summarized the work of Ranade, Naoroji, and Romesh Dutt in a popularized idiom, urged the adoption of handlooms as a way of generating employment and competing with Lancashire cloth against proposals of heavy capital investment in Indian textile factories, and warned against the colonial state's "hypnotic conquest of the mind." The colonial state proscribed the text in 1910, but by then it had sold more than ten thousand copies, had been summarized in a shorter pamphlet titled *Krishaker sarbanash* (Ruin of the Peasantry), had structured *swadeshi* street plays, and more significantly, had assumed the status of mandatory reading for an entire generation of *swadeshi* activists.[9]

In the early 1900s, the colonial government instituted a series of authoritarian checks (including the interception of all letters addressed from Paris, London, Berlin, Berkeley, and San Francisco from nationalist organizations in exile) on the circulation and production of "seditious works."[10] These measures were directed against works produced within colonial India as well as against the astonishing proliferation of journals, articles, and pamphlets generated in a global trans-imperial field. The increase in nationalist organizations in this trans-imperial field included Ghadar (San Francisco, Palo Alto, Berkeley), the Revolutionary Party (London and Paris), and the

Free India Society (London, Paris, and Berlin). Among the publications proscribed were socialist journals like the *Indian Sociologist*, the *Gaelic American*, and *Justice* produced by Indian students in Berkeley and Stanford under the leadership of Har Dayal, professor of philosophy at Stanford University, and often ingeniously wrapped in catalogs of Paris firms such as *Bon Marché*, as well as pamphlets by Sudhindra Nath Bose, a professor of politics at the University of Iowa.[11] Other proscribed publications produced outside colonial India included *Swadeshi Bharat* (Independent India), *Oh Martyrs: Speeches of Indian Nationalists*, Joseph Mazzinni's autobiography (in translation), *Swaraj, Universal Dawn, Talwar* (a periodical published from Berlin), *Infamies of Liberal Rule in India, Bharat Mein Angrezi Hakumat* (British Rule in Bharat), *Sipahi guddhar itihas* (History of the Sepoy Mutiny), and *Naveen Hindustan* (Young India).[12] The numerous works marked as "seditious" largely circulated from "hand to hand, until the relay would be disrupted by a dawn raid and the last reader, usually a schoolboy or some unemployed youth in a mufassil town," was taken with the "offending object" to the local police station.[13]

These long-distance imagings of the nation remarkably conformed to institutional nationalist critiques of colonial rule.[14] An instance of this resonance were various pamphlets circulated within colonial India and written by "Indian" migrant laborers employed on the San Francisco Railway in 1906–7. A pamphlet from 1906, which begins with the salutation "Bande Mataram" (hail to the motherland), reiterates key aspects of the nationalist critique of colonial economic policies and urges fellow nationals to awaken to the fact that

> the English have kept you ignorant of progress and liberty, and continually instill into you the lesson of slavery. . . . Slowly they are stealing away from you all your produce and money, and in the course of time you have been reduced to such abject poverty that you have become the absolute slaves of the English. . . . Passing the whole of your servitude in hunger and privation, your faces have become the colour of the earth; and this is the reason why the English speak of you as "black man." . . . You and the English are both of the same original stock—you are both *Aryans*. But they have reduced you to the status of animals. . . . *the English take out of your motherland the money earned by your labour, 65 crores of rupees and send it to England, and there hundreds and thousands, without moving a hand or foot, are supplied by your labour*. . . . Consider how *Bharat* be-

came so poor? How did you become so poor? . . . It is through subju-
gation to a foreign rule.[15]

The circulation of such works and their constitutive force in "manufacturing rebels" and transforming "nurseries into revolutionary cells" became
increasingly apparent at the turn of the century, especially in Bengal.[16] During this period, secondary school and college students became a chief constituency for an increasingly militant and violent *swadeshi* movement. The
spread of *swadeshi* practices in schools included the refusal by students to
write examinations on foreign paper; solidarity marches conducted barefoot
that both protested state violence against *swadeshi* activists and signaled national mourning; and various forms of social ostracism of fellow students
who consumed foreign products, including such measures as throwing acid
on the foreign-made clothes of fellow students (44–46).

The colonial state instituted a set of draconian measures against schools,
teachers, and students patronizing and distributing proscribed works and
engaging in activities deemed seditious. In 1905, the Bengal government
officially condemned the political activities of students, and local officials
were enlisted to report any students involved in boycotts, picketing, and
practices of social ostracism. School and college authorities were warned
that failure to report and prevent such activities would result in the dismissal of school functionaries and the revocation of state grants-in-aid programs for schools and colleges, the privilege of competing for government
scholarships, and official recognition of the institutions.[17] Although many of
the students involved in such practices were either heavily fined or more often expelled from educational institutions, the colonial state's repressive
measures did not fully stem the force of counterhegemonic national pedagogical activities.

In November 1905, Satish Chandra Mukherjee, Gooroodass Banerjee,
Brajendra Nath Seal, and Rabindranath Tagore, among others, designed
the outlines of a National Council of Education. They denounced colonial
educational institutions, especially Calcutta University, which by 1918, with
twenty-seven thousand students, was one of the largest universities in the
world, as *gulam khanas* or a "house for manufacturing slaves." More crucially, they elaborated a programmatic national educational program and established the Bengal National College (BNC) and Bengal Technical Institute in Calcutta in 1906, and a number of primary and secondary schools
that neither accepted state financial aid nor requested official recognition as
counterpedagogical sites.[18] The National Council of Education sought to
impart "Education—literary as well as Scientific and Technical—on Na-

tional lines and exclusively under National Control" through the use of the vernaculars and independently produced textbooks, with a "special importance" accorded to "a knowledge of the country, its Literature, History and Philosophy and incorporating with the best Oriental ideals of life and thought the best assimilable ideals of the West."[19]

The faculty at the BNC reads like a dream roster of *swadeshi* intellectuals and activists. It included Aurobindo Ghose (principal), Satish Chandra Mukherjee (superintendent), Radha Kumund Mukherjee, Benoy Kumar Sarkar, B. B. Ranade, and Sakharam Ganesh Deuskar (author of *Desher katha*), and there was as well a regular lecture series by Rabindranath Tagore, R. C. Bonnerjee, Gooroodass Banerjee (the first "Indian" vice-chancellor of Calcutta University), and A. K. Coomaraswamy (the noted art historian) (61–64). Symptomatic of *swadeshi*'s productivist orientation, the curriculum conjoined intellectual and manual labor. Formal training in mechanical and chemical engineering was hitched to a manufacturing unit geared toward local and regional *swadeshi* enterprises. As Satish Mukherjee, the superintendent of the BNC observed, "the combination of practical teaching and a sort of factory work on a small scale," was a "unique feature of this institution" and the first experiment along these lines in colonial India (70). The productivist logic of such experiments informed the juxtaposition of *swadeshi* products of the BNC workshop—scientific technical instruments, chemical and medical lab tools—alongside British commodities at various public exhibitions. A January 1908 article from the British-run Calcutta newspaper the *Statesman* reluctantly observed that "side by side with the Swadeshi products were specimens of English manufacture, and the difference was very slight and sometimes indeed the balance lay with the Indian" (quoted at 70). National education was rapidly becoming, in the words of one admiring *swadeshi* activist, "a sort of all-India commodity" (76). The ideological and disciplinary domain of educational institutions had passed by the turn of the century, particularly in Bengal, from a colonial to a national developmentalist project.

Among the most extraordinary products of Bengal National College was Narendranath Bhattacharya (1887–1954), who, under the assumed name of Manabendra Nath Roy (acquired in Palo Alto, Calif.), became a central Marxist theorist and revolutionary of the twentieth century. The son of an impoverished Brahmin village schoolteacher, Roy was expelled at age eighteen, in 1905, from Harinabhi Anglo-Sanskrit School for organizing a *swadeshi* rally. He became a prominent figure in the so-called terrorist underground movement from 1907 onward, while studying at the newly instituted Bengal National College and later at the Bengal Technical Institute, an education he financed by running a tea stand on Clive Street, Calcutta. Facing certain imprisonment for various activities (he led the first officially categorized "political robbery" in 1907 as well as others in 1909 and 1915), he fled colonial India in 1915 and embarked on an anticipated short mission to acquire funds and ammunition from Germany and Japan for the underground *swadeshi*-inspired movement.[20] He did not return until 1930. During those intervening decades, he established the Communist Party of Mexico in 1919 (he first read Marx at the New York Public Library in 1917), and the Community Party of India in 1920 (established in Tashkent). He also authored more than 130 works, including *An Indian Communist Manifesto* (1920), the famous *Supplementary Thesis* in response to Lenin's *Theses on the National and Colonial Question* (1920), and *Revolution and Counter-Revolution in China* (1930). And he served on the executive committee and presidium of the Comintern in various capacities, including chairman of the Eastern Commission and official emissary to China in 1927, until a final, bitter break with the Comintern in 1929.

In numerous works, Roy theorized nationalism as a historically specific misrecognition, as a chimerical overcoming, of the structurally engendered problem of class inequalities and global capitalism. In the specific instance of Indian nationalism, he argued that it substituted a structural critique of capitalism for a restorative civilizational project that refused to recognize that "post-British India cannot and will not become pre-British India."[21] Its social logic necessarily entailed, for Roy, the negation of the radical impulse rooted in popular (worker and peasant) struggles in favor of a reactionary absolutization of an indeterminate past. During his long imprisonment in a colonial prison in the 1930s, Roy elaborated a distinctive materialist philosophy of "radical humanism" that departed from the increasingly sclerotic character of orthodox Marxism. It resonated with and drew from not only the works of such heterodox Marxists as Ernst Bloch, Georg Lukács, and Antonio Gramsci but from the utopian vision of autonomy authored by *swadeshi* activists at the turn of the century. Indeed, Roy upheld the lived experience of the *swadeshi* movement as the animating force field of his life's work.

> When, as a schoolboy of fifteen, I began my political life, which may end in nothing, I wanted to be free. Independence, complete and absolute, is a new-fangled idea. The old-fashioned revolutionaries thought in terms of freedom. In those days, we had not read Marx. We did not know about the existence of the proletariat. Still, many spent their lives in jail and went to the gallows. There was no proletariat to propel them.

They were not conscious of class struggle. They did not have the dream of Communism. . . . I began my political life with that spirit, and I still draw my inspiration rather from that spirit than from the three volumes of *Capital* or three-hundred volumes by the Marxists.[22]

And so the experiential and conceptual coordinates of freedom as articulated by the *swadeshi* movement continued to hold sway for a former radical nationalist turned Marxist revolutionary on a global scale.

PURSUING AUTONOMY: *SWADESHI* BHARAT

Swadeshi practices such as the boycott of British products, the fostering of indigenous capital and enterprise, the valorization of a productive, self-sacrificing laboring subject as the normative national, the institution of a range of nationalist cultural and social organizations, and the like sought to secure the *autonomy* of the imagined national space of Bharat. Within the more abstract argot of nationalist political economy, autonomy had signaled a modern developmentalist project grounded in conceptions of the nation as the natural scale of capital accumulation. The meaning of autonomy, as recast by *swadeshi* activists and intellectuals, came to occupy a more expansive semantic and social field. Autonomy entailed the actualization in everyday practices of the presumed organic character of indigenous practices, institutions, and categories of understanding. As such, it implied a doubled critique of both the differentiating logic of colonial practices and the negative freedom endorsed by classical liberalism that, according to *swadeshi* activists, an earlier generation of Congress leaders had uncritically accepted.

Although *swadeshi* activists reiterated the critique of colonial economic policies elaborated by the first generation of Congress leaders, they condemned the reformist and constitutional program of the INC. As the institutional expression of an "old patriotism" still mired in an "ardent admiration for Europe," the Congress had continued to regard "bondage" as a "school of freedom."[23] Building on the nationalist critique of classical political economy, *swadeshi* activists explicitly thematized the limits of one of its constitutive expressions, namely, classical liberalism. In opposition to the formalistic and negative ideal of freedom of classical liberalism rooted in a self-regulating market and isolated monads, *swadeshi* activists sought to recover what Bipin Pal called the "specific law of our own National Being" grounded in "our social and political philosophy." The "fundamental ideals of Indian nationalism" were based, in this view, in an organic social cement of "association, not isolation; cooperation, not competition; . . . duty and not right."[24] More crucially, *swaraj*, as "the accepted political ideal of the Indian nationalists," did not, according to Pal, "connote the same thing as what is called 'independence' in English" (85). Rather the "correct rendering of *swaraj*" was "autonomy and not independence," for "autonomy is a positive, while independence is a negative concept" (86). Against the intermonadic relations envisioned by classical liberalism, *swadeshi* activists sought to realize a strong form of autonomy founded on the dialectical unity of various isolated freedoms (social and individual, spiritual and material) in a perceived organic social formation.

The central task concerned concretizing, in the here and now, what Tagore, the poet-philosopher of the movement in its initial phase, called a *swadeshi samaj*, or an autonomous indigenous society constituted through collective and individual practices of self-reliance, self-sufficiency, and sacrifice. In a famous July 1904 public address, "Our *Swadeshi Samaj*," Tagore elaborated the lineaments of an ethics of indigeneity that shaped the everyday politics of the *swadeshi* movement as well as subsequent Gandhian ideologies and strategies of mobilization. Key elements of this vision included the organization of cooperative enterprises, the critique of consumption practices, the emphasis on labor practices oriented toward the accumulation of spiritual and material *shakti* (power), the forging of rural grass-roots development projects, and the institution of mass education schemes through received folk media (the example of Armenian nationalists in Russia was seen as exemplary in this regard). Although Tagore would later become one of the most strident critics of nationalism and especially abjure the exclusionary Hindu underpinnings of dominant nationalism, there was in this early moment no hesitation about proclaiming that the "common ground" for the envisioned *swadeshi samaj* would "not be un-Hindu, it will be more especially Hindu."[25] It was precisely the perceived humanist kernel of Hinduism that would "unite us in concrete relations with this *Bharatvarsha* of ours, the resort of our gods, the retreat of our *rishis* [Hindu sages], the motherland of our ancestors" (21). The establishment of early colonial rule had, he noted, coincided with the protracted loss of Bharat's former glory marked by a resistance to novelty, the substitution of a "womanish *shakti* of thrift and conservation" for a "masculine adventurous curiosity," and a pervasive succumbing to a "policy of funk" (29, 31). Tagore observed: "At his onslaught [the Britisher] the defensive barriers of our crouching, run-away *samaj* [society] began to give way in places, and through the gaps the Outside, in dread of which we had shrunk into ourselves, came hurtling in upon us. Now who shall thrust it back? With this breaking down of our enclosure we discovered two things — how wonderfully strong we had been, how miserably weak we have become" (30). Collective acts of sacrifice, likened to the "vast *Yajnas*" (Vedic ritual sacrifices) of "old days," would work as a national barricade against the "fatal embrace" of colonial domination that had "introduced its tentacles through and through our social fabric, from our educational institutions to the shops dealing with our daily necessities" (19, 23). The adoption of renunciatory practices conjoined with a productivist ethic would constitute the specifically *swadeshi* strategy for national material and spiritual accumulation. Such efforts would gather the fragmented energies of what had become a "broken-up *samaj*" and unleash the "undying *shakti* of *Bharat*" (20, 32).

The *swadeshi* movement did not represent a retreat from or of the political. It contested both narrow institutional understanding of politics and the formalistic conception of rights enshrined in classical liberalism and permanently deferred in a colonial state. What it rejected outright was the relegation of the political to the "speechifying" sanctified precincts of the INC, what Tagore called the "book-learned . . . watch-and-chain-bedecked assembly" (19). It was precisely because the colonial state had no organic affiliation with indigenous society that attempts to seek transformations in state policy only entailed the successive loss of autonomy — "the government in our country — the *Sarkar* has no relations with our social organizations — the *Samaj;* so that whatever we may seek from the former must be paid for out of our freedom" (6). The reformist, state-centered orientation of institutional nationalism simply affirmed the intimacy between a neglect of the inner logic of indigenous institutions and the condition of bondage. For as Tagore suggested, "have we not signed away our birthright to the white man — are not our very tastes put for sale in his shops?" (8). The making of a *swadeshi samaj* necessitated, in other words, delimiting what Etienne Balibar, following Fichte, calls the "the internal borders of freedom" as necessary preparatory work, as the enabling "condition of the liberation of the external borders."[26] *Swadeshi samaj* was envisioned as at once a space of refuge from an increasingly interventionist colonial state, a site of resistance to the further loss of the distinctive destiny, the "God-given function of India," and a space for redeeming the inner logic of indigenous institutions and practices.[27] The practical activity of establishing substantive autonomy — the continual performance of the unique logic of indigenous practices, categories, and institutions — required nothing more, and nothing less, than becoming "our true selves, consciously, actively and with our full strength *(shakti)*" (31). The relationship between the national self and the larger national whole was, in this reckoning, one of deep intimacy, direct immediacy, and reciprocal inherence. Nationals bore within themselves the organic whole of the imagined community, and individual actions and dispositions shaped, in turn, the larger community.

One of the most commonly invoked examples of an organic national society and economy within *swadeshi* discourse was Japan. Within the geopolitical imaginary of *swadeshi,* Japan occupied, especially after its victory over Russia in 1905, a central normative significance. It figured prominently — in economic, philosophical, and literary texts, folk songs and popular discourse — as an example of a nation that had achieved capitalist development without surrendering its unique cultural essence and autonomy. Tagore held up Japan as an archetypical instance of a nation that had resisted the totalizing sway of a formal, instrumental rationality that ceaselessly converted the other into the same, transformed organic relations into a mechanical social cement, and attenuated the individual into "a machine, a tool, for the furtherance of some interest." Although Japan's victory had been waged through the "mechanical" means of war, its nationals had not become "parts of a machine," for "every Japanese solider was something more than a machine . . . they all remained related to their Mikado and their country in a reverential self-dedication" (16). Japan's "efficient modern war" did not translate into a battlefield peopled by automatons blindly fulfilling an imposed logic and going to "their death like pawns moved by an unknown player." The instrumental, life-destroying, and mechanical orientation of an alien and alienating colonial modernity could only be overcome through a willed embrace of the animating sociocultural spirit common to both Japan and Bharat, namely, that of "sacrifice" and "self-immolation" (17).

In his post-*swadeshi* internationalist humanist incarnation, Tagore would rethink this fantastic misrecognition of Japan's imperial war machine and emergent fascist ideologies of a homogeneous national-social body. During his travels to Southeast Asia, China, Japan, and the United States in 1916–17, he emphasized the complex imbrication of self-understood anti-hegemonic nationalisms within the alienating structures of modernity. Driven by a "desire to turn themselves into a machine of power" in a world-historical context defined by the proliferation of "national carnivals of materialism," Japan was for the post-*swadeshi* Tagore one more instance of the disastrous "logic of the Nation."[28] Instead of the embodiment of organic solidarity or genuine autonomy, Japanese society stood for an "all-pervading mental slavery" manifest in the "voluntary submission of the whole people" to the "clipping of their freedom by their government" (39, 141). In a controversial public address in Tokyo, he argued that the hegemonic aspirations of the Japanese national-imperial project rested on a doubled conflation of modernization (capitalist development) with modernism and Europe:

> I must warn . . . that modernizing is a mere affectation of modernism, just as affectation of poesy is poetizing. It is nothing but mimicry, only affectation is louder than the original, and it is too literal. . . . Modernism is not in the dress of the Europeans; or in the hideous structures where their children are interned when they take their lessons; or in the square houses with flat straight wall-surfaces, pierced with parallel lines of windows, where these people are caged in their lifetime . . . these are not modern, but merely European. True modernism . . . is independence of thought and action, not tutelage under European schoolmasters. (93–94)

Although Japanese newspapers praised the "poetic qualities" of this address, they also relegated it, as Tagore ruefully observed, to the "poetry of a defeated people" (53). The self-conscious celebration of the subject-position of those without a nation, the valorization of the special destiny of "we of no nations of the world," was, unlike the *swadeshi samaj* address of 1904, explicitly antinationalist. From this standpoint, the nation form was both an expression and product of the abstract, impersonal structure of capitalist modernity that everywhere "turned souls into commodities and life into compartments, which, with its iron claws, scratches out the heart of the world and knows not what it has done" (60). The proliferation of the ideologies, institutions, and practices of the nation form, the "advent" of more "people into the arena of nationality," only increased the numbers of "bond-slaves" of a globe-spanning and mechanistic capitalist modernity (54, 60).

Tagore's critique of the exclusionary "civilization of power" instantiated in the nation form carried a distinctively utopian imprimatur (33). This utopian impulse, developed during the *swadeshi* era, informed his condemnation of the increasingly abstract, scientific, and systematic forms of governance in both national and colonial contexts that ignored the fact that "we, who are governed, are not a mere abstraction" (24). The "national machinery of commerce and politics" was only capable of turning out "neatly compressed bales of humanity which have their use and high market value," but which "savoring of gigantic manufacture" would forever ensnare "personal humanity" into "iron hoops" (16–17). In this regard, Tagore's early *swadeshi* formulations of autonomy and his subsequent antinationalist liberal humanism were both steeped in a resolutely utopian understanding of collec-

tive and individual practices of autonomy. However, the politics of autonomy as enshrined in dominant *swadeshi* practice and discourse, from which
Tagore decisively broke by 1907, was more firmly rooted within an
avowedly nativist and nationalist episteme.

The pursuit of autonomy was, for swadeshists, both an expression and a
product of the fact that Bharat was a "distinct" and "individual social organism" in relation to other formally similar national spaces in a global
grid.[29] Bipin Pal's claim that "the nation is not a mere collection of individuals" but an "organism" with an "end unto itself" expressed the consolidation
of territorial nativist and organicist conceptions of Bharat.[30] Expressing a
key ideological motif of *swadeshi*, Pal, akin to Aurobindo Ghose, figured the
nation as an organic entity against the secular temporality that underwrote
the "merely civic" vocation of "Western nationalism."[31] Consider, for instance, the following statement:

> Every object is a thought of God — materialized; every man is the Spirit
> of God — incarnated. So is every nation the manifestation and revela-
> tion of a Divine Ideal. In a nation, the individuals composing it stand in
> an organic relation to one another and to the whole of which they are
> limbs and organs. . . . An organism is logically prior to the organs. . . .
> Individuals are born, individuals die, — but the nation liveth for ever.
> The Deity, the divine-Ideal, the Logos of God, which *Bande Mataram*
> [hail to the motherland] reveals, is eternal.[32]

Such organicist visions of nationhood derived their affective force from a
specific conception of Hinduism as "more than a mere system of theology
and ethics" (106). As the perceived substance of indigenous practices and
institutions, Hinduism had "developed directly into a unique universality"
that was at once "national and universal" (106–7). For *swadeshi* intellectuals, the humanism of Hinduism derived from its notion of imminent divinity
insofar as "man is made not out of the image, not in the image, but of the
substance of the Maker" (147). Building upon a distinctive philosophical-
religious tradition that rejected the distinction between the concrete and
abstract universal (the *Apara* or *Saguna* versus *Para* or *Nirguna Brahmin* or
Godhead), Pal configured the relationship between the self and the national
whole as an ontological unity. In the "true organic conception of the whole,
while actually it is revealed through its parts, logically it is equally implied,
not partially but fully, in each one of these parts . . . this is the universal
character of all organic wholes."[33] Swadeshists transposed a specific Hindu
religious-philosophical schema — one that emphasized the originary unity of

organic wholes and apparently discrete parts—onto the terrain of everyday political contention. They thus provided explicit philosophical-religious
content to popular nativist understandings, condensed in conceptions of
India as Bharat, of the relationship between nation, territory, history, and
personhood.

The ideal of autonomy and the preconditions for its realization were no
different, in this view, from the "longing for salvation" contained in the
Vedantic notion of *mumukshutwa*. The desire for autonomy, likened to *mumukshutwa* by both Pal and Ghose, hinged on not only the objective "existence of bondage" but also a subjective "keen sense of it."[34] The first step
toward "civic and spiritual salvation" entailed grasping that, just as in "true
Vedantic culture," the "whole" did not negate the apparent diversity of the
"phenomenal world" but rather was dialectically entwined within it. In this
view, the problem of "British sovereignty" could not be tackled by "false and
fanciful abstractions" unmoored from the inner logic of an organic national
whole. Substantive autonomy demanded, on a subjective register, the "full
and uninterrupted consciousness" that the colonial regime was "foreign and
not national, and can never be so" (69). The apprehension of the "mayic"
or illusory sovereignty of the colonial regime required the interiorization
of the authentic reality and deeper structure of an organic national whole
expressive of and rooted within the perceived universality and humanism
of Hinduism. Autonomy in this strong sense, its conjoined political and
philosophical-religious meaning, would remain impossible until the generalization of a radical consciousness and the objective attainment of "a Free
State" constituted by "Free Citizens." Only then, Pal observed, "can we
recognize, can we actualize, can we objectify, can we bring it before ourselves, our own natural freedom. . . . it is in the life of a free citizen in a free
state wherein you realize that freedom of God, which is self-restraint, self-
regulation and self-determination for the purpose of self-realization" (147).
The pursuit of substantive autonomy, the forging of a *swadeshi samaj*, demanded the transformation of socioeconomic and cultural fields, categories
of perception, and practices of the self in accord with an organic national
whole and on the terrain of the everyday.

By the last third of the nineteenth century, the iconic figure of Bharat
Mata had become the visual embodiment of the autonomy of the imagined
nation and the exemplar of national yearnings for authentic cultural artifacts and practices seemingly exempt from colonial mediation. During the
swadeshi era, Bharat Mata became a ubiquitous figurative presence: songs,
novels, visual representations (from popular *bazaar* images to the famous
painting of Bharat Mata by Abanindranath Tagore), and collective prac-

tices testify to the progressive Hinduization and feminization of the imagined body politic.[35] Commodities produced within the sacred space of Bharat Mata were endowed with a fetish value. Conceived as lying outside the orbit of the alienating and racially discriminatory sphere of colonial exchange, home manufactures were invested with a transcendental national significance. In particular, handlooms became the concrete, material symbols of the imagined simplicity and purity of village life, of folklore, of a distinctive Indian tradition, of forms of life opposed to and outside of the modern colonial era. *Swadeshi* both exalted an absolute space of national belonging and expressed a mythical sense of time, of mythic national origins and permanence.

It also mapped onto the self-understood universality of elite national imaginings the competing universality of everyday Hindu devotional practices. *Swadeshi* folk songs, for instance, exhorted nationals to work against an exploitative and alien colonial regime from the standpoint of an organic and concrete vision of national space as Bharat Mata. These songs index the ways in which the world market and the space it encompassed came to be felt as a palpable presence in everyday life. The following popular song from the 1870s is exemplary:

> The weaver and the blacksmith are crying day and night.
> They cannot find their food by plying their trade.
> Even threads and needles come from distant shores.
> Even matchsticks are not produced in the country.
> Whether in dressing themselves or producing their domestic utensils
> or even in lighting their oil-lamps . . .
> In nothing are the people independent of the foreign master . . .
> Swarms of locust from a distant island coming to these shores
> have eaten up all its solid grains leaving only the chaff for the
> starving children of the soil.[36]

Among the most famous of the folk songs from the turn of the century was the following:

> We may be poor, we may be small,
> But we are a nation of seven crores [seventy million].
> . . . .
> Defend your homes, protect your shops,
> Don't let the grain from our barns be looted abroad.
> We will eat our own coarse grain and wear the rough, home-spun cloth,

What do we care for lavender and imported trinkets?
Foreigners drain away our mother's [Bharat Mata's] milk,
Will we simply stand and watch? [37]

Such folks songs articulated, in a different timbre, Tagore's warning that just as the "European mills are killing our handicrafts, so is the all pervading machinery of an alien Government destroying our simple old village organization." [38] Under the combined force of the distended geographies of the world market and the differentiating effects of colonial practices — the intensified immiseration of a subsistence peasantry, devastating famines, high inflation, and record levels of peasant indebtedness — the very "soil" of the nation had "dried up." As a consequence, the "village community, the mother of nations" was threatened with extinction because its "life-giving institutions" lay "uprooted and . . . floating" like "dead wood logs down the stream of time" (70).

Perhaps the most foundational category within the popular *swadeshi* imaginary was that of Bharat Mata — the very locus of a determinate slide from nation to Hindu deity. Among the most enduring instantiations of this slippage was Bankim Chandra Chattopadhyay's (1838–94) celebrated hymn "Bande Mataram" (Hail to the Motherland), composed initially as a song in 1875. The song — later inserted into his famous novel *Anandmath,* which bristled with an anti-Muslim ideology — became *the* slogan at mass nationalist rallies, the so-called terrorist underground societies that advocated direct violent action and were spawned by the movement. It retains, in the contemporary period, the dubious status of the anthem of the violent and aggressive Hindu nationalist movement.

The song deifies national territorial space as the Hindu goddess Durga, the slayer of demons and the female instantiation of Shiva, the lord of destruction in the Hindu pantheon. The song begins by recounting the nurturing bounty of the motherland, the space of an original fullness, which is successively transfigured into the image of Durga and the destructive, castrating goddess Kali (also a manifestation of Durga), who exhorts the several million armed hands of her progeny to enrich her power and by extension their own. [39] This image of the motherland — which condenses a temporal movement from the glorious mother of an ancient past, the dispossessed mother of the present, and the triumphant, all-conquering mother of the future — was mobilized against both the colonial state and Muslims. By 1908, the colonial government declared the proclamation of the slogan — *Bande Mataram* — illegal in public spaces. [40] In certain instances, houses inscribed with the slogan were pulled down, and struggles ensued about whether shouting the slogan from within houses, schools, and institutional sites constituted a violation of this draconian law. Such legislation, however, did not stem the tide of practices both within and outside colonial India that sought to render visible, against the abstraction of colonial state space, an organic, concrete national space.[41]

The highly ritualized performances that accompanied vows to the nation in numerous cities and villages exemplify the way the notion of a common economic collective was rendered both palpable and fundamentally Hindu. These vows were commonly enacted by ceremonial bathing in the Ganges followed by the donning of locally produced cloth and the tying of symbolic braids or *rakhis* (which signify kinship relations among Hindus) to signal the unbroken unity of the national collective forged through the making of a productive national laboring body and the consumption of indigenously produced goods. The transposition of one imaginary of kinship onto the categorical form of the nation symbolically coded the bodies of nationals as instantiations of Bharat Mata. The religious idiom of many collective performances of *swadeshi* vows by diverse groups (cobblers, artisans, *dhobis*, weavers, students) included swearing upon a sword or a copy of the Gita, and reciting Sanskrit mantras. In the case of the famous *anushilan* societies (which combined gymnastic training with religious instruction) and underground "terrorist" cells of Bengal, pledges were enacted upon a map of Bharat Mata in a complex structure of primary *(adya)* and final *(antya)* vows.[42] The imagined national space and economy of Bharat became, through such collective practices, a site for the transmutation of the raw, accidental fatalities of everyday life into the transcendent solidarity of an organically constituted nation.

The interpenetration of an anticolonial political-economic project with quotidian devotional practices was the very signature of *swadeshi* repertoires of contention. Colonial district officials in Agra and Allahabad in 1908 and 1909, for instance, kept a stringent check on what were seen as "clear innovations" in everyday religious practice that amounted to "more or less deliberate attempts to foster seditious and disloyal feelings." The focus of such anxieties was the novel form of *Ramlila* (part of the annual Hindu festival based on the epic Ramayana) processions in Agra and Allahabad that juxtaposed Hindu deities with nationalist figures (Rani of Jhansi, Lokmanya Tilak, and Aurobindo Ghose) and superimposed images of female deities on the map of colonial India to figure Bharat Mata. Such figurative and cartographic representations of Bharat Mata were placed on a platform and paraded through the streets accompanied by shouts of "Bande Mataram" and "Bharat Mata ki jai."[43] National imaginings were expressed as well by the use of Hindu iconography on the coins and medals circulated in various provinces that were variously used as legal tender in *swadeshi* shops and enterprises, as ornaments, as "charm lockets for success," as prizes at schools, and as national badges. The front of some of these coins was inscribed with the words *swadeshi nishka* (pure gold), a figure of Lakshmi (the Hindu goddess of wealth), and the phrase *Tat-sat Bharat* (That is true, India). On the back of the coins, the year according to the Hindu calendar was recorded (*Kali yuga* 5006). Some of the most commonly distributed medals were stamped on the front with the nationalist slogan *Bande Mataram* and on the back with a figure of Lakshmi, along with a prayer for national wealth and prosperity.[44] The emergence of *swadeshi* currency in an era of high inflation, combined with the depreciating value of state fiduciary money or the silver-standard rupee, expressed the desire to concretize an authentic sphere of everyday exchange exempt from the relations of unequal exchange that defined colonial state space.

Sumit Sarkar and Ranajit Guha have provided different diagnoses of the "failure" of the *swadeshi* movement. For Sarkar, the constitutive limits of the movement lay in its inability to translate the urban and middle-class provenance of its animating "economic interests" into a popular agrarian politics.[45] Ranajit Guha has emphasized the predominance of coercion over consent in *swadeshi* strategies of mobilization as a failure of ethical-political leadership.[46] Methods of ostracism associated with the abrogation of Hindu caste prohibitions and rituals, for instance, were pervasively deployed against those violating the socioeconomic sanctity of the nation (108–16). The coercive, violent aspect of *swadeshi* practices was evident in the use of caste excommunication, the withdrawal of ritual services (not just by priests but also by doctors, lawyers, barbers, and washermen), the boycott of wedding and funeral ceremonies, as well as physical intimidation. These measures were directed against those either "serving the alien regime as police officials, prosecuting lawyers, crown witnesses, etc., or by failing — as landlords — to ban the sale of foreign goods within their estates, as grocers — to stop retailing Liverpool salt. Among the victims, too, were those who could be said to have transgressed the new *acara* [discipline] by refusing to go through the ritual of oath-taking in support of *Swadeshi* or wear *rakhi* on their wrists as a token of solidarity" (112). *Swadeshi* thus reactivated a "traditional" disciplinary idiom linked to Hindu religious doctrines and sanctions in an effort to actualize substantive autonomy on the scale of both the imagined nation and everyday practices. There is indeed considerable irony in the fact that *swadeshi*'s vision of the spread of autonomy and self-regulation into the hands of what Bipin Pal called a "composite Indian com-

munity" was pursued through coercive and violent measures that disproportionately targeted subaltern social classes.[47] Yet it is also impossible to
account for this central tension — shaped by but not reducible to the class
provenance of the movement's leadership or a failure of ethical-political
leadership as such — without exploring the ideological contours of territorial
nativist visions of nationhood and the global context of their emergence.

THE "IDOLATRY OF GEOGRAPHY": PUTTING ABSTRACTIONS IN PLACE

The idealist and organicist predicates of *swadeshi* visions of nationhood were,
despite their own self-presentation, intelligible products of a specific historical conjuncture and geopolitical field. The decades between the late 1870s
and 1914 marked the unprecedented dissemination of nationalist movements in both colonized and imperial-national contexts in Europe, South
Asia, and East Asia. These nationalist movements were distinguished by
widely shared particularistic and organic conceptions of nationhood,
evinced in the novel emphasis placed on a common territory, language, ethnicity, and race as the essential markers of nationhood. Late-nineteenth and
early-twentieth-century nationalisms discursively converged around an in-
vocation of an already existent, internally homogenous, and externally distinctive nation; widely shared organic understandings of the relationship
between people, history, territory, and state; and a profoundly statist orientation that reflected the progressive conjoining of the link between nationhood and statehood. These discursive elements fueled and expressed a
transnational politics of closure that found concrete expression in a range of
practices. These included the stress placed on cultural and linguistic purity;
the emergence of protectionist economic policies and immigration controls
in Europe, America, and Japan; the rise of mass mobilization campaigns in
colonial India and China that sought to regulate practices of consumption
and production as part of a larger effort to produce an autonomous national
space; and the popularization and attempted naturalization of imperial ideologies in Europe, North America, and Japan. The growing "intertextual-
ity" or discursive overlap between diverse nationalist movements was expressive of, and rooted within, a common historical conjuncture and
transnational field. The global field of the early twentieth century was
marked by the emergence of a transposable, dynamic, and durable nation
form in conjunction with the complex re- and de-territorialization of social
relations wrought by colonial and capitalist expansion.[48]

It was during the *swadeshi* era that radical nationalists recast the notion of

Bharat Mata in an explicitly idealist philosophical framework, one whose underlying epistemology of comparison bears an uncanny resemblance to contemporary theorizations of difference. Although conceptions of Bharat Mata in popular geohistorical discourse from the 1870s onward had borne an unmarked relationship to everyday Hindu idioms and devotional practices, *swadeshi* activists such as Bipin Pal and Aurobindo Ghose self-consciously elaborated its meaning in idealizing and idealist terms, welding together upper-caste Hindu philosophical traditions of thought and popular Shakta devotional practices.[49] Within the terms of this high philosophical nativist discourse, Bharat Mata was represented as an archaic spiritual essence, a transcendent "regulative Idea of the universe," expressive of the universality of Hinduism and Indian nationhood.[50] Despite conceding the formal similarity between notions of Bharat Mata, contemporary German nationalist notions of the Fatherland, and older European notions of *patrie,* Bipin Pal insisted that the "nation as mother" as "applied to India by its children" was radically distinct in substance and could not therefore be grasped with reference to European concepts and histories. What distinguished the Indian concept of nation-as-mother from apparently similar European formations was that it "had no metaphor behind it" (83). It was not a "mere idea or fancy," nor could it be reduced to the "mere civic sentiment" that underwrote what he called the "secular patriotism of Europe" (84, 108). Yet, despite this strong assertion of radical difference, Pal invoked Mazzini's (whose works were widely taught in *swadeshi* curriculum) definition of nationality as the "individuality of peoples" to suggest a singular self-conscious being or personality particular to every national formation (94). In other words, a singular self-conscious being marks out "different humans units from one another," and on a global scale, "this differentiation between the collective life and character of different social units constitutes the very soul and essence of the nation idea."[51] The "mother" in *motherland* was a "distinct personality" in the specifically Hegelian sense of a conscious, self-mediating Spirit that evolves through a succession of its temporal forms toward absolute knowledge of itself and which was conceived by "the Hindu . . . [as] behind his own history and evolution."[52] As a lived actuality rather than a conceptual abstraction, Bharat Mata was at once a "physical and spiritual, geographical and social" entity, and what is more, the "cult of the Mother among us . . . our love of the land and people" was an "organic part of our ideal of the love of God" (108).

The concept of Bharat Mata was rooted, according to Pal, within the "old universal" principles constitutive of all systems of Hindu-Brahminical philosophical thought: the structuring dynamic of *purusha* (the principle of change coded as a masculine essence) and *prakriti* (the principle of permanence coded as feminized nature or earth) (87, 88). The relationship between these two principles was, for Pal, that of a fundamental unity of opposites that structured in common the otherwise distinct Vedantic, Vaishnava, and Shaivite traditions. The conception of mother "associated with our geographical habitat," that is, the "personality behind [Hindu] history and evolution," represented *prakriti* as *shakti* (primordial, universal power) (88). Drawing a parallel between Hegel's conception of the unfolding of reason as one in which "the self separates itself from itself to return to itself to be itself," Pal suggests that Bharat Mata, the embodiment of *prakriti*, was "that through which the Divine realizes Himself in His Own Being" (89). Pal transposed Hegel's idea of the Absolute as the subject-object of history into nation-as-mother, which was identified as the "dynamic element in our ethical consciousness . . . as providence in history . . . as that which works out different changes through which the universe is evolving itself. . . . It is Raciality in the history and evolution of races. It is the spirit of Nationality in national life and evolution" (92).

Pal insisted that the conception of Bharat Mata was not, as British colonial ideology averred, a "rank superstition" or "sinister fanaticism" (106–7). Nor was it an instance of what Hegel called a "Pure Being," equivalent to a "Pure Nothing," which severed from the particular remains an empty abstraction. Quite the converse; Bharat Mata embodied, for Pal, the fact that the "universal cannot exist without the particular." Unlike the "worldly, merely political aspirations" of European nationalism that could not grasp the unity of the universal and the particular and consequently never attain "the dignity of a philosophy, or the sanctity of religion," the Indian concept of nation-as-mother was a lived actuality, one that was at once universal and particular, abstract and concrete.[53] More crucially, it was a constitutive element of the phenomenology of Hinduism-as-lived, of the performative logic of everyday Hindu devotional practices. Tied to the "peculiarly Hindu conception of the Motherhood of God," it was continually enacted in the "concrete experiences of motherhood in our own mothers first, dimly, as through a glass, and next in the motherhood of our own wives in which we ourselves also so largely participate, — directly and almost face to face — that we can see and seize the Motherhood of God."[54] Given this dense philosophical-religious referential context (one that was resolutely Brahminical and patriarchal), it was not surprising, Pal argued, that "outsiders" who know Bharat Mata only as India could only apprehend her as "a mere bit of earth . . . as only a geographical expression" (106). It was "absolutely impossible for the European or American to clearly understand . . . this strange idealization of our land . . . the Cult of the Mother among us" (107). Pal acknowledged the novelty of the constellation of nation and mother, the fact that it was only in recent decades that "all these old and traditional gods and goddesses who had lost their hold upon the modern educated mind have been reinstalled with a new historic and nationalist interpretations in the thoughts and sentiments of the people" (105). Yet he nonetheless presented his project as the recovery of the original pure meaning of Bharat Mata.

In a move paradigmatic of modern idealist and nativist projects that slide from a critique of the present to a promised escape from history as such, Pal sought to endow the concept of Bharat Mata with a transcendent meaning by retrieving its original and, therefore, final reference. The generalization of Bharat Mata in repertoires of mass mobilization and everyday cultural landscapes had, he argued, resulted in the denudation of its original meaning as the "idealization and spiritualization of the collective life and functions of our society . . . as the apotheosis of our Race-Spirit and National Organism." Against this debasement of Bharat Mata, born of the "imitation of foreign ideas and ideals" and the "uncritical study of European histories and concepts," Pal strained to redeem its auratic value (109). He attempted to secure for his fellow nationals — especially the constituency of "modern educated" Hindu middle classes, whom colonialism had severed from the "ancient realities of their language and literature"—the ultimate guarantee of the organic, the primal, the originary (83). The semantic privilege accorded to original and pure meanings was part of the same ideological force field that posited Hindus as originary core nationals. Yet such an attempt only reinforced the status of Bharat Mata as exemplary of "frozen emanations," namely, words "that are sacred without sacred content."[55] For one of the constitutive contradictions of the "jargon of authenticity" and other cognate projects of modernist reenchantment is that they gather force precisely with the disintegration of auratic values and meanings in everyday life. A spectacular instance of this was Gandhi's inauguration of the Bharat Mata temple in the ancient pilgrimage city of Benares, United Provinces, in 1936 (in 1983, Hindu nationalist groups constructed another Bharat Mata temple in Haridwar, UP). Unlike the familiar array of Hindu deities, the inner sanctum of this temple contains a large relief map of India drawn to scale and carved in marble. What Rabindranath Tagore came to condemn as the nationalist "idolatry of geography" has few more concrete expressions than the inner sanctum of the Bharat Mata temple.[56]

Swadeshi's vision of a territorially delimited and organically constituted national space and economy was part of the project of producing a homogenous and singular nationality. However, the specifically upper-caste Hindu categories that oriented *swadeshi* practices of mass mobilization and the territorial nativist epistemology within which they were embedded were shot through with internal hierarchies and exclusions. Although all existing indigenous social groups that inhabited the imagined space of Bharat comprised the common economic collective and were deemed nationals, they were not understood as national in the same fashion and degree.

The quixotic quest for authenticity and purity resulted in the marginalization of particular social groups whose alleged foreignness was set up as signs of exteriority. This conceptualization informs, for instance, the way the boycott of foreign commodities was applied to Muslim professionals, shop owners, and peasants, who often refused to patronize the higher-priced *swadeshi* shops out of economic compulsion. The equivalence posited between the consumption of "foreign" goods and ritual pollution and impurity was extended to the paradigmatic foreign body within the nation, that is, Muslims, and informed the series of violent "Hindu–Muslim" riots that occurred between 1906 and 1908.[57] The fact that *swadeshi* was opposed by dominant Muslim social and political groups for a complex of reasons — including the specific political economy of agrarian relations in Bengal structured in the form of a predominantly Muslim peasantry and a land-owning Hindu elite — represented the practical refutation of the universalistic self-understanding of dominant nationalism.

One of the elements of this opposition, which exceeded both the instrumental logic of colonial political engineering and a straightforward logic of class antagonism, was the profound anxiety invoked by *swadeshi*'s nativism. Mohamed Ali's 1912 editorial titled "The Communal Patriot" articulated the unacknowledged violent social logic of the nativist and idealist inflection of dominant Indian nationalism. Ali was a leading figure of the Muslim League, established in 1906 following the colonial policy of instituting separate electorates for Muslims and Hindus in limited, self-governing institutions. He later assumed a central role in the next mass mobilization phase of nationalism, that is, the *khilafat* movement (the movement in favor of the restoration of the caliphate in Turkey) in the 1920s. Among the deepest ironies of the Indian nationalist movement is that the *khilafat* movement, which was explicitly extraterritorial in its orientation and focus, was the only sustained campaign that brought together Hindus and Muslims on an equal footing. Ali's essay sought to show why the "patriotism in vogue" had taken the mutually exclusive forms of "Hindu or Muslim" conceptions of nationhood rather than a "truly Indian nationalism."[58] With specific reference to dominant Congress nationalism, he observed:

If the past could not offer a chart or a compass for the new voyage [of nationalism], clearly the fault lay with the Muslims who viciously strayed into *Bharat* and demolished its political features and landmarks. Instead of accepting philosophically what could not be undone, they began to quarrel with history. This attitude speedily produced amongst the majority of the educated Hindus the unfortunate habit of ignoring the one great reality of the Indian situation — the existence of about 70 million Muslims who had made a permanent home in this country. Whatever may be the inspiration of Hinduism as a religious creed, the educated Hindus made it a rallying symbol for political unity. The aspiration for self-government arrested all movements for social reform, which the early impulse toward liberalism had called forth amongst the educated Hindus. Past history was ransacked for new political formulas; and . . . "nationality" and "patriotism" began to be associated with Hinduism. The Hindu "communal patriot" sprang into existence with "*Swaraj*" as his war cry. He refuses to give quarter to the Muslims unless the latter quietly stifles his individuality and becomes completely Hinduized. He knows, of course, the use of the word like "India" and "Territorial Nationality" and they form an important part of his vocabulary. But the Muslims weigh on his consciousness, all the same, as a troublesome irrelevance; and he would thank his stars if some great exodus or even a geological cataclysm could give him riddance. . . . The spectacle of a go-ahead Hinduism, dreaming of self-government and playing with its ancient gods clad in the vesture of democracy, dazes the . . . Muslim. (76–77)

The figure of the "Muslim" was the permanent spectral presence within territorial nativist conceptions of nationhood. Generated from the margins of dominant Indian nationalism, Ali's articulation of the anxiety invoked by a "go-ahead Hinduism, . . . playing with its ancient gods clad in the vesture of democracy," elaborated the experiential tensions at the core of *swadeshi* nationalism: the fact that it proffered a powerful critique of the differentiating and discriminatory logic of colonial structures yet also produced new differentiations of its own. It poignantly expressed the effects of the interpellation of the figure "Muslim" as a problematic particularity against an imagined Hindu/Indian universality, as an "alien . . . a meddlesome freak . . . who wantonly interfered with the course of Indian History." An ideologically overburdened figure, the "Muslim" was held hostage to a historicist reading of the past that rendered him a "prisoner in the dock," one who was forever being "called upon to justify" all manner of "strange incidents . . . raked up from his long and eventful career" (77). Written more than ninety years ago, Ali's critique continues to haunt a contemporary political field defined by the intensification of violent nativist ideologies and one in which Indian Muslims are still held responsible for the perceived "original sin" of the 1947 partition of India.

In a 1913 essay titled "Pan Islamism," Bipin Pal, a self-understood secularist, observed that *swadeshi* nationalism had led to the "the foolish and suicidal ambition of once more re-establishing either a single Hindu state or a confederacy of Hindu states in India. Some people, thus, secretly interpreted *Swaraj* as Hindu *Raj*."[59] He even acknowledged that the "*swadeshi* propaganda developed a particularly pronounced Hindu ideal, which was naturally interpreted by some at least of the Mahomedan leaders in the country as a distinct and real menace to their own political future" (371). However, rather than attempting to render Muslim opposition intelligible in terms of the limits of dominant nationalism or the specific political economy of agrarian relations in Bengal, he merely asserted the dominant Indian nationalist position. He argued:

> Had they [Muslims] thrown themselves heart and soul into this new Nationalist Movement in India, this excessive Hindu emphasis might have been very easily removed. For then the *Swadeshi* movement would have developed into a purely economic and political propaganda fully representative of the composite Indian people. But they held aloof. . . . It was perhaps, well that it should have been so. For this Hindu nationalism will gradually help the evolution of a real Federal nationalism among us, which seems clearly to be the ideal-end and the ultimate aim of modern historic evolution in India. (371)

Pal's assertion that the category *Muslim,* unlike the category *Hindu,* connotes neither "geographical habitat" nor "political associations and obligations," underlay his identification of "Pan-Islamism" as the "common enemy of Indian nationalism in its truest and broadest sense as well as of the present government in India" (389). The rendering of the category *Muslim* as intrinsically supranational and supraterritorial expressed the workings of a territorial nativist vision of nationhood that asserted a privileged organic territorial relationship between Hindus and the imagined nation. More crucially, it bracketed the ways in which both Muslim nationalism and Pan-Islamism in late colonial India were concrete responses, as various historians have shown, to the threat posed by both colonial rule and dominant Indian nationalism.[60]

The ontological privilege accorded to Hinduism as a "unique universality" and the substantive essence of Indian nationhood was instantiated in a range of practices and institutions, and it fueled the Hinduization of Indianness and the Indianization of Hinduness.[61] Universalized thus, the specifically upper-caste Hindu content of dominant practices and discourses of nationhood remained unmarked, especially against the hallucinogenic visibility of the category *Muslim*. Paradoxically, territorial nativism enabled the persistent self-understanding of dominant Indian nationalism as secular. From this perspective, contrary to one of the most consistent claims of institutional nationalism and indeed contemporary secular discourse, the problem lay not with religious difference or religiously marked identities as such but with a nationalism that disavowed its own territorial nativism. *Swadeshi* marked a sharper crystallization of the conflictual construction of Hindu and Muslim identities and their hierarchical and differential placement within the imagined national space. Yet this ran directly counter to nationalist objectives, which were not to re-create the exclusions of colonialism but to forge an inclusive and autonomous society, not to allow doubt about the historical and social heterogeneity of the imagined national community but to exhibit its essential unity.

THE WELDING OF *SWADESHI* AND *SWARAJ*

Swadeshi was a paradigmatic instance of a territorial nativist vision of nationhood. As an encompassing "ideology of pure materials," its logic extended beyond the valorization of coarse homespun cloth and indigenous commodities.[62] For it attempted to render an ethic of indigeneity, with its idealist and nativist inflections, as a categorical imperative in diverse socioeconomic, cultural, philosophical, and aesthetic fields. In 1906, Surendranath Banerjea asserted: "we must be *swadeshi* in all things, *swadeshi* in our thoughts . . . in our educational methods and industrial development."[63] Elsewhere, he noted the ways the generalization of *swadeshi* practices and ideologies had created a

> strange atmosphere. . . . Young and old, rich and poor, literate and illiterate, all breathe it, and all are swayed and moved and even transported by the invisible influence that is felt. Reason halts; judgment is held in suspense; it is one mighty impulse that moves the heart of the commu-

nity and carries everything before it. An eminent doctor told me that . . .
a girl-patient of his, not more than six years old, cried out in her delir-
ium that she would not take any foreign medicine.[64]

Decades of resolutions and meetings of the Indian National Congress
denounced the constitutive disjuncture of history, territory, and people
under colonial rule. Expressed within the categories of high Brahminical
philosophical-religious discourse, the motif of a national epiphany dominated *swadeshi* discourse.

> The first thing in Vedantic culture is *Nithiavastha Vichara Vivaha,* "mine
> and not mine," the "self and the not self." This discrimination is the very
> first thing in Vedantic culture. The very first thing in the culture of the
> ideal of *Swaraj* [self-rule] is discrimination between the national self
> and that which is not the national self. The idea of *Swaraj* has been re-
> vealed to us only recently and why? Because for over a 100 years we
> never looked upon the British government as *Pararashtra* as a foreign
> government.[65]

Although the counterhegemonic aspirations of the *swadeshi* movement
were expressed in a specifically upper-caste and urban-centered (if not always urban-oriented) Hindu categorical idiom, it would be erroneous to
conceive nationalism's territorial nativism as produced within a hermetically
sealed-off cultural/spiritual domain or as an atavistic upsurge of tradition in
the face of an abstractly conceived process of modernization. Rather,
swadeshi's nativism was a multiply refracted expression of the perceived
threat of the abstract and differentiating logic of colonial structures and
global capitalist expansion. The expansive thrust of capitalism and the differentiating effects of colonial practices produced both movements of territorial closure as well as ongoing imperial expansion.

If *swadeshi* was particularist without (that is, in relation to the colonial
state and the world market), it understood itself as universalist within the
national space of Bharat. Within an absolute and sovereign space of nationness, inequalities and differences would, it was believed, disappear. Pitched
against what Pal identified as the "invasion of British capital" and what
Ranade saw as the "foreign merchants hand that now trafficks direct with
our producers in the remotest villages," the movement sought to establish an
autonomous national economic and cultural complex.[66] The spatial fetish-
ism of *swadeshi,* as manifest in the desire to constitute a continuous,
homogenous, sovereign space of nationness, only becomes intelligible with

reference to the simultaneous homogenization and differentiation of socio-economic relations constitutive of colonial state space.

The growing recognition of cultural and economic differentiation within colonial India spurred yearnings for an organic cultural and economic order. A central task for many nationalists at the turn of the century was to reconcile the internal unevenness that defined colonial space into a coherent national whole. V. G. Kale articulated the increasingly visible fact of spatiotemporal unevenness as a dominant fact of Indian political economy. He argued that while "certain spots in the country" were "completely Westernized . . . in several others a juxta-position of the Western and Eastern, the new and the old" was predominant.[67] Kale observed that an "Indian craftsman" from the ancient world of "Ashoka or Kalidasa," returning to the "scenes of his activities now," would be struck by the coexistence of apparently distinct social and organizational forms:

> He would indeed be astonished at the sight of the steam engine, the telegraph wire and the gigantic machinery working in a factory, but he would probably not fail to recognize the familiar handloom, wooden plough and bullock cart of this own day. . . . The incongruity of bullock carts laboriously threading their way through the crowded streets of Bombay with their small burden of a few cotton bales while motor cars and electric tram cars whizzed past them every moment . . . typifies the curious evolution that is going on in the country. . . . The most primitive forms of industry and organization may be witnessed side by side with the most up-to-date factories and machines. (124)

The spectacular coexistence of contending space-times, of distinct socioeconomic and cultural forms within a single formation, propelled the nativist and idealist inflection of late-nineteenth and early-twentieth-century nationalism. The problem of internal differentiation and fragmentation drove the nationalist imperative of forging an economically and culturally homogenous national space-time, it animated later Gandhian attempts to restore apparently organic socioeconomic and cultural forms, and it proffered a normative vocabulary for strong assertions of a distinct "Indian" modernity.

The search for an authentic national community and an absolute space of nationness (Bharat Mata) became more intense with the increasing relativization of particularistic communities and spaces. If colonial rule had disrupted the presumed organic unity of people and territory (Bharat Mata), *swadeshi* attempted to restore the organic inherence of parts and whole through the forging of an autonomous national space and economy. If processes of commodification entailed the historically novel individualization of social subjects as market participants, *swadeshi* sought to reconstitute social subjects as productive laboring subjects and concrete nationals. If the contradictory logic of colonial practices along with the deterritorializing dynamic of the world market threatened to undermine what were imagined as fixed social identities, *swadeshi* practices sought to reterritorialize identities that had allegedly become disembedded from an organic whole on a specifically national scale. What such a construction enabled was the conception of capitalism as an "outside" that impinged on rather than constituted and shaped from within. Yet the historical emergence and constitution of *swadeshi* attests to the way this alleged outside constructed and constituted imaginings of an imagined self-enclosed, sacral "inside."

The attempted regulation of a national economic sphere was produced within and against the perceived deterritorializing boundlessness of a British-dominated global sphere of circulation and production. It was rooted within and expressive of a globally articulated movement toward the creation of distinctive, state-defined, and state-protected national political-economic and cultural spaces. As Romesh Dutt argued in 1903:

> The *Swadeshi* movement is one which all nations of the world are seeking to adopt in the present day. Mr. Chamberlain is seeking to adopt it by a system of imperial Protection, Mr. Balfour seeks to adopt it by a scheme of Retaliation. France, Germany, the United States and all British Colonies [that is, white-settler colonies granted fiscal autonomy] adopt it by building up a wall of prohibitive duties. We have no control over our fiscal legislation, we adopt the *Swadeshi* Scheme therefore by a laudable resolution to use our home manufactures, so far as practicable, in preference to foreign manufactures.[68]

Recognizing the limits imposed by Britain's economic hegemony and colonial rule, the proponents of *swadeshi* sought to constitute, nonetheless, a self-moving national economy. As Bipin Pal remarked, "Protection, with a view to controlling foreign markets, is absolutely impossible under present circumstances. But we can, by regulating consumption, have some sort of protection for our indigenous arts and industries."[69] To combat the hegemony of British capital, nationalists advocated a strategy of capital accumulation whose specifically *swadeshi* or Indian character would be founded on practices of self-sufficiency, autonomy, and self-reliance. In concrete terms, this meant the protection, fostering, and amalgamation of dispersed indigenous joint-stock capitals, the advocacy of productivist ideologies of labor, and the practices of consumption regulated and restricted by a spirit of abnegation and asceticism. *Swadeshi* nationalism attempted to domesticate, to territorialize, the abstract temporal dynamic of capital within a concrete national space. Condensed in Surendranath Banerjea's rhetorical question was a core ideological impulse of *swadeshi:* "If protection by legislative enactment is impossible, may we not, by fiat of the national will, afford industries such protection as may lie in our powers?"[70] A number of studies have extensively recorded the precise empirical links between the nationalist movement and indigenous capitalists.[71] The *swadeshi* movement spurred the establishment, for instance, of the Tata Industrial Steel Company (TISCO) in 1907, the Bank of India and Canara Bank in 1906, the Bank of Baroda and Punjab and Sind Bank in 1908, and the Central Bank of India in 1911. Moreover, it was critical in the phenomenal growth of the indigenous textile industry (which produced machine-made copies of homespun for rural areas) as well as in the growth of the chemical industry, shipping, tobacco, leather, and insurance.[72] The same formal relationship between the colonial state and capital imbued the nationalist envisioning of a sovereign national state. Despite Gandhi's later conceptually radical reformulation, *swadeshi* was a movement for the *nationalization* of capital, not its abolition.

Nationalism's aggressively normative and modernist temporal vision had profoundly statist implications. Within late-nineteenth-century nationalist discourse, the uncontested Other of development was "barbarism," and there could be no "going back to barbarism . . . that will not aid national growth."[73] Institutional nationalism sought to secure for the spatial particularity of the Indian nation a niche in the world-historical dynamic of industrialization. This developmental and productivist orientation, a product of the hierarchical global order of capital, privileged the modern form of a developmental national state. Only a centralized, developmental state was considered adequate to the task of regulating and directing the national economy and realizing uniform development of the national whole. The demand for an autonomous national state that would fulfill the universal promise of development was made by the Indian National Congress on the basis of "a universal humanity" and the presumed existence of a bounded economic and cultural collective (19, 267). As stressed by Ranade, the anticipated sovereign state was conceived as the "national organ for taking care of national needs."[74] The broad nationalist argument was strikingly akin to later Gerschenkronian formulations of late development. For given the nation's "late entry into the field of world competition," an interventionist state that directly entered the sphere of production as mobilizer and manager of national resources could alone lay the foundation for the expansion of capital.[75] In a 1907 *swadeshi* address, Gokhale (a "moderate" nationalist) argued that only a state pursuing "a judicious system of protection" could "ensure conditions under which new infant industries can stand on their own legs" by erecting a "protection wall around" in the manner of other national states, such as "America — already one of the richest nations in the world has done . . . and the case is the same with France and Germany."[76] The key constituents of the postcolonial state's industrialization strategy — import substitution, mixed economy, and the privilege accorded to capital-intensive industries — were already present, in embryonic form, in the work of these early nationalists.

In an 1890 address that inaugurated the institution of indigenous industrial enterprises, Ranade declared as a "civic virtue" the attempt to

> [o]rganize labour and capital by co-operation, and import freely foreign skill and machinery, till we learn our lessons properly and need no help. . . . This is the civic virtue we have to learn, and according as we learn it or spurn it we shall win or lose in the contest. I feel certain that it will soon become the creed of the whole nation and ensure the permanent triumph of the modern spirit in the ancient land.[77]

The ultimate goal of achieving an autarkic, self-sufficient national economy, a Listian dream par excellence, underwrote the conceptual welding of *swaraj* and *swadeshi*. As Pal observed:

> What shall we do the moment we have *swaraj?* We shall do what every nation or almost every nation has done under the circumstances under which we live now. We shall impose a heavy prohibitive protective tariff upon every inch of textile fabric that comes from Manchester. We shall impose a protective prohibitive tariff upon every blade of knife that comes from Leeds and Sheffield.[78]

Given the nativist and idealist inflection of *swadeshi*'s political-economic imaginary, it was pervasively held that the envisioned "reconstructed Indian economy" would necessarily follow the "Indian genius and tradition" such that "industrial development would follow the course indicated by our past historical tradition, draw inspiration and strength for guidance from our own Indian past" (270). This argument echoed a broader nationalist faith in not only the indigenous roots of a distinctive Indian modernity but also the possibility of forging a unique and pacific path of capitalist growth.

In a striking formulation of the thesis of a distinct and autonomous Indian modernity, Radhakamal Mukherjee argued:

> Our economic structure is as modern as that of the West, and it will pursue a line of evolution not towards the so-called modern or Western industrialism, but towards a fuller and more determinate Indian economic order. . . . In the interests not only of Indian culture but also of Universal Humanity, India must have her own industrial life and destiny. . . . The synthetic vision of India will be the sorely needed corrective of the rigid, analytical, mechano-centric standpoint (of western industrialism).[79]

The *swadeshi*-era signification of Hinduism as a "unique Universality" anchored the claim that the immediate particularity of Indian society was sublated by a deeper, fundamental universality.[80] Indian national development was therefore not a particularistic concern but in the very interest of "Universal Humanity." By this same logic, a Bharat or India foreign to itself, as was the case under colonial rule, was the very sign of alienated humanity. Although this line of reasoning shaped the persistently universalistic self-understanding of *swadeshi* nationalism, it neither did nor could smooth over its multiple internal contradictions. One of the deep tensions within the *swadeshi* political-economic imaginary was that the productivist economic strategies advanced threatened to undermine the assumed "synthetic" and organic character of the Indian nation. On the one hand, nationalism pitted the assumed "synthetic" organic unity of indigenous institutions against the "analytical, mechano-centric" character of Western society.[81] This fissure parallels the specifically modern binarism between *Gemeinschaft/Gesellschaft*—the traditional, organically linked community versus the alienated society engendered by the dissolution of all organic links. On the other hand, nationalism sought capitalism without *Gesellschaft*, industrial development without the attendant structural tensions. This contradictory stance presaged the limits of later mid-twentieth-century dependency paradigms that construed national sovereignty (and an absolute political-economic space) as a barricade against the force of global capitalism, thereby constructing an absolute opposition between sovereignty and capital and bracketing their institutional intertwinement in the nation form. Although critical of what Romesh Dutt denounced as the "age of imperialism, the unending struggle for material interest, for conquests, annexations, extension of markets," nationalists grounded the possibility of *swaraj* in the promise of a self-enclosed, self-sufficient economic and cultural space.[82] This welding of *swaraj* with *swadeshi* was the ideological nub of late-nineteenth and early-twentieth-century nationalism in colonial India. Left unasked, until Gandhi's entry in the 1920s, were questions about the systemic linkages between capitalism, social violence, and the nation form.

The sovereignty of the future nation-state, as envisaged by nationalists, hinged on its capacity as a developmental vehicle for the nation. The developmentalism of late-nineteenth-century nationalist discourse presaged both the conceptual framework of the Indian National Congress party's 1945 election manifesto and the planning ideologies of the postcolonial national state during the 1950s and 1960s.[83] The postcolonial nation-state, especially during its Nehruvian incarnation, grounded its legitimacy on both democratic representativeness and the orchestration of a rational, state-centered plan of development. This doubled legitimacy was a product of the nationalist argument against colonialism. Yet the imperative of developing the national collective, regarded as an undifferentiated whole in class, caste, religious, and regional terms, and the productivist agenda of state developmental agencies also entailed the marginalization of subaltern social groups and classes. The institutionalization of economic planning as a specialized bureaucratic activity relegated to nonrepresentative institutions (such as the planning commission) has marked the attenuation of democratic representativeness and Gandhian-inspired *swadeshi* visions of a popular and sovereign national economic collective forged from below.

The contemporary neoliberal state/capital configuration has not signaled the retreat or withdrawal of the state. It has rather taken the form of a selective privileging of particular urban-regional nodes (Hyderabad, Bangalore), spheres (most strikingly, information technology), and class constellations (Hindu, urban, middle class, and avidly consumerist) as the economic motors of national development. Contemporary processes of political and economic restructuring have not only reinforced territorially grounded assertions of nationalism tied to an exclusionary and violent Hindutva ideology but generated new forms of sociospatial and economic unevenness. Yet they have also spurred a resurgence of an array of popular practices and social movements that oppose transnational capital and self-consciously invoke the inherited vision of a popular and sovereign national economic collective. The dual imperative of *swadeshi* and *swaraj*, forged in the late nineteenth century, continues to shape on-going struggles about the political economy of nationhood.

CONCLUSION

O n the eve of his departure for a tour of Southeast Asia in July 1927, Rabindranath Tagore addressed a group of nationalist activists and intellectuals assembled at Calcutta University. His speech, later published as a separate volume titled *Greater India,* began by charting the familiar lines of his opposition to what he had elsewhere called the mechanistic "logic of the nation."[1] Propelled by the "dust storm of modern history," Indian nationalists had succumbed to the global "hunger" for the central "political feast" of the age, namely, the goal of a sovereign nation-state.[2] Seduced by a statist imaginary, they were in danger, Tagore warned, of eclipsing "the eternal grace of India [*Bharat*]" that lay in the capacity to "see all as part of ourselves" (its imminent universalism) and its "acceptance of sacrifice" (its spiritual essence) (198, 199). Without an "identification of our own personality," the realization of the "inner truth" of Bharat would remain an unattainable dreamworld. Tagore had helped author the vision of autonomy that anchored *swadeshi* visions of Bharat as an organically constituted nation, as both a space of refuge and a site of resistance to colonialism. In his post-*swadeshi* antinationalist incarnation, he sought the "inner truth" of India in a literal and imaginative Greater India that was roughly congruent to a Pan-Asian world. It was still possible to witness the "real wealth" of India, to experience the visible "surplus of her cultural life" based on centuries of accumulating interconnections in this "far-off field" across "oceanic barriers." Built on an "ethic of sacrifice" rather than the "infliction of suffering," the shared "truth" of this Pan-Asian world enabled "us to feel those who are distant and different to be near and meaningful to us." Tagore urged a spatial and ideological realignment of dominant anticolonial nationalism beyond the "barriers of external geography" and the nation form toward this organically interlinked Pan-Asian world (198).

In a remarkable passage, Tagore uncannily presages recent subalternist attempts to contain the multitemporal and multiscalar dynamic of capitalism and the transformations wrought by colonialism in the static, if admittedly "hyper-real," geopolitical category of *Europe.*[3] He observed:

> If we follow the course of our modern political self-assertion we touch foreign history at its starting point. In a feverish political urge we had

to imagine ourselves to be dream-made Mazzinis, Garibaldis and Wash-
ingtons; in our economic life we were caught in the labyrinth of imaginary Bolshevism, Syndicalism or Socialism. These mirage-like mani-
festations are not the natural outgrowths of Indian history, but are
fantasies born of our recent misfortune and hunger. As the film of this
dream-cinema is being unrolled before our eyes, we see the trade-mark
"Made in Europe" flashed in the corners, betraying the address of the
factory where the film originated.[4]

Entranced by the phantasmagoria of a globally ascendant national "dream-
cinema" that was, for Tagore, irreducibly European in origin and content,
Indians qua nationalists would remain passive spectators and consumers of
histories and products "Made in Europe." Tagore powerfully articulates
here the predicament of societies and peoples who bore the ideological stigmata of being historical "latecomers" in an era that seemed, for many colonized intellectuals, as that of the mechanical reproduction of European colonial and capitalist domination.

Tagore's turn-of-the-century articulation of a *swadeshi samaj*, an autonomous national society grounded in collective practices of sacrifice, had
long morphed into a liberal, humanist internationalism premised on an in-
dividualist and individualizing ethic. Yet his address captures, in a poetic
register, the long echo of *swadeshi:* the intimacy between a political-economic
vision of autarky (made in Bharat) and a substantively autonomous cultural
space (whether located in the bounded national community of Bharat or in
a wider Pan-Asian arena). His liberal internationalism shared with *swadeshi*
discourse an encompassing ethic of indigeneity and the self-conscious pursuit of forms of sociality and personhood untouched by the perceived abstract logic of capitalism and exempt from the geographies of domination
that constituted colonial worlds. What held together these apparently distinct formations beyond their common intellectual genealogy were their
roots within the problem of colonial unevenness, the shared grappling with
the mundane and spectacular differentiations wrought by the production of
a distinctive colonial state space.

The attempt to secure an autonomous space-time, one not beholden to
what Tagore identified as the "mirage" of Europe, resonates with many of
the normative and conceptual impulses that have informed recent claims of
an alternate modernity and radical singularity. Animated by a shared
utopian longing, such formulations also contain a certain willed forgetting
of their own conditions of possibility. For what makes possible both projects
of radical autonomy and teleological accounts of the replication of social and

cultural forms is the historically specific dialectic between the universaliz-ing drive of capitalism and the multiple forms of unevenness that are its in-ternal supplement. Although capitalist modernity might have the determi-nate appearance — like a mirage — of constituting an "empty, homogenous time" and an "abstract homogenous space," it also contains within itself the principle of its own negation in the form of internal differentiation and fragmentation.[5]

The problematic of unevenness is a constitutive element of the doubled dynamic of capital and the phenomenological experience of modernity. Yet, as I have argued, the problem of unevenness in colonial India was shaped by features that set it apart, that rendered it distinctive. This was expressed in the particular relationship between colonial state space and the imperial economy, in the temporally accelerated articulation between novel and re-ceived forms and idioms, in the disjuncture between the space of the pro-duction of value and the space of its realization, and in the simultaneous ho-mogenization and differentiation of socioeconomic relations on multiple spatial scales. As a lived reality, colonial state space was a multiply-refracted force field. Its effects were manifest in the making of novel conceptions of space and time, in the radical re-signification of a range of locally inflected sociopolitical categories (Aryavarta, Hindustan, Bharat, *swaraj*, *swadeshi*, Bharat Mata), in the forging of an insurgent nationalist political economy, and in the utopian charge of *swadeshi* visions of autonomy. The colonial car-tography of socioeconomic and cultural differentiations animated popular attempts to estrange the colonial familiar and provisioned the ground for the nationalist appropriation of colonial state space as the locus of an imagined national space and economy.

There may well be, as David Harvey argues, "no outer resolution to the inner contradictions of capitalism," no stable institutional and spatial fix to the contradictions that have shaped its dynamic historical geography apart from a thoroughgoing internal transformation.[6] Yet, in a specific historical conjuncture and global field, the nation form came to represent for many an-ticolonial activists in South Asia, as elsewhere, the embodiment of a form of universality grounded in particularity, of sustained economic growth, and the institutional medium for either resolving or regulating socioeconomic unevenness. The authors of the political economy of nationhood elaborated the problem of unevenness and differentiation on multiple spatial scales and in different spheres. Dadabhai Naoroji, among others, focused on the ex-tractive relationship between Britain and India (commonly figured as that between bloated city and bleeding countryside) and identified the imperial scale-making project of a range of colonial policies. The celebrated "drain thesis"—the foundational category of the economic critique of colonialism—inverted the claims of material and moral progress generated by the colonial state and provided such positivist indices as national per capita income estimates in order to render palpable the impoverishment of what was seen as a bounded national space and economy.[7] M. G. Ranade, and later G. V. Joshi and Vaman Kale, analyzed the generation of "dependent" colonial economies in relation to the international division of labor that underwrote relations of unequal exchange in terms that contested and exceeded the axiomatic presuppositions of classical political economy.[8] Others, such as Romesh Dutt and Radhakamal Mukherjee, directed attention to the deepening internal differentiation of the imagined nation evinced in the violent articulation of local and village economies with the world market, accelerated urban-rural polarization and massive rural migration, deepening class polarities, the reified separation between intellectual and manual labor, and the toll wrought by recurrent devastating famines.[9] In their attempt to envision a nationalist political economy against the abstractions of classical political economy and the contradictions of colonial space, Indian nationalists assembled a strongly autarkic vision of the nation as the natural scale of capital accumulation and as the collective embodiment of indigenous labor.

If the project of Indian economics was a product of the lived contradictions of colonial space, it was also inseparably part of the transnational ascendancy of statist developmentalist frameworks in the late nineteenth century. These presented a profound challenge to the political-economic imaginary and regulatory order that underwrote Britain's globe-spanning imperial economy. The promise of state-directed economic development conjured by the German historical school and List was explicitly intended for aspiring imperial powers ("civilized nations" such as Germany and the United States) suffering under the perceived dual yoke of classical political economy and Britain's global economic hegemony. Indian nationalists, especially *swadeshi* activists, did more than simply extend the categories of Listian developmentalism and the German historical school beyond the Atlantic circuit of its initial formulation. By refracting and reworking the problem of political-economic autonomy and development with specific reference to colonial unevenness, they radicalized its political signification, deepened its social reference, and transformed the "original" in turn. Listian developmentalism, as recast in a range of colonial and peripheral contexts—from late-nineteenth-century India to twentieth-century Korea and Kemalist Turkey—had a socially radical afterlife outside its original constituency precisely because of its articulation with distinctive forms of spatial unevenness and experiences of temporal nonsynchronicity.

Ironically, an exploration of the insurgent nationalist political economy forged by Indian nationalists returns to focus the now forgotten origins of the term *postcolonial*. The term was first used in the context of modes of articulation debates in South Asian political economy in the early 1970s.[10] This is ironic in light of not only the decline of political economy in South Asian historiography and colonial studies more generally but the predominant epistemological and discourse-centered preoccupations of the interdisciplinary field designated as postcolonial theory. This is a point not just about the different political and conceptual vocations that characterize projects in distinct historical conjunctures but about the dangers of eclipsing from view the deeply impassioned politics of political-economic and cultural autonomy fashioned by anticolonial struggles.

In our current historical moment, the spectral gathering of imperial projects, revisionist apologias for empire, and the proximate aftereffects of neoliberal restructuring threatens to bludgeon the critical legacy of anticolonial struggles. Indian nationalists, like many anticolonial activists in East Asia, Africa, and the Middle East, had sought to realize the dream of political-economic and cultural autonomy, to overcome what Gandhi called the *khudaro* or barbarism of colonialism and capitalism, to achieve a substantively noncolonial future. We know all too well, of course, the shattering of this promise by both internal tensions and external constraints, of the transformation of utopian visions into legitimating ones, of the hollowing out of the critical and radically futural impulse of diverse anticolonial projects. Yet anticolonial movements—from the Haitian revolution of the 1790s that radicalized enlightenment frameworks even though it was rendered "unthinkable" in its time to the twentieth-century era of decolonization that fueled Bandung national developmentalism and the Non-Aligned Movement that transposed *swadeshi's* vision of autonomy unto a wider geopolitical field—did secure the right of collective self-determination and economic autonomy, if only in a formal sense, beyond the particular regions of Europe and America.[11] The contemporary conjunction between imperial projects and neoliberal economic fatalism seems poised to render debates on "postcoloniality," especially those that bracket political economy, ever more scholastic. The point here is not to embrace an uncritical view of anticolonial struggles. It is rather the importance of not confining our analysis to what Theodore Adorno identified as the historicist underpinnings of the "loathsome question" of what is "living and what is dead" about past works and struggles, of their message and meaning for the present.[12] We might ask instead the antihistoricist question of what our shared global present signifies from the standpoint of anticolonial struggles for autonomy.

One of the aims of this work has been to demonstrate that a focus on the structural and experiential contradictions of colonialism does not mandate an ersatz return to the crude determinations or tight teleologies of orthodox Marxism. Nor does it entail glossing over the expressive negotiations, creative transpositions, and forms of social agency that challenged and refashioned apparently immutable structures of domination. It suggests rather the value of a sustained focus on the "regulated improvisations" in both collective practices and conceptual frameworks — engendered within the interstices of contradictory social formations — that effect durable transformations.[13] The formation and generalization of the categories *national economy* and *national space*, within and against colonial state space and a Britain-centered global economy, attest to the reciprocal determination between contradictory structures and forms of agency, political economy and cultural imaginaries, meaning and materiality.

This book has sought to overcome the limits of methodological nationalism, which has enshrined categories such as *national space* and *national economy* as natural and has authorized the incarceration of multiscalar and multitemporal processes within state-delimited territorial boundaries. By adopting a historical-geographical perspective, it has elaborated the intimate relations between the production of an uneven colonial space, key global dynamics, and the nationalization of everyday categories of understandings in a specific historical conjuncture. These processes operated on overlapping and intersecting spatial scales. They did not emerge outward from original, pregiven social relations and spaces, nor did they constitute simple, linear links. Rather their relation was that of a complex movement of accumulating interconnections within a specific global field. For all their apparent polysemy, they were closely entwined, rooted in, and reflective of the production of a simultaneously interdependent, hierarchically organized, and profoundly uneven global space.

The constitutive elements of Indian nationalism — the territorial nativist envisioning of Bharat as an organic national whole; the tension between a universalistic conception of development and a particularistic vision of nationhood; the *swadeshi*-borne faith in forging a uniquely pacific path of industrialization that would yield capitalist development without *Gesellschaft* — were expressed and shaped through particular cultural and social logics and categories of understanding. Yet Indian nationalism was not a singular formation set apart from the global field of its emergence and constitution. The attempt to secure an alternate gestalt grounded in the perceived singularity of indigenous institutions and practices was a historically specific response embedded within a particular global field. The idea of nationhood as the culmination of an inner dialectic, as the expression of a singular organic formation, had become a key motif of late-nineteenth and early-twentieth-century nationalist discourse across diverse regional contexts. Confronted with the convulsive transformations wrought by colonialism and capitalism, many nationalists in colonial India, as elsewhere, interpreted and translated the historical dislocations of the present in and through a nativist, historicist, and idealist idiom. Territorial nativism was part of the global politics of territorial closure that defined the historical-geographical field of the late nineteenth and early twentieth centuries.

Yet, at the same time, the particular form of territorial nativism forged by an upper-caste and ascendant Hindu middle class in the last third of the nineteenth century in colonial India had concretely local effects. It is only by exploring the historical production of the spatial and temporal matrices of nationalist imaginings that the internal relationship between nationalism and communalism becomes evident. By providing a critical account of the formation of a territorial nativist episteme, this work has sought to suggest that neither nationalism nor communalism can be grasped in themselves, conceived independently of one another. Rather they stood in a dialectical relationship to one another in the form of historically specific internal contraries. As the inner lining of territorial nativist visions of nationhood, communalism was integral to the constitution of dominant ideologies and practices of Indian nationalism, even as it appeared to exceed their ideological horizon. The formal ideological symmetry between nationalism and communalism was manifest in their common orientation toward the realization of the modern phantasm of sociocultural purity, the presumptive organic identity between individuals and larger collectivities, and the imaging of particular groups as the bearers of the stigmata of otherness, belatedness, and insufficient authenticity. The discourse of communalism and nationalism was never very far apart. They have a joint descent in the territorial nativist conception of India as Bharat as elaborated between 1860 and 1880.

Territorial nativism conferred an ontological privilege to Hinduism as a unique universality and to upper-caste Hindus as the organic core nationals. It did so not on explicitly religious grounds but through a historicist understanding of the liaison between territory, history, and collective identity. It is impossible to understand the persistently secular self-understanding of dominant Indian nationalism much less the ways in which it figured the "Muslim" as a problematic particularity within an imagined national whole without reference to this historical and epistemological formation. The mobilizing *swadeshi* vision of an autonomous national space and economy and the attempt to actualize it on the terrain of everyday practices carried a

utopian surplus. Yet, underwritten by a distinctively territorial nativist episteme, the movement also engendered and sharpened differentiations of its
own. We cannot focus on the utopian drift of *swadeshi* imaginaries without a
simultaneous account of the ways in which it held Muslims hostage, as
Muhammad Ali warned, to a historicist reading of the past.[14] Nor can we
ignore the violent tensions that continued to haunt institutional nationalism
long after the formal end of the *swadeshi* movement.

The contemporary Hindu nationalist project has redrawn everyday institutional landscapes, normative horizons, and political discourse. It has reworked the nationalized educational curriculum, especially history textbooks, along the thin, brutal lines of Hindutva, which not only pushes the
obsessive archaism of early nationalist historiography to an absurd extreme
but seeks to erase what even Raja Shiva Prasad insisted on in the early
1870s as the difference between poetic, religious time and concrete historicity.[15] Such pedagogical projects appear guaranteed to generate anew nativist and historicist ideologies as common sense. What is more, we are increasingly witness to the proliferation of both state and popular violence
toward Muslims, who are seen as lacking a presumed organic connection to
the national whole and made to collectively bear the burden of the presumed
"original sin" of partition. The form and level of violence in recent years —
from Ayodhaya to Bombay to Gujarat — seem to signal a departure from the
simple marginalization toward the active exteriorization (in both political
and symbolic terms) of the Indian Muslim population. They have certainly
prompted a visceral recognition of the active presence of the 1947 partition — the blood-soaked materialization of national space that yielded the
sovereign states of India and Pakistan — in everyday political landscapes
and discourses.[16]

Many of these developments have been fashioned by institutional logics
and political shifts in the last few decades. Yet they also represent the brutal actualization of the embedded contradictions of territorial nativist conceptions of India as a bounded national space and economy as first forged
during the late nineteenth and early twentieth centuries. The uncanny presence of ideologies, projects, and subjectivities that belong as much to a supposedly superseded past as to the present should provide the impetus and
occasion for a focus on the actually existing contradictions of the nation
form and its longer-run relationship to the dynamic and uneven historical
geography of capital. Critical historical and political practice hinges on the
identification of those elements in the present, or the repressed possibilities
and hopes of apparently past struggles, that contain the potential of mediating between the actual and the possible. We need to heed the spirit, although

not the nationalist impulse, of Bipin Pal's exhortation to attend to the "actualities of the present."[17] Only then can we begin to fashion genuinely critical projects that are not rooted in the ideology of the nation form, nativist and organicist visions of community, or particularizing frameworks that veer uncomfortably close to the politics of closure that Hindutva seeks to actualize. Moving beyond the multiple guises of methodological nationalism represents an initial step toward this larger effort.

NOTES

Introduction

1. Jawaharlal Nehru, *The Discovery of India* (Delhi: Oxford University Press, 1985), 59–60.

2. For an incisive account of Nehru's vision for modern India, see Sunil Khilnani, *The Idea of India* (London: Farrar, Straus and Giroux, 1997).

3. For analyses of contemporary transformations, see Samir Amin, "The Challenge of Globalization," *Review of International Political Economy* 3, 2 (1996): 216–59; Neil Brenner, "Beyond State-Centrism? Space, Territoriality and Geographical Scale in Globalization Studies," *Theory and Society* 28, 1 (1999): 39–78; Manuel Castells, *The Information Age: Economy, Society and Culture*, vols. 1 and 2 (Oxford: Blackwell, 1997); Jean Comaroff and John L. Comaroff, eds., *Millennial Capitalism and the Culture of Neoliberalism* (Durham, N.C.: Duke University Press, 2001); Peter Dicken, *Global Shift: Transforming the World Economy* (New York: Guilford Press, 1998); David Harvey, *Spaces of Hope* (Berkeley: University of California Press, 2000); Harvey, *The Condition of Postmodernity* (Cambridge, Mass.: Blackwell, 1990); Joachim Hirsch, "The Nation-State, Globalization and Democracy," *Review of International Political Economy* 1, 2 (1995): 267–84; Bob Jessop, "Reflections on the (Il)logics of Globalization," in *Globalization and the Asia Pacific*, ed. Peter Dicken, Kris Olds, Phillip Kelly, and Henry Yeung (London: Routledge, 1999); Saskia Sassen, *Globalization and Its Discontents* (New York: New Press, 1998). For accounts that regard current processes as signaling the potential end of the nation-state and nationalism, see Arjun Appadurai, *Modernity at Large: Cultural Dimensions of Globalization* (Minneapolis: University of Minnesota Press, 1996); and Appadurai, "Sovereignty without Territoriality: Notes for a Postnational Geography," in *The Geography of Identity*, ed. Patricia Yaeger (Ann Arbor: University of Michigan, 1996); David Held, "The Decline of the Nation-State," in *New Times: The Changing Face of Politics in 1990s*, ed. Stuart Hall and Martin Jacques (London: Lawrence and Wishart, 1990); Held, *Democracy and the Global Order* (London: Polity Press, 1995); Michael Hardt and Antonio Negri, *Empire* (Cambridge: Harvard University Press, 2000).

4. Michael Mann, "Has Globalization Ended the Rise and Rise of the Nation-State?" *Review of International Political Economy* 4, 3 (1997): 472–96; Jan Art Scholte, "Global Capitalism and the State," *International Affairs* 73, 3 (1997):

427–52; Robert Wade, "Globalization and Its Limits: Reports of the Death of the National Economy Are Greatly Exaggerated," in *National Diversity and Global Capitalism,* ed. Susanne Berger and Robert Dore (Ithaca, N.Y.: Cornell University Press, 1996).

5. Phillip Abrams, "Notes on the Difficulty of Studying the State," *Journal of Historical Sociology* 1, 1 (1977): 15.

6. Henri Lefebvre, *The Production of Space,* trans. Donald Nicholson-Smith (Cambridge, Mass.: Blackwell, 1991), 88.

7. Benedict Anderson, introduction to *Mapping the Nation,* ed. Gopal Balakrishnan (London: Verso, 1996), 2.

8. The literature on Indian nationalism is extensive and impossible to cite fully. Early studies were organized in the form of either uncritical celebrations of Indian nationalism, such as Pattabhi Sitaramaya, *History of the Indian National Congress,* vol. 1, *1885–1935* (Delhi: S. Chand, 1969), or class-theoretical Marxian analyses exemplified by R. P. Dutt, *India Today* (Bombay: People's Publishing House, 1949); Bipin Chandra, *The Rise and Growth of Economic Nationalism in India, 1880–1905* (1966; reprint, Delhi: Longman, 1972); and A. R. Desai, *Social Background of Indian Nationalism* (Bombay: Popular Book Depot, 1948). Others provided institutional histories such as John Mclane, *Indian Nationalism and the Early Congress* (Princeton: Princeton University Press, 1977). The early Cambridge school focused on such themes as Indian "collaboration" and worked within a modernization framework that bracketed structural relations of domination as exemplified by Anil Seal, *The Emergence of Indian Nationalism: Competition and Collaboration in the Late Nineteenth Century* (Cambridge: Cambridge University Press, 1968); and John Gallagher, Gordon Johnson, and Anil Seal, eds., *Locality, Province and Nation* (Cambridge: Cambridge University Press, 1973). For a recent Cambridge school account that posits nationality as already imminent in the early nineteenth century, see Christopher Bayly, *Origins of Nationality in South Asia: Patriotism and Ethical Governance in the Making of Modern India* (Delhi: Oxford University Press, 1998). The subaltern studies collective has transformed the practice and texture of research on Indian nationalism in recent decades. See, in particular, Shahid Amin, *Event, Metaphor, Memory: Chauri Chaura, 1922–1992* (Berkeley: University of California Press, 1995); Ranajit Guha, "On Some Aspects of the Historiography of Colonial India," in *Subaltern Studies,* vol. 1, ed. Ranajit Guha (Delhi: Oxford University Press, 1982); and Guha, "An Indian Historiography of India," in *Dominance without Hegemony* (Cambridge: Harvard University Press, 1997); Partha Chatterjee, *Nationalist Thought and the Colonial World: A Derivative Discourse* (1986; reprint, Minneapolis: University of Minnesota, 1993); Chatterjee, *The Nation and Its Fragments: Colonial and Post-*

Colonial Histories (Princeton: Princeton University Press, 1993); Sudipta Kaviraj, "The Imaginary Institution of India," in *Subaltern Studies*, vol. 7, ed. Partha Chatterjee and Gyanendra Pandey (Delhi: Oxford University Press, 1992); Gyanendra Pandey, *The Ascendancy of the Congress in Colonial North India* (Delhi: Oxford University Press, 1978); Pandey, *The Construction of Communalism in Colonial North India* (Delhi: Oxford University Press, 1990); and Sumit Sarkar, *A Critique of Colonial India* (Delhi: Oxford University Press, 1985). For nonsubalternist accounts of nationalism, see Sugata Bose and Ayesha Jalal, eds., *Nationalism, Democracy, and Development: State and Politics in India* (Delhi: Oxford University Press, 1998); Mushirul Hasan, *Nationalism and Communal Politics in India, 1916–1928* (Delhi: Manohar Publications, 1979); Hasan, *Islam and Indian Nationalism: Reflections on A. K. Azad* (Delhi: Manohar Publications, 1992); Sumathi Ramaswamy, *Passions of the Tongue: Language Devotion in Tamil Nadu* (Berkeley: University of California Press, 1997); Sumit Sarkar, *The Swadeshi Movement in Bengal, 1903–8* (Delhi: Oxford University Press, 1973); Tanika Sarkar, *Hindu Wife, Hindu Nation: Community, Religion and Cultural Nationalism* (London: Hurst, 2001); David Ludden, ed., *Contesting the Nation: Religion, Community and the Politics of Democracy in India* (Philadelphia: University of Pennsylvania Press, 1996); and Peter Van der Veer, *Religious Nationalism: Hindus and Muslims in India* (Berkeley: University of California Press, 1994). For the specific literature on Muslim nationalism, see chapter 8 of this work.

See chapter 5 of this work for an elaboration of the elision of the spatial dimensions of nationalist discourse within the highly sophisticated debates about nationalist historiography initiated by subalternist historians.

9. Lefebvre, *Production of Space.*
10. For exemplary studies of the phenomenon of unevenness in a political-economic register, see David Harvey, *The Limits to Capital* (Chicago: University of Chicago Press, 1982); Neil Smith, *Uneven Development* (Cambridge, Mass.: Blackwell, 1984). For analyses of forms of cultural and socioeconomic unevenness, see Ernst Bloch, *Heritage of Our Times*, trans. Neville and Stephen Plaice (Berkeley: University of California Press, 1991); and Bloch, "Nonsynchronism and the Obligation to Its Dialectics, *New German Critique* 11 (1977): 22–38; Henri Lefebvre, *Critique of Everyday Life*, vol. 1, trans. John Moore (London: Verso: 1991); Lefebvre, *Production of Space;* Harry Harootunian, *Overcome by Modernity: History, Culture, and Community in Interwar Japan* (Princeton: Princeton University Press, 2000); and Harootunian, *History's Disquiet: Modernity, Cultural Practice, and the Question of Everyday Life* (New York: Columbia University Press, 2000).
11. Pierre Bourdieu, *Outline of a Theory of Practice* (Cambridge: Cambridge University Press, 1977); Bourdieu, *The Logic of Practice* (Stanford: Stanford Uni-

versity Press, 1988); Bourdieu, *In Other Words: Essays towards a Reflexive Sociology*, trans. Mathew Adamson (Oxford: Polity Press, 1990); Craig Calhoun, "Habitus, Field and Capital: The Question of Historical Specificity," in *Bourdieu: Critical Perspectives*, ed. C. Calhoun, E. Lipuma, and M. Postone (Chicago: University of Chicago Press, 1993); Nobert Elias, *The Civilizing Process* (Oxford: Blackwell, 1978); Anthony Giddens, *Central Problems in Social Theory: Action, Structure and Contradiction in Social Analysis* (Berkeley: University of California Press, 1990); Moishe Postone, *Time, Labor and Social Domination* (Cambridge: Cambridge University Press, 1993); William Sewell, "A Theory of Structure: Duality, Agency and Transformation," *American Journal of Sociology* 98, 1 (1992): 1–29.

12. Geoff Eley and Ronald Suny, *Becoming National: A Reader* (New York: Oxford University Press, 1996), 24.

13. Rogers Brubaker, *Nationalism Reframed: Nationhood and the National Question in the New Europe* (Cambridge: Cambridge University Press, 1996); Craig Calhoun, *Nationalism* (Minneapolis: University of Minnesota Press, 1998); John Hall, ed., *The State of the Nation: Ernest Gellner and the Theory of Nationalism* (Cambridge: Cambridge University Press, 1998); Michael Mann, "A Political Theory of Nationalism and Its Excesses," in *Notions of Nationalism*, ed. Sukumar Periwal (Budapest: Central European University Press, 1995).

14. Karl Deutsch, *Nationalism and Social Communication* (1966; reprint, Cambridge: MIT Press, 1978); Hugh Seton-Watson, *Nations and States* (Boulder, Colo.: Westview Press, 1977).

15. Ernest Gellner, *Nations and Nationalism* (Ithaca, N.Y.: Cornell University Press, 1983); Elie Kedourie, *Nationalism in Asia and Africa* (London: Weidenfeld and Nicolson, 1970).

16. Eric Hobsbawm, *Nations and Nationalism since 1780* (Cambridge: Cambridge University Press, 1990).

17. Charles Tilly, "States and Nationalism in Europe, 1492–1992," *Theory and Society* 23, 1 (1994): 131–46; Michael Mann, *The Sources of Social Power*, vol. 2 (Cambridge: Cambridge University Press, 1993).

18. Michael Hechter, *Internal Colonialism: The Celtic Fringe in the British National Development* (New York: Transaction Books, 1975); Tom Nairn, *The Break-up of Britain: Crisis and Neo-Nationalism* (London: New Left Books, 1977).

19. See William Sewell, "Historical Events as Transformations of Structures," *Theory and Society* 25, 6 (1997): 841–81; and Sewell, "Three Temporalities: Towards an Eventful Sociology," in *The Historic Turn in the Human Sciences*, ed. Terence McDonald (Ann Arbor: University of Michigan, 1996).

20. Benedict Anderson's 1983 work, *Imagined Communities: Reflections on the Origins and Spread of Nationalism* (rev. ed., London: Verso, 1991), is arguably the single

most influential work on nationalism in recent memory. For a detailed elaboration of the influence of Anderson, see Eley and Suny, *Becoming National;* and Manu Goswami, "Rethinking the Modular Nation Form: Towards a Sociohistorical Conception of Nationalism," *Comparative Studies in Society and History* 44, 4 (2002): 770–99.

21. Homi Bhabha, ed., *Nation and Narration* (London: Routledge, 1990); Katherine Verdery, "Whither Nation and Nationalism?" in *Mapping the Nation,* ed. Gopal Balakrishnan (London: Verso, 1996).

22. Calhoun, *Nationalism.* For a counterargument, see Benedict Anderson, *The Spectre of Comparisons: Nationalism, Southeast Asia and the World* (London: Verso, 1998).

23. For an elaboration of this argument, see Goswami, "Rethinking the Modular Nation Form."

24. Brubaker, *Nationalism Reframed,* 16.

25. The "invention of tradition" thesis that gained broad currency during the early 1980s sought to historicize and materialize nationalist ideology. However, intrinsic to the notion of invention was the assumed existence of a real national history or nation obscured by disingenuous or duped political and economic elites. Although the "invention of tradition" thesis broke from approaches that took nationalism at its own word, it tended to fix nationalism, in the last instance, on one side of the divide between ideology and objectivity. In this context, Benedict Anderson's conceptualization of the nation as an "imagined community" moved discussions of nationalism beyond the previous bind of adjudicating between the reality versus the fiction of the concept "nation." See Eric Hobsbawm and Terence Ranger, eds., *The Invention of Tradition* (Cambridge: Cambridge University Press, 1983).

26. See, e.g., works by J. Borneman, *Belonging in the Two Berlins: Kin, State, Nation* (Cambridge: Cambridge University Press, 1992); Michael Billig, *Banal Nationalism* (London: Sage, 1995); Chatterjee, *Nationalist Thought in the Colonial World* and *Nation and Its Fragments;* Paul Gilroy, "*There Ain't No Black in the Union Jack*": *The Cultural Politics of Race and Nation* (Chicago: University of Chicago Press, 1987); Eley and Suny, *Becoming National;* Marilyn Ivy, *Discourses of the Vanishing: Modernity, Phantasm, Japan* (Chicago: University of Chicago Press, 1995); Andrew Parker and Doris Russo, eds., *Nationalisms and Sexualities* (London: Routledge, 1992); Tzvetan Todorov, *On Human Diversity: Nationalism, Racism, and Exoticism in French Thought,* trans. Catherine Porter (Cambridge: Harvard University Press, 1993); Nira Yuval-Davis and Flora Anthias, *Women, Nation, State* (London: Macmillan, 1989); Verdery, "Whither Nation and Nationalism?"

27. Pierre Bourdieu and Loïc Wacquant, *An Invitation to Reflexive Sociology* (Chi-

cago: University of Chicago Press, 1992), 105. For an important exception, see Etienne Balibar, "The Nation Form: History and Ideology," in *Race, Nation, Class: Ambiguous Identities,* ed. E. Balibar and I. Wallerstein (London: Verso, 1991).

28. Etienne Balibar, *Masses, Classes, Ideas* (London: Routledge, 1994), 202.

29. Nicos Poulantzas, *State, Power, and Socialism,* trans. Patrick Camiller (London: Verso, 2000), 97.

30. Calhoun, *Nationalism,* 5.

31. A focus on the transposability of the nation form departs from Benedict Anderson's account of the modular reproduction of nationalist models and strategies. For an account of the transposable, durable, doubled, and dynamic character of the nation form, see Goswami, "Rethinking the Modular Nation Form."

32. Stuart Hall, "The Local and the Global: Globalization and Ethnicity," in *Culture, Globalization and the World System: Contemporary Conditions for the Representation of Identity,* ed. Anthony King (Minneapolis: University of Minnesota Press, 1997), 22.

33. Peter Sahlins, *Boundaries: The Making of France and Spain in the Pyrenees* (Berkeley: University of California Press, 1978); Eugene Weber, *Peasants into Frenchmen: The Modernization of Rural France, 1871–1914* (Stanford: Stanford University Press, 1976); Thongchai Winichakul, *Siam Mapped: A History of the Geo-Body of the Nation* (Honolulu: University of Hawaii Press, 1994); and Firoozeh Kashani-Sabet, *Frontier Fictions: Shaping the Iranian Nation, 1804–1946* (Princeton: Princeton University Press, 1999) focus on the construction of particular national territorial boundaries. Mathew Edney, *Mapping an Empire: The Geographical Construction of British India, 1765–1843* (Chicago: University of Chicago Press, 1997), focuses solely on techniques of imperial mapping and official discourses rather than the social production of space or the spatiality of nationalist and popular imaginings.

34. Anderson, *Imagined Communities;* Winichakul, *Siam Mapped;* Sumathi Ramaswamy, "Catastrophic Cartographies: Mapping the Lost Continent of Lemuria," *Representations* 67 (1999): 92–129; and Ramaswamy, "History at Land's End: Lemuria in Tamil Spatial Fables," *Journal of Asian Studies* 59, 3 (2000): 575–602.

35. Nadia Abu el-Haj, "Translating Truths: Nationalism, the Practice of Archaeology and the Remaking of Past and Present in Contemporary Jerusalem," *American Ethnologist* 25, 2 (1998): 166–88; David Hooson, ed., *Geography and Identity* (Cambridge, Mass.: Blackwell, 1994).

36. Anderson, *Imagined Communities;* Eric Kaufmann, "Naturalizing the Nation": The Rise of Naturalistic Nationalism in the United States and Canada," *Com-*

parative Studies in Society and History 40, 4 (1998): 666–95; Liisa Malkki, "National Geographic: The Rooting of Peoples and the Territorialization of National Identity among Scholars and Refugees," *Cultural Anthropology* 7, 1 (1992): 22–44; Kashani-Sabet, *Frontier Fictions;* Ramaswamy, "Catastrophic Cartographies" and "History at Land's End"; Oliver Zimmer, "In Search of Natural Identity: Alpine Landscapes and the Reconstruction of the Swiss Nation," *Comparative Studies in Society and History* 40, 4 (1998): 637–65.

37. The most striking exception to metaphorical and physical-territorial understandings of national space is Nicos Poulantzas's chapter on "The Nation" in *State, Power, and Socialism.* Poulantzas elaborates a brilliant, if largely ignored, theorization of the role of the nation-state in establishing and regulating the spatial and temporal matrices of everyday life.

38. Lefebvre, *Production of Space.* See chapter 1 of this work for a broader discussion of Lefebvre's theory of the production of social space and the debates spawned in the critical geography literature.

39. Poulantzas, *State, Power, and Socialism,* 49–122.

40. It is beyond the scope of this work to explore the apparent homology between the nation form and the commodity form. Like the commodity form, the nation form has a dynamic, doubled, durable, and transposable structure. For an account of the nation form as dynamic, doubled, and transposable, see Goswami, "Rethinking the Modular Nation Form." The extension of the commodity form, for instance, generates, without resolving a range of spatiotemporal contradictions. For example, the commodity is both abstract, universal and concrete, particular; it is both an exchange-value and a use-value; the worker is both an abstract, interchangeable unit of labor power and a concrete individual; money operates both as international currency and as national money and the like.

41. World systems theorists have long emphasized the globalizing thrust of capital accumulation processes and analyzed its relation to the system of territorial (including national) states. They conceive the nation form, however, as a functional emanation of a "world capitalist economy." See, in particular, Giovanni Arrighi, *The Long Twentieth Century: Money, Power and the Origins of Our Times* (London: Verso, 1994); and Immanuel Wallerstein, *Historical Capitalism* (London: New Left Books, 1983); and Wallerstein, *Mercantilism and the Consolidation of the World Economy,* vol. 2 of *The Modern World System* (New York: Academic Press, 1980). An important exception within this framework is Balibar's location of the emergence of the nation form within the historical context of imperial expansion in his essay "The Nation Form." He repudiates attempts to deduce the nation-state from capitalist relations of production as well as teleological schemas that posit it as the mechanical outcome of a deter-

ministic unfolding of capitalist modes of production. Instead, he locates the emergence of nation-states with reference to the historical conjunction of the making of a world economy and early forms of imperialism.

42. Brubaker, *Nationalism Reframed*, 15.

43. John Agnew, "The Territorial Trap: The Geographical Assumptions of inter-national Relations Theory," *Review of International Political Economy* 1, 1 (1994): 53–80; Pierre Bourdieu, "Rethinking the State: Genesis and Structure of the Bureaucratic Field," in *State/Culture: State-Formation after the Cultural Turn*, ed. George Steinmetz (Ithaca, N.Y.: Cornell University Press, 1999); Brenner, "Beyond State Centrism"; Peter Taylor, "Embedded Statism and the Social Sciences," *Environment and Planning A* 28, 11 (1996): 1917–28; Immanuel Wallerstein, *Unthinking Social Science: The Limits of Nineteenth Century Paradigms* (Cambridge: Polity Press, 1991). For analyses, from different disciplinary perspectives, that attempt to move beyond a nation-state centric frame, see Prasenjit Duara, "Transnationalism in the Era of Nation-States," *Development and Change* 29, 4 (1998): 647–70; Duara, *Rescuing History from the Nation* (Chicago: University of Chicago Press, 1997); Rebecca Karl, *Staging the World: Chinese Nationalism at the Turn of the Twentieth Century* (Durham, N.C.: Duke University Press, 2002); Paul Gilroy, *The Black Atlantic: Modernity and Double Consciousness* (Cambridge: Harvard University Press, 1993); Sydney Mintz, *Sweetness and Power: The Place of Sugar in World History* (New York: Viking Penguin, 1985); Eric Wolf, *Europe and the People without History* (Berkeley: University of California Press, 1982).

44. The term *deep structure* derives from Sewell's compelling theorization of the dialectical relationship between structure and agency in "A Theory of Structure: Duality, Agency and Transformation."

45. Pierre Bourdieu, *Masculine Domination* (Stanford: Stanford University Press, 2001), 82.

46. For sympathetic overviews of the subaltern studies collective, see Florencia Mallon, "The Promise of and Dilemma of Subaltern Studies: Perspectives from Latin American History," *American Historical Review* 99, 4 (1994): 1491–515; Gyan Prakash, "Subaltern Studies as Postcolonial Criticism," *American Historical Review* 99, 4 (1994): 1475–90; Prakash, "Writing Post-Orientalist Histories of the Third World," *Comparative Studies in Society and History* 32, 2 (1990): 383–408; Walter Mignolo, *Local Histories/Global Designs: Coloniality, Subaltern Knowledges, and Border Thinking* (Princeton: Princeton University Press, 2000); Gayatri Chakravorty Spivak, "Can the Subaltern Speak?" in *Marxism and the Interpretation of Cultures*, ed. Cary Nelson and Lawrence Grossberg (Urbana: University of Illinois Press, 1988); and Spivak, "Subaltern Studies: Deconstructing Historiography," in *Selected Subaltern*

Studies, ed. Ranajit Guha and Gayatri C. Spivak (Delhi: Oxford University Press, 1988). For critiques of subaltern studies from different perspectives, see Vinayak Chaturvedi, introduction to *Mapping Subaltern Studies and the Post-colonial*, ed. V. Chaturvedi (London: Verso, 2000); Frederick Cooper, "Conflict and Connection: Rethinking African History," *American Historical Review* 99, 4 (1994): 1516–45; Rosalind O'Hanlon, "Recovering the Subject: Subaltern Studies and Histories of Resistance in Colonial South Asia," *Modern Asian Studies* 22, 1 (1988): 189–224; Rosalind O'Hanlon and David Wash-brook, "After Orientalism: Culture, Criticism, and Politics in the Third World," *Comparative Studies in Society and History* 34, 1 (1992): 141–67; Sumit Sarkar, "The Decline of the Subaltern in Subaltern Studies," in *Writing Social History* (Delhi: Oxford University Press, 1997); and Sarkar, "Orientalism Re-visited: Saidian Frameworks in the Writing of Modern Indian History," in Chaturvedi, *Mapping Subaltern Studies and the Postcolonial*. Also see Gayatri C. Spivak's recent critical reworking of the project of subaltern history and post-colonial studies in *A Critique of Postcolonial Reason: Toward a History of the Vanishing Present* (Cambridge: Harvard University Press, 1999).

47. Chatterjee, *Nationalist Thought and the Colonial World*, 1–35.

48. Ibid., 169; also see 36–52.

49. Frantz Fanon, *The Wretched of the Earth*, trans. Constance Farrington (New York: Grove, 1965), 204.

50. Chatterjee, *Nationalist Thought and the Colonial World*, 43.

51. In the powerful conclusion of *Nationalist Thought and the Colonial World*, Chatterjee alludes to, without fully exploring, the location of "universal Reason" within the dynamic of capitalist modernity. He observes "ever since the Age of Enlightenment, Reason in its universalizing mission has been parasitic upon a much more lofty, much more mundane, palpably material and singu-larly invidious force, namely the universalistic urge of capital" (168).

52. Chatterjee, *The Nation and Its Fragments*, 6. Chatterjee argues: "Anti-colonial nationalism creates its own domain of sovereignty within colonial society . . . by dividing the world of social institutions and practices into two domains — the material and the spiritual. The material is the domain of the 'outside,' of the economy and of statecraft, of science and technology, a domain where the West has proved its superiority and the East has succumbed. . . . The spiri-tual, on the other hand, is an 'inner' domain bearing the 'essential' marks of cultural identity. This formula is, I think, a fundamental feature of anti-colonial nationalisms in Asia and Africa."

53. The most sophisticated and provocative instance of this argument is Dipesh Chakrabarty's *Provincializing Europe: Postcolonial Thought and Historical Difference* (Princeton: Princeton University Press, 2000); and Chakrabarty, *Habitations*

of Modernity: Essays in the Wake of Subaltern Studies (Chicago: University of Chicago Press, 2002). Also see Dipesh Chakrabarty, "Marx after Marxism: History, Subalternity and Difference," *Meanjin* 52 (1993): 421–34. Gyan Prakash has argued that an adequate analysis of colonialism has not taken place because, "while there are many examples of critiques of liberal historiography and of its complicity with imperialism, the revision of the discipline from the place of 'otherness' is yet to occur." See Gyan Prakash, *After Colonialism: Imperial Histories and Postcolonial Displacements* (Princeton: Princeton University Press, 1994), 5. Such a revision, he suggests, would entail the documentation "not only of a record of domination but also . . . to mark those subaltern positions and knowledges that could not be properly recognized and named, only 'normalized' by colonial discourses" (5–6). Vicente Rafael presents his analysis of practices of conversion in colonial Philippines as an attempt to "translate between a local history which remains proximate yet irreducibly foreign to me," and the claim that his "intervention in the critique of colonial discourse" lies in its ability to register the "radically heterogeneous inhabiting the specifically local." See Vicente Rafael, *Contracting Colonialism: Translation and Christian Conversion in Tagalog Society under Early Spanish Rule* (Durham, N.C.: Duke University Press, 1993), xiv.

54. Prakash, *After Colonialism*, 5.

55. For a recent argument along these lines, see Gyan Prakash, *Another Reason: Science and the Imagination of Modern India* (Princeton: Princeton University Press, 1999). In his incisive account of colonial science's functioning as a cultural discourse and modality of power, Prakash argues for the "undeniably different" character of "Indian modernity" (13). He observes: "Navigating between the bank of the Vedas and the bank of modern science and technology, but holding neither one nor the other fixed, India appears simultaneously as something altogether new and unmistakably old, at once undoubtedly modern and irreducibly Indian. Therein lies Indian modernity's pervasive presence and precarious existence" (14). Also see Partha Chatterjee's argument in *The Nation and Its Fragments* that his critique of universalizing narratives is articulated from a position of alterity recoded as an "Indian exceptionalism" (13).

56. Charles Tilly, *Big Structures, Large Processes, Huge Comparisons* (New York: Russell Sage, 1984).

57. Fernand Braudel, in *The Perspective of the World: Civilization and Capitalism, Fifteenth–Eighteenth Centuries* (London: Harper and Row, 1979), provides an account of an uneven worldwide space-time defined by processes of intensified socioeconomic interdependence within which "spaces of silence" are temporally simultaneous (18). Yet the notion of "spaces of silence" tends to reproduce the notion of peoples and spaces without history. For a fundamen-

tal rethinking of the abstract temporal dynamic of capitalism that attributes a temporal directionality but not a telos to the capital relation, see Postone, *Time, Labor and Social Domination.* For an analysis of contemporary processes of global restructuring as multiscalar and multitemporal, see Jessop, "(Il)logics of Globalization."

58. The specificity of "colonial modernity" has become a central problematic for historians and social theorists linked to the subaltern studies collective. For a provocative attempt to rethink temporality, capital, and difference from a subalternist perspective, see Chakrabarty, *Provincializing Europe.* For arguments, in varying registers, about the singularity and particularity of an "Indian" modernity, see Chatterjee, *Nation and Its Fragments;* and Prakash, *Another Reason.* For an account of cultural unevenness as a central dynamic of a "coeval modernity," see Harootunian, *Overcome by Modernity* and *History's Disquiet.* For a compelling analysis of "subaltern modernity" that deploys Henri Lefebvre's theorization of social space without a strong claim of irreducible difference, see Fernando Coronil, *The Magical State: Nature, Money, and Modernity in Venezuela* (Chicago: University of Chicago Press, 1997).

59. For an impassioned plea against narratives of "third world" belatedness and insufficiency that follow from teleological and evolutionary historicist conceptions of modernity, see Chakrabarty, *Provincializing Europe.* Also, see Partha Chatterjee's critique of an authorized sociological determinism that erases the historical specificity of colonial formations in *Nationalist Thought and the Colonial World.*

60. Harootunian, *Overcome by Modernity,* xvi.

61. Coronil, *Magical State,* 7.

62. Lefebvre, *Production of Space,* 88.

63. Dilip Gaonkar, ed., *Alternative Modernities* (Durham, N.C.: Duke University Press, 2001); Chatterjee, *Nation and Its Fragments;* Prakash, *Another Reason;* and Timothy Mitchell, ed., *Questions of Modernity* (Minneapolis: University of Minnesota Press, 2000).

64. For a strong critique of the limits of the idea of an "alternative modernity" particular to colonial and postcolonial societies, see Harry Harootunian, "Ghostly Comparisons: Anderson's Telescope," *Diacritics* 29, 4 (1999): 135–49. Also see Crystal Bartolovich and Neil Lazarus, eds., *Marxism, Modernity and Postcolonial Studies* (Cambridge: Cambridge University Press, 2002); Arif Dirlik, *The Postcolonial Aura: Third World Criticism in the Age of Global Capitalism* (Boulder, Colo.: Westview Press, 1997); Aijaz Ahmad, *In Theory: Classes, Nations, Literatures* (London: Verso, 1994); and Spivak, *Critique of Postcolonial Reason,* for differing attempts to interrogate the internal relationships between postcolonial theory and contemporary capitalism.

65. For an account of the literature on colonial governmentality in South Asian historiography, see chapter 1 of this work. For influential Foucauldian analyses of colonialism in the wider field of colonial studies, see Timothy Mitchell, *Colonizing Egypt* (Berkeley: University of California Press, 1991); and Anne Stoler, *Race and the Education of Desire: Foucault's History of Sexuality and the Colonial Order of Things* (Durham, N.C.: Duke University Press, 1995). For prominent exceptions to the broader discursivist trend within colonial studies, see John Comaroff and Jean Comaroff, *Of Revelation and Revolution: The Dialectics of Modernity on a South African Frontier,* vol. 2 (Chicago: University of Chicago Press, 1997); and Jean Comaroff and John Comaroff, *Of Revelation and Revolution: Christianity, Colonialism and Consciousness in South Africa,* vol. 1 (Chicago: University of Chicago Press, 1991); Frederick Cooper, *Decolonization and African Society: The Labor Question in French and British Africa* (Cambridge: Cambridge University Press, 1996); Catherine Hall, *Civilizing Subjects: Metropole and Colony in the English Imagination, 1830–1867* (Chicago: University of Chicago Press, 2002); Thomas Holt, *The Problem of Freedom: Race, Labor and Politics in Jamaica and Britain, 1832–1938* (Baltimore: Johns Hopkins University Press, 1992); Mahmood Mamdani, *Citizen and Subject: Contemporary Africa and the Legacy of Late Colonialism* (Princeton: Princeton University Press, 1996); Michel-Rolph Trouillot, *Silencing the Past: Power and the Production of History* (Boston: Beacon Press, 1995); Louise Young, *Japan's Total Empire: Manchuria and the Culture of Wartime Imperialism* (Berkeley: University of California Press, 1998). These works forge an analytical path that recalls, in varying ways, an earlier generation of scholars of colonialism, most notably George Balandier, "The Colonial Situation: Theoretical Approaches," in *Social Change: The Colonial Situation,* ed. Immanuel Wallerstein (New York: John Wiley, 1966); C. L. R. James, *The Black Jacobins* (1938; reprint, New York: Vintage, 1963); Mintz, *Sweetness and Power;* and Wolf, *Europe and the People without History.*

66. Comaroff and Comaroff, *Revelation and Revolution,* 2:18. For programmatic reviews of the broad trajectory of colonial studies from different perspectives, see Nicholas Dirks, ed., *Colonialism and Culture* (Ann Arbor: University of Michigan Press, 1992); Frederick Cooper and Anne Stoler, eds., *Tensions of Empire: Colonial Cultures in a Bourgeois World* (Berkeley: University of California Press, 1997); and Frederick Cooper, "Decolonizing Situations: The Rise, Fall, and Rise of Colonial Studies, 1951–2001," *French Politics, Culture and Society* 20, 2 (2002): 47–76.

67. For non-economistic readings of capitalism, see Georg Lukács, *History and Class Consciousness,* trans. Rodney Livingstone (Cambridge: MIT Press, 1990); Postone, *Time, Labor and Social Domination;* Derek Sayer, *Capitalism and*

Modernity: An Excursus on Marx and Weber (London: Routledge, 1991); and
Sayer, *The Violence of Abstraction: The Analytical Foundations of Historical Materialism* (London: Basil Blackwell, 1987).

68. Janet Abu-Lughod, "Going beyond Global Babble," in *Culture, Globalization
and the World-System: Contemporary Conditions for the Representation of Identity*, ed.
Anthony King (Minneapolis: University of Minnesota Press, 1997). By suggesting parallels between the late-nineteenth/early-twentieth-century moment
of colonial and capitalist expansion and contemporary processes of global sociospatial restructuring, I do not mean to overlook the qualitative differences—geopolitical, institutional, structural, and technological—that define
the present. However, attention to the long-run history of global restructuring mitigates the more excessive claims of radical novelty made on behalf of
contemporary processes. A focus on the long-run historical geography of capital also provides an antidote to neoliberal ideologies that proclaim the realization of a fully globalized world either in the present or at some future moment. Such deeply ideological projections ignore the structural phenomenon
of unevenness intrinsic to the dynamic of capitalism as well as historically
specific forms of resistance that impose limits on the realization of a fully
globalized world.

69. Walter Benjamin, *Illuminations* (New York: Schocken Books, 1968), 261.

Chapter One

1. Quoted in Bernard Cohn, "Representing Authority in Colonial India," in *An
Anthropologist among the Historians* (Delhi: Oxford University Press, 1987),
633.

2. Cohn, *Anthropologist among the Historians*; and Bernard Cohn, *Colonialism and
Its Forms of Knowledge* (Princeton: Princeton University Press, 1996. For a critical elaboration of Edward Said's foundational problematic of Orientalism in
the South Asian context, see Carol Breckenridge and Peter Van der Veer,
eds., *Orientalism and the Postcolonial Predicament* (Philadelphia: University of
Pennsylvania, 1993). For analyses of caste as a principal invention of colonial
sociologies of knowledge, see Bernard Cohn, "The Census, Social Structure,
and Objectification in South Asia," in *Anthropologist among the Historians*; Arjun
Appadurai, "Number in the Colonial Imagination," in *Modernity at Large*,
114–38; Nicholas B. Dirks, *Castes of Mind: Colonialism and the Making of Modern
India* (Princeton: Princeton University Press, 2001); Ronald Inden, *Imagining
India* (Oxford: Blackwell, 1990); and Rashmi Pant, "The Cognitive Status of
Caste in Colonial Ethnography: A Review of Some Literature of the North
West Provinces and Oudh," *Indian Economic and Social History Review* 24,
2 (1987): 145–62. For an analysis of the colonial genealogy of political-

religious identities and discourses, see Pandey, *Construction of Communalism in Colonial North India*. For studies of disciplinary practices in the field of colonial medicine that targeted the body as a site of regulation, see David Arnold, *Colonizing the Body: State Medicine and Epidemic Disease in Nineteenth-Century India* (Berkeley: University of California Press, 1993). On colonial discourses on criminality and related classificatory techniques, see Anand Yang, ed., *Crime and Criminality in British India* (Tucson: University of Arizona Press, 1995); and Sanjay Nigam, "Disciplining and Policing the 'Criminals by Birth,' Part 2: The Development of a Disciplinary System, 1871–1900," *Indian Economic and Social History Review* 27, 3 (1990): 257–87. On the colonial reordering of nature, see David Arnold and Ramachandra Guha, eds., *Nature, Culture, Imperialism: Essays on the Environmental History of South Asia* (Delhi: Oxford University Press, 1995). For critical accounts of the colonial epistemologies that underlay the reworking of personal and criminal law, see Cohn, *Anthropologist among the Historians* and *Colonialism and Its Forms of Knowledge;* Indrani Chatterjee, *Gender, Slavery and Law in Colonial India* (Delhi: Oxford University Press, 1999); Thomas Metcalfe, *Ideologies of the Raj* (Cambridge: Cambridge University Press, 1996); Michael R. Anderson, "Islamic Law and the Colonial Encounter," in *Institutions and Ideologies,* ed. David Arnold and Peter Robb (London: Curzon, 1993), 165–85; Radhika Singha, *A "Despotism of Law": British Criminal Justice and Public Authority in North India, 1772–1837* (Delhi: Oxford University Press, 1998); and Janaki Nair, *Women and the Law in Colonial India* (Delhi: Kali for Women, 1996).

3. For an early Foucauldian perspective on the colonial state, see Bernard Cohn and Nicholas B. Dirks, "Beyond the Fringe: The Nation-State, Colonialism and the Technologies of Power," *Journal of Historical Sociology* 1, 2 (1988): 224–29. Within the field of South Asian historiography, the rubric of "governmentality" has been most fully developed by Chatterjee, *Nation and Its Fragments;* Dirks, *Castes of Mind;* David Scott, "Colonial Governmentality," *Social Text* 43 (1995): 191–200; D. Scott, *Refashioning Futures: Criticism after Postcoloniality* (Princeton: Princeton University Press, 1999); and Prakash, *Another Reason.* Also see Sudipta Kaviraj, "On the Construction of Colonial Power: Structure, Discourse, Hegemony," in *Contesting Colonial Hegemony: State and Society in Africa and India,* ed. D. Engels and S. Marks (London: British Academic Press, 1994); and U. Kalpagam, "Colonial Governmentality and the 'Economy,'" *Economy and Society* 29, 3 (2000): 418–38.

4. Lefebvre, *Production of Space,* 88.

5. There is an extensive literature on the social production of scale and scalar politics in the critical geography field. See, in particular, Neil Brenner, "The Limits to Scale? Methodological Reflections on Scalar Structuration,"

Progress in Human Geography 15, 4 (2001): 525–48; Neil Smith, "Homeless/ Global: Scaling Places," in *Mapping the Futures,* ed. J. Bird, B. Curtis, T. Putnam, and T. Tickner (London: Routledge, 1993), 87–119; and Eric A. Swyngedouw, "Neither Global nor Local: 'Glocalization' and the Politics of Scale," in *Spaces of Globalization: Reasserting the Power of the Local,* ed. K. R. Cox (New York: Guilford Press, 1997).

6. Lefebvre, *Production of Space,* 191.

7. See, e.g., Bourdieu, *Outline of a Theory of Practice* and *Logic of Practice;* Giddens, *Central Problems in Social Theory;* and Sewell, "Theory of Structure."

8. For the scattered, if much mined, reflections on space by Michel Foucault, see "Of Other Spaces," *Diacritics* 16, 1 (1986): 22–27; and Foucault, "Questions on Geography," in *Power/Knowledge,* ed. Colin Gordon (London: Harvester Press, 1980). Emile Durkheim, *The Elementary Forms of Religious Life,* trans. Joseph Swain (1915; reprint, New York: Free Press, 1965). For influential phenomenological perspectives on space, see Gaston Bachelard, *The Poetics of Space,* trans. Maria Jolas (Boston: Beacon Press, 1994); and Michel de Certeau, *The Practice of Everyday Life,* trans. Steven Rendall (Berkeley: University of California Press, 1984).

9. For instances of explicitly Foucauldian and Heideggerian perspectives on colonial and postcolonial space, see Satish Deshpande, "Hegemonic Spatial Strategies: The Nation-Space and Hindu Communalism in Twentieth-Century India," *Public Culture* 10, 2 (1998): 249–83; Mitchell, *Colonizing Egypt;* John Noyes, *Colonial Space: Spatiality in the Discourse of German Southwest Africa, 1884–1915* (Philadelphia: Harwood Publishers, 1992). For an insightful and highly influential anthropological perspective on contemporary spatial politics and formations, see Akhil Gupta and James Ferguson, "Beyond Culture: Space, Identity, and the Politics of Difference," *Cultural Anthropology* 7, 1: 6–23. For an innovative spatial history, influenced by Said, see Paul Carter, *The Road to Botany Bay: An Exploration of Landscape and History* (Chicago: University of Chicago Press, 1989).

10. For related readings of Henri Lefebvre, see Neil Brenner, Bob Jessop, Martin Jones, and Gordon Macleod, eds., *State/Space: A Reader* (Oxford: Blackwell, 2003), 1–27; Neil Brenner, "Global, Fragmented, Hierarchical: Henri Lefebvre's Geographies of Globalization," *Public Culture* 10, 1: 137–69; Coronil, *Magical State;* Harvey, *Condition of Postmodernity;* Andrew Merrifield, "Place and Space: A Lefebvrian Reconciliation," *Transactions of the Institute of British Geographers* 18, 4 (1993): 516–31; Poulantzas, *State, Power, and Socialism,* 93–122; Kristin Ross, *The Emergence of Social Space: Rimbaud and the Paris Commune* (Minneapolis: University of Minnesota, 1994). Also see Doreen Massey, *Space, Place, Gender* (Minneapolis: University of Minnesota Press, 1994); Ed-

ward Soja, *Post-Modern Geographies: The Reassertion of Space in Critical Social Theory* (London: Verso, 1989); and David Gregory and John Ury, eds., *Social Relations and Spatial Structures* (London: Macmillan, 1994).

11. Lefebvre, *Production of Space*, 337.

12. See Benjamin, *Illuminations*, 261. For compelling readings of Benajmin's conception of capitalist temporality, see Peter Osborne, *The Politics of Time: Modernity and Avant-Garde* (London: Verso 1995); Harootunian, *History's Disquiet*; and Susan Buck-Morss, *Dialectics of Seeing: Walter Benjamin and the Arcades Project* (Cambridge: MIT Press, 1989).

13. Lefebvre, *Production of Space*, 306.

14. Also see Lefebvre, *Critique of Everyday Life*, vol. 1.

15. For a theorization of capitalism as a historically specific form of social mediation, see Postone, *Time, Labour and Social Domination*. Also see Sayer, *Violence of Abstraction* and *Capitalism and Modernity*. For a paradigmatic analysis that locates reification within the antinomies of the commodity form, see Lukács, "Reification and the Consciousness of the Proletariat," in *History and Class Consciousness*.

16. Lefebvre, *Production of Space*, 281.

17. Brenner, "Global, Fragmented, Hierarchical," 147. Also see Fernando Coronil's analysis of the contradictory effects of state spatial and economic strategies in *The Magical State* and Arjun Appadurai's account of the limits of statist attempts to produce locality in *Modernity at Large*, 182–89. For an analysis of state territorialization from a different analytical perspective, see Peter Vandergeerst and Nancy Peluso, "Territorialization and State Power in Thailand," *Theory and Society* 35 (1995): 385–426.

18. For an elaboration of this reading, see Harvey, *Limits to Capital* and *Condition of Postmodernity*; Brenner, "Global, Fragmented, Hierarchical" and "Beyond State-Centrism?"; and Jessop, "Reflections on the (Il)logics of Globalization." The categories of *deterritorialization* and *reterritorialization* in these works depart from their more prevalent metaphoric usage in historical and cultural studies that largely follow the work of Deleuze and privilege the moment of deterritorialization as constitutive of capitalism and what has come to be called globalization. Perhaps the most striking instance of this trend — one that reiterates rather than challenges neoliberal ideologies of frictionless circulation and an absolute opposition between state and capital — is Hardt and Negri's *Empire*.

19. Karl Marx, *Grundrisse: Foundations of the Critique of Political Economy*, trans. Martin Nicolaus (New York: Vintage Books, 1973), 408.

20. Harvey, *Limits to Capital*, 416. Also see Neil Smith, "The Satanic Geographies of Globalization," *Public Culture* 10, 1: 169–92; and Smith, *Uneven Development*.

21. Osborne, *Politics of Time*, 165.

22. Chakrabarty, *Provincializing Europe*, 47–71; Frederick Cooper, "Colonizing Time: Work Rhythms and Labour Conflict in Colonial Mombassa," in Dirks, *Colonialism and Culture*.

23. See Chakrabarty, *Provincializing Europe*, 47–71.

24. See, in particular, John Agnew and Stuart Corbridge, *Mastering Space: Hegemony, Territory and International Political Economy* (London: Routledge, 1995); Michael Geyer and Charles Bright, "For a Unified History of the World in the Twentieth Century," *Radical History Review* 39:69–91; Eric Hobsbawm, *Industry and Empire: From 1750 to the Present Day* (Cambridge: Cambridge University Press, 1986); Mann, *Sources of Social Power*, vol. 2; Wolf, *Europe and the People without History*.

25. Arrighi, *Long Twentieth Century*, 54. Also see Robert Cox, *Production, Power and World Order* (New York: Columbia University Press, 1987).

26. Arrighi, *Long Twentieth Century*, 58.

27. Hobsbawm, *Industry and Empire*, 139.

28. Mann, *Sources of Social Power*, 265.

29. Lefebvre, *Production of Space*, 350.

30. Arrighi, *Long Twentieth Century*; Giovanni Arrighi and Beverly Silver, *Chaos and Governance in the Modern World System* (Minneapolis: University of Minnesota Press, 1999); Karl Polanyi, *The Great Transformation: The Political and Economic Origins of Our Times* (Boston: Beacon Press, 1957); Anwar Shaikh, "Foreign Trade and the Law of Value, Part 1," *Science and Society* 43, 3 (1979): 281–302; and Shaikh, "Foreign Trade and the Law of Value, Part 2," *Science and Society* 44, 1 (1980): 27–57.

31. See Shaikh, "Foreign Trade and the Law of Value," pts. 1 and 2, for a sharp critique. Also see Coronil, *Magical State*, 39–41. For a provocative reading of Adam Smith, see Emma Rothschild, *Economic Sentiments: Adam Smith, Condorcet, and the Enlightenment* (Cambridge: Harvard University Press, 2001).

32. See Arrighi, *Long Twentieth Century*, 55–57; S. James and D. Lake, "The Second Face of Hegemony: Britain's Repeal of the Corn Laws and the American Walker Tariff of 1846," *International Organization* 43, 1 (1989): 1–29; Patrick O'Brien and G. A. Pigman, "Free Trade, British Hegemony and the International Economic Order in the Nineteenth Century," *Review of International Studies* 18, 2 (1992): 89–114; Hobsbawm, *Industry and Empire*, 134–53; and Polanyi, *Great Transformation*. Also see J. Gallagher and R. E. Robinson, "The Imperialism of Free Trade," *Economic History Review*, 2d ser., 6:1–15.

33. Lefebvre, *Production of Space*, 32. The colonial Indian army was, as David Washbrook notes, *the* "army of British imperialism, formal and informal, which operated worldwide, opening up markets of the industrial revolution,

subordinating labor forces to the domination of capital and bringing benighted civilizations enlightened values." Washbrook, "South Asia, the World
System and World Capitalism," *Journal of Asian Studies* 49, 3 (1990): 481. It
was deployed in Afghanistan in the 1870s and early 1880s, in the final conquest of Burma in the late 1880s, against the Mahdi uprisings of 1885–86
and 1896 in Sudan, the Boxer Rebellion of 1900 in China, the Boer War in
South Africa during 1899–1902, in Tibet in 1902–3, and the Persian Gulf in
the first decade of the twentieth century. Also see A. Offer, "The British Empire, 1870–1914: A Waste of Money?" *Economic History Review* 46, 2: 215–38.

34. Lance Davis and Robert Huttenback, "The Export of British Finance,
    1865–1914," *Journal of Imperial and Commonwealth History* 13, 3 (1985): 50–51.
    Leland Jenks, *The Migration of British Capital to 1875* (1927; reprint, London:
    Nelson, 1971); and Daniel Thorner, *Investment in Empire: British Railway and
    Steam Shipping Enterprise in India, 1825–1849* (Philadelphia: University of Penn-
    sylvania, 1950), provide the figure of 150 million in railway investment. B. R.
    Tomlinson, *Political Economy of the Raj, 1914–47: The Economics of Decolonization
    in India* (London: Cambridge University Press, 1979), 4, provides a figure of
    200 million.

35. Jenks, *Migration of British Capital to 1875*, 207; Thorner, *Investment in Empire*,
    viii. Also see Lance Davis and Robert Huttenback, *Mammon and the Pursuit of
    Empire: The Political Economy of British Imperialism, 1860–1912* (Cambridge:
    Cambridge University Press, 1986).

36. See Eric Stoke's classic analysis, *The English Utilitarians and India* (Oxford:
    Clarendon Press, 1959), for the ascendancy of utilitarian thought.

37. Bernard Semmel, "Philosophical Radicals and Colonialism," *Journal of Eco-
    nomic History* 21, 4 (1961): 513.

38. See Lionel Robbins, *Robert Torrens and the Evolution of Classical Economics* (Lon-
    don: Macmillan, 1958), 225–31, 254–57.

39. John Stuart Mill, *Principles of Political Economy* (1848; reprint, London: Long-
    mans, Green, 1909), 727–28.

40. Harvey, *Limits to Capital*, 431–38. Harvey deploys the term *spatial fix* to refer
    to periodic attempts to resolve the contradictions of capital accumulation
    through the production of particular spatial and political-regulatory infra-
    structures and frameworks. It is a central category of his broader theorization
    of the multiple spatiotemporal contradictions of capitalism, such as the ten-
    sion between extending markets through the annihilation of space by time
    and the simultaneous need for fixed infrastructure (with a long turnover
    time) to enable rapid movements through space.

41. This quotation and those that follow in this paragraph are quoted in Mintz,
    Sweetness and Power, 42.

42. Lefebvre, *Production of Space*, 21.

43. Jenks, *Migration of British Capital to 1875*, 208.

44. *Annual Register*, 1858 (IOL), 259.

45. The Stracheys were central administrative figures of the post-1858 regime. Their "contribution," as they wrote, could only be described as "insignificant by a false affectation of modesty. There is hardly a great office of the State from that of Lieutenant-Governor or Member of Council downward, which one or other of us has not held, and there is hardly a great department of the administration for the management of which, at some time, one or another of us has not been responsible." John Strachey and Richard Strachey, *The Finances and Public Works of India from 1869 to 1881* (London: K. Paul, Trench, 1882), vii.

46. Finance Records, July 1874, no. 9, 562, IOL.

47. Edward Davidson, *The Railways of India: With an Account of Their Rise, Progress and Construction* (London: E. and F. N. Spon, 1868), 3–4 (emphasis added).

48. Thorner, *Investment in Empire*, 177–78.

49. Jenks, *Migration of British Capital to 1875*, 210–11.

50. Hyde Clark, *Colonization, Defence and Railways in Our Indian Empire* (London: John Weale, 1857), 222. Also see Clark, *Practical and Theoretical Considerations on the Management of Railways in India* (London: John Weale, 1848).

51. Hyde Clark, "Railways in India," *Railway Register*, September 1845, 2:178, 181–92. Quoted in Thorner, *Investment in Empire*, 10.

52. Anonymous, Letter to Lord John Russell on the Subject of the East India Railways, 1848, quoted in Thorner, *Investment in Empire*, 8.

53. Thorner, *Investment in Empire*, 152.

54. *Parliamentary Returns on Indian Railways, 1854–61*, L/PWD/5/24, 112–16, IOL.

55. Jenks, *Migration of British Capital to 1875*, 227.

56. Daniel Headrick, *The Tentacles of Progress: Technology transfer in the Age of Imperialism* (New York: Oxford University Press, 1988), 53–54.

57. Jenks, *Migration of British Capital to 1875*, 231.

58. J. N. Westwood, *Railways of India* (Vancouver: David and Charles, 1974), 37.

59. Thomas Bazley to Mayo, August 9, 1869, Lord Mayo Papers, Cambridge University Library.

60. Evidence of Danvers, *Parliamentary Papers*, H.C. 327, vol. 8, sess. 1872, 2049, IOL. Also see Juland Danvers, *Indian Railways: Their Past History, Present Conditions, and Future Prospects* (London: E. Wilson, 1877).

61. Memorandum by Louis Mallet, Financial Proceedings, 1871–76, 12–14, L/F/5/19, IOL.

62. Ian J. Kerr, *Building the Railways of the Raj, 1850–1900* (Delhi: Oxford University Press, 1997), 19–21.

63. Phillip Bagwell, *The Transport Revolution* (London: Routledge, 1974), 99–102; Also see Frank Dobbins, *Forging Industrial Policy: The United States, Britain, and France in the Railway Age* (Cambridge: Cambridge University Press, 1994).

64. John McGuire, "The World Economy, the Colonial State, and the Establishment of the Indian National Congress," in *The Indian National Congress and the Political Economy of India, 1885–1985*, ed. Mike Shepperdson and Colin Simmons (London: Avebury, 1983), 7.

65. Strachey and Strachey, *Finances and Public Works of India from 1869 to 1881*, 7–8. For the emergence of a globally organized British imperial communications network, see Paul Kennedy, "Imperial Cable Communications and Strategy, 1870–1914," in *The War Plans of the Great Powers, 1880–1914*, ed. Paul Kennedy (London: Allen and Unwin, 1979); Nigel Thrift, "Transport and Communications, 1730–1914," in *An Historical Geography of England and Wales*, ed. R. A. Dodgon and R. A. Butlin (London: Academic Press, 1990).

66. The Upper Ganges Canal consisted of a 568-mile main canal and 3,293 miles of subsidiary channels. The canal was five times larger in length than all the irrigation lines of Egypt and Lombardy considered together and a third longer than the Pennsylvania Canal, which was the largest navigation canal in the United States. Financed by private loans raised in London, the canal was marred by serious design flaws, and the East India Company was forced to undertake the necessary repair work. For an account of this project, see Ian Stone, *Canal Irrigation in British India: Perspectives on Technological Change in a Peasant Society* (Cambridge: Cambridge University Press, 1984), 18.

67. See Robert B. Buckley, *The Irrigation Works of India and Their Financial Results* (London: E. and F. Spon, 1880), 189.

68. Stone, *Canal Irrigation in British India*, 23–25.

69. Lord Canning's Minute on Private Companies for Canals and Irrigation, November 29, 1858, Home Department Revenue Branch, Proceedings, February 11, 1859, no. 1/4, NAI.

70. The comparable expenditure on railways during this period was 23.9 million pounds. *Report of the Indian Famine Commission, 1879*, in *Parliamentary Papers*, 1881, pt. 2, 147, 27, IOL.

71. *Report of the Indian Irrigation Commission, 1901–3* (London: HMSO, 1903), 1, 11:102–3, IOL.

72. David Gilmartin, "Scientific Empire and Imperial Science: Colonialism and Irrigation Technology in the Indus Basin," *Journal of Asian Studies* 53, 4 (1994): 1127–49; Elizabeth Whitcombe, *Agrarian Conditions in Northern India: The United Provinces under British Rule, 1860–1900* (Berkeley: University of California Press, 1972); Also see Prakash, *Another Reason*, 61–63. For a dis-

senting view about the effects of irrigation, see Stone, *Canal Irrigation in British India.*

73. Whitcombe, *Agrarian Conditions in Northern India,* 61–120; Gilmartin, "Scientific Empire and Imperial Science."

74. Home Department, to the Government, NWP, June 2, 1870, in NWP Revenue Proceedings no. 56, Index no. 1, December 3, 1870, IOL.

75. Quoted in A. H. Harrington, "Economic Reform in Rural India," *Calcutta Review* 80 (1885): 435.

76. For the recurring iteration of the state as the supreme landlord, see Minute by John Strachey, May 19, 1859, Home Judicial Proceedings, September 16, 1862; Minute by Sir William Muir, June 12, 1877, Finance Department Collections, c/140, 110, IOL. Also see Strachey and Strachey, *Finances and Public Works of India,* in which they note that "The State in India has always possessed, both in theory and in practice, the greater share of the property in India, and has been entitled to receive from the occupier such portion of the surplus profit after defraying the expenses of cultivation as it has appeared possible or expedient to take" (14).

77. An exemplary instance of the reiteration of this conception is B. H. Baden-Powell, *The Land Systems of British India,* vols. 1 and 2 (Oxford: Clarendon Press, 1892). Also see S. Ambirajan, *Classical Political Economy and British Policy in India* (Cambridge: Cambridge University Press, 1978), 171–80; and Stokes, *English Utilitarians and India,* 287–323, for the continued resonance of conceptions of the state as the universal landlord.

78. Baden-Powell, *Land Systems of British India,* 1:239.

79. For the role of the state in geological, forestry, and agricultural research, see Roy Macleod and Deepak Kumar, eds., *Technology and the Raj: Western Technology and Technical Transfers to India, 1700–1947* (Delhi: Sage Publications, 1995).

80. David Ludden, *An Agrarian History of South Asia,* vol. 4 *of The New Cambridge History of India* (Cambridge: Cambridge University Press, 1999), 180–90.

81. Ranajit Guha, *A Rule of Property for Bengal: An Essay on the Idea of Permanent Settlement* (1962; reprint, Durham, N.C.: Duke University Press, 1996).

82. Ramchandra Guha, *The Unquiet Woods: Ecological Change and Peasant Resistance in the Himalayas* (Delhi: Oxford University Press, 1989); R. P. Tucker, "The British Colonial System and the Forests of the Western Himalayas," in *Global Deforestation and the Nineteenth Century World Economy,* ed. R. P. Tucker and J. F. Richards (Durham, N.C.: Duke University Press, 1983); K. Sivaramakrishnan, "Colonialism and Forestry in India: Imagining the Past in Present Politics," *Comparative Studies in Society and History* 37, 1 (1995): 3–40. For accounts written by the major players in forestry legislation and policy making,

see B. H. Baden-Powell, "On the Defects of the Existing Forest Law (Act VII of 1865) and Proposals for a New Forest Act," in *Report of the Proceedings of the Forest Conference, 1873–74*, ed. B. H. Gamble and J. S. Gamble (Calcutta: Superintendent of Government Printing, 1875); Dietrich Brandis, *Progress of Forestry in India* (London: McFarlane and Erskine, 1884); and *Suggestions Regarding Forest Administration in the North-Western Provinces and Oudh* (Calcutta: Government of India Press, 1882).

83. B. H. Baden–Powell and J. S. Gamble, eds., *Report of the Proceedings of the Forest Conference, 1873–1874* (Calcutta: Superintendent of Government Printing, 1875). For detailed accounts, see Ramchandra Guha, "An Early Environmental Debate: The Making of the 1878 Forest Act," *Indian Economic and Social History Review* 27, 1:65–84. Sivaramakrishnan, "Colonialism and Forestry in India."

84. Baden-Powell, *Land Systems of British India,* 1:358.

85. Sivaramakrishnan, "Colonialism and Forestry in India," 14–15.

86. Department of Revenue, Agriculture, and Commerce (Forests) Proceedings, nos. 18–20, 1880, 15–16, NAI.

87. See, in particular, Sivaramakrishnan, "Colonialism and Forestry in India"; and Ramchandra Guha and Madhav Gadgil, "State Forestry and Social Conflict in British India: A Study in the Ecological Bases of Agrarian Protest," *Past and Present* 123:141–77.

88. For the global dominance of German forestry science, see James Scott, *Seeing Like a State: How Certain Schemes to Improve the Human Condition Have Failed* (New Haven: Yale University Press, CT, 1999), 13–16. Key works in the field of ecological imperialism include Guha, *Unquiet Woods;* Whitcombe, *Agrarian Conditions in Northern India;* R. P. Tucker, "The Depletion of India's Forests under British Imperialism: Planters, Foresters and Peasants in Assam and Kerala," in *The Ends of the Earth,* ed. D. Worster (Cambridge: Cambridge University Press). Also see Mike Davis's passionately argued *Late Victorian Holocausts: El Nino, Famines and the Making of the Third World* (London: Verso, 2001), on the dialectic between ecological disasters and free-trade market principles in colonial India.

89. Sivaramakrishnan, "Colonialism and Forestry in India," 10.

90. *Report of a Committee on the Classification of Public Works Expenditures and the Various Returns Exhibiting Which Are Required by the Governments of India,* quoted in Ambirajan, *Classical Political Economy and British Policy in India,* 247 (emphasis added).

91. Ludden, *Agrarian History of South Asia,* 181.

92. Ian Derbyshire, "Economic Change and the Railways in North India,

1860–1914," *Modern Asian Studies* 21, 3 (July 1987): 521–45; Whitcombe, *Agrarian Conditions in Northern India,* 64–68.

93. For a detailed history of colonial labor migrations, see Hugh Tinker, *A New System of Slavery: The Export of Indian Labour Overseas* (Oxford: Oxford University Press, 1974).

94. Stone, *Canal Irrigation in British India,* 1984.

95. For railway-aided expansion in agricultural production in this region, see John Hurd, "Railways," in *The Cambridge Economic History of India,* ed. Dharma Kumar and Meghnad Desai, vol. 2, *1757–1970* (Cambridge: Cambridge University Press, 1983), 737–61. For irrigation-propelled shifts in agricultural productions, see Ian Stone, "Canal Irrigation and Agrarian Change: The Experience of the Ganges Canal Trace, Muzaffarnagar District (U.P)," in *Economy and Society: Essays in Indian Economic and Social History,* ed. K. N. Chaudhari and Clive Dewey (Delhi: Oxford University Press, 1979), 86–112. For more general analysis of the commercialization of agricultural production in UP during this period, see Shahid Amin, *Sugarcane and Sugar in Gorakhpur: An Inquiry into Peasant Production for Capitalist Enterprise in Colonial India* (Delhi: Oxford University Press, 1984); and Whitcombe, *Agrarian Conditions in Northern India.*

96. For accounts of urban-centered industrial and financial enterprises in different regional locales, see Amiya Kumar Bagchi, *Private Investment in Empire, 1900–1939* (Cambridge: Cambridge University Press, 1972); and Bagchi, *The Political Economy of Underdevelopment* (Cambridge: Cambridge University Press, 1982); Rajnarayan Chandravarkar, "Industrialization in India before 1947: Conventional Approaches and Alternative Perspectives," *Modern Asian Studies* 19, 3 (1985): 623–68; C. J. Dewey, "The Government of India's "New Industrial Policy," 1900–1925: Formation and Failure," in Chaudhari and Dewey, *Economy and Society;* Colin Simmons, "Deindustrialization, Industrialization and the Indian Economy c. 1850–1947," *Modern Asian Studies* 19, 3 (1985): 593–622; and Daniel Thorner and Alice Thorner, "De-Industrialization in India, 1881–1931," in *Land and Labour in India,* ed. Daniel Thorner and Alice Thorner (Philadelphia: University of Pennsylvania Press, 1962). For a sophisticated analysis of Bengal's regional agrarian political economy in relation to the wider British imperial economy for a later period, see Sugata Bose, *Agrarian Bengal: Economy, Social Structure and Politics, 1919–1947* (Cambridge: Cambridge University Press, 1986). Also see Binay B. Chaudhuri, "Growth of Commercial Agriculture in Bengal, 1859–1885," *Indian Economic and Social History Review* 7, 2 (1970): 25–60. For an account of agricultural trends across and between subregions in a cotton-growing region, see Sumit Guha, *The*

Agrarian Economy of the Bombay Deccan, 1818–1941 (Oxford: Oxford University Press, 1985). Also see Neil Charlesworth, *Peasants and Imperial Rule: Agriculture and Agrarian Society in the Bombay Presidency, 1850–1935* (Cambridge: Cambridge University Press).

97. Ludden, *Agrarian History of South Asia,* 181.

98. Hurd, "Railways," 752–53, 758.

99. Agnew, "Territorial Trap"; Agnew and Corbridge, *Mastering Space;* Dobbins, *Forging Industrial Policy;* Mann, *Sources of Social Power,* vol. 2; Wolf, *Europe and the People without History.*

100. Frederick Lehmann, "Great Britain and the Supply of Railway Locomotives to India: A Case Study of Economic Imperialism," *Indian Economic and Social History Review* 2, 4 (October 1965): 300. Also see Lehmann, "Railway Workshops, Technology Transfer, and Skilled Labour Recruitment in Colonial India, *Journal of Historical Research* 20, 1 (1977): 49–61.

101. Hurd, "Railways," 745.

102. B. R. Tomlinson, *The Economy of Modern India, 1860–1970* (Cambridge: Cambridge University, 1993), 51–61.

103. K. N. Chaudhari, "Foreign Trade and Balance of Payments, 1757–1947," in Kumar and Desai, *Cambridge Economic History of India,* 853–54. There was also a concomitant expansion in the status of colonial India as a source for raw cotton. In 1858, exports to Britain amounted to 132.7 million pounds of cotton, or only 13 percent of total cotton imports in Britain. Two years later, exports from colonial India increased to 392.7 million pounds and comprised 75 percent of total British imports. Although cotton exports declined after the end of the American civil war and the collapse of the speculative cotton boom, the volume of exports never fell below the prewar level (849).

104. On the integration of markets, see Michelle McAlpin, "Price Movements and Fluctuations in Economic Activity (1860–1947)," in Kumar and Desai, *Cambridge Economic History of India,* 878–904; Tomlinson, *Economy of Modern India,* 61. Also see Anand Yang, *Bazaar India: Markets, Society, and the Colonial State in Bihar* (Berkeley: University of California Press, 1998), 112–60, for a compelling account of bazaars as a chief locus for the production of social categories and material practices.

105. For a detailed account of this formation understood in terms of a distinctive colonial mode of production, see Hamza Alavi and John Harriss, eds., *Sociology of "Developing Societies": South Asia* (New York: Monthly Review Press, 1989); Hamza Alavi, *Capitalism and Colonial Production* (London: Croom Helm, 1982); Bagchi, *Political Economy of Underdevelopment;* Jairus Banaji, "For a Theory of Colonial Modes of Production," *Economic and Political Weekly* 23 (1973): 2498–502.

106. See Davis, *Late Victorian Holocausts*, table P1, 7, for different figures. Also see Amartya Sen, *Poverty and Famines: An Essay on Entitlement and Deprivation* (New York: Oxford University Press, 1981).

107. Davis, *Late Victorian Holocausts*, 31–32.

108. See, in particular, Shahid Amin, "Small Peasant Commodity Production and Rural Indebtedness: The Culture of Sugarcane in Eastern UP, 1880–1920," in *Subaltern Studies*, vol. 1, ed. Ranajit Guha (Delhi: Oxford University Press, 1984); Jairus Banaji, "Capitalist Domination and the Small Peasantry: Deccan Districts in the Late Nineteenth Century," *Economic and Political Weekly* 12, 33–34 (1977): 1375–404; Bose, *Agrarian Bengal*; Charlesworth, *Peasants and Imperial Rule*; Chaudhuri, "Growth of Commercial Agriculture in Bengal"; Ravinder Kumar, *Western India in the Nineteenth Century: A Study of the Social History of Maharashtra* (London: Routledge and Kegan Paul, 1968); Ludden, *Agrarian History of South Asia*; Whitcombe, *Agrarian Conditions in Northern India*. For a related account of the contradictions within colonial policies in relation to forms of coerced labor, see Gyan Prakash, *Bonded Histories: Genealogies of Labor Servitude in Colonial India* (Cambridge: Cambridge University Press, 1991).

109. Cohn, "Representing Authority in Colonial India" and *Colonialism and Its Forms of Knowledge*.

110. Bernard Cohn, "The Study of Indian Society and Culture," in *Anthropologist among the Historians*, 158–65; and Louis Dumont, "The 'Village Community' from Munro to Maine," *Contributions to Indian Sociology* 9 (1966): 67–89.

111. Cohn, "Study of Indian Society and Culture," 162.

112. M. B. Nanavati and J. J. Ajaria, *The Indian Rural Problem* (Bombay: Indian Society of Agricultural Economists, 1960).

113. Amin, "Small Peasant Commodity Production and Rural Indebtedness"; Bose, *Agrarian Bengal*; Banaji, "Capitalist Domination and the Small Peasantry"; Kumar, *Western India in the Nineteenth Century*; Whitcombe, *Agrarian Conditions in Northern India*.

114. Chatterjee, *The Nation and Its Fragments*, 16–24.

115. Marx, *Grundrisse*, 731–732.

116. Thorner, *Investment in Empire*, 392.

117. McGuire, "World Economy, the Colonial State, and Establishment of the Indian National Congress," 48, 44. Also see Michael Edelstein, *Overseas Investment in the Age of High Imperialism: The United Kingdom, 1850–1914* (New York: Columbia University Press, 1982).

118. Marx, *Grundrisse*, 227–28.

119. Arrighi, *Long Twentieth Century*, 239–300; Gabriel Ardant, "Financial Policy and Economic Infrastructure of Modern States and Nations," in *The Forma-*

tion of National States in Europe, ed. Charles Tilly (Princeton: Princeton University Press, 1975); Cox, *Production, Power, and World Order,* 111–20; Mann, *Sources of Social Power,* vol. 2; Charles Maier, "Consigning the Twentieth Century to History: Alternative Narratives for the Modern Era," *American Historical Review* 105, 3 (2000): 807–31; John Vincent Nye, "The Myth of Free-Trade Britain and Fortress France: Tariffs and Trade in the Nineteenth Century," *Journal of Economic History* 51, 1 (1991): 23–46; Polanyi, *Great Transformation;* Paul Bairoch, "European Trade Policy, 1815–1914," in *The Cambridge Economic History of Europe,* ed. Peter Mathias and Sidney Pollard (Cambridge: Cambridge University Press, 1989).

120. On the specificity of nationally regulated capitalism, see Amin, "Challenge of Globalization"; M. Dunford and M. Perrons, *The Arena of Capital* (London: Macmillan, 1983); Claudia von Braunmuhl, "On the Analysis of the Bourgeois Nation-State within the World Market Context," in *State and Capital,* ed. J. Holloway and S. Picciotto (Austin: University of Texas Press, 1978).

121. Polanyi, *Great Transformation.*

122. Max Weber, *General Economic History,* trans. Frank Knight (New York: Crowell-Collier, 1961), 249. Elsewhere Weber emphasized the "memorable alliance" between "rising states and the sought-after and privileged capitalist powers" as a "major factor in creating modern capitalism. . . . Neither the trade nor the monetary policies of the modern states . . . can be understood without this peculiar political competition and 'equilibrium,' that is, interstate competition for mobile capital." Max Weber, *Economy and Society* (Berkeley: University of California Press, 1978), 1:353–54.

123. Polanyi, *Great Transformation,* 201.

124. In terms of physical-territorial expansion, the British Empire increased, as Eric Hobsbawm notes, "by some 4 million square miles . . . France by 3.5 million. Germany acquired more than 1 million, Belgium and Italy just under 1 million square miles. The USA acquired more than some 100,000 . . . [and] Japan . . . the same amount." Hobsbawm, *The Age of Empire, 1875–1914* (New York: Random House, 1989), 59.

125. Paul Bairoch, *The Economic Development of the Third World since 1900* (Berkeley: University of California Press, 1975), 309–11.

126. Wolf, *Europe and the People without History.*

127. Marcello de Cecco, *Money and Empire: The International Gold Standard, 1870–1914* (Totowa, N.J.: Rowman and Littlefield, 1975), 36.

128. Alan Milward, *The Economic Effects of the Two World Wars on Britain* (London: Macmillan, 1970), 45.

129. Michael Barratt-Brown, *The Economics of Imperialism* (Harmondsworth: Penguin Books, 1974), 133–36; Cecco, *Money and Empire,* 29–38; Francois

Crouzet, *The Victorian Economy* (London: Methuen, 1982), 370; S. B. Saul, *Studies in British Overseas Trade, 1870–1914* (Liverpool: Liverpool University Press, 1960), 62; Tomlinson, *Economy of Modern India,* 15. Also see Dietmar Rothermund, "An Aspect of the Monetary Policy of British Imperialism," *Indian Economic and Social History Review* 7, 1 (1970): 91–108; and S. Ambirajan, *Political Economy and Monetary Management, 1776–1914* (Madras: East-West Press, 1984).

130. S. B. Saul, "The Economic Significance of 'Constructive Imperialism,'" *Journal of Economic History* 17, 2 (1957): 173–92.

131. All quotations of Lord Hamilton in this paragraph are from MSS C-126/5-1903, June 19, Lord Hamilton to Lord Curzon, IOL.

132. A. J. H. Latham, *The International Economy and the Underdeveloped World, 1865–1914* (New York: Oxford University Press, 1978); Sunanda Sen, *Colonies and the Empire: India, 1890–1914* (Calcutta: Orient Longman, 1992); Wallerstein, *Historical Capitalism and Mercantilism and the Consolidation of the European World Economy.*

133. For a detailed discussion, see Cecco, *Money and Empire,* 62–76.

134. John Maynard Keynes was employed at the India Office in London for two years. For a justification and explanation of the sterling exchange system, see John Maynard Keynes, *Indian Currency and Finance* (1913; reprint, London: Macmillan, 1924). Keynes was appointed to the Royal Commission on Indian Currency and Finance in 1913, shortly after the completion of his work.

135. Cecco, *Money and Empire,* 62. Also see Saul, *Studies in British Overseas Trade.*

136. A. G. Chandavarkar, "Money and Credit, 1858–1947," in Kumar and Desai, *Cambridge Economic History of India,* 770.

137. Sugata Bose and Ayesha Jalal, *Modern South Asia: History, Culture and Political Economy* (Delhi: Oxford University Press, 2002), 100. The exact figures of the annual drain remains the subject of some debate. See Barratt-Brown, *Economics of Imperialism,* 85; and Tomlinson, *Economy of Modern India,* 13–14, for competing figures.

138. The statements in the epigraphs are given as quoted in Bipin Chandra Pal, *The New Economic Menace to India* (Madras: Ganesh and Co., 1920), 81, 83.

Chapter Two

1. See Anthony Giddens, *The Nation-State and Violence,* vol. 2 of *A Contemporary Critique of Historical Materialism* (Berkeley: University of California Press, 1985), for an analysis of the reflexive processes of state consolidation.

2. Appadurai, "Number in the Colonial Imagination," in *Modernity at Large.* Also see N. G. Barrier, ed. *The Census in British India: New Perspectives* (Delhi: Ox-

ford University Press, 1981); Frank Conlon, "The Census of India as a Source for the Historical Study of Religion and Caste," in Barrier, *Census in British India;* and Pant, "Cognitive Status of Caste in Colonial Ethnography."

3. R. S. Smith, "Rule-by-Records and Rule-by-Reports: Complementary Aspects of the British Imperial Rule of Law," *Contributions to Indian Sociology* 19, 1 (1985): 153–76.

4. Cohn, *Historian among the Anthropologists* and *Colonialism and Its Forms of Knowledge.*

5. See Dirks, *Castes of Mind,* for a theorization of colonial rule as an ethnographic state.

6. Exemplary of the commercial dictionaries produced during this period is the multivolume dictionary on economic products by George Watt, *A Dictionary of the Economic Products of India,* 7 vols. (London: W. H. Allen and Co., 1885–96); and Watt, *The Commercial Products of India* (London: John Murray, 1908). Also see William Crooke, *A Glossary of North Indian Peasant Life* (1879; reprint, Delhi: Oxford University Press, 1989); William Hoey, *A Monograph on Trade and Manufactures in Northern India* (Lucknow: American Methodist Press, 1880); and B. H. Baden-Powell, *Handbook of the Economic Products of the Punjab,* 2 vols. (Roorkee: Thomason Civil Engineering College Press, 1868–72).

7. Finance Department, no. 27, April 7, 1860, Form of and Method of Keeping Indian Accounts, 1860–1900, L/F/5/97, IOL.

8. *Report of the Commissioner of Inquiry into the Constitution and Mode of Conduct in the Business of the Financial Department and of the Offices and Audit and Account Attached to That Department* (Calcutta: Military Orphan Press, 1864), 13. Also included in L/F/5/97 cited in the previous note.

9. Finance Department, no. 27, April 7, 1860, Form of and Method of Keeping Indian Accounts, 1860–1900, L/F/5/97, IOL.

10. System of Account in Vogue in the Bombay, Madras and Bengal Presidency, 1857–58, Finance Department memorandum, June 1872, Form of and Method of Keeping Indian Accounts, 1860–1900, Finance Department, L/F/5/97, IOL.

11. *Report of the Commissioner of Inquiry into the Constitution and Mode of Conduct in the Business of the Financial Department,* 39.

12. For a general history of accounting in colonial and postcolonial India, see G. P. Kapadia, "History of the Accountancy Profession in India (New Delhi: Institute of Chartered Accountants of India, 1973). For a Foucauldian analysis of the "economy" as a discursive effect generated by practices of accounting, statistical representation, and discourses of accountability, see Kalpagam, "Colonial Governmentality and the 'Economy'"; and U. Kalpagam, "Colonial-

ism, Rational Calculations and Idea of the Economy," *Economic and Political Weekly* 32, 4 (1997): 2–12.

13. Legislative Department, May 1882, part A, 9–107, Proc. no. 23, Abstract of the Proceedings of the Legislative Council, of the governor-general of India, August 3, 1881, NAI.

14. See, in particular, Weber, *Economy and Society*, 1:85–107; Max Weber, *The Protestant Ethic and the "Spirit" of Capitalism and Other Writings*, trans. Peter Baehr and Gordon C. Wells (New York: Penguin Books, 2002), 36–363; and Weber, *General Economic History*.

15. See, in particular, Ian Hacking, *The Taming of Chance* (Cambridge: Cambridge University Press, 1990); Mary Poovey, *A History of the Modern Fact: Problems of Knowledge in the Sciences of Wealth and Society* (Chicago: University of Chicago Press, 1998); and Poovey, "Figures of Arithmetic, Figures of Speech: The Discourse of Statistics," in *Questions of Evidence: Proof, Practice, and Persuasion across the Disciplines*, ed. James Chandler, Arnold Davidson, and Harry Harootunian (Chicago: University of Chicago Press, 1994). For an analysis of accounting procedures focused on their internal logic rather than their historicity, see Kalpagam, "Colonial Governmentality and the 'Economy.'"

16. Poulantzas, *State, Power, and Socialism*, 110.

17. Lefebvre, *Production of National Space*, 96.

18. David Ludden, "India's Developmental Regime," in Dirks, *Colonialism and Culture*, 261.

19. Appadurai, "Number in the Colonial Imagination," in *Modernity at Large*, 120.

20. Proceedings of the Revenue Department, NWP, July 1875, no. 9, 21, IOL.

21. Proceedings of the Revenue Department, NWP, November 1875, 9, 3, IOL. Also see Proceedings of the Revenue, Agriculture, and Commerce Department, January 1871, 54, IOL; Proceedings of the Revenue Department, August 1876, no. 92-124, IOL.

22. Proceedings of the Revenue Department, NWP, November 1875, no 9, 3, IOL.

23. Proceedings of the Revenue Department, August 1876, no. 92-124, 144, IOL.

24. Proceedings of the Revenue Department, January 1871, 54, IOL.

25. Proceedings of the Revenue Department, NWP, March 1875, no. 5, 4, IOL.

26. Proceedings of the Revenue Department, NWP, August 1876, 129, IOL.

27. John Strachey, *India: Its Administration and Progress* (London: George Allen and Unwin, 1888), 297.

28. Proceedings of the Revenue Department, NWP, November 1875, 7, IOL.

29. Bourdieu, *In Other Words*, 76.

30. Ripon's address to the Edinburgh Philosophical Institution, November 10,

1885, as quoted in S. R. Mehrotra, *The Emergence of the Indian Nation Congress* (Delhi: Vikas Publications, 1971), 134.

31. Lefebre, *Production of Space*, 89.

32. Selections from vernacular newspapers, NWP 1868, 7, IOL.

33. General Proceedings, NWP, April 1865, 86, IOL.

34. Selections from vernacular newspapers, 1870, 12, IOL.

35. Bholanauth Chunder, *The Travels of a Hindoo to Various Parts of Bengal and Upper India*, vol. 1 (London: Trubner, 1869), 437–38.

36. Crooke, *Glossary of North Indian Peasant Life*, 169.

37. Karl Marx, *Capital: A Critique of Political Economy*, vol. 1, trans. Ben Fowkes (New York: Vintage Books, 1977), 227, 209.

38. Irfan Habib, "Monetary System and Prices," in *The Cambridge Economic History of India*, ed. Tapan Raychudhari and Irfan Habib, vol. 1, *1200–1750* (Cambridge: Cambridge University Press, 1982); Habib, "A System of Trimetallism in the Age of 'Price Revolution': Effects of the Silver Influx on the Mughal Monetary System," in *The Imperial System of Mughal India*, ed. John Richards (London: Oxford University Press, 1987); Frank Perlin, "Money Use in Pre-Colonial India and the International Trade in Currency Media," in Richards, *Imperial System of Mughal India*; Sanjay Subrahmanyam, ed., *Money and the Market in India, 1100–1700* (Delhi: Oxford University Press, 1994). For an influential account in policy terms, see James Princep, *Essays on Indian Antiquities, History, Numismatics, and Paleographic of the Late James Princep, to which are added his useful tables, illustrative of Indian History, chronology, modern coinages, weights, measures etc*, ed. with notes by Edward Thomas (London: J. Murray, 1858).

39. Financial Series, L/F/5/17, 22–23, IOL. Also see Princep, *Essays on Indian Antiquities, History, Numismatics, and Paleographic of the Late James Princep*, 4–26.

40. For important accounts of merchant credit relations as mediated through kinship and caste-based networks, see Chris Bayly, *Rulers, Townsmen, Bazaars: North Indian Society in the Age of British Expansion* (Cambridge: Cambridge University Press, 1983), 374–93; and David Rudner, "Banker's Trust and the Culture of Banking among the Nattukottai Chettiars of Colonial South India," *Modern Asian Studies* 23, 3 (1989): 417–58. For works on the early colonial period that emphasize the entanglements of markets with forms of sovereignty and the cultural logics of exchange, see Kumkum Chatterjee, *Merchants, Politics, and Society in Early Modern India* (Leiden: E. J. Brill, 1996); Sudipta Sen, *Empire of Free Trade* (Philadelphia: University of Pennsylvania Press: 1998). For an analysis of the formation of *bazaars* over the longue durée from the late eighteenth to the early twentieth century, emphasizing the ways in which they worked as a practical refutation of Orientalist and official discourses on the Indian village, see Yang, *Bazaar India*; K. N. Chaudhari,

*Asia before Europe: Economy and Civilization of the Indian Ocean from the Rise of Is-
lam to 1750* (Cambridge: Cambridge University Press, 1990); and Chaudhari,
The Trading World of Asia and the East India Company, 1600–1760 (Cambridge:
Cambridge University Press, 1978), represent exemplary social histories of
merchant networks in the precolonial and early colonial era.

41. Princep, *Essays on Indian Antiquities, History, Numismatics, and Paleographic of the
Late James Princep*, 4–26.

42. See, in particular, Claude Markovits, *The Global World of Indian Merchants,
1750–1947: Traders of Sind from Bukhara to Panama* (Cambridge: Cambridge
University Press, 2000); Sanjay Subrahmanyam, ed., *Merchants, Markets and
the State in Early Modern India, 1770–1870* (Delhi: Oxford University Press,
1990); Rajat Kanta Ray, "Asian Capital in the Age of European Domination:
The Rise of the Bazaar, 1800–1914," *Modern Asian Studies* 29, 3 (1995):
449–554; Assiya Siddiqi, ed., *Trade and Finance in Colonial India* (Delhi: Oxford University Press, 1995); Lakshmi Subramaniam, *Indigenous Capital and
Imperial Expansion: Bombay, Surat and the West Coast* (Delhi: Oxford University
Press, 1996).

43. Princep, *Essays on Indian Antiquities, History, Numismatics, and Paleographic of the
Late James Princep*, 28.

44. Quoted in Jehangir C. Coyajee, *The Indian Currency System, 1835–1926*
(Madras: Thompson and Co., 1930), 5.

45. Minute of the Dispatch to the Secretary of State Respecting a Paper Currency, by the Right Honourable James Wilson, December 25, 1859, *Parliamentary Papers*, 1860, V/4/49, 7, IOL.

46. British India, according to the act, "denoted the territories that are or may be
vested in her Majesty by the Statute 21 and 22 Vic. 106 . . . except the settlement of Prince of Wales Island, Singapore and Malacca." Act XIX of 1861,
An Act to Provide for a Government Paper Currency, as quoted in B. B. Dasgupta, *Paper Currency in India* (Calcutta: Calcutta University, Senate House,
1927), 299.

47. Amiya Kumar Bagchi, *The Evolution of the State Bank of India*, vol. 2: *The Era of
the Presidency Banks, 1876–1920* (Delhi: State Bank of India and Sage Publications, 1997), 39.

48. Marx, *Capital*, 1:226.

49. *Report of the Commission to Enquire into the Operation of Act XIX of 1861 Being Act to
Provide for a Government Paper Currency*, vol. 1 (Calcutta: Superintendent of
Government Press, 1867). Also contained in V/26/302/1, IOL.

50. Crooke, *Glossary of North Indian Peasant Life*, 168.

51. Bagchi, *Evolution of the State Bank of India*, vol. 2; and Ray, "Asian Capital in
the Age of European Domination." For a later period, see G. Balachandran,

"Towards a Hindu Marriage: Anglo-Indian Monetary Relations in Inter-War India, 1917–1935," *Modern Asian Studies* 28, 3 (1994): 614–47.

52. *Report of the Commission to Enquire into the Operation of Act XIX of 1861*, 1:84.

53. Charles Northcote Cooke, *The Rise, Progress, and Present Condition of Banking in India* (Calcutta: P. M. Cranenburgh, 1863), 21.

54. Ray, "Asian Capital in the Age of European Domination," 496.

55. *Index and Appendices to the Evidence Taken before the Committee Appointed to Inquire into the Indian Currency* (London: Eyre and Spottiswoode for HMSO, 1899), 70.

56. Bagchi, *Evolution of the State Bank of India*, 2:24–64.

57. L. C. Jain, *Indigenous Banking in India* (London: Macmillan, 1929), 95–96. Also see Bagchi, *Evolution of the State Bank of India*, 2:44–50; and Ray, "Asian Capital in the Age of European Domination," 497–99.

58. Quoted in K. Bashyam and K. Y. Adiga, *The Negotiable Instruments Act, 1881*, 4th ed. (Calcutta: Butterworth and Co., 1927), 17–18.

59. See, in particular, Sripati Charan Roy, *Customs and Customary Law in British India* (Calcutta: Hare Press, 1911); Bagchi, *Evolution of the State Bank of India*, vol. 2. For an account of the juridical reworking of indigenous merchant practice, see Ritu Birla, "Hedging Bets: The Politics of Commercial Ethics in Late Colonial India," Ph.D. dissertation, Columbia University, 1999.

60. For the concept of "time-space compression," see Harvey, *Condition of Postmodernity*.

61. Roy, *Customs and Customary Law in British India*, 541; and Cooke, *Rise, Progress, and Present Condition of Banking in India*, 82–83.

62. See, in particular, Albert S. J. Baster, *The Imperial Banks* (London: P. S. King and Son, 1929); Compton Mackenzie, *Realms of Silver: One Hundred Years of Banking in the East* (London: Routledge and Kegan Paul, 1954). Also see Bagchi, *Evolution of the State Bank of India*, vol. 2; and Ray, "Asian Capital in the Age of European Domination."

63. Finance Department, 1863, no. 1, *Parliamentary Papers*, vol. 39, 1865, 62–63, IOL.

64. Dasgupta, *Paper Currency in India*, 90, 92.

65. From Officiating Secretary to the Board of Revenue, NWP, to the Secretary of Government, NWP, in *Report of the Commission to Enquire into the Operation of Act XIX of 1861*, 1:88.

66. The Assistant Collector of Treasury, Futtehpore, NWP, in *Report of the Commission to Enquire into the Operation of Act XIX of 1861*, 1:248–50.

67. On the universalization of lower-denominational notes, see Dasgupta, *Paper Currency in India*, 90–94. For shifts in banking networks and regulatory practices, see Bagchi, *Evolution of the State Bank of India*, vol. 2; and Ray, "Asian

Capital in the Age of European Domination." On juridical shifts in negotiable instruments, see Bashyam and Adiga, *Negotiable Instruments Act;* and Roy, *Customs and Customary Law in British India.*

68. The Respectful Memorial of the Bombay Association to Sir John Lawrence, Viceroy and Governor-General of India, in Council, February 8, 1864, *Parliamentary Papers,* vol. 39, 1865, 5, IOL.

69. Dadabhai Naoroji, *Poverty and Un-British Rule in India* (1901; reprint, Delhi: Government of India Publications, 1962), 92. Also see Naoroji, *Indian Exchange and Bimetallism* (London: Longmans, Green and Co., 1886).

70. Keynes, *Indian Currency and Finance,* 178.

71. Some of the works include B. R. Ambedkar, *The Problem of the Rupee: Its Origins and Its Solution* (London: P. S. King and Sons, 1923); L. C. Jain, *The Monetary Problems of India* (London: Macmillan, 1920); Vaman Govind Kale, *Indian Industrial and Economic Problems* (Madras: G. A. Naksan and Co., 1917); Kale, *Currency Reform in India* (Poona: Aryabhushan Press, 1919); Naoroji, *Poverty and Un-British Rule in India;* Findlay Shirras, *Indian Finance and Banking* (London: Macmillan, 1920).

72. Bourdieu, *In Other Words,* 134.

Chapter Three

1. For instances of modernization-theoretic analyses that reiterate official discourse on railways as the very sign of modernity, see Hurd, "Railways"; and Moriss D. Morris, "The Growth of Large-Scale Industry to 1947," in Kumar and Desai, *Cambridge Economic History of India,* vol. 2. For an analysis of the impact of railways on markets see, John Hurd, "Railways and the Expansion of Markets in India, 1861–1921," *Explorations in Economic History* 12, 3 (1975): 263–88; McAlpin, "Price Movements and Fluctuations in Economic Activity." On peasant rationality and income distribution, see Michelle Burge McAlpin, "Railroads, Prices and Peasant Rationality: India, 1860–1900," *Journal of Economic History* 34, 3 (1974): 662–84; and McAlpin, "The Effects of Expansion of Markets on Rural Income Distribution in Nineteenth Century India," *Explorations in Economic History* 12 (1975): 289–302. For analyses of railways in terms of economic imperialism, see Lehmann, "Great Britain and the Supply of Railway Locomotives to India"; Ranajit Das Gupta, "Capital Investment and Transport Modernisation in Colonial India," in *Essays in Honour of Professor S. C. Sarkar* (Delhi: People's Publishing House, 1976); and Sunil Sen, "Marx on Indian Railways," in *Das Kapital Centenary Volume: A Symposium,* ed. Mohit Sen and M. B. Rao (Delhi: People's Publishing House, 1968). On questions of technology transfer, see Headrick, *Tentacles of Progress;* and Lehmann, "Railway Workshops, Technology Transfer, and Skilled

Labour Recruitments in Colonial India." For an important account of the railway campaign and levels of investment, see Thorner, *Investment in Empire;* and W. J. Macpherson, "Investment in Indian Railways, 1845–1875," *Economic History Review* 8, 2 (1955): 177–86. For the economic impact of railways in different regional contexts, see Derbyshire, "Economic Change and Railways in North India"; and Mukul Mukherjee, "Railways and Their Impact on Bengal's Economy, 1870–1920," *Indian Economic and Social History Review* 17, 2: 191–209.

2.   For an account of the managerial practices, focused on colonial contractors, in the building of railways, see Kerr, *Building the Railways of the Raj;* and Kerr, introduction to *Railways in Modern India,* ed. I. Kerr (Delhi: Oxford University Press, 2001). For insightful accounts of labor struggles at different historical moments, see Dipesh Chakrabarty, "Early Railwaymen in India: 'Dacoity' and 'Train Wrecking,' 1860–1900," in *Essays in Honour of Professor S. C. Sarkar;* David Arnold, "Industrial Violence in Colonial India," *Comparative Studies in Society and History* 22 (1980): 234–55; and Lajpat Jagga, "Colonial Railwaymen and British Rule: A Probe into Railway Labour and Agitation in India, 1919–1922," *Studies in History* 111, 1–2: 1981, 103–45. For an interesting account of colonial technology—including a brief account of railways—as instruments of colonial governmentality, see Prakash, *Another Reason: Science and the Imagination of Modern India.* For a compelling historical ethnography on the making of the Anglo-Indian community and the colonial railway lines, see Laura Bear, "Traveling Modernity: Capitalism, Community and Nation in the Colonial Governance of Indian Railways," Ph.D. dissertation, University of Michigan, 1998.

3.   George Macgeorge, *Ways and Works in India, Being an Account of the Public Works in That Country from the Earliest Times up to the Present Day* (Westminster: Archibald Constable and Co., 1894), 220.

4.   Davidson, *Railways of India,* 3–6. Marx commented that railways in colonial India would not only be the "forerunner of modern industry," but that the "modern industry, resulting from the railway system will dissolve the hereditary divisions of labour upon which rest the Indian castes, those decisive impediments to Indian progress and Indian power." The fact that this did not quite occur shaped the predominant lack narratives on industrialization in subsequent Marxist and nationalist economic historiography of late colonial India. See Karl Marx, "The Future Results of British Rule in India," in *On Colonialism* (Moscow: Progress Publishers, 1978), 84, 85.

5.   Appadurai, "Number in the Colonial Imagination," in *Modernity at Large,* 134. For the objectification of caste as a social category and its shifting meanings

in colonial discourse, see the classic essay by Bernard Cohn, "The Census, Social Structure, and Objectification in South Asia," in *An Anthropologist among the Historians*; and Dirks, *Castes of Mind*.

6. Bipin Chandra Pal, *Memories of My Life and Times in the Days of My Youth, 1857–1884* (1884; reprint, Calcutta: Bipinchandra Pal Institute, 1973), 152–53.

7. *Report from the Select Committee on East India (Railways)*, C.416, 1857–58, IOL.

8. Headrick, *Tentacles of Progress*, 56–57.

9. Michael Freeman, *Railways and the Victorian Imagination* (New Haven: Yale University Press, 1999), 114, 118.

10. Public Works Department Proceedings, January 1865, P/217/38, IOL.

11. John Brunton, *John Brunton's Book; Being the Memories of John Brunton, Engineer, from a manuscript in his own hand written for his grandchildren and now printed* (1864; reprint, Oxford: Clarendon Press, 1939), 105.

12. Quoted in Sir William Patrick Andrew, *Indian Railways as Connected with British Empire in the East* (London: W. H. Allen and Co., 1884), xxxvii.

13. John Brunton, Minutes of Proceedings of the Institution of Civil Engineers, 22 (1862–63), 455–56, quoted in Kerr, *Building the Railways of the Raj*, 98.

14. James Berkley, "On Indian Railways," Minutes of Proceedings of the Institution of Civil Engineers, 19 (1859–60), quoted ibid., 115.

15. Kerr, *Building the Railways of the Raj*, 105–10.

16. "Regulations for Pay and Promotions," in *Proceedings of the Railway Conference* (Simla: Government of India Press, 1900).

17. K. M. Hassan, *Report on the Representation of Muslims and Other Minority Communities in the Subordinate Railway Service* (Simla: Government of India Press, 1932).

18. Davidson, *Railways of India*, 100.

19. *Administration Report on Indian State Railways from their Commencement to the End of 1879–1880*, 1881, Appendix CC, X, V/24/3532, IOL.

20. For an excellent historical ethnography of the making of an Anglo-Indian community on the railway lines, see Bear, "Traveling Modernity." For a classic account of racialization and racial identities in colonial contexts more generally, see Stoler, *Race and the Education of Desire*; and Anne Stoler, "Rethinking Colonial Categories: European Communities and the Boundaries of Rule," in Dirks, *Colonialism and Culture*.

21. *Administration Report on Indian State Railways from their Commencement to the End of 1879–1880*, 1881, Appendix C, XII, V/24/3532, IOL.

22. Public Works Department Proceedings, NWP, 1873, 7, 132–33, IOL.

23. Selections from vernacular newspapers, NWP, May 31, 1871, 250, IOL.

24. Westwood, *Railways of India*, 80–82.

25. Public Works Department Proceedings, NWP, November 1864, 464–65, IOL.

26. Westwood, *Railways of India*, 73.

27. Public Works Department Proceedings, NWP, June 1865, 10, 3, IOL.

28. Horace Bell, *Railway Policy in India* (London: Rivington, Percival and Co., 1894), 73.

29. Freeman, *Railways and the Victorian Imagination*, 110–14.

30. A Petition to British Government praying for certain reforms in the Railway Arrangements for the convenience of native passengers, 1867, T37184(c), IOL. The British-Indian Association, established in 1866, consisted of north Indian regional elites who sought to represent "Indian" demands to the colonial state and the British Parliament.

31. Chunder, *Travels of a Hindoo to Various Parts Of Bengal and Upper India*, 2:130.

32. Public Works Department Proceedings, NWP, 1871, no. 10, 135–36, IOL.

33. Ibid., NWP, 1871, no. 7, 77–78, IOL.

34. Selections from vernacular newspapers, 1869, l/R/5/46, 245–46, IOL.

35. Public Works Department Proceedings, NWP, 1869, no. 6, 9, IOL.

36. Selections from vernacular newspapers, 1869, l/R/5/46, 351, and 1872, 527, IOL.

37. Railway thieves were registered under the 1911 Criminal Tribes Act. For a suggestive account, see Chakrabarty, "Early Railwaymen in India."

38. M. K. Gandhi, *An Autobiography: The Story of My Experiments with Truth*, trans. Mahadev Desai (Boston: Beacon Press, 1993).

39. For insightful accounts of labor protests in the 1920s, see Arnold, "Industrial Violence in Colonial India"; and Jagga, "Colonial Railwaymen and British Rule."

40. Cited in V. G. Kale, *Introduction to the Study of Indian Economics* (Poona: Aryabhushan Press, 1918), 198 (epigraph).

41. Wolfgang Schivelbusch, *The Railway Journey: The Industrialization of Time and Space in the Nineteenth Century* (Berkeley: University of California Press, 1986), 36.

42. M. K. Gandhi, *Hind Swaraj and Other Writings*, ed. Anthony J. Parel (1910; reprint, Cambridge: Cambridge University Press, 1997), 48–49 (epigraph), 47. The term *civilization,* as used by Gandhi, explicitly referred to the industrial revolution. He argued, "Let it be remembered that Western Civilization is only a hundred years old, or to be more precise fifty. Within this short span the Western people appear to have been reduced to a state of cultural anarchy." See M. K. Gandhi, *The Collected Works of Mahatma Gandhi* (Delhi: Nehru Memorial Museum and Library, 1960), 8:374.

43. Gandhi, *Hind Swaraj*, 48.

44. See note 1 by the editor of *Hind Swaraj*, about Gandhi's use of the *sudharo/kudharo* dichotomy.

45. For an account of the adoption of this transnational marketing campaign during the 1970s in Japan, see Ivy, *Discourses of the Vanishing*, 48.

46. *Asian Age*, October 7, 1997.

Chapter Four

1. For general analyses of colonial education with varying emphases, see Aparna Basu, *The Growth of Education and Political Development in India, 1898–1920* (Delhi: Oxford University Press, 1974); Stokes, *English Utilitarians and India;* Bruce McCully, *English Education and the Origins of Indian Nationalism* (New York: Columbia University Press, 1942); and Gauri Viswanathan, *Masks of Conquest: Literary Study and British Rule in India* (New York: Columbia University Press, 1989).

2. Viswanathan, *Masks of Conquest*, 146.

3. Dispatch by Charles Wood, *Parliamentary Papers*, 1854, vol. 147, IOL.

4. For works that focus on the constitution of a bilingual elite intelligentsia, see David Kopf, *British Orientalism and the Bengal Renaissance* (Berkeley: University of California Press, 1969). On national consciousness, see McCully, *English Education and the Origins of Indian Nationalism;* Basu, *Growth of Education and Political Development in India;* and Ainslie Embree, *India's Search for National Identity* (New York: Alfred Knopf, 1968). For important accounts of colonial hegemony in the educational field, see Ranajit Guha, "An Indian Historiography of India," in *Dominance without Hegemony* (the essay was first published as a separate volume in 1988); and Viswanathan, *Masks of Conquest.*

5. Revenue Proceedings, NWP, 1873, no. 10, IOL.

6. Selections from Records of Government, NWP, 1858, vol. 3, 427–28, 313, IOL.

7. General Proceedings, NWP, July 1876, 23, IOL.

8. Selections from Records of Government, NWP, 1858, 314, IOL.

9. Revenue Proceedings, NWP, December 1874, 42, IOL.

10. Whitcombe, *Agrarian Conditions in Northern India*, 122–28.

11. *Report of the Land Revenue Settlement, Lucknow District*, Oudh Settlement Reports, comp. H. H. Butts, 1873, 7, IOL.

12. Christopher Bayly, *Empire and Information: Intelligence Gathering and Communication in India, 1780–1870* (Cambridge: Cambridge University Press, 1996), 309.

13. *Final Report on the Settlement of Moradabad District*, Government of NWP, comp. E. B. Alexander, 1881, 92, IOL.

14. Abstract of the reports of surveys and of other geographical operations in India, 1871, 16, IOL.

15. Whitcombe, *Agrarian Conditions in Northern India*, 126–28. Until the late 1870s, the system was based on calculating the so-called ideal rental, with the state directly appropriating 50 percent. In the early 1880s, the notion of the ideal rent was abandoned in favor of the actual or so-called natural rent.

16. Quoted in Baden-Powell, *Land Systems of British India*, 1:333.

17. *Report of the Land Revenue Settlement, Lucknow District*, 14.

18. *Report on the Final Settlement of Fatehpur District*, Government of NWP, comp. A. B. Patterson, 1878, 53, IOL.

19. Baden-Powell, *Land Systems of British India*, 1:350.

20. *Report of the Land Revenue Settlement, Lucknow District*, 14–15.

21. C. H. T. Crosthwaite, *Notes on the North-Western Provinces of India, by a District Officer* (London: E. Arnold, 1870), 5.

22. The following account of district administration is derived from Whitcombe, *Agrarian Conditions in Northern India*, 236. Also see P. Carnegy, *A Note on the Land Tenures and Revenue Assessments of Upper India* (London: Longmans, Green, 1874).

23. Minute by Sir William Muir, Lieutenant Governor, Revenue Proceedings, NWP, 1868, 14, IOL.

24. The various laws relating to *patwaris* were codified by the NWP Land Revenue Act XIX of 1873, amended by Act XV of 1886; the Oudh Land Revenue Act XVII of 1876; the NWP and Oudh Kanungo and Patwari Act XIII of 1882, amended by Act IX of 1889.

25. Crosthwaite, *Notes on the North-Western Provinces of India*, 5.

26. Revenue Proceedings, NWP, November 1878, no. 12, IOL.

27. Baden-Powell, *Land Systems of British India*, 1:358.

28. A *lakh* is 100,000 rupees.

29. Revenue Proceedings, NWP, August–October 1864, 73–74, IOL.

30. *Report on the Administration of the NWP*, 1875–76, xiii, IOL.

31. Baden-Powell, *Land Systems of British India*, 1:27.

32. Revenue Proceedings, NWP, November–March, 1864, 74, IOL.

33. General Proceedings, NWP, November 1870, no. 4, 46–49, IOL.

34. J. A. Baines, "The Distribution and Movement of Population in India," *Journal of the Royal Statistical Society*, March 1893, 15–16.

35. See, e.g., Bayly, *Empire and Information*, 300–302. For the empiricist grounding of British geography as a disciplinary formation, see Meredith Bowen, *Empiricism and Geographical Thought from Francis Bacon to Alexander von Humboldt* (Cambridge: Cambridge University Press, 1981).

36. General Proceedings, NWP, 1867, 42–43, IOL.

37. Pal, *Memories of My Life and Times*, 30.

38. General Proceedings, NWP, 1867, 44, IOL.

39. Bourdieu, *In Other* Words, 138.

40. Abstract of the reports of surveys and of other geographical operations in India, 1871, 18, IOL.

41. Malkki, "National Geographic," 26.

42. See, e.g., Anderson, *Imagined Communities;* and Winichakul, *Siam Mapped.*

43. Selections from vernacular newspapers, *Oudh Punch*, September 11, 1877, 635–36, IOL.

44. Petition sent to the British Government praying for certain reforms in Public Instruction and concerning the education of natives through the vernaculars, 1869, cat. no. T371842, no. 5, 4, IOL.

45. Bipin Chandra Pal, *Swadeshi and Swaraj* (1907; reprint, Calcutta: Yuganyanti Prakashak, 1954), 257.

46. Guha, "Indian Historiography of India," in *Dominance without Hegemony.*

47. Ibid.; Chatterjee, *Nation and Its Fragments*, 76–115; Kaviraj, "The Imaginary Institution of India"; and Sudipta Kaviraj, *The Unhappy Consciousness: Bankimchandra Chattopadhyaya and the Formation of Nationalist Discourse in India* (Delhi: Oxford University Press, 1995).

48. Guha, "Indian Historiography of India," in *Dominance without Hegemony*, 195. Guha argues that "no historiography of colonial India would be truly Indian except as a critique of the very fundamental of the power relations which constituted colonialism itself."

49. Poulantzas, *State, Power, and Socialism*, 100.

50. Sewell, "Theory of Structure."

Chapter Five

1. Guha, "Indian Historiography of India," in *Dominance without Hegemony*. Guha reworks his original characterization of the first generation of historical works in Bengali as still caught in a "mythic drift," in the more recent work *History at the Limit of World-History* (New York: Columbia University Press, 2002), 10–13. Here he characterizes Ram Ram Basu's *Raja pratapaditya caritra* (1801) as part of a global process of historicization, coeval with European colonial expansion, and more crucially, as emblematic of the emergence of modern historiography in colonial India. His subsequent attempt in the same work to posit an equivalence between Sanskritic categories in ancient Vedic texts (located in an indeterminate past) and modern forms of historical consciousness represents more than a simple inversion of British colonial histori-

ography's rejection of vernacular modalities of writing and historical memory. It elides the historicity of social categories and enacts a willed forgetting of colonial transformations.

2. See, e.g., Chatterjee, *Nation and Its Fragments*, chaps. 4 and 5; Kaviraj, *Unhappy Consciousness*; Kaviraj, "Imaginary Institution of India"; and Indira Chowdhury, *The Frail Hero and Virile History: Gender and the Politics of Culture in Colonial Bengal* (Delhi: Oxford University Press, 1998). This scholarship has opened up many productive insights, but it has also reproduced an undifferentiated and ideal-typical understanding of *Puranic-itihas*. For accounts that emphasize regionally specific and historically varied Puranic modalities and genres, see Sumit Sarkar, *Writing Social History* (Delhi: Oxford University Press, 1997), 1–49; Vasudha Dalmia, "Vernacular Histories in Late-Nineteenth Century Banaras: Folklore, Puranas and the New Antiquarianism," *Indian Economic and Social History Review* 38, 1 (2001): 59–79; Prachi Deshpande, "Narratives of Pride: Historical Memory and Regional Identity in Maharasthra, India, c. 1870–1960," Ph.D. dissertation, Tufts University, 2002; Narayana Rao, David Schulman, and Sanjay Subrahmanyam, eds., *Textures of Time: Writing History in South India, 1600–1800* (Delhi: Permanent Black, 2001).

3. The continuist civilizational narrative imbues popular Hindutva discourse, the more specialized industry of postcolonial Puranic studies in India (see n. 8 in this chapter), and its orientalist variants in the American academy.

4. Commonly regarded as consisting of eighteen major chronicles, Puranas were composed by Brahminical *sutas* (or royal panegyrists) between 500 B.C. and A.D. 500 and were based on collations of much earlier material that were diverse in both form and content. See, in particular, Romila Thapar, *A History of India* (Baltimore: Penguin Books, 1965–66), 1:28–30; Thapar, *History and Beyond* (Delhi: Oxford University Press, 2000); Ludo Rocher, *The Puranas*, vol. 2 of *The History of Indian Literature* (Wiesbaden: Otto Harrassowitz, 1986); and Narayana Velcheru Rao, "Puranas as Brahminic Ideology," in *Purana Perennis: Reciprocity and Transformation in Hindu and Jaina Texts*, ed. Wendy Doniger (Albany: State University of New York Press, 1993).

5. Guha, "Indian Historiography of India," in *Dominance without Hegemony*, 180–83; Chatterjee, *Nation and Its Fragments*, 77–84; Uma Chakravarti, "Whatever Happened to the Vedic Dasi? Orientalism, Nationalism and a Script for the Past," in *Recasting Women: Essays in Colonial History*, ed. K. Sangari and Sudesh Vaid (Delhi: Kali for Women, 1989), 36–38.

6. Chatterjee, *Nation and Its Fragments*, 80; Chakravarti, "Whatever Happened to the Vedic Dasi?" 36–38.

7. Quoted in Chatterjee, *Nation and Its Fragments*, 78.

8. See, e.g., Dineshchandra Sircar, *Studies in the Geography of Ancient and Medieval India* (Delhi: Motilal Banarsidass, 1971); Sircar, *Cosmography and Geography in Early Indian Literature* (Calcutta: Indian Studies, Past and Present, 1967); Sircar, "Ancient Indian Cartography," in *The Indian Archives*, vol. 5 (Delhi: National Archives of India, 1951); Maya Prasad Tripathi, *Development of Geographical Knowledge in Ancient India* (Varanasi: Bharatiya Vidya Prakashan, 1969); Amarnath Das, *India and Jambu Island* (Delhi: Vidya Publishers, 1985). For a widely influential British colonial account, see Alexander Cunningham, *The Ancient Geography of India* (London: Trubner, 1871). For a late-nineteenth-century instance of a geographical dictionary of Puranic categories, see Nundo Lal Dey, *The Geographical Dictionary of Ancient and Medieval India* (1899; reprint, Delhi: Oriental Books, 1971).

9. Constituent Assembly Debates, vol. 9, no. 38, September 17 and 18, 1949, p. 1674, http://alfa.nic.in/debates.htm.

10. Tripathi, *Development of Geographical Knowledge in Ancient India*, 182.

11. Syed Muzafer Ali, *The Geography of the Puranas* (Delhi: People's Publishing House, 1966), 109.

12. Sircar, "Ancient Indian Cartography," 60, as quoted in Susan Gole, *Indian Maps and Plans from the Earliest Times to the Advent of European Surveys* (Delhi: Manohar Publications, 1989), 17.

13. Ibid. Also see Susan Gole, *Early Maps of India* (Delhi: Sanskriti in association with Arnold Heinemann Publishers, 1976); Gole, *A Series of Early Printed Maps of India in Facsimile* (Delhi: Jayaprints, 1980); and Gole, *India within the Ganges* (Delhi: Jayaprints, 1983).

14. Exemplary of these is a Puranic-inspired Jain painting from around the sixteenth century that configures the *Madhya Loka* or Middle World as an "infinite series of concentric circular bands which represent alternating bodies of land and water." Kay Talwar and Kalyan Krishna, *Pigment Paintings on Cloth* (Ahmedabad: Calico Museum, 1979), 93. Jain geographical works shared many categories in common with Puranic accounts (e.g., Bharata, Jambud-vipa). However, they also contained many unique temporal conceptions and geographical imaginings (such as the division of the world into thirty-two concentric circles). See Sircar, *Cosmography and Geography in Early Indian Literature*; Sircar, *Studies in the Geography of Ancient and Medieval India*; and Tripathi, *Development of Geographical Knowledge in Ancient India*.

15. Gole, *Indian Maps and Plans*, 26–28.

16. Ibid., 14; Francis Wilford, "An Essay on the Sacred Isles of the West," *Asiatick Researches* 8 (1805); Andre Wink, *Land and Sovereignty in India: Agrarian Society and Politics under the Eighteenth Century Maratha Swarajya* (Cambridge: Cambridge University Press, 1986), 290. For a discussion of Puranic scales

and measures, see Tripathi, *Development of Geographical Knowledge in Ancient India*, 246–47.

17. Tripathi, *Development of Geographical Knowledge in Ancient India*, 244.

18. Gole, *Indian Maps and Plans*, 25.

19. James Blaut, *The Colonizer's Map of the World* (Berkeley: University of California Press, 1993); Harvey, *Condition of Postmodernity*, 240–60; Winichakul, *Siam Mapped*.

20. In a brilliant analysis of the historicity of spatiotemporal matrices, Poulantzas argues that the "appearance of frontiers in the modern sense of the term: that is to say, limits capable of being shifted along a serial and discontinuous loom which everywhere fixes insides and outsides" was embedded within and specific to modern capitalism. See Poulantzas, *State, Power, and Socialism*, 104.

21. Inden, *Imagining India*, 257.

22. Quoted in Chatterjee, *Nation and Its Fragments*, 79.

23. Sircar, *Cosmography and Geography in Early Indian Literature*, 19; K. M. Panikkar, *The Ideas of Sovereignty and State in Indian Political Thought* (Bombay: Bharatiya Vidya Bhavan, 1963), 92–100; Wink, *Land and Sovereignty in India*.

24. John Ruggie, "Territoriality and Beyond: Problematizing Modernity in International Relations," *International Organization* 47, 1 (1993): 139–74; and Agnew, "Territorial Trap."

25. Wink, *Land and Sovereignty in India*, 14. Also see Sumit Guha's account of the status of Maratha genealogies as instruments for encoding rights and constructing custom, "Rights and Wrongs in the Maratha Country: Antiquity, Custom and Power in the Eighteenth Century India," in *Changing Concepts of Rights and Justice in South Asia*, ed. Sumit Guha and Michael Anderson (Delhi: Oxford University Press, 1998), 14–29.

26. Postone, *Time, Labor and Social Domination*, 186–225.

27. Quoted in Chatterjee, *Nation and Its Fragments*, 78.

28. Sarkar, *Writing Social History*, 7.

29. See Moishe Postone's discussion of concrete versus abstract time in *Time, Labor and Social Domination*, 200–216. Romila Thapar has argued that the linear time and sequential forms of reckoning coexisted with cyclical temporal schemas in various Puranas. See Thapar, *History and Beyond*. For a classic colonial attempt to "rationalize" Puranic temporal schemas, see Alexander Cunningham, *Book of Indian Eras, with Tables for Calculating Indian Dates* (1883; reprint, Varanasi: Indological Book House, 1970).

30. Benjamin, "Theses on the Philosophy of History," in *Illuminations*, 261.

31. Chatterjee, *Nation and Its Fragments*, 80.

32. Guha, "Indian Historiography of India," in *Dominance without Hegemony*, 183. For an even more problematic reversal from this earlier position, see the dis-

cussion in this chapter's n. 1 of Ranajit Guha's more recent engagement with vernacular historical works in *History at the Limit of World-History*.

33. Sarkar, *Writing Social History*, 309–11.

34. Rosalind O'Hanlon, *Caste, Conflict and Ideology: Mahatma Jotirao Phule and Low Caste Protest in Nineteenth Century Western India* (Cambridge: Cambridge University Press, 1985), 164–65.

Chapter Six

1. Bipin Chandra Pal, *The Soul of India* (Madras: Tagore and Co., 1923), 70.

2. Bayly, *Empire and Information*, 245. For an excellent account of the formation of a Hindi public sphere from the 1920s to the 1940s, see Francesca Orsini, *The Hindi Public Sphere, 1920–1940: Language and Literature in the Age of Nationalism* (Delhi: Oxford University Press, 2002).

3. Bayly, *Empire and Information*; Sanjay Joshi, *Fractured Modernity: Making of a Middle Class in Colonial North India* (Delhi: Oxford University Press, 2001).

4. Chunder, *Travels of a Hindoo to Various Parts of Bengal and Upper India*, 1:389.

5. General Proceedings, NWP, June 10, 1865, 162, IOL.

6. Quoted in Bayly, *Empire and Information*, 343.

7. Selections from the Records of Government, NWP, vol. 3, 1855, IOL.

8. General Proceedings, NWP, 1877, 12, IOL.

9. Ibid., July 1876, 23; and April 1882, 20, IOL.

10. Bayly, *Empire and Information*, 349.

11. Copy of Correspondence between the Government of India and the Secretary of State for India on the Subject of Act No. IX of 1878, "An Act for the Better Control of Publications in Oriental Languages," *Parliamentary Papers*, 1878, vol. 57, C2040, 66–67, IOL.

12. Rajah Shiva Prasad, *Itihas timirnasak* (Allahabad: Government Press, 1864), IOL.

13. Sajun K. Lal, "Rajah Shiv Pershad: Early Life and Career," in *Indica: Indian Historical Research Institute Silver Jubilee Commemoration Volume* (Bombay: Heras Institute of Indian History and Culture, 1953).

14. Bayly, *Empire and Information*, 234.

15. General Proceedings, NWP, 1876, nos. 1–3, "Annual Report on the Progress of Education, NWP, 1874–75," 36–37, P/837, IOL.

16. Shiva Prasad's role as architect of official caste and religious categories began with the NWP- and Awadh-wide census survey of 1865. In his commentary on the report, Prasad noted in a positivist vein, "appendix B contains much valuable and interesting information, though mixed with much that is worthless, badly arranged, and sometimes contradictory. The reader will often find the statement that Aheer is derived from ahi, a snake . . . he will meet with

such glaring errors as the following: Domes come from Arabia; the Cashmere Pundits, who attempt to pass themselves off as an offshoot of the Brahmin class, are in reality Kayasths ... it is not probably that Domes, who are generally considered to belong to aborigines of India, would have come from Arabia. . . . there is no reason to suppose that Cashmere Pundits are in reality Kayasths." Revenue Proceedings, NWP, 1867, "Report of the Census of the NWP and Awadh, 1865," November 1867, 119–20, P/438/57, IOL.

17. On Prasad's specific role, see Amrit Rai, *A House Divided: The Origin and Development of Hindi/Hindavi* (Delhi: Oxford University Press, 1984), 269–71; and David Lelyveld, *Aligarh's First Generation: Muslim Solidarity in British India* (Princeton: Princeton University Press, 1977), 98, 109. For an insightful account of the political contestation over Hindi and Urdu as distinctive, racialized language formations, see David Lelyveld, "The Fate of Hindustani," in *Orientalism and the Postcolonial Predicament: Perspectives on South Asia*, ed. Carol Breckenridge and Peter Van der Veer (Philadelphia: University of Pennsylvania Press, 1993).

18. Quoted in Christopher King, "Images of Virtue and Vice: The Hindi–Urdu Controversy in Two Nineteenth-Century Hindi Plays," in *Religious Controversy in British India: Dialogues in South Asian Languages*, ed. Kenneth Jones (Albany: State University of New York Press, 1992), 124.

19. Sayyid Khan regarded Prasad as a long-standing opponent and "blamed" his apparent endorsement of Hindi for the "rise of Hindu–Muslim enmity." See Lelyveld, *Aligarh's First Generation*, 98. In the early 1880s, Prasad became embroiled in debates with proponents of orthodox Hinduism as well as Hindu social reformers, including Dayanand. In 1885, Prasad wrote a critical commentary titled *Nivedan* (Lucknow: Munshi Nawal Kishore, 1888), Vernacular Text (VT) 1233, IOL, in response to Dayanand's influential work *Satyarth Prakash*.

20. Pal, *Memories of My Life and Times*, 442.

21. General Proceedings, NWP, 1876, no. 16, 21, IOL.

22. Ibid., no. 18, 22, IOL.

23. In 1851, Prasad published a work on the rise and fall of the Sikhs, titled *Shkhaon ka udaya aur asta*, that closely followed the Sikh war of 1846–47 (VT 152, IOL). His 1849 work on the lives of exemplary women, titled *Vamamanoranjana*, was widely disseminated in both private and government schools in the context of intensifying debates over the status of women. He translated as well the Laws of Manu under the Hindi title *Manava dharamasara* in 1856.

24. H. L. Singh, "Modern Historical Writings in Hindi," in *Historians of India,*

Pakistan and Ceylon, ed. C. H. Phillips (London: Oxford University Press, 1961), 461–63.

25. Quoted in Vasudha Dalmia, *The Nationalization of Hindu Traditions: Bharatendu Harishchandra and Nineteenth-Century Banaras* (Delhi: Oxford University Press, 1997), 330.

26. All quotations in this paragraph are from Prasad, *Itihas timirnasak* (1864), preface, 14156, IOL.

27. Raja Shiva Prasad, *Itihasa-timiranasaka* (Benares: Medical Hall Press, 1873), preface, 279/4, IOL. Note the different spelling of this text in the Blumhardt Catalogue, Vernacular Text (VT) Collections, from the first edition of 1864.

28. Dalmia, *Nationalization of Hindu Traditions,* 330–32. Also see her insightful discussion of early Hindi journalism in Benares during this period (227–32).

29. Prasad, *Itihasa-timiranasaka* (1873), 7. All translations of vernacular sources are mine unless otherwise noted.

30. General Proceedings, NWP, April 17–18, 1875, Report from Director of Public Instruction, P/54, IOL.

31. Ibid., July 1876, Annual Record of Native Publications under Act XXV of 1867, no. 19, 24, P/837, IOL.

32. Prasad, *Itihasa-timiranasaka* (1873), 18.

33. It is important to note here the central influence of Max Muller (1823–1900), Orientalist scholar par excellence, in later nationalist historiography. A product of the German romanticist movement, Max Muller translated the full texts of the Vedas and authored the racialization of the previously linguistic-philological category of Aryans. The idealist and idealizing vision of Hinduism in later nationalist historiography bore a relationship of elective affinity with German romanticist discourse, which posited "ancient" Hindu philosophy as the ancestor of modern idealism.

34. For the shifting significations of the category *Arya* in colonial discourse and Orientalist scholarship, see Thomas Trautmann, *Aryans and British India* (Berkeley: University of California, 1997); Susan Bayly, "Caste and 'Race' in the Colonial Ethnography of India," in *The Concept of Race in South Asia,* ed. Peter Robb (Delhi: Oxford University Press, 1995), 165–218; Dirks, *Castes of Mind,* 142–44, 245–46; Joan Leopold, "The Aryan Theory of Race in India, 1870–1920," *Indian Economic and Social History Review* 7, 2 (1970): 271–97. For an account of racialized categories in nationalist discourses of the twentieth century, see Christophe Jaffrelot, "The Idea of the Hindu Race in the Writings of Hindu Nationalist Ideologues in the 1920s and 1930s: A Concept between Two Cultures," in Robb, *Concept of Race in South Asia;* Kenneth Jones, *Arya Dharm: Hindu Consciousness in Nineteenth-Century Punjab* (Berkeley: Uni-

versity of California Press, 1976); and Sumathi Ramaswamy, "Remains of the
Race: Archaeology, Nationalism and the Yearning for Civilization in the Indus Valley," *Indian Economic and Social History Review* 38, 2 (2001): 105–45. For
oppositional Dalit imaginaries in later periods, see O'Hanlon, *Caste, Conflict
and Ideology;* and Ramaswamy, "Remains of the Race."

35. For an elaboration of this argument, see Chakravarti, "Whatever Happened
to the Vedic Dasi?," and Lata Mani, "Contentious Traditions: The Debate on
Sati in Colonial India," in Sangari and Vaid, *Recasting Women.*

36. Prasad, *Itihasa-timiranasaka* (1873), 87.

37. H. M. Elliot, *The History of India as Told by Its Own Historians: The Muhammaden
Period*, ed. by John Dowson from the posthumous papers of the late Sir H. M.
Elliot, 8 vols. (London: Trubner, 1876–77).

38. Prasad, *Itihasa-timiranasaka* (1873), preface.

39. Elliot, *History of India as Told by Its Own Historians*, xx.

40. .Prasad, *Itihasa-timiranasaka* (1873), 96.

41. For an analogous formation in Bengali histories, see Chatterjee, *Nation and Its
Fragments*, 109–10.

42. Henry Maine was the first to introduce the positivist categories of Comte and
Taine into the field of comparative and historical jurisprudence. His most fa-
mous formulation was that of "village republics," or more specifically, Indian
village communities as residual Aryan institutions. His major works include
Ancient Law (London: J. Murray, 1883) and *Village Communities in the East and
West* (London: J. Murray, 1871).

43. *Englishman*, March 19, 1866, 128, NAI.

44. Poulantzas, *State, Power, and Socialism*, 114.

45. My discussion is based on a reading of more than forty historical and geographical works that were used as textbooks in the United Provinces and
Bengal and can be found under Vernacular Text Collections (VT) in the relevant J. F. Blumhardt catalogues, IOL. The works are listed in the bibliography under "Hindi-Language Texts" and "Bengali-Language Texts" in the
IOL. I have used the original spellings of the titles as found in the VT Collections, IOL.

46. Bapudeva Sastri, *Bhugola-varnana* (Mirzapur: Orphan Press, 1857), 1, VT
120, IOL.

47. Pandit Sitarama, *Bhugol o itihas Lalitpur* (1869), preface, VT 121, IOL.

48. For surveys of historical works in different vernaculars such as Bengali,
Marathi, Kannada, and Assamese, see Tarasankar Banerjee, ed., *Historiography in Modern Indian Languages, 1800–1947* (Calcutta: Naya Prokash, 1987);
and Dilip Kumar Ganguly, *History and Historians in India* (New Delhi: Abhinav Publications, 1984).

49. Raja Shiva Prasad, *Bhugola hastamalaka,* 6th ed. (Allahabad, 1874), 1–2, VT 1307, IOL.

50. Pandit Mulacanda, *Bhugol o itihas Lucknow* (1872), 26, IOL.

51. Vishnu Vittal Srikhande, *Bhugol Bharat ke shalaon ke liya* (Lucknow: Navala Kisore, 1877), 23, VT 108, IOL.

52. Anonymous, *Bhugol darpan* (Agra School Book Society, 1842), 1, VT 17, IOL. Also see textbooks from the 1840s and 1850s, mentioned above and listed in the bibliography under Hindi and Bengali texts in the IOL.

53. Prasad, *Bhugola hastamalaka,* 59–62.

54. James Grant Duff, *A History of the Mahrattas* (London: Longmans, Rees, Orme, Brown and Green, 1826); James Tod, *Annals and Antiquities of Rajasthan or the Central and Western Rajpoot States of India* (1829; reprint, London: Oxford University Press, 1829); Joseph Davey Cunningham, *A History of the Sikhs from the Origin of the Nation to the Battle of the Sutlej* (1849; reprint, Delhi: S. Chand, 1966); John Watson and Kaye Wilson, eds., *The People of India: A Series of Photographic Illustrations, with Descriptive Letterpress of the Races and Tribes of Hindustan,* vols. 1–8 (London: India Museum, 1868–75).

55. There is a vast literature on the colonial construction of reified categories of caste and religion in such interlinked arenas as Orientalist scholarship, the reworking of legal codes and practices, and everyday administrative practice. Some important works in this field include Appadurai, "Number in the Colonial Imagination," in *Modernity at Large;* Cohn, *An Anthropologist among the Historians* and *Colonialism and Its Forms of Knowledge;* Dirks, *Castes of Mind;* Ludden, *Contesting the Nation;* Sandra Freitag, *Collective Action and Community: Public Arenas in the Emergence of Communalism in North India* (Berkeley: University of California Press, 1989); Inden, *Imagining India;* Pandey, *Construction of Communalism in Colonial North India;* Lata Mani, *Contentious Traditions: The Debate on Sati in Colonial India* (Berkeley: University of California Press, 1998); Van der Veer, *Religious Nationalism.*

56. Chunder, *Travels of a Hindoo to Various Parts of Bengal and Upper India,* 1:370–71.

57. Appadurai, "Number in the Colonial Imagination," in *Modernity at Large,* 134.

58. Irfan Habib, *An Atlas the Mughal Empire: Political and Economic Maps with Detailed Notes, Bibliography and Index* (Delhi: Oxford University Press, 1982), 122.

59. Irfan Habib, foreword, in Gole, *Early Maps of India,* viii–ix.

60. Joseph Schwartzberg, ed., *A Historical Atlas of South Asia* (New York: Oxford University Press, 1992), 507.

61. H. Blochmann, "Contributions to the Geography and History of Bengal (Muhammadan Period)," *Journal of the Royal Asiatic Society of Bengal* 42

(1873); Gole, *Indian Maps and Plans from the Earliest Times to the Advent of European Surveys;* Joseph Schwartzberg, "South Asian Cartography," in *The History of Cartography,* vol. 2 (Chicago: University of Chicago Press, 1987).

62. Bayly, *Empire and Information,* 305.

63. Pandit Ramajasana, *Bhugol-candrika* (Allahabad: Government Press, 1865), 104, VT 156, IOL.

64. Anonymous, *Bhugol zila Meerut* (1878), 1, VT 14160, IOL.

65. Prasad, *Bhugola-Hastamalaka,* 2.

66. Pandit Mohan Lal, *Awadh ka bhugol* (1876), 2, IOL.

67. Munshi Iswariprasada, *Jagadbhhugola* (1868–69), 14, VT 155, IOL.

68. Pal, *Memories of My Life and Times,* 205.

69. Bharatendu Harischandra, *Bharatendu samagra,* ed. Hemant Sharma (Varanasi: Pracharak granthavali pariyojana, Hindi pracharak samasthan, 1987), 253–54.

70. For an incisive reading of the gendered iconography of nationalism, see Anne McClintock, *Imperial Leather: Race, Gender, and Sexuality in the Colonial Context* (London: Routledge, 1995), 352–91.

71. Selections from vernacular newspapers, 1877, 315–25, IOL.

72. One of the most striking examples of such a work is Bhudeb Mukhopadhyay's 1876 Bengali work titled *Svapnalabdha bharatbarser itihas.* See Chatterjee, *Nation and Its Fragments,* 111–12.

73. Sarkar, *Hindu Wife, Hindu Nation,* 51.

74. Sarkar, *Writing Social History,* 313.

75. On the practice of *darshan,* see Diane Eck, *Darsan: Seeing the Divine Image in India* (New York: Columbia University Press: 1998); on Shakta devotional practices, see Sarkar, *Writing Social History,* 282–357. For an analysis of the relationship between *darshan* and nationalist discourse, particularly in the work of Tagore, see Chakrabarty, *Provincializing Europe,* 173–78.

76. My analysis departs from Dipesh Chakrabarty's claim that nationalist imaginings of Bharat Mata indexed an "age-old" subjectless religious modality that had survived intact and signaled the "irreducible heterogeneity in the constitution of the political." See Chakrabarty, *Provincializing Europe,* 177, 178.

77. Sitalaprasada Upadhyaya, *Duradarsi yogi: Bharat ka saccha swapna* (Ghazipur: Hanuman Press, 1892), VT 155, IOL.

78. Pal, *Soul of India,* 50.

Chapter Seven

1. Marx, *Grundrisse,* 104–5. Also see Sayer, *Violence of Abstraction,* 125–49.

2. For descriptive histories of economic nationalists, see Ajit Dasgupta, *A History of Indian Economic Thought* (London: Routledge, 1993); B. N. Ganguli, *Indian*

Economic Thought: Nineteenth Century Perspectives (Delhi: Gian, 1977); V. B. Singh, *From Naoroji to Nehru: Six Essays in Indian Economic Thought* (Delhi: Macmillan, 1975); and Joseph Spengler, *Indian Economic Thought* (Durham, N.C.: Duke University Press, 1971). For an especially influential analysis of economic nationalism, see Chandra, *Rise and Growth of Economic Nationalism in India.*

3. For a recent instance of this distinction, see Sanjay Seth, "Rewriting Histories of Nationalism: The Politics of 'Moderate Nationalism' in India, 1870–1905," *American Historical Review* 104, 1 (1999): 95–116.

4. Naoroji, *Poverty and Un-British Rule in India,* 192; Mahadev Govind Ranade, *Ranade's Economic Writings,* ed. Bipan Chandra Pal (Delhi: Gian, 1990), 322–49.

5. Ranade, *Ranade's Economic Writings,* 338.

6. Naoroji, *Poverty and Un-British Rule in India,* 191.

7. Ranade, *Ranade's Economic Writings,* 324.

8. G. V. Joshi, *Writings and Speeches of G. V. Joshi* (Poona: Aryabhushan Press, 1912), as quoted in Vaman Govind Kale, *Introduction to the Study of Indian Economics* (Poona: Aryabhushan Press, 1918), 196–97.

9. Indian National Congress Papers, vol. 1, 1885–1900, 121, NAI.

10. Susan Buck-Morss, "Envisioning Capital: Political Economy on Display," *Critical Inquiry* 21, 2 (1995): 439. Also see Polanyi, *Great Transformation,* 11–30. For a dissenting view articulated from a Foucauldian perspective, see Timothy Mitchell, *Rule of Experts: Egypt, Techno-Politics, Modernity* (Berkeley: University of California Press, 2002); and Mitchell, "Fixing the Economy," *Cultural Studies* 12, 1 (1998): 82–101. In *Rule of Experts,* Mitchell argues that "no political economist of the eighteenth or nineteenth century wrote about an object called the economy. The term economy in that period carried the older meaning of thrift and in a larger sense referred to the proper husbanding of resources and the intelligent management of their circulation. The idea of the economy did not emerge until the middle decades of the twentieth century" (4). He locates the concept of the economy as the "totality of monetized relations within a defined space" in the mid-twentieth century with the formation of Keynesian economics. This perspective simply transposes Foucault's specific understanding of governmentality as grounded in an economizing logic into the social category of the economy in a transhistorical fashion. It ignores, of course, the concept of the national economy developed within the German historical school and, more crucially, conflates the notion of totality with the formalistic models of neoclassical and Keynesian macroeconomics. It also brackets a long tradition of Marxian engagements with the historicity of conceptions of the economy as an objective, bounded and external realm. For

an account of the specificity of Keynesian economics and conceptions of a national economy without an occlusion of the sociohistorical iterations of this category, see Hugo Radice, "The National Economy: A Keynesian Myth?" *Capital and Class* 22 (spring 1984): 111–40.

11. Within the classical Marxian tradition, Luxemburg and Lukács in particular elaborated the historicity of this conception of the economy. See Rosa Luxembourg, *Die Akkumulation des Kapitals: Ein Beitrag zur ökonomischen Erklärung des Imperialismus* (Berlin: Buchhandlung Vorwärts Paul Singer, 1913); and Lukács, *History and Class Consciousness*, esp. 4–8, 104–7. In a similar vein, E. P. Thompson argued that "the very category of economics—the notion that it is possible to isolate economic from non-economic social relations—was the product of a particular phase of capitalist evolution." E. P. Thompson, *The Poverty of Theory* (London: Merlin, 1978), 82–83.

12. Friedrich List, *Das Nationale System der Politischen Oekonomie* (Jena: Verlag von Gustav Fischer, 1910). For the English translation, see List, *The National System of Political Economy* (New York: Augustus Kelly, 1966). For an account of List's importance in China, Japan, and especially the United States, see the comprehensive biography by William Otto Henderson, *Friedrich List, Economist and Visionary, 1789–1846* (London: F. Cass, 1983), 26. Also see William O. Henderson, "Friedrich List and the Social Question," *Journal of European Economic History* 10:697–708. For a juxtaposition of List and Marx in a triumphal ideological idiom, see Roman Sporzluk, *Communism and Nationalism: Friedrich List and Karl Marx* (New York: Oxford University Press, 1988). For an incisive analysis of List's work, see David Levi-Farr, "Friedrich List and the Political Economy of the Nation-State," *Review of International Political Economy* 4, 1 (1997): 154–78. Also see Friedrich List, *The Natural System of Political Economy*, trans. W. O. Henderson (Totowa, N.J.: F. Cass, 1983),; and List, "Outlines of American Political Economy," in *Life of Friedrich List and Selections from His Writings*, ed. M. Hirst (London: Smith, Elder, 1909), 147–272.

13. Bipan Chandra notes the influence of List, as well as Sismondi and Carey, on Ranade but does so only in passing and without engaging their works. See Chandra, in *Ranade's Economic Writings*, ed. Bipan Chandra, xiv, xviii.

14. List had spent more than a decade, from the early 1820s until 1832, in Harrisburg, Pennsylvania, developing not only close intellectual links with figures such as Henry Clay, Nicholas Biddle, and Mathew Carey but helping to plan canal and railway systems.

15. List, *National System of Political Economy*, 174.

16. The German terms are from List, *Nationale System der Politischen Oekonomie*, 267, 268, 290, 291.

17. Johann Fichte, *Der geschlossne Handelsstaat* (Leipzig: F. Eckardt, 1910).

18. List, *National System of Political Economy*, 35–36.

19. Karl Marx, "Draft of an Article on Friedrich List's *Das Nationale System der Politischen Oekonomie*," in *Collected Works*, vol. 4 (Moscow: Progress Publishers, 1975), 276.

20. List's theory was mobilized as the economic rationale for German unification in the 1880s. During World War II, it was deployed as a defense of a pan-German nation. It has more recently been summoned to legitimate the European Union. See, e.g., E. N. Roussakis, *Friedrich List, the Zollverien, and the Uniting of Europe* (Bruges: College of Europe, 1968).

21. Henry Carey, *The Harmony of Interests: Agricultural, Manufacturing and Commercial* (1851; reprint, New York: A. M. Kelley, 1967); and Carey, *Principles of Political Economy* (Philadelphia: Carey, Lea and Blanchard, 1837–40). Also see John Rae, *Statement of Some New Principles on the Subject of Political Economy* (Boston: Hillard, Gray, 1834).

22. Marx, *Grundrisse*, 883.

23. Harvey, *Limits to Capital*, 439.

24. Marx, *Grundrisse*, 887.

25. Harvey, *Limits to Capital*, 439.

26. Marx, "Draft of an Article on List's *Nationale System der Politischen Oekonomie*," 281.

27. See, in particular, Brenner, "Beyond State-Centrism?" 39–78; Agnew, "Territorial Trap," 53–80; and Wallerstein, *Unthinking Social Science*.

28. Ranade, *Ranade's Economic Writings*, 322–50.

29. Alavi, *Capitalism and Colonial Production*, 65.

30. Joshi, "Writings and Speeches," as quoted in Kale, *Introduction to the Study of Indian Economics*, 189.

31. Indian National Congress Papers, vol. 11, 1902, 44–45, NAI.

32. For a history of this epithet, see Antoinette Burton, "Tongues Untied: Lord Salisbury's 'Black Man' and the Boundaries of Imperial Democracy," *Comparative Studies in Society and History* 43, 2 (2000): 632–59. Also see Rozina Visram, *Ayahs, Lascars and Princes: Indians in Britain, 1700–1947* (London: Pluto, 1986); and Jonathan Schneer, *London 1900: The Imperial Metropolis* (New Haven: Yale University Press, 1999), for an account of Naoroji's years in London. Naoroji was the first to employ the term *swaraj* to signify "national self-government," in his 1906 presidential address to the Indian National Congress. For a detailed biography, see R. P. Masani, *Dadabhai Naoroji: The Grand Old Man of India* (London: Allen and Unwin, 1939).

33. Naoroji, *Poverty and Un-British Rule in India*, 283.

34. Marx drew on Naoroji's analysis of "unrequited exports" to argue for the central importance of such imperial financial transfers in Britain's national econ-

omy. See Marx, *Capital*, chap. 35. Also see Ganguli, *Indian Economic Thought*, 136–37.

35. For a detailed account of the basis for competing figures during this period, see Kale, *Introduction to the Study of Indian Economics*, 155–57.

36. Colonial officials included Lord Curzon in 1901, and F. G. Atkinson in 1908 and 1909; nationalist economists and British socialists included William Digby in 1901, B. N. Sharma in 1921, Findlay Shirras in 1922, Shah and Khambatta in 1924, Wadia and Joshi in 1925, and V. K. R. V. Rao in 1936. See V. K. R. V. Rao, *An Essay on India's National Income, 1925–1929* (London: Allen and Unwin, 1939), for an account of various attempts. Rao's work was the recipient of both the Adam Smith Prize in Political Economy from Cambridge University and the first Dadabhai Naoroji Memorial Prize in 1936.

37. Naoroji, *Poverty and Un-British Rule in India*, 201–2.

38. Naoroji corresponded and worked with the British Socialist leader Henry Hyndman for twenty years and carried on an extensive correspondence with the Austo-Hungarian Marxist Karl Kautsky. Naoroji Papers, Private Collection, NAI.

39. William Digby, *"Prosperous" British India: A Revelation from Official Research* (London: Allen and Unwin, 1901).

40. Karl Marx, *On Colonialism* (Moscow: Foreign Language Publishing House, 1962), 304. Also see Marx, *Capital*, vol. 3, chap. 35, for an analysis of the drain as unrequited exports.

41. Arya Mitra, May 9, 1878, 368, L/R/55, selections from the vernacular newspapers published in the Punjab, North-Western Provinces, Oudh, and Central Provinces, IOL.

42. For a detailed examination of this contentious process, see Peter Harnetty, *Imperialism and Free Trade: Lancashire and India in the Mid Nineteenth Century* (Manchester: Manchester University Press, 1977).

43. Minute, July 13, 1879, India Council Minute Book, no. C/128, 367–70, IOL.

44. Further Papers Relating to Import Duties upon Cotton Goods, no. 1, extract from J. Strachey's statement in V/4/55, 1878–79, *Parliamentary Papers*, vol. 55, IOL.

45. Nasimi Agra, January 30, 1879, selections from the vernacular newspapers published in the Punjab, North-Western Provinces, Oudh, and Central Provinces, IOL.

46. *Hindi Pradip* was a newspaper edited by Balkrishan Bhatt (who later, in 1885, joined the Indian National Congress).

47. Hindi Pradip, July 1879, selections from the vernacular newspapers published in the Punjab, North-Western Provinces, Oudh, and Central Provinces, IOL.

48. Home Department (Political) Proceedings, March 1908, 42, 44, NAI.

49. Ibid., April 1912, no. 3, NAI.

50. Romesh Chunder Dutt, *The Economic History of India under Early British Rule*, vol. 1 (1902; reprint, New York: Augustus Kelley, 1969), preface, xvi. Also see Dutt, *The Economic History of India in the Victorian Age*, vol. 2 (1904; reprint, New York: Burt Franklin, 1970); Dutt, *Open Letters to Lord Curzon on Famines and Land Assessments in India* (London: Trubner, 1900); Dutt, *England and India, 1785–1885* (London: Chatto and Windus, 1897); Dutt, *A History of Civilization in Ancient India* (London: Chatto and Windus, 1882); Dutt, *Peasantry of Bengal* (Calcutta: Modern Book Agency, 1874).

51. Dutt, *Economic History of India under Early British Rule*, 1:xv.

52. Pal, *New Economic Menace to India*, 70.

53. Chris Bayly, *The Local Roots of Indian Politics: Allahabad, 1880–1920* (Oxford: Clarendon Press, 1975), 133.

54. Sitaramaya, *History of the Indian National Congress*, 117–18.

55. Strachey, *India*, 5–7.

56. Indian National Congress Papers, vol. 1, 1890, 109, NAI.

57. Ibid., 1895, 173.

58. Malkki, "National Geographic," 26–27.

59. Indian National Congress Papers, vol. 1, 1895, 133, NAI.

60. Kale, *Introduction to the Study of Indian Economics*. Also see Kale, *Indian Industrial and Economic Problems*, and *Currency Reform in India*.

61. Kale, *Introduction to the Study of Indian Economics*, 3.

62. Subramania Aiyar, *Some Economic Aspects of British Rule in India* (Madras: Swadesamitran Press, 1903), was, for instance, exemplary of this school.

63. Radhakamal Mukherjee, *The Foundations of Indian Economics*, with an introduction by Patrick Geddes (London: Longmans, Green, 1916).

64. Mukherjee's extensive engagement with German economic sociologists such as Werner Sombart was driven, in part, by a search for an alternate pathway and form of industrial development. See, in particular, his discussion of alternatives to mass-scale industrialization, esp. ibid., 358–79.

65. See, e.g., Radhakamal Mukherjee, *The Indian Working Class* (Bombay: Hind Kitabs, 1945). For instances of works directly inspired by Mukherjee during the late 1920s and 1930s, see B. Shiva Rao, *The Industrial Worker in India* (London: Allen and Unwin, 1939); and Palamadai Lokanathan, *Industrial Welfare in India* (Madras: Methodist Publishing House, 1929).

66. Mukherjee, *Foundation of Indian Economics*, xix.

67. See, in particular, the remarkable theorization of uneven development elaborated by Kozo Uno, *Principles of Political Economy: Theory of a Pure Capitalist Society*, trans. Thomas T. Sekine (1945; reprint, Brighton, Sussex: Harvester,

1980). For an analysis of Marxist historiography in China, see Arif Dirlik, *Revolution and History: Origins of Marxist Historiography in China, 1919–1937* (Berkeley: University of California Press, 1978).

68. Mukherjee, *Foundations of Indian Economics,* 415.

69. Theodor Adorno, *The Jargon of Authenticity,* trans. Knut Tornowski and Frederic Will (Evanston, Ill.: Northwestern University Press, 1973), 116.

70. Mukherjee, *Foundations of Indian Economics,* 328.

Chapter Eight

1. For detailed accounts, see Chris Bayly, "The Origins of Swadeshi: Cloth and Indian Society," in *The Social Life of Things,* ed. Arjun Appadurai (Cambridge: Cambridge University Press, 1986), 285–328; Ranajit Guha, "Discipline and Mobilize," in *Dominance without Hegemony,* 100–150; and especially Sarkar, *Swadeshi Movement in Bengal.* Also see Haridas Mukherjee and Uma Mukherjee, *India's Fight for Freedom or the Swadeshi Movement, 1905–1906* (Calcutta: Firma K. L. Mukhopadhyay, 1958); and Mukherjee and Mukherjee, *A Phase of the Swadeshi Movement, National Education, 1905–1910* (Calcutta: Chuckerverty, Chatterjee, 1953).

2. Naoroji, *Poverty and Un-British Rule in India,* 183 (emphasis in the original).

3. The INC meeting of 1906 also adopted resolutions on national education, boycott, and *swaraj.* See Indian National Congress Papers, vol. 11, 1906, 85, NAI.

4. B. R. Nanda, *Gokhale: The Indian Moderates and the British Raj* (Princeton: Princeton University Press, 1977), 24. Ranade's sartorial style, personal comportment, cultural and literary tastes, scholarly research, and political efforts exemplified the construction of a *swadeshi* habitus.

5. Home Department, Judicial Proceedings, August 1880, nos. 203–5, NAI.

6. For a detailed examination of Curzon's attempted reforms, see Basu, *Growth of Education and Political Development in India.* The School Text-Book Committee of 1900 announced as imperative a greater control over textbooks, because ever since the Tilak sedition trial of 1897 there had been a growing sense "that many of vernacular books patronized [in indigenous schools] contained lessons capable of being used as apologies for disloyalty." Educational Proceedings A, February 1900, Proc. 40–54, NAI; Secretary of State's Dispatch, no. 19, Educational Proceedings, December 16, 1897, NAI.

7. Educational Proceedings A, June 1901, enclosure to Proc. 47, NAI.

8. Ibid., April 1916, no. 3, NAI.

9. Sarkar, *Swadeshi Movement in Bengal,* 269–70. Other pamphlets that conformed to the genre of popular nationalist political economy included Charunchandra Basu Majumdar's 1905 *Bartaman samashya o swadeshi andolan* (Present-Day

Problems and the Swadeshi Movement), written as a dialogue between a *swadeshi* activist and a peasant; Gispati Kabyatirtha's 1907 work, *Bideshi bhishkar o swadeshi mahatmya* (Expulsion of the Foreign and the Virtues of the Indigenous); and the labor organizer Surjyakumar Ghosal's 1908 work, *Bharate annakashta* (Scarcity in India).

10. Home Department (Political) Proceedings, April 1911, no. 7, deposit; Home Department (Political) Proceedings A, July 1913, nos. 4–6, NAI.

11. Home Department (Political) Proceedings, December 1907, no. 9, NAI.

12. Ibid., April 1911, no. 7, deposit, NAI.

13. Guha, *Dominance without Hegemony*, 212.

14. Among these were various publications from the Ghadr (revolution) organization from San Francisco on the subject of the "national drain." Home Department (Political) Proceedings A, July 1913, nos. 4–6, NAI.

15. Home Department (Political) Proceedings, August 1907, no. 36, deposit, NAI.

16. Basu, *Growth of Education and Political Development in India*, 42–56.

17. Circular issued by R. W. Carlyle, Officiating Chief Secretary to the Governor of Bengal, Home Department (Public) Proceedings A, August 1906, nos. 261–71, NAI.

18. See Basu, *Growth of Education and Political Development in India*, 107; Mukherjee and Mukherjee, *Phase of the Swadeshi Movement*, 38–55.

19. Mukherjee and Mukherjee, *Phase of the Swadeshi Movement*, 47.

20. For a detailed biographical account, see M. N. Roy, *Selected Works of M. N. Roy, 1917–1922*, ed. Sibnarayan Ray (Delhi: Oxford University Press, 2000), 1:1–19.

21. M. N. Roy, "India in Transition," in *Selected Works of M.N. Roy*, 1:352.

22. M. N. Roy, *New Orientation: Lectures Delivered at the Political Study Camp Held at Dehradun from May 8–18, 1946* (Calcutta: South Asia Books, 1999), 121–22.

23. Pal, *Swadeshi and Swaraj*, 18, 56.

24. Bipin Pal, *Nationality and Empire: A Running Study of Some Current Indian Problems* (Calcutta and Simla: Thacker, Spink, 1916), 86.

25. Rabindranath Tagore, *Greater India* (Madras: S. Ganesan, 1921), 32.

26. Etienne Balibar, "Fichte and the Internal Border," in *Masses, Classes, Ideas*, 67.

27. Tagore, *Greater India*, 32.

28. Rabindranath Tagore, *Nationalism* (1917; reprint, Westport, Conn.: Greenwood Press, 1973), 39, 141, 55.

29. Pal, *Nationality and Empire*, 86.

30. Pal, *Swadeshi and Swaraj*, 252.

31. Pal, *Soul of India*, 15.

32. Pal, *Swadeshi and Swaraj*, 289.

33. Pal, *Soul of India*, 15.

34. Pal, *Swadeshi and Swaraj*, 64.

35. For a detailed account of various images and figures of Bharat Mata, see Sugata Bose, "Nation as Mother: Representations and Contestations of India in Bengali Literature and Culture," in *Nationalism, Democracy, and Development: State and Politics in India*, ed. Sugata Bose and Ayesha Jalal (Delhi: Oxford University Press, 1996), 50–75.

36. The song was drawn from a popular novel by Babu Manmohan Bose titled *Banghadeep-pararajya*. See Pal, *Memories of My Life and Times*, 207.

37. Quoted in Bayly, "Origins of Swadeshi," 327.

38. Tagore, *Greater India*, 70.

39. For an insightful reading, see Tanika Sarkar, "Imagining Hindurashtra: The Hindu and the Muslim in Bankim Chandra's Writings," in *Contesting the Nation: Religion, Community and the Politics of Democracy*, ed. David Ludden (Philadelphia: University of Pennsylvania Press, 1996), 173.

40. Home Department (Political) Proceedings, October 1910, no. 20, NAI.

41. A pamphlet titled *Bande mataram*, published by nationalists in exile associated with the socialist revolutionary party—-which included figures such as Madame Cama and Hemant Kannungo—-was smuggled into and widely distributed in colonial India, at the International Socialist Conference on August 27, 1910, and at the Egyptian conference held in Brussels. Home Department (Political) Proceedings, April 1911, no. 7, deposit, NAI.

42. Sarkar, *Swadeshi Movement in Bengal*, 312–13.

43. Home Department (Political) Proceedings, August 1911, no. 14, NAI.

44. Ibid., January 1908, no. 8, NAI.

45. Sarkar, *Swadeshi Movement in Bengal*.

46. Guha, "Discipline and Mobilize," in *Dominance without Hegemony*.

47. Pal, *Nationality and Empire*, 86.

48. For a fuller elaboration of this argument, see Goswami, "Rethinking the Modular Nation Form."

49. For an extraordinary analysis of the socially embedded theological innovations of *swadeshi* discourses on Hinduism, see Andrew Sartori, "The Categorical Logic of a Colonial Nationalism: Swadeshi Bengal, 1904–1908," *Comparative Studies of South Asia, Africa and the Middle East* (2003) 23, 1. Also see Sarkar, *Writing Social History*, esp. 186–215 and 282–357, for an account of popular Shakta practices and doctrinal innovations.

50. Pal, *Soul of India*, 90.

51. Pal, *Nationality and Empire*, 75.

52. Pal, *Soul of India*, 94.

53. Pal, *Nationality and Empire*, 77.

54. Pal, *Soul of India*, 107.

55. Adorno, *Jargon of Authenticity*, 9.

56. Rabindranath Tagore, "A Vision of Indian History," in *A Tagore Reader*, ed. Amiya Chakravarty (Boston: Beacon Press, 1966), 196.

57. Sarkar, *Swadeshi Movement in Bengal*, 79–82.

58. Mohamed Ali, "The Communal Patriot," in *Select Writings and Speeches of Maulana Mohamed Ali*, ed. Afzal Iqbal (Lahore: Islamic Book Foundation, 1987), 75, 76.

59. Pal, *Nationality and Empire*, 388.

60. See, in particular, Faisal Devji, "Muslim Nationalism: Founding Identity in Colonial India," Ph.D. dissertation, University of Chicago, 1993; Ayesha Jalal, *Self and Sovereignty: Individual and Community in South Asian Islam since 1850* (Delhi: Oxford University Press, 2001); and Jalal, "Exploding Communalism: The Politics of Muslim Identity in South Asia," in Bose and Jalal, *Nationalism, Democracy and Development*, 76–103. For general histories of Muslim nationalism, see Hasan, *Islam and Indian Nationalism*; Mushirul Hasan, ed., *Communal and Pan-Islamic Trends in Colonial India* (New Delhi: Manohar Publications, 1985); Hasan, *Nationalism and Communal Politics in India*; Lelyveld, *Aligarh's First Generation*; Barbara Metcalf, *Islamic Revival in British India: Deoband, 1860–1900* (Princeton: Princeton University Press, 1982). Also see Manu Goswami, "The Production of India: Colonialism, Nationalism and Territorial Nativism," Ph.D. dissertation, University of Chicago, chap. 9.

61. Pal, *Swadeshi and Swaraj*, 106–7. Also see Goswami, "Production of India," chap. 9.

62. Adorno, *Jargon of Authenticity*, 50.

63. Quoted in Mukherjee and Mukherjee, *India's Fight for Freedom*, 198.

64. Surendranath Banerjea, *A Nation in Making: Being the Reminiscences of Fifty Years of Public Life* (London: Oxford University Press, 1925), 197.

65. Home Department (Public) Proceedings, December 1907, 282, NAI.

66. Ibid., 274; Ranade, *Ranade's Economic Writings*, 273.

67. Kale, *Introduction to the Study of Indian Economics*, 124.

68. Romesh Dutt, speech at the Benares Industrial Conference, 1903, as quoted in Kale, *Introduction to the Study of Indian Economics*, 221.

69. Home Department (Public) Proceedings, December 1907, 259, NAI.

70. Indian National Congress Papers, vol. 11, 1902, 12, NAI.

71. For analyses, focused on later decades, of the concrete links between the INC and indigenous capitalists, see Claude Markovits, *Indian Business and Nationalist Politics, 1931–39* (Cambridge: Cambridge University Press, 1985); and Dwijendra Tripathi, *Business and Politics in India: A Historical Perspective* (New Delhi: Manohar Publications, 1991). Also see John Mclane, "The Drain of

Wealth and Indian Nationalism at the Turn of the Century, *Indian Economic and Social History Review* 1, 1 (1963); Sarkar, *Critique of Colonial India;* and Sarkar, *Swadeshi Movement in Bengal.*

72. Simon R. B. Leadbeater, *The Indian Cotton-Mill Industry and the Legacy of Swadeshi, 1900–1985* (Delhi: Sage Publications, 1993); and Amit Bhattacharya, *Swadeshi Enterprise in Bengal, 1900–1920* (Jadavpur, Calcutta: INA Press, 1986).

73. Home Department (Public) Proceedings, December 1907, 250, NAI.

74. Ranade, *Ranade's Economic Writings,* 344.

75. For an elaboration of this argument, see Pal's speeches recorded in Home Department (Public) Proceedings, December 1907, 298, NAI.

76. As quoted in Kale, *Introduction to the Study of Indian Economics,* 223.

77. Ranade, *Ranade's Economic Writings,* 277–78.

78. Home Department (Public) Proceedings, December 1907, 273, NAI.

79. Mukherjee, *Foundations of Indian Economics,* 462–63.

80. Pal, *Swadeshi and Swaraj,* 106–7.

81. Mukherjee, *Foundations of Indian Economics,* 463.

82. Dutt, *England and India,* 23.

83. The INC election manifesto of 1945 stated, "The most vital and urgent of India's problems is how to remove the curse of poverty and raise the standard of the masses. . . . The state must own or control key and basic industries and services, mineral resources, railways, waterways, shipping, and other means of public transport. Currency and exchange, banking and insurance, must be regulated in the national interest." As quoted in A. M. Zaidi, *A Tryst with Destiny: A Study of Economic Policy Resolutions of the INC Passed during the Last One Hundred Years* (Delhi: Prakashan, 1985), 79–81.

Conclusion

1. Tagore, *Nationalism,* 60. Also see Tagore, *Greater India.*

2. Rabindranath Tagore, "From Greater India," in Chakravarty, *Tagore Reader,* 198, 197.

3. For a provocative elaboration of the thesis that received "European" frameworks cannot adequately register forms of difference, see Chakrabarty, *Provincializing Europe,* 37. For related arguments yet with important internal differences, see Guha, *History at the Limit of World-History;* Prakash, *Another Reason;* Chatterjee, *Nation and Its Fragments.*

4. Tagore, "From Greater India," 197–98.

5. Benjamin, *Illumination*s, 261; Lefebvre, *Production of Space,* 287.

6. Harvey, *Limits to Capital,* 414.

7. Naoroji, *Poverty and Un-British Rule in India, Indian Exchange and Bimetallism,* and *Speeches and Writings.*

8. Ranade, *Ranade's Economic Writings* and *Essays on Indian Economics;* Joshi, *Writings and Speeches of G. V. Joshi;* Kale, *Introduction to the Study of Indian Economics* and *Indian Industrial and Economic Problems.*

9. Mukherjee, *Foundations of Indian Economics, Economic Problems of Modern India,* and *Indian Working Class;* Dutt, *Economic History of India under Early British Rule, Economic History of India in the Victorian Age, Open Letters to Lord Curzon on Famines and Land Assessments in India,* and *England and India.*

10. Hamza Alavi, "The Postcolonial State," *New Left Review* 74 (1972): 59–82. Also see Alavi, "India and the Colonial Mode of Production," *Socialist Register* 4 (1975): 160–97.

11. Michel Rolph-Trouillot provides an inspired reading of the silencing of the Haitian revolution both in its time and subsequent historiography in *Silencing the Past.* Also see C. L. R. James's classic work, *The Black Jacobins.*

12. Theodore Adorno, "Aspects of Hegel's Philosophy," in *Hegel: Three Studies,* trans. Shierry Weber Nicholsen (Cambridge: MIT Press, 1993), 1.

13. Bourdieu, *Outline of a Theory of Practice.*

14. Ali, "Communal Patriot."

15. Prasad, *Itihas-timirnasaka* (1873), 5–6.

16. During the last decade, there has been an extraordinary surge of extraordinary analyses of the partition from different conceptual and thematic frameworks. These include Urvashi Butalia, *The Other Side of Silence: Voices from the Partition of India* (Delhi: Kali for Women, 1998), Joya Chatterjee, *Bengal Divided: Hindu Communalism and Partition, 1932–1947* (Cambridge: Cambridge University Press, 1995); and Gyanendra Pandey, *Remembering the Partition* (Cambridge: Cambridge University Press, 2001).

17. Pal, *Swadeshi and Swaraj,* 40.

BIBLIOGRAPHY

ARCHIVAL SOURCES

India Office Library and Records (IOL), British Museum, London

English-Language Texts
Education Department Proceedings, North-Western Provinces (NWP) and Oudh
Finance Department collections
Finance Miscellaneous series
Finance Proceedings
General Proceedings, NWP and Oudh
Home Department, General Proceedings
Home Department, Judicial Proceedings
Home Department, Public Proceedings
Public Works Department Proceedings
Public Works Department Proceedings, NWP and Oudh
Railways Department Proceedings
Report on External Commerce
Revenue, Agriculture, and Commerce Department Proceedings
Selections from the Records of the Government, NWP and Oudh
Selections from the Educational Records of the Government of India
Selections from the Records of the Government of India
Selections from the vernacular newspapers published in the Punjab, NWP, Oudh,
    and Central Provinces
Statistical abstracts for British India
Vernacular Text Collection, comp. J. F. Blumhardt, catalogue of the IOL

Hindi-Language Texts (Vernacular Text Collection, IOL)
Anonymous. 1840. *Bhugol o itihas o jyothish sankshaep katha* (Geography, History,
    Astrology: A Succinct Account).
Anonymous. 1879. *Prasnottara Bharatvarsha ke ithasa ke vishaya men* (A Catechism
    on the History of India). Agra. 14156.
Basudev, Pandit. 1870. *Bhugol zillah Jalaun* (The Geography of Jalaun District).
Caudhuri, Madhusudana. 1877. *Bharatavarsha ka bhugthranth* (The Physical Geog-
    raphy of India). VT 129.

Chaudhuri, Budhinata. 1871. *Prithvi-itihasa* (The History of the Earth). VT 120.

Dayal, Devi. 1877. *Bhugol o itihas Farukhabad* (The Historical Geography of Farukhabad).

Dhar, Pandit Bansi. 1870. *Bhugol* (Geography).

———. 1870. *Bhugol Meerut* (The Geography of Meerut).

Iswariprasada, Munshi. 1868–69. *Jagadhbhugola* (Geography of the World). VT 155.

Karimuddin. 1869. *Bharatavarshiay vrttantaprakasa* (History of India). 279/4.

Lal, Pandit Khuj Bihari. 1848. *Bhugol suchan* (Geography Textbook).

Lal, Pandit Mohan. 1876. *Awadh ka bhugol* (The Geography of Awadh).

Lala, Krshna. 1862. *Bhugolasara* (An Elementary Geography of India). 14160.

———. 1867. *Bhugola-prakasa* (Simple Geography of Europe and Asia). VT 155.

Lala, Munshi Dori. 1876. *Madhya Pradesh ka bhugol* (The Geography of Madhya Pradesh). VT 112.

Lala, Ranta. 1851. *Bhugola-darpana* (Elementary Geography). 279/4.

Maganlal, Pandit. 1872. *Awadh ka bhugol* (The Geography of Awadh).

Mukarji, Niranjana. 1874. *Bharatvashiya rajadarpana* (Political History of India). 279/5.

Mukherjee, Babu Narayan. 1875. *Bharat varshiya darpan* (History of India).

Mukhopadyaya, Rajakrshna. 1878. *Sube Bangal ka itihasa* (A History of Bengal). Trans. Sivarayana Trivedi. VT 111.

Mulacanda, Pandit. 1870. *Bharatkhand ka varnan* (Geography of India).

———. 1870. *Bhugol dipak* (A Short Geography of India). VT 110.

———. 1871. *Bhugola zila Jalaun* (Geography of the District of Jalaun). VT 110.

———. 1872. *Bhugol o itihas Lucknow* (The Historical Geography of Lucknow, 1872).

Mulye, Vasundeva Ballala. 1876. *Bhugol vidya* (Geographical Knowledge).

———. 1876. *Itihasasara* (A Short History of India). VT 112.

Prabulala. 1872. *Madhyapradesa ka bhugola* (Geography of the Central Provinces). VT 108.

Prasad, Rajah Shiva. 1851. *Sikhaon ka udaya aur asta.* VT 152.

———. 1864. *Itihas timirnasak.* 3 vols. Allahabad: Govt Press.

———. 1873. *Itihas-timirnasaka.* 3 vols. Benares: Medical Hall Press.

———. 1874. *Bhugola hastamalaka*, 6th ed. (Geography of the World: Crystal Clear). VT 1307.

———. 1888. *Nivedan.* Lucknow: Munshi Nawal Kishore. VT 1233.

Ramajasana, Pandit. 1865. *Bhugol-candrika* (The Geography of the World). VT 156.

Ramalala, Munasi. 1871. *Bhugol o itihas Hamirpur* (The Historical Geography of Hamirpur). VT 110.

Ramaprasada, Munshi. 1869. *Bhugola-varnana* (Description of Geography). 14160.

Ramlal, Munshi. 1871. *Bhugol o itihas Etawah* (The Historical Geography of Etawah).

Sastri, Bapudeva. 1857. *Bhugol varnan* (Description of Geography). VT 120.

Simha, Ganapata. 1878. *Chota bugola-varnana* (Geography of India). VT 108.

Singh, Umrao. 1874, *Pascimottara desiya bhugola* (The Geography of the North-Western Provinces). VT 108.

Sitarama, Pandit. 1869. *Bhugol o itihas Lalitpur* (The Historical Geography of Lalitpur). VT 121.

Sivanarayana. 1872. *Avadha desiya bhugola* (The Geography of Awadh). VT 112.

Srikhande, Vishnu Vittal. 1877. *Bhugol Bharat ke shalaon ke liya* (Geography for Indian Students). VT 108.

Taradatta. 1871. *Bhugola Kurmacala* (Geography of the Kumaon). VT 110.

Upadhyaya, Sitalaprasada. 1892. *Duradarsi yogi: Bharat ka saccha swapna* (A Brief Account of the State of Bharat, Past and Present, Written in the Form of a True Dream). VT 155.

Vasudeva, Ravi. 1874. *Bangal ka itihas* (History of Bengal).

Bengali-Language Texts (Vernacular Text Collection, IOL)

Chattopadhyaya, Sasibhushana. 1878. *Bharatavarsher vivarana* (Geography of India). 14131.

Chattopadhyaya, Tarincharana. 1878. *Bhugolvarana* (A Geography of the World). 14131.

Datta, Udaykrishna. 1879. *Bhugolsara* (A Geography of the World). 14131

Mukhopadhyay, Bhudeb. 1876. *Svapnalabdha bharatbarser itihas* (History of India as Revealed in a Dream).

Mukhopadhyaya, Haranachandra. 1868. *Asiyar vivarana* (Geography of Asia). 14131.

Mukhopadyaya, Harimohana. 1870. *Vangadeser viseshavivarana* (Geography of Bengal for the Use of Schools). 14131.

Raya, Krishnachandra. 1880. *Bharataverser bhuvrittanta* (Geography of India). 14131.

Sarkar, Pyaricharana. 1862. *Bharatvarsher bughola vrittanta* (Geography of India). 14131.

Cambridge University Library, Manuscript Collection

Lord Mayo Papers

National Archives (NAI), Delhi

Dadabhai Naoroji Papers, private collection
Education Department Proceedings
Foreign and Political Department Proceedings
Home Department (Political) Proceedings
Home Department (Public) Proceedings
Home Department (Revenue Branch) Proceedings
Indian National Congress Papers, 1885–1920
Papers Relating to Individual Acts of Government of India
Public Works Department Proceedings

Nehru Memorial Museum and Library (NMML), Delhi

Journal of Poona Sarvajanik Sabha
Papers of the Oudh Branch of the British-India Association, 1863–67

PUBLISHED GOVERNMENT RECORDS

Administration Report on Indian State Railways from their Commencement to the End of 1879–1880. Appendix CC, X, V/24/3532. 1881.

Annual Register. 1858.

Final Report on the Settlement of Moradabad District. NWP Settlement Reports. Comp. E. B. Alexander. 1881.

Index and Appendices to the Evidence Taken before the Committee Appointed to Inquire into the Indian Currency. Indian Currency Committee of 1898 (Fowler Committee). London: Eyre and Spottiswoode for HMSO, 1899.

Proceedings of the Railway Conference. Simla: Government of India Press, 1900.

Report from the Select Committee on East India (Railways). C416. 1857–58.

Report of the Commission to Enquire into the Operation of Act XIX of 1861 Being Act to Provide for a Government Paper Currency. Vol. 1. Calcutta: Superintendent Government Printing, 1867.

Report of the Commissioner of Inquiry into the Constitution and Mode of Conduct in the Business of the Financial Department and of the Offices and Audit and Account Attached to That Department. Calcutta: Military Orphan Press, 1864.

Report of the Indian Famine Commission, 1879. Parliamentary Papers. 1881.

Report of the Indian Irrigation Commission, 1901–3. London: HMSO, 1903.

Report of the Land Revenue Settlement, Lucknow District. Oudh Settlement Reports. Comp. H. H. Butts. 1873.

Report of the Proceedings of the Forest Conference, 1873–1874. Ed. B. H. Baden-Powell and J. S. Gamble. Calcutta: Superintendent of Government Printing, 1875.

Report on the Final Settlement of Fatehpur District. NWP Settlement Reports. Government of North-Western Provinces. Comp. A. B. Patterson. 1878.

Report on the Representation of Muslims and Other Minority Communities in the Subordinate Railway Service. By K. M. Hassan. Simla: Government of India Press, 1932.

Suggestions Regarding Forest Administration in the North-Western Provinces and Oudh. By D. Brandis. Calcutta: Government of India Press, 1882.

PUBLISHED SOURCES

Abrams, Phillip. 1988. "Notes on the Difficulty of Studying the State." *Journal of Historical Sociology* 1, 1: 58–89.

Abu el-Haj, Nadia. 1998. "Translating Truths: Nationalism, the Practice of Archaeology and the Remaking of Past and Present in Contemporary Jerusalem." *American Ethnologist* 25, 2: 166–88.

Abu-Lughod, Janet. 1997. "Going beyond Global Babble." In *Culture, Globalization and the World-System: Contemporary Conditions for the Representation of Identity,* ed. Anthony King. Minneapolis: University of Minnesota Press.

Adam, John, and Robert West. 1979. "Money, Prices and Economic Development in India, 1861–1895." *Journal of Economic History* 39, 1: 55–68.

Adorno, Theodore. 1973. *The Jargon of Authenticity.* Trans. Knut Tornowski and Frederic Will. Evanston, Ill.: Northwestern University Press.

———. 1993. "Aspects of Hegel's Philosophy." In *Hegel: Three Studies.* Trans. Shierry Weber Nicholsen. Cambridge: MIT Press.

Agnew, John. 1994. "The Territorial Trap: The Geographical Assumptions of International Relations Theory." *Review of International Political Economy* 1, 1: 53–80.

Agnew, John, and Stuart Corbridge. 1995. *Mastering Space: Hegemony, Territory and International Political Economy.* London: Routledge.

Ahmad, Aijaz. 1994. *In Theory: Classes, Nations, Literatures.* London: Verso.

Aiyar, Subrahmanya. 1903. *Some Economic Aspects of British Rule in India.* Madras: Swadesamitran Press.

Alavi, Hamza. 1972. "The Postcolonial State." *New Left Review* 74:59–82.

———. 1975. "India and the Colonial Mode of Production." *Socialist Register* 4:160–97.

———. 1982. *Capitalism and Colonial Production.* London: Croom Helm.

Alavi, Hamza, and John Harriss, eds. 1989. *South Asia.* New York: Monthly Review Press.

Ali, Mohamed. 1987. "The Communal Patriot." In *Select Writings and Speeches of Maulana Mohamed Ali*. Ed. Afzal Iqbal. Lahore: Islamic Book Foundation.

Ali, Syed Muzafer. 1966. *The Geography of the Puranas*. Delhi: People's Publishing House.

Ambirajan, S. 1968. *Classical Political Economy and British Policy in India*. Cambridge: Cambridge University Press.

———. 1984. *Political Economy and Monetary Management, 1776–1914*. Madras: East-West Press.

Ambedkar, B. R. 1923. *The Problem of the Rupee: Its Origins and Its Solution*. London: P. S. King and Sons.

Amin, Samir. 1996. "The Challenge of Globalization." *Review of International Political Economy* 3, 2: 216–59.

Amin, Shahid. 1982. "Small Peasant Commodity Production and Rural Indebtedness: The Culture of Sugarcane in Eastern UP, 1880–1920." In *Subaltern Studies*, vol. 1, ed. Ranajit Guha. Delhi: Oxford University Press.

———. 1984. *Sugarcane and Sugar in Gorakhpur: An Inquiry into Peasant Production for Capitalist Enterprise in Colonial India*. Delhi: Oxford University Press.

———. 1995. *Event, Metaphor, Memory: Chauri Chaura, 1922–1992*. Berkeley: University of California Press.

Anderson, Benedict. 1991. *Imagined Communities: Reflections on the Origins and Spread of Nationalism*. Rev. ed. London: Verso.

———. 1996. Introduction to *Mapping the Nation*, ed. Gopal Balakrishnan. London: Verso.

———. 1998. *The Spectre of Comparisons: Nationalism, Southeast Asia and the World*. London: Verso.

Anderson, Michael R. 1993. "Islamic Law and the Colonial Encounter." In *Institutions and Ideologies*, ed. David Arnold and Peter Robb. London: Curzon.

Andrew, William Patrick. 1884. *Indian Railways as Connected with British Empire in the East*. London: W. H. Allen and Co.

Appadurai, Arjun. 1996. *Modernity at Large: Cultural Dimensions of Globalization*. Minneapolis: University of Minnesota.

———. 1996. "Sovereignty without Territoriality: Notes for a Postnational Geography." In *The Geography of Identity*, ed. Patricia Yaeger. Ann Arbor: University of Michigan.

Ardant, Gabriel. 1975. "Financial Policy and Economic Infrastructure of Modern States and Nations." In *The Formation of National States in Europe*, ed. Charles Tilly. Princeton: Princeton University Press.

Arnold, David. 1980. "Industrial Violence in Colonial India." *Comparative Studies in Society and History* 22:34–55.

———. 1993. *Colonizing the Body: State Medicine and Epidemic Disease in Nineteenth-Century India.* Berkeley: University of California Press.

Arnold, David, and Ramchandra Guha, eds. 1995. *Nature, Culture, Imperialism: Essays on the Environmental History of South Asia.* Delhi: Oxford University Press.

Arnold, Edwin. 1865. *The Marquis of Dalhousie's Administration of British India.* Vol. 2. London: Saunders, Otley and Co.

Arrighi, Giovanni. 1994. *The Long Twentieth Century: Money, Power and the Origins of Our Times.* London: Verso.

Arrighi, Giovanni, and Beverly Silver. 1999. *Chaos and Governance in the Modern World System.* Minneapolis: University of Minnesota Press.

Bachelard, Gaston. 1994. *The Poetics of Space.* Trans. Maria Jolas. Boston: Beacon Press. Originally published 1964, in French.

Baden-Powell, B. H. 1868–72. *Handbook of the Economic Products of the Punjab.* Vols. 1 and 2. Roorkee: Thomason Civil Engineering College Press.

———. 1875. "On the Defects of the Existing Forest Law (Act VII of 1865) and Proposals for a New Forest Act." In *Report of the Proceedings of the Forest Conference, 1873–74,* ed. B. H. Baden-Powell and J. S. Gamble. Calcutta: Superintendent of Government Printing.

———. 1892. *The Land Systems of British India.* Vols. 1 and 2. Oxford: Clarendon Press.

Baden-Powell, B. H., and J. S. Gamble, eds. 1875. *Report of the Proceedings of the Forest Conference, 1873–1874.* Calcutta: Superintendent of Government Printing.

Bagchi, Amiya Kumar. 1972. *Private Investment in India, 1900–1939.* Cambridge: Cambridge University Press.

———. 1976. "De-Industrialization in India in the Nineteenth Century: Some Theoretical Implications." *Journal of Development Studies* 12, 2: 135–64.

———. 1982. *The Political Economy of Underdevelopment.* Cambridge: Cambridge University Press.

———. 1997. *The Evolution of the State Bank of India.* Vol. 2, *The Era of the Presidency Banks, 1876–1920.* Delhi: State Bank of India and Sage Publications.

Bagwell, Phillip. 1974. *The Transport Revolution.* London: Routledge.

Baines, J. A. 1893. "The Distribution and Movement of Population in India." *Journal of the Royal Statistical Society,* March, 15–16.

Bairoch, Paul. 1975. *The Economic Development of the Third World since 1900.* Berkeley: University of California Press.

———. 1989. "European Trade Policy, 1815–1914." In *The Cambridge Economic History of Europe,* ed. Peter Mathias and Sidney Pollard. Cambridge: Cambridge University Press.

———. 1993. *Economics and World History: Myths and* Paradoxes. Chicago: University of Chicago Press.

Bakhtin, Mikhail. 1981. *The Dialogic Imagination.* Ed. M. Holquist. Austin: University of Texas Press.

Balachandran, G. 1994. "Towards a Hindu Marriage: Anglo-Indian Monetary Relations in Inter-War India, 1917–1935." *Modern Asian Studies* 28, 3: 615–47.

Balandier, Georges. 1966. "The Colonial Situation: Theoretical Approaches." In *Social Change: The Colonial Situation,* ed. Immanuel Wallerstein. New York: John Wiley.

Balibar, Etienne. 1991. "The Nation Form: History and Ideology." In *Race, Nation and Class: Ambiguous Identities,* ed. E. Balibar and I. Wallerstein. London: Verso.

———. 1994. *Masses, Classes, Ideas.* London: Routledge.

Banaji, Jairus. 1972. "For a Theory of Colonial Modes of Production." *Economic and Political Weekly* 23:2498–502.

———. 1977. "Capitalist Domination and the Small Peasantry: Deccan Districts in the Late Nineteenth Century." *Economic and Political Weekly* 12, 33–34: 1375–404.

Banerjea, Surendranath. 1925. *A Nation in Making: Being the Reminiscences of Fifty Years of Public Life.* London: Oxford University Press.

Banerjee, Tarasankar. 1987. *Historiography in Modern Indian Languages, 1800–1947.* Calcutta: Naya Prokash.

Barratt-Brown, Michael. 1974. *The Economics of Imperialism.* Harmondsworth: Penguin Books.

Barrier, Gerald, ed. 1981. *The Census in British India: New Perspectives.* Delhi: Oxford University Press.

Bartolovich, Crystal, and Neil Lazarus, eds. 2002. *Marxism, Modernity and Postcolonial Studies.* Cambridge: Cambridge University Press.

Bashyam, K., and K. Y. Adiga. 1927. *The Negotiable Instruments Act, 1881.* 4th ed. Calcutta: Butterworth and Co.

Baster, Albert S. J. 1929. *The Imperial Banks.* London: P. S. King and Son.

Basu, Aparna. 1974. *The Growth of Education and Political Development in India, 1898–1920.* Delhi: Oxford University Press.

Bayly, Christopher. 1975. *The Local Roots of Indian Politics: Allahabad, 1880–1920.* Oxford: Clarendon Press.

———. 1983. *Rulers, Townsmen, Bazaars: North Indian Society in the Age of British Expansion, 1770–1870.* Cambridge: Cambridge University Press.

———. 1986. "The Origins of Swadeshi: Cloth and Indian Society." In *The Social Life of Things: Commodities in Cultural Perspective,* ed. Arjun Appadurai. Cambridge: Cambridge University Press.

———. 1996. *Empire and Information: Intelligence Gathering and Social Communication in India, 1780–1870.* Cambridge: Cambridge University Press.

———. 1998. *Origins of Nationality in South Asia: Patriotism and Ethical Governance in the Making of Modern India.* Delhi: Oxford University Press.

Bayly, Susan. 1995. "Caste and 'Race' in the Colonial Ethnography of India." In *The Concept of Race in South Asia,* ed. Peter Robb. Delhi: Oxford University Press.

Bear, Laura. 1998. "Traveling Modernity: Capitalism, Community and Nation in the Colonial Governance of the Indian Railways." Ph.D. dissertation, University of Michigan.

Bell, Horace. 1894. *Railway Policy in India.* London: Rivington, Percival and Co.

Benjamin, Walter. 1968. *Illuminations.* New York: Schocken Books.

Bhabha, Homi. 1990. *Nation and Narration.* London: Routledge.

Bhattacharyya, Amit. 1986. *Swadeshi Enterprise in Bengal, 1900–1920.* Jadavpur, Calcutta: INA Press.

Billig, Michael. 1995. *Banal Nationalism.* London: Sage Publications.

Birla, Ritu. 1999. "Hedging Bets: The Politics of Commercial Ethics in Late Colonial India." Ph.D. dissertation, Columbia University.

Blaut, J. M. 1993. *The Colonizer's Map of the World.* Berkeley: University of California Press.

Bloch, Ernst. 1991. *Heritage of Our Times.* Trans. Neville and Stephen Plaice. Berkeley: University of California Press. Originally published 1962, in German.

———. 1977. "Nonsynchronism and the Obligation to Its Dialectics." *New German Critique* 11 (spring): 22–38.

Blochmann, H. 1873. "Contributions to the Geography and History of Bengal (Muhammadan Period)." *Journal of the Royal Asiatic Society of Bengal* 42.

Born, K. E. 1983. *International Banking in the Nineteenth and Twentieth Century.* Berg: Leamington Spa.

Borneman, J. 1992. *Belonging the Two Berlins: Kin, State, Nation.* Cambridge: Cambridge University Press.

Bose, Sugata. 1986. *Agrarian Bengal: Economy, Social Structure, and Politics, 1919–1947.* Cambridge: Cambridge University Press.

———. 1996. "Nation as Mother: Representations and Contestations of India in Bengali Literature and Culture. In *Nationalism, Democracy, and Development: State and Politics in India,* ed. Sugata Bose and Ayesha Jalal. Delhi: Oxford University Press.

———, ed. 1990. *South Asia and World Capitalism.* Delhi: Oxford University Press.

Bose, Sugata, and Ayesha Jalal. 2002. *Modern South Asia: History, Culture and Political Economy.* Delhi: Oxford University Press.

———, eds. 1998. *Nationalism, Democracy and Development: State and Politics in India.* Delhi: Oxford University Press.

Bourdieu, Pierre. 1977. *Outline of a Theory of Practice.* Trans. Richard Nice. Cambridge: Cambridge University Press.

———. 1988. *The Logic of Practice.* Stanford: Stanford University Press.

———. 1990. *In Other Words: Essays towards a Reflexive Sociology.* Trans. Mathew Adamson. Stanford: Stanford University Press.

———. 1999. "Rethinking the State: Genesis and Structure of the Bureaucratic Field." In *State/Culture: State-Formation after the Cultural Turn,* ed. George Steinmetz. Ithaca, N.Y.: Cornell University Press.

———. 2001. *Masculine Domination.* Trans. Richard Nice. Stanford: Stanford University Press.

Bourdieu, Pierre, and Loïc Wacquant. 1992. *An Invitation to Reflexive Sociology.* Chicago: University of Chicago Press.

Bowen, Meredith. 1981. *Empiricism and Geographical Thought from Francis Bacon to Alexander von Humboldt.* Cambridge: Cambridge University Press.

Brandis, D. 1884. *Progress of Forestry in India.* London: McFarlane and Erskine.

Braudel, Fernand. 1979. *The Perspective of the World: Civilization and Capitalism, Fifteenth–Eighteenth Centuries.* London: Harper and Row.

Braunmuhl, Claudia von. 1978. "On the Analysis of the Bourgeois Nation-State within the World Market Context." In *State and Capital,* ed. J. Holloway and S. Picciotto. Austin: University of Texas Press.

Breckenridge, Carol, and Peter Van der Veer. 1993. *Orientalism and the Postcolonial Predicament.* Philadelphia: University of Pennsylvania.

Brenner, Neil. 1997. "Global, Fragmented and Hierarchical: Henri Lefebvre's Geographies of Globalization." *Public Culture* 10, 1: 137–69.

———. 1999. "Beyond State-Centrism? Space, Territoriality, and Geographical Scale in Globalization Studies." *Theory and Society* 28, 1: 39–78.

———. 2001. "The Limits to Scale? Methodological Reflections on Scalar Structuration." *Progress in Human Geography* 15, 4: 525–48.

Brenner, Neil, Bob Jessop, Martin Jones, and Andrew Macleod, eds. 2003. *State/Space: A Reader.* Oxford: Blackwell.

Brubaker, Rogers. 1996. *Nationalism Reframed: Nationhood and the National Question in the New Europe.* Cambridge: Cambridge University Press.

Brunton, John. [1864] 1939. *John Brunton's Book; Being the Memories of John Brunton, Engineer, from a manuscript in his own hand written for his grandchildren and now printed.* Reprint. Oxford: Clarendon Press.

Buchanan, D. 1934. *The Development of Capitalist Enterprise in India.* New York: Macmillan.

Buckley, Robert B. 1880. *The Irrigation Works of India and Their Financial Results.* London: E. and F. Spon.

Buck-Morss, Susan. 1989. *Dialectics of Seeing: Walter Benjamin and the Arcades Project.* Cambridge: MIT Press.

———. 1995. "Envisioning Capital: Political Economy on Display." *Critical Inquiry* 21, 2: 434–67.

Burton, Antoinette. 2000. "'Tongues Untied: Lord Salisbury's 'Black Man' and the Boundaries of Imperial Democracy." *Comparative Studies in Society and History* 43, 2: 632–59.

Butalia, Urvashi. 1998. *The Other Side of Silence: Voices from the Partition of India.* Delhi: Kali for Women.

Calhoun, Craig. 1993. "Habitus, Field and Capital: The Question of Historical Specificity." In *Bourdieu: Critical Perspectives,* ed. C. Calhoun, E. Lipuma, and M. Postone. Chicago: University of Chicago Press.

———. 1994. *Social Theory and the Politics of Identity.* Cambridge, Mass.: Blackwell.

———. 1998. *Nationalism.* Minneapolis: University of Minnesota.

Carey, Henry Charles. 1837–40. *Principles of Political Economy.* Philadelphia: Carey, Lea and Blanchard.

———. [1851] 1967. *The Harmony of Interests: Agricultural, Manufacturing and Commercial.* Reprint. New York: A. M. Kelley.

Carnegy, P. 1874. *A Note on the Land Tenures and Revenue Assessments of Upper India.* London: Longmans, Green.

Carter, Paul. 1989. *The Road to Botany Bay: Explorations in Landscape and History.* Chicago: University of Chicago Press.

Castells, Manuel. 1997. *The Information Age: Economy, Society and Culture.* Vols. 1 and 2. Oxford: Blackwell.

Chakrabarty, Dipesh. 1976. "Early Railwaymen in India: 'Dacoity' and 'Train Wrecking,' 1860–1900." In *Essays in Honour of Professor S. C. Sarkar.* Delhi: People's Publishing House.

———. 1989. *Rethinking Working Class History: Bengal, 1890–1940.* Princeton: Princeton University Press.

———. 1993. "Marx after Marxism: History, Subalternity and Difference." *Meanjin* 52:421–34.

———. 2000. *Provincializing Europe: Postcolonial Thought and Historical Difference.* Princeton: Princeton University Press.

———. 2002. *Habitations of Modernity: Essays in the Wake of Subaltern Studies.* Chicago: University of Chicago Press.

Chakravarti, Uma. 1989. "Whatever Happened to the Vedic Dasi? Orientalism, Nationalism and a Script for the Past." In *Recasting Women: Essays in Colonial History,* ed. K. Sangari and Sudesh Vaid. Delhi: Kali for Women.

Chandavarkar, A. G. 1983. "Money and Credit, 1858–1947." In *The Cambridge Economic History of India,* ed. Dharma Kumar and Meghnad Desai, vol. 2, *1747–1947.* Cambridge: Cambridge University Press.

Chandra, Bipan. 1972. *The Rise and Growth of Economic Nationalism in India, 1880–1905.* Delhi: Longman.

———. 1979. *Nationalism and Colonialism in Colonial India.* Delhi: Longman.

———. 1985. *Communalism in Modern India.* Delhi: Longman.

———. 1988. *India's Struggle for Independence, 1854–1947.* Delhi: Longman.

Chandra, Sudhir. 1992. "Communal Consciousness in Late Nineteenth Century Hindi Literature." In *Communal and Pan-Islamic Trends in Colonial India,* ed. M. Hasan. New Delhi: Manohar Publications.

Chandravarkar, Rajnarayan. 1985. "Industrialization in India before 1947: Conventional Approaches and Alternative Perspectives." *Modern Asian Studies* 19, 3: 623–68.

Charlesworth, Neil. 1982. *British Rule and the Indian Economy, 1800–1914.* London: Macmillan.

———. 1985. *Peasants and Imperial Rule: Agriculture and Agrarian Society in the Bombay Presidency, 1850–1935.* Cambridge: Cambridge University Press.

Chatterjee, Indrani. 1999. *Gender, Slavery and Law in Colonial India.* Oxford: Oxford University Press.

Chatterjee, Joya. 1995. *Bengal Divided: Hindu Communalism and Partition, 1932–1947.* Cambridge: Cambridge University Press.

Chatterjee, Kumkum. 1996. *Merchants, Politics and Society in Early Modern India.* Leiden: E. J. Brill.

Chatterjee, Partha. [1986] 1993. *Nationalist Thought and the Colonial World: A Derivative Discourse.* Reprint. Minneapolis: University of Minnesota Press.

———. 1993. *The Nation and Its Fragments: Colonial and Post-Colonial Histories.* Princeton: Princeton University Press.

Chaturvedi, Vinayak. 2000. Introduction to *Mapping Subaltern Studies and the Postcolonial,* ed. Vinayak Chaturvedi. London: Verso.

Chaudhari, K. N. 1978. *The Trading World of Asia and the English East India Company, 1660–1760.* Cambridge: Cambridge University Press.

———. 1983. "Foreign Trade and Balance of Payments, 1757–1947." In *The Cambridge Economic History of India,* ed. Dharma Kumar and Meghnad Desai, vol. 2, *1757–1970.* Cambridge: Cambridge University Press.

———. 1990. *Asia before Europe: Economy and Civilization of the Indian Ocean from the Rise of Islam to 1750.* Cambridge: Cambridge University Press.

Chaudhuri, Binay B. 1970. "The Growth of Commercial Agriculture in Bengal, 1859–1885." *Indian Economic and Social History Review* 7, 2: 25–60.

Chowdhury, Indira. 1998. *The Frail Hero and Virile History: Gender and the Politics of Culture in Colonial Bengal*. Delhi: Oxford University Press.

Chunder, Bholanauth. 1869. *The Travels of a Hindoo to Various Parts of Bengal and Upper India*. 2 vols. London: Trubner and Co.

Clark, Hyde. 1848. *Practical and Theoretical Considerations on the Management of Railways in India*. London: John Weale.

———. 1858. *Colonization, Defence and Railways in Our Indian Empire*. London: John Weale.

Cohn, Bernard. 1990. *An Anthropologist among the Historians and Other Essays*. Delhi: Oxford University Press.

———. 1996. *Colonialism and Its Forms of Knowledge*. Princeton: Princeton University Press.

Cohn, Bernard, and Nicholas B. Dirks. 1988. "Beyond the Fringe: the Nation-State, Colonialism and the Technologies of Power." *Journal of Historical Sociology* 1, 2: 224–29.

Comaroff, Jean, and John Comaroff. 1991. *Of Revelation and Revolution: Christianity, Colonialism, and Consciousness in South Africa*. Vol. 1. Chicago: University of Chicago Press.

———, eds. 2001. *Millennial Capitalism and the Culture of Neoliberalism*. Durham, N.C.: Duke University Press.

Comaroff, John, and Jean Comaroff. 1997. *Of Revelation and Revolution: The Dialectics of Modernity on a South African Frontier*. Vol. 2. Chicago: University of Chicago Press.

Conlon, Frank, 1981. "The Census of India as a Source for the Historical Study of Religion and Caste." In *Census in British India*, ed. G. Barrier. Delhi: Oxford University Press.

Cooke, Charles Northcote. 1863. *The Rise, Progress, and Present Condition of Banking in India*. Calcutta: P. M. Cranenburgh.

Cooper, Frederick. 1992. "Colonizing Time: Work Rhythms and Labour Conflict in Colonial Mombassa." In *Colonialism and Culture*, ed. Nicholas B. Dirks. Ann Arbor: University of Michigan Press.

———. 1994. "Conflict and Connection: Rethinking African History." *American Historical Review* 99, 4: 1516–45.

———. 1996. *Decolonization and African Society: The Labor Question in French and British Africa*. Cambridge: Cambridge University Press.

———. 2002. "Decolonizing Situations: The Rise, Fall, and Rise of Colonial Studies, 1951–2001." *French Politics, Culture and Society* 20, 2: 47–76.

Cooper, Frederick, and Anne L. Stoler, eds. 1997. *Tensions of Empire: Colonial Cultures in a Bourgeois World*. Berkeley: University of California Press.

Coronil, Fernando. 1997. *The Magical State: Nature, Money, and Modernity in Venezuela*. Chicago: University of Chicago Press.

Cox, Robert. 1987. *Production, Power and World Order: Social Forces in the Making of History*. New York: Columbia University Press.

Coyajee, Jehangir C. 1930. *The Indian Currency System, 1835–1926*. Madras: Thompson and Co.

Crooke, William. [1879] 1989. *A Glossary of North Indian Peasant Life*. Reprint. Delhi: Oxford University Press.

———. 1897. *The North-Western Provinces of India: Their History, Ethnology and Administration*. London: Methuen.

Crosthwaite, C. H. T. 1870. *Notes on the North-Western Provinces of India, by a District Officer*. London: E. Arnold:.

Crouzet, Francois. 1982. *The Victorian Economy*. London: Methuen.

Cunningham, Alexander. 1871. *The Ancient Geography of India*. London: Trubner and Co.

———. [1883] 1970. *Book of Indian Eras, with Tables for Calculating Indian Dates*. Reprint. Varanasi: Indological Book House.

Cunningham, Joseph Davey. [1849] 1966. *A History of the Sikhs from the Origin of the Nation to the Battle of the Sutlej*. Reprint. Delhi: S. Chand.

Dalmia, Vadudha. 1997. *The Nationalization of Hindu Traditions: Bharatendu Harischandra and Nineteenth-Century Banaras*. Delhi: Oxford University Press.

———. 2001. "Vernacular Histories in Late-Nineteenth Century Banaras: Folklore, Puranas and the New Antiquarianism." *Indian Economic and Social History Review* 38, 1: 59–79.

Danvers, Juland. 1877. *Indian Railways: Their Past History, Present Conditions, and Future Prospects*. London: E. Wilson.

Das, Amarnath. 1985. *India and Jambu Island*. Delhi: Vidya Publishers.

Das Gupta, Ranajit. 1976. "Capital Investment and Transport Modernisation in Colonial India." In *Essays in Honour of Professor S. C. Sarkar*. Delhi: People's Publishing House.

Dasgupta, Ajit. 1993. *A History of Indian Economic Thought*. London: Routledge.

Dasgupta, B. B. 1927. *Paper Currency in India*. Calcutta: Calcutta University, Senate House.

Datta, Bhabatosh. 1978. *Indian Economic Thought: Twentieth-Century Perspectives*. Delhi: Tata McGraw Hill.

Davidson, Edward. 1868. *Railways of India: With an Account of Their Rise, Progress and Construction*. London: E. and F. N. Spon.

Davis, Lance, and Robert Huttenback. 1985. "The Export of British Finance, 1865–1914." *Journal of Imperial and Commonwealth History* 13:3.

———. 1986. *Mammon and the Pursuit of Empire: The Political Economy of British Im-perialism, 1860–1912.* Cambridge: Cambridge University Press.

Davis, Mike. 2001. *Late Victorian Holocausts: El Nino, Famines and the Making of the Third World.* London: Verso.

de Cecco, Marcello. 1975. *Money and Empire: The International Gold Standard, 1870–1914.* Totowa, N.J.: Rowman and Littlefield.

de Certeau, Michel. 1984. *The Practice of Everyday Life.* Trans. Steven Rendall. Berkeley: University of California Press.

Derbyshire, Ian. 1987. "Economic Change and Railways in North India, 1860–1914." *Modern Asian Studies* 21, 3: 521–45.

Desai, A. R. 1948. *Social Background of Indian Nationalism.* Bombay: Popular Book Depot.

Deshpande, Prachi. 2002. "Narratives of Pride: Historical Memory and Regional Identity in Maharashtra, India, c. 1870–1960." Ph.D. dissertation, Tufts University.

Deshpande, Satish. 1998. "Hegemonic Spatial Strategies: The Nation-Space and Hindu Communalism in Twentieth-Century India." *Public Culture* 10, 2: 249–83.

Deutsch, Karl. [1966] 1978. *Nationalism and Social Communication.* Reprint. Cambridge: MIT Press.

Devji, Faisal. 1993. "Muslim Nationalism: Founding Identity in Colonial India." Ph.D. dissertation, University of Chicago.

Dewey, C. J. 1979. "The Government of India's 'New Industrial Policy,' 1900–1925: Formation and Failure." In *Economy and Society: Studies in Indian Economic and Social History,* ed. K. N. Chaudhari and C. J. Dewey. Delhi: Oxford University Press.

Dey, Nundo Lal. [1899] 1971. *The Geographical Dictionary of Ancient and Medieval India.* Reprint. Delhi: Oriental Books.

Dicken, Peter. 1998. *Global Shift: Transforming the World Economy.* New York: Guilford Press.

Digby, William. 1901. *"Prosperous" British India: A Revelation from Official Records.* London: Allen and Unwin.

Dirks, Nicholas. 1987. *The Hollow Crown: Ethnohistory of an Indian Kingdom.* Cambridge: Cambridge University Press.

———. 2001. *Castes of Mind: Colonialism and the Making of Modern India.* Princeton: Princeton University Press.

———., ed. 1992. *Colonialism and Culture.* Ann Arbor: University of Michigan.

Dirlik, Arif. 1978. *Revolution and History: Origins of Marxist Historiography in China, 1919–1937.* Berkeley: University of California Press.

———. 1997. *The Postcolonial Aura: Third World Criticism in the Age of Global Capitalism.* Boulder, Colo.: Westview Press.

Dobbins, Frank. 1994. *Forging Industrial Policy: The United States, Britain, and France in the Railway Age.* Cambridge: Cambridge University Press.

Duara, Prasenjit. 1997. *Rescuing History from the Nation.* Chicago: University of Chicago Press.

———. 1998. "Transnationalism in the Era of Nation-States." *Development and Change* 29, 4: 647–70.

Duff, James Grant. 1826. *A History of the Mahrattas.* London: Longmans, Rees, Orme, Brown and Green.

Dumont, Louis. 1966. "The 'Village Community' from Munro to Maine." *Contributions to Indian Sociology* 9:67–89.

Dunford, M., and M. Perrons. 1983. *The Arena of Capital.* London: Macmillan.

Durkheim, Emile. [1915] 1965. *The Elementary Forms of Religious Life.* Trans. Joseph Swain. Reprint. New York: Free Press.

Dutt, R. P. 1949. *India Today.* Bombay: People's Publishing House.

Dutt, Romesh C. 1874. *Peasantry of Bengal.* Calcutta: Modern Book Agency.

———. 1882. *A History of Civilization in Ancient India.* London: Chatto and Windus.

———. 1897. *England and India, 1785–1885.* London: Chatto and Windus.

———. 1900. *Open Letters to Lord Curzon on Famines and Land Assessments in India.* London: Trubner.

———. [1902] 1969. *The Economic History of India under Early British Rule.* Vol. 1. Reprint. New York: Augustus Kelley.

———. [1904] 1970. *The Economic History of India in the Victorian Age.* Vol 2. Reprint. New York: Burt Franklin.

Eck, Diane. 1998. *Darsan: Seeing the Divine Image in India.* New York: Columbia University Press.

Edelstein, Michael. 1982. *Overseas Investment in the Age of High Imperialism: The United Kingdom, 1850–1914.* New York: Columbia University Press.

Edney, Mathew. 1997. *Mapping an Empire: The Geographical Construction of British India, 1765–1843.* Chicago: University of Chicago Press.

Eley, Geoff, and Ronald Suny. 1996. *Becoming National: A Reader.* New York: Oxford University Press.

Elias, Norbert. 1978. *The Civilizing Process.* Oxford: Blackwell.

Elliot, H. M., and J. M. Dowson. 1867–77. *The History of India as Told by Its Own Historians: The Muhamman Period.* Ed. John Dowson from the posthumous papers of the late Sir H. M. Elliot. 8 vols. London: Trubner.

Embree, Ainslie. 1968. *India's Search for National Identity.* New York: Alfred Knopf.

Fanon, Frantz. 1965. *The Wretched of the Earth.* Trans. Constance Farrington. New York: Grove.

Farnie, D. A. 1979. *The English Cotton Industry and the World Market, 1815–96.* London: Oxford University Press.

Fichte, Johann Gottlieb. [1800] 1910. *Der geschlossne Handelsstaat.* Reprint. Leipzig: F. Eckardt.

Foucault, Michel. 1978. *Discipline and Punish: The Birth of the Prison.* Trans. Alan Sheridan. New York: Pantheon.

———. 1980. "Questions on Geography." In *Power/Knowledge,* ed. Colin Gordon. London: Harvester Press.

———. 1986. "Of Other Spaces." *Diacritics* 16, 1: 22–27.

———. 1991. "Governmentality." In *The Foucault Effect: Studies in Governmentality,* ed. G. Burchell, C. Gordon, and P. Miller. Chicago: University of Chicago Press.

Freeman, Michael. 1999. *Railways and the Victorian Imagination.* New Haven: Yale University Press.

Freitag, Sandria. 1989. *Collective Action and Community: Public Arenas and the Emergence of Communalism in North India.* Berkeley: University of California Press.

Gallagher, John, Gordon Johnson, and Anil Seal. 1973. *Locality, Province and Nation.* Cambridge: Cambridge University Press.

Gallagher, John, and Ronald Robinson. 1953. "The Imperialism of Free Trade." *Economic History Review* 6, 1: 1–15.

Gandhi, M. K. [1910] 1997. *Hind Swaraj and Other Writings.* Ed. Anthony J. Parel. Reprint. Cambridge: Cambridge University Press.

———. 1958–89. *The Collected Works of Mahatma Gandhi.* 90 vols. Delhi: Nehru Memorial Museum and Library.

———. 1993. *An Autobiography: The Story of My Experiments with Truth.* Trans. Mahadev Desai. Boston: Beacon Press.

Ganguli, B. N. 1977. *Indian Economic Thought: Nineteenth Century Perspectives.* Delhi: Gian.

Ganguly, Dilip Kumar. 1984. *History and Historians in India.* New Delhi: Abhinav Publications.

Gaonkar, D., ed. 2001. *Alternative Modernities.* Durham, N.C.: Duke University Press.

Gellner, Ernest. 1983. *Nations and Nationalism.* Ithaca, N.Y.: Cornell University Press.

Geyer, Michael, and Charles Bright. 1987. "For a Unified History of the World in the Twentieth Century." *Radical History Review* 39:69–91.

———. 1995. "World History in a Global Age." *American Historical Review* 100, 4 (October): 1034–60.

Giddens, Anthony. 1987. *The Nation-State and Violence.* Vol. 2 of *A Contemporary Critique of Historical Materialism.* Berkeley: University of California Press.

————. 1991. *Central Problems in Social Theory: Action, Structure and Contradiction in Social Analysis.* Berkeley: University of California Press.

Gilmartin, David. 1994. "Scientific Empire and Imperial Science: Colonialism and Irrigation Technology in the Indus Basin." *Journal of Asian Studies* 53, 4: 1127–49.

Gilroy, Paul. 1987. *"There Ain't No Black in the Union Jack": The Cultural Politics of Race and Nation.* Chicago: University of Chicago Press.

————. 1993. *The Black Atlantic: Modernity and Double Consciousness.* Cambridge: Harvard University Press.

Gole, Susan. 1976. *Early Maps of India.* With a foreword by Irfan Habib. Delhi: Sanskriti in association with Arnold-Heinemann Publishers.

————. 1980. *A Series of Early Printed Maps of India in Facsimile.* Delhi: Jayaprints.

————. 1983. *India within the Ganges.* Delhi: Jayaprints.

————. 1989. *Indian Maps and Plans from the Earliest Times to the Advent of European Surveys.* New Delhi: Manohar Publications.

Gopal, Sarvepalli. 1966. *British Policy in India, 1858–1905.* Cambridge: Cambridge University Press.

Goswami, Manu. 1998. "From Swadeshi to Swaraj: Nation, Economy, Territory in Colonial South Asia, 1870–1907." *Comparative Studies in Society and History* 40, 4: 609–36.

————. 1998. "The Production of India: Colonialism, Nationalism and Territorial Nativism, 1870–1920." Ph.D. dissertation, University of Chicago.

————. 2002. "Rethinking the Modular Nation Form: Towards a Sociohistorical Understanding of Nationalism." *Comparative Studies in Society and History* 44, 4: 770–99.

Gregory, David, and John Ury, eds. 1994. *Social Relations and Spatial Structures.* London: Macmillan.

Grierson, George A. 1889. "The Modern Vernacular Literature of Hindustan." *Journal of the Asiatic Society of Bengal* (Calcutta), pt. 1 for 1888. Special issue.

Guha, Ramchandra. 1989. *The Unquiet Woods: Ecological Change and Peasant Resistance in the Himalaya.* Delhi: Oxford University Press.

————. 1990. "An Early Environmentalist Debate: The Making of the 1878 Forest Act." *Indian Economic and Social History Review* 27, 1: 65–84.

Guha, Ramchandra, and Madhav Gadgil. 1989. "State Forestry and Social Conflict in British India: A Study in the Ecological Bases of Agrarian Protest." *Past and Present* 123: 141–77.

Guha, Ranajit. [1962] 1996. *A Rule of Property for Bengal: An Essay on the Idea of Permanent Settlement.* Reprint. Durham, N.C.: Duke University Press.

————. 1982. "On Some Aspects of the Historiography of Colonial India." In *Subaltern Studies,* vol. 1, ed. Ranajit Guha. Delhi: Oxford University Press.

———. 1988. "The Prose of Counter-Insurgency." In *Selected Subaltern Studies,* ed. Ranajit Guha and Gayatri Spivak. New York: Oxford University Press.

———. 1997. *Dominance without Hegemony: History and Power in Colonial India.* Cambridge: Harvard University Press.

———. 2002. *History at the Limit of World-History.* New York: Columbia University Press.

Guha, Sumit. 1985. *The Agrarian Economy of the Bombay Deccan, 1818–1941.* Delhi: Oxford University Press.

———. 1998. "Rights and Wrongs in the Maratha Country: Antiquity, Custom and Power in the Eighteenth Century India." In *Changing Concepts of Rights and Justice in South Asia,* ed. Sumit Guha and Michael Anderson. Delhi: Oxford University Press.

Gupta, Akhil, and James Ferguson. 1992. "Beyond Culture: Space, Identity and the Politics of Difference." *Cultural Anthropology* 7, 1: 6–23.

Habib, Irfan. 1982. *An Atlas of the Mughal Empire: Political and Economic Maps with Detailed Notes, Bibliography and Index.* Delhi: Oxford University Press.

———. 1982. "Monetary System and Prices." In *The Cambridge Economic History of India,* ed. Tapan Raychudhari and Irfan Habib, vol. 1, *1200–1750.* Cambridge: Cambridge University Press.

———. 1987. "A System of Trimetallism in the Age of 'Price Revolution': Effects of the Silver Influx on the Mughal Monetary System." In *The Imperial System of Mughal India,* ed. John Richards. London: Oxford University Press.

Hacking, Ian. 1990. *The Taming of Chance.* Cambridge: Cambridge University Press.

Hall, Catherine. 2002. *Civilizing Subjects: Metropole and Colony in the English Imagination, 1830–1867.* Chicago: University of Chicago Press.

Hall, John, ed. 1998. *The State of the Nation: Ernest Gellner and the Theory of Nationalism.* Cambridge: Cambridge University Press.

Hall, Stuart. 1997. "The Local and the Global: Globalization and Ethnicity." In *Culture, Globalization and the World System: Contemporary Conditions for the Representation of Identity,* ed. Anthony King. Minneapolis: University of Minnesota Press.

Hardt, Michael, and Antonio Negri. 2000. *Empire.* Cambridge: Harvard University Press.

Hardy, P. D. 1980. *The History of Topographical Maps; Symbols, Pictures and Surveys.* Thames and Hudson: London.

Harischandra, Bharatendu. 1987. *Bharatendu samagra.* Ed. Hemant Sharma. Varanasi: Pracharak granthavali pariyojana, Hindi pracharak samasthan.

Harnetty, Peter. 1977. *Imperialism and Free Trade: Lancashire and India in the Mid Nineteenth Century.* Manchester: Manchester University Press.

Harootunian, Harry. 1999. "Ghostly Comparisons: Anderson's Telescope." *Diacritics* 29, 4: 135–49.

———. 2000. *History's Disquiet: Modernity, Cultural Practice, and the Question of Everyday Life.* New York: Columbia University Press.

———. 2000. *Overcome by Modernity: History, Culture, and Community in Interwar Japan.* Princeton: Princeton University Press.

Harrington, A. H. 1885. "Economic Reform in Rural India." *Calcutta Review* 80:435–59.

Harvey, David. 1984. *Limits to Capital.* Midway Reprint. Chicago: University of Chicago Press.

———. 1990. *The Condition of Postmodernity: An Enquiry into the Origins of Cultural Change.* Cambridge, Mass.: Blackwell.

———. 2000. *Spaces of Hope.* Berkeley: University of California Press.

Hasan, Mushirul. 1979. *Nationalism and Communal Politics in India, 1916–1928.* New Delhi: Manohar Publications.

———. 1992. *Islam and Indian Nationalism: Reflections on A. K. Azad.* New Delhi: Manohar Publications.

———., ed. 1985. *Communal and Pan-Islamic Trends in Colonial India.* New Delhi: Manohar Publications.

Headrick, Daniel. 1988. *The Tentacles of Progress: Technology Transfer in the Age of Imperialism, 1850–1940.* New York: Oxford University Press.

Hechter, Michael. 1975. *Internal Colonialism: The Celtic Fringe in British National Development.* New York: Transaction Books.

Held, David. 1990. "The Decline of the Nation-State." In *New Times: The Changing Face of Politics in the 1990s,* ed. Stuart Hall and Martin Jacques. London: Lawrence and Wishart.

———. 1995. *Democracy and Global Order.* London: Polity.

Henderson, William Otto. 1981. "Friedrich List and the Social Question." *Journal of European Economic History* 10:697–708.

———. 1983. *Friedrich List, Economist and Visionary, 1789–1846.* London: F. Cass.

Hindley, Clement. 1929. "Indian Railway Developments." *Asiatic Review* 25.

Hirsch, Joachim. 1995. "The Nation-State, Globalization and Democracy." *Review of International Political Economy* 1, 2: 267–84.

Hobsbawm, Eric. 1986. *Industry and Empire: From 1750 to the Present Day.* London: Penguin.

———. 1987. *The Age of Empire, 1875–1914.* New York: Random House.

———. 1990. *Nations and Nationalism since 1780.* Cambridge: Cambridge University Press.

Hobsbawm, Eric, and Terence Ranger, eds. 1983. *The Invention of Tradition.* Cambridge: Cambridge University Press.

Hoey, William. 1880. *A Monograph on Trade and Manufactures in Northern India.* Lucknow: American Methodist Press.

Holt, Thomas. 1992. *The Problem of Freedom: Race, Labor and Politics in Jamaica and Britain, 1832–1938.* Baltimore: Johns Hopkins University Press.

Hooson, David, ed. 1994. *Geography and National Identity.* Cambridge, Mass.: Blackwell.

Hurd, John. 1975. "Railways and the Expansion of Markets in India, 1861–1921." *Explorations in Economic History* 12, 3: 263–88.

———. 1983. "Railways." In *The Cambridge Economic History of India,* ed. Dharma Kumar and Meghnad Desai, vol. 2, *1757–1970.* Cambridge: Cambridge University Press.

Inden, Ronald. 1990. *Imagining India.* Oxford: Blackwell.

Iqbal, Afzal, ed. 1987. Select *Writings and Speeches of Maulana Mohamed Ali.* Lahore: Islamic Book Foundation.

Ivy, Marilyn. 1995. *Discourses of the Vanishing: Modernity, Phantasm, Japan.* Chicago: University of Chicago Press.

Jaffrelot, Christophe. 1995. "The Idea of the Hindu Race in the Writings of Hindu Nationalist Ideologues in the 1920s and 1930s: A Concept between Two Cultures." In *The Concept of Race in South Asia,* ed. Peter Robb. Delhi: Oxford University Press.

Jagga, Lajpat. 1981. "Colonial Railwaymen and British Rule: A Probe into Railway Labour and Agitation in India, 1919–1922." *Studies in History* 111, 1–2: 103–45.

Jain, L. C. 1920. *The Monetary Problems of India.* London: Macmillan.

———. 1929. *Indigenous Banking in India.* London: Macmillan.

Jalal, Ayesha. 1996. "Exploding Communalism: The Politics of Muslim Identity in South Asia." In *Nationalism, Democracy and Development: State and Politics in India,* ed. Sugata Bose and Ayesha Jalal. Delhi: Oxford University Press.

———. 2001. *Self and Sovereignty: Individual and Community in South Asian Islam since 1850.* Delhi: Oxford University Press.

James, C. L. R. [1938] 1963. *The Black Jacobins: Toussaint L'Ouverture and the San Domingo Revolution.* Reprint. New York: Vintage Books.

James, S., and D. Lake. 1989. "The Second Face of Hegemony: Britain's Repeal of the Corn Laws and the American Walker Tariff of 1846." *International Organization* 43, 1: 1–29.

Jenks, Leland. [1927] 1971. *The Migration of British Capital to 1875.* Reprint. London: Nelson.

Jessop, Bob. 1999. "Reflections on the (Il)logics of Globalization." In *Globalization and the Asia Pacific,* ed. Peter Dicken, Kris Olds, Phillip Kelly, and Henry Yeung. London: Routledge.

Jones, Kenneth. 1976. *Arya Dharm: Hindu Consciousness in Nineteenth-Century Punjab.* Berkeley: University of California Press.

———. 1981. "Religious Identity and the Indian Census." In *Census in British India,* ed. G. Barrier. Delhi: Oxford University Press.

Joshi, G. V. 1912. *Writings and Speeches of G. V. Joshi.* Poona: Aryabhushan Press.

Joshi, Sanjay. 2001. *Fractured Modernity: Making of a Middle Class in Colonial North India.* Delhi: Oxford University Press.

Kale, Vaman Govind. 1917. *Indian Industrial and Economic Problems.* Madras: G. A. Naksan and Co.

———. 1918. *Introduction to the Study of Indian Economics.* Poona: Aryabhushan Press.

———. 1919. *Currency Reform in India.* Poona: Aryabhushan Press.

Kalpagam, U. 1997. "Colonialism, Rational Calculations and Idea of the Economy." *Economic and Political Weekly* 32, 4: 2–12.

———. 2000. "Colonial Governmentality and the 'Economy.'" *Economy and Society* 29, 3: 418–38.

Kapadia, G. P. 1973. *History of the Accountancy Profession in India.* Delhi: Institute of Chartered Accountants of India.

Karl, Rebecca. 2002. *Staging the World: Chinese Nationalism at the turn of the Twentieth Century.* Durham, N.C.: Duke University Press.

Kashani-Sabet, Firoozeh. 1999. *Frontier Fictions: Shaping the Iranian Nation, 1804–1946.* Princeton: Princeton University Press.

Kaufmann, Eric. 1998. "Naturalizing the Nation: The Rise of Naturalistic Nationalism in the United States and Canada." *Comparative Studies in Society and History* 40, 4: 666–95.

Kaviraj, Sudipta. 1992. "The Imaginary Institution of India." In *Subaltern Studies,* vol. 7, ed. Partha Chatterjee and Gyanendra Pandey. Delhi: Oxford University Press.

———. 1994. "On the Construction of Colonial Power: Structure, Discourse, Hegemony." In *Contesting Colonial Hegemony: State and Society in Africa and India,* ed. D. Engels and S. Marks. London: British Academic Press.

———. 1995. *The Unhappy Consciousness: Bankimchandra Chattopadhyay and the Formation of Nationalist Discourse in India.* Delhi: Oxford University Press.

Kedourie, Elie. 1970. *Nationalism in Asia and Africa.* London: Weidenfeld and Nicolson.

Kennedy, P. 1979. "Imperial Cable Communications and Strategy, 1870–1914." In *The War Plans of the Great Powers, 1880–1814,* ed. P. Kennedy. London: Allen and Unwin.

Kern, Stephen. 1983. *The Culture of Time and Space, 1880–1918.* Cambridge: Harvard University Press.

Kerr, Ian. 1995. *Building the Railways of the Raj, 1850–1900*. Delhi: Oxford University Press.

———. 2001. Introduction to *Railways in Modern India*, ed. Ian Kerr. Delhi: Oxford University Press.

Keynes, John Maynard. [1913] 1924. *Indian Currency and Finance*. Reprint. London: Macmillan.

Khilnani, Sunil. 1997. *The Idea of India*. London: Farrar, Straus and Giroux.

King, Christopher. 1992. "Images of Virtue and Vice: The Hindi–Urdu Controversy in Two Nineteenth-Century Hindi Plays." In *Religious Controversy in British India: Dialogues in South Asian Languages*, ed. Kenneth Jones. Albany: State University of New York Press.

Kipling, Rudyard. [1885] 1989. *Complete Verse*. Reprint. New York: Random House.

Kopf, David. 1968. *British Orientalism and the Bengal Renaissance*. Berkeley: University of California Press.

Kumar, Dharma, and Meghnad Desai, eds. 1983. *Cambridge Economic History of India*. Vol. 2, *1757–1970*. Cambridge: Cambridge University Press.

Kumar, Ravinder. 1968. *Western Indian in the Nineteenth Century: A Study of the Social History of Maharashtra*. London: Routledge and Kegan Paul.

Lal, Sujan K. 1953. "Rajah Shiv Pershad: Early Life and Career." In *Indica: Indian History Research Institute Silver Jubilee Commemoration Volume*. Bombay.

Latham, A. J. H. 1978. *The International Economy and the Underdeveloped World, 1865–1914*. New York: Oxford University Press.

Leadbeater, Simon R. B. 1993. *The Indian Cotton-Mill Industry and the Legacy of Swadeshi, 1900–1985*. Delhi: Sage Publications.

Lefebvre, Henri. 1991. *Critique of Everyday Life*. Vol. 1. Trans. John Moore. London: Verso. Originally published 1958, in French.

———. 1991. *The Production of Space*. Trans. Donald Nicholson-Smith. Oxford: Blackwell. Originally published 1978, in French.

Lehmann, Frederick. 1965. "Great Britain and the Supply of Railway Locomotives to India: A Case Study of Economic Imperialism." *Indian Economic and Social History Review* 2, 4: 297–306.

———. 1977. "Railway Workshops, Technology Transfer, and Skilled Labour Recruitment in Colonial India." *Journal of Historical Research* 20, 1: 49–61.

Lelyveld, David. 1977. *Aligarh's First Generation: Muslim Solidarity in British India*. Princeton: Princeton University Press.

———. 1993. "The Fate of Hindustani." In *Orientalism and the Postcolonial Predicament: Perspectives on South Asia*, ed. Carol Breckenridge and Peter van der Veer. Philadelphia: University of Pennsylvania Press.

Leopold, Joan. 1970. "The Aryan Theory of Race in India, 1870–1920." *Indian Economic and Social History Review* 7, 2: 271–97.

Levi-Farr, David. 1997. "Friedrich List and the Political Economy of the Nation-State." *Review of International Political Economy* 4, 1: 154–78.

Leyshon, Andrew, and Nigel Thrift. 1997. *Money/Space: Geographies of Monetary Transformation.* London: Routledge.

List, Friedrich. [1827] 1909. "Outlines of American Political Economy." In *Life of Friedrich List and Selections from His Writings,* ed. M. Hirst, 147–272. Reprint. London: Smith, Elder.

———. [1838] 1983. *The Natural System of Political Economy.* Trans. and ed. W. O. Henderson. Reprint. Totowa, N.J.: F. Cass.

———. [1841] 1966. *The National System of Political Economy.* Reprint. New York: Augustus Kelly.

———. [1841] 1910. *Das Nationale System der Politischen Oekonomie.* Reprint. Jena: Verlag von Gustav Fischer.

Lokanathan, Palamadai. 1929. *Industrial Welfare in India.* Madras: Methodist Publishing House.

Ludden, David. 1979. "Patronage and Irrigation in Tamil Nadu: A Long-Term View." *Indian Economic and Social History Review* 8, 4: 347–65.

———. 1992. "India's Developmental Regime." In *Colonialism and Culture,* ed. Nicholas B. Dirks. Ann Arbor: University of Michigan.

———. 1993. "World Economy and Village India, 1600–1900." In *South Asia and World Capitalism,* ed. Sugata Bose. Delhi: Oxford University Press.

———. 1999. *An Agrarian History of South Asia.* Vol. 4. of *The New Cambridge History of India.* Cambridge: Cambridge University Press.

———, ed. 1994. *Agricultural Production and Indian History.* Delhi: Oxford University Press.

———. 1996. *Contesting the Nation: Religion, Community and the Politics of Democracy in India.* Philadelphia: University of Pennsylvania Press.

Lukács, Georg. 1990. *History and Class Consciousness.* Trans. Rodney Livingstone. Cambridge: MIT Press.

Lutt, J. 1974. *Hindu Nationalism in Uttar Pradesh.* Stuttgart: Ernst Klett Verlag.

Luxembourg, Rosa. 1913. *Die Akkumulation des Kapitals: Ein Beitrag zur ökonomischen Erklärung des Imperialismus.* Berlin: Buchhandlung Vorwärts Paul Singer.

Macgeorge, George. 1894. *Ways and Works in India: Being an Account of the Public Works in That Country from the Earliest Times up to the Present Day.* Westminster: Archibald Constable and Co.

Mackenzie, Compton. 1954. *Realms of Silver: One Hundred Years of Banking in the East.* London: Routledge and Kegan Paul.

Macleod, Roy, and Deepak Kumar, eds. 1995. Technology and *the Raj: Western Technology and Technical Transfers to India, 1700–1947.* Delhi: Sage Publications.

Macpherson, W. J. 1955. "Investment in Indian Railways, 1845–1875." *Economic History Review* 8, 2: 177–86.

Maier, Charles. 2000. "Consigning the Twentieth Century to History: Alternative Narratives for the Modern Era." *American Historical Review* 105, 3: 807–31.

Maine, Henry Sumner. 1871. *Village Communities in the East and West.* London: J. Murray.

———. 1883. *Ancient Law.* London: J. Murray.

Malkki, Liisa. 1992. "National Geographic: The Rooting of Peoples and the Territorialization of National Identity among Scholars and Refugees." *Cultural Anthropology* 7, 1: 24–44.

Mallon, Florencia. 1994. "The Promise and Dilemma of Subaltern Studies: Perspectives from Latin American History." *American Historical Review* 99, 4: 1491–515.

Mamdani, Mahmood. 1996. *Citizen and Subject: Contemporary Africa and the Legacy of Late Colonialism.* Princeton: Princeton University Press.

Mani, Lata. 1989. "Contentious Traditions: The Debate on Sati in Colonial India." In *Recasting Women: Essays in Colonial History,* ed. Kumkum Sangari and Sudesh Vaid. Delhi: Kali for Women.

———. 1998. *Contentious Traditions: The Debate on Sati in Colonial India.* Berkeley: University of California Press.

Mann, Michael. 1993. *The Sources of Social Power.* Vol. 2, *The Rise of Classes and Nation-States.* Cambridge: Cambridge University Press.

———. 1995. "A Political Theory of Nationalism and Its Excesses." In *Notions of Nationalism,* ed. Sukumar Periwal. Budapest: Central European University Press.

———. 1997. "Has Globalization Ended the Rise and Rise of the Nation-State? *Review of International Political Economy* 4, 3: 472–96.

Markovits, Claude. 1995. *Indian Business and Nationalist Politics, 1931–39.* Cambridge: Cambridge University Press.

———. 2000. *The Global World of Indian Merchants, 1750–1947: Traders of Sind from Bukhara to Panama.* Cambridge: Cambridge University Press.

Marx, Karl. 1962. *On Colonialism.* Moscow: Foreign Language Publishing House.

———. 1973. *Grundrisse: Foundations of the Critique of Political Economy.* Trans. Martin Nicolaus. New York: Vintage Books.

———. 1975. *Capital: A Critique of Political Economy.* Vol. 3. Moscow: Foreign Language Publishing House.

———. 1975. "Draft of an Article on Friedrich List's *Das Nationale System der Politischen Oekonomie.*" In *Collected Works,* vol 4. Moscow: Progress Publishers.

———. 1977. *Capital: A Critique of Political Economy.* Vol. 1. Trans. Ben Fowkes. New York: Vintage Books.

———. 1978. "The Future Results of British Rule in India." In *On Colonialism*. Moscow: Progress Publishers.

Masani, R. P. 1939. *Dadabhai Naoroji: The Grand Old Man of India*. London: Allen and Unwin.

Massey, Doreen. 1994. *Space, Place, Gender*. Minneapolis: University of Minnesota Press.

McAlpin, Michelle Burge. 1974. "Railroads, Prices and Peasant Rationality: India, 1860–1900." *Journal of Economic History* 34, 3: 662–84.

———. 1975. "The Effects of Expansion of Markets on Rural Income Distribution in Nineteenth Century India." *Explorations in Economic History* 12:289–302.

———. 1983. "Price Movements and Fluctuations in Economic Activity." In *The Cambridge Economic History of India*, ed. Dharma Kumar and Megnad Desai, vol. 2, *1757–1970*. Cambridge: Cambridge University Press.

McClintock, Anne. 1995. *Imperial Leather: Race, Gender, and Sexuality in the Colonial Contest*. London: Routledge.

McCully, Bruce. 1942. *English Education and the Origins of Indian Nationalism*. New York: Columbia University Press.

McGuire, John. 1988. "The World Economy, the Colonial State, and the Establishment of the Indian National Congress." In *The Indian National Congress and the Political Economy of India, 1885–1985*, ed. Mike Shepperdson and Colin Simmons. London: Avebury.

Mclane, John. 1963. "The Drain of Wealth and Indian Nationalism at the Turn of the Century." *Indian Economic and Social History Review* 1, 1.

———. 1977. *Indian Nationalism and the Early Congress*. Princeton: Princeton University Press.

Mehrotra, S. R. 1971. *The Emergence of the Indian Nation Congress*. Delhi: Vikas Publications.

Merrifield, Andrew. 1993. "Place and Space: A Lefebvrian Reconciliation." *Transactions of the Institute of British Geographer*, 18, 4: 516–31.

Metcalf, Barbara. 1982. *Islamic Revival in British India: Deoband, 1860–1900*. Princeton: Princeton University Press.

Metcalf, Thomas. 1996. *Ideologies of the Raj*. Cambridge: Cambridge University Press.

Mignolo, Walter D. 2000. *Local Histories/Global Designs: Coloniality, Subaltern Knowledges, and Border Thinking*. Princeton: Princeton University Press.

Mill, John Stuart. [1848] 1909. *Principles of Political Economy*. Reprint. London: Longmans, Green.

Milward, Alan. 1970. *The Economic Effects of the Two World Wars on Britain*. London: Macmillan.

Mintz, Sidney. 1985. *Sweetness and Power: The Place of Sugar in World History*. New York: Viking Penguin.

Misra, B. B. 1978. *The Indian Middle Classes*. Delhi: Longman.

Mitchell, Timothy. 1991. *Colonizing Egypt*. Berkeley: University of California Press.

———. 1998. "Fixing the Economy." *Cultural Studies* 12, 1: 82–101.

———. 2002. *Rule of Experts: Egypt, Techno-Politics, Modernity*. Berkeley: University of California Press.

———., ed. 2000. *Questions of Modernity*. Minneapolis: University of Minnesota.

Mookerji, Radhakumud. 1914. *The Fundamental Unity of India*. London: Longmans, Green.

Moriss, Morris D. 1983. "The Growth of Large-Scale Industry to 1947." In *The Cambridge Economic History of India*, ed. Dharma Kumar and Meghnad Desai, vol. 2, *1757–1970*. Cambridge: Cambridge University Press.

Mukherjee, Haridas, and Uma Mukherjee. 1953. *A Phase of the Swadeshi Movement, National Education, 1905–1910*. Calcutta: Chuckerverty, Chatterjee.

———. 1958. *India's Fight for Freedom or the Swadeshi Movement, 1905–1906*. Calcutta: Firma K. L. Mukhopadhyay.

Mukherjee, Mridula. 1985. "Commercialization and Agrarian Change in Pre-Independence Punjab." In *Essays on the Commercialization of Indian Agriculture*, ed. K. N. Raj, N. Bhattacharya, and S. Guha. Delhi: Oxford University Press.

Mukherjee, Mukul. 1980. "Railways and Their Impact on Bengal's Economy, 1870–1920." *Indian Economic and Social History Review* 17, 2: 191–209.

Mukherjee, Radhakamal. 1916. *The Foundations of Indian Economics*, with an introduction by Patrick Geddes. London: Longmans, Green.

———. 1939–41. *Economic Problems of Modern India*. London: Macmillan.

———. 1945. *The Indian Working Class*. Bombay: Hind Kitabs.

Mukhopadyay, Subodh Kumar. 1981. *Evolution of Historiography in Modern India*. Calcutta: K. P. Bagchi.

Mullhall, Michael. 1880. *The Progress of the World in Arts, Agriculture, Commerce, Manufactures, Instruction, Railways and Public Works*. London: Trubner.

Nair, Janaki. 1996. *Women and the Law in Colonial India*. Delhi: Kali for Women.

Nairn, Tom. 1977. *The Break-up of Britain: Crisis and Neo-Nationalism*. London: New Left Books.

Nanavati, M. B., and J. J. Anjaria. 1960. *The Indian Rural Problem*. Bombay: Indian Society of Agricultural Economists.

Nanda, B. R. 1977. *Gokhale: The Indian Moderates and the British Raj*. Princeton: Princeton University Press.

Naoroji, Dadabhai. 1886. *Indian Exchange and Bimetallism*. London: Longmans, Green.

———. [1901] 1962. *Poverty and Un-British Rule in India*. Reprint. Delhi: Government of India Publications.

———. 1917. *Speeches and Writings*. Madras: Nateson and Co.

Nehru, Jawaharlal. [1946] 1985. *The Discovery of India*. Reprint. Delhi: Oxford University Press.

Nigam, Sanjay. 1990. "Disciplining and Policing the 'Criminals by Birth.' Part 2: The Development of a Disciplinary System, 1871–1900." *Indian Economic and Social History Review* 27, 3: 257–87.

Noyes, John. 1992. *Colonial Space: Spatiality in the Discourse of German Southwest Africa, 1884–1915*. Philadelphia: Harwood Publishers.

Nye, John Vincent. 1991. "The Myth of Free-Trade Britain and Fortress France: Tariffs and Trade in the Nineteenth Century." *Journal of Economic History* 51, 1: 23–46.

O'Brien, Patrick, and G. A. Pigman. 1992. "Free Trade, British Hegemony and the International Economic Order in the Nineteenth Century." *Review of International Studies* 18, 2: 89–114.

Offer, A. 1993. "The British Empire, 1870–1914: A Waste of Money?" *Economic History Review* 46, 2: 215–38.

O'Hanlon, Rosalind. 1985. *Caste, Conflict and Ideology: Mahatma Jotirao Phule and Low Caste Protest in Nineteenth Century Western India*. Cambridge: Cambridge University Press.

———. 1988. "Recovering the Subject: Subaltern Studies and Histories of Resistance in Colonial South Asia." *Modern Asian Studies* 22, 1: 189–224.

O'Hanlon, Rosalind, and David Washbrook. 1992. "After Orientalism: Culture, Criticism, and Politics in the Third World." *Comparative Studies in Society and History* 34, 1: 141–67.

Orsini, Francesca. 2002. *The Hindi Public Sphere, 1920–1940: Language and Literature in the Age of Nationalism*. Delhi: Oxford University Press.

Osborne, Peter. 1995. *The Politics of Time: Modernity and Avant-Garde*. London: Verso.

Pal, Bipin Chandra. [1884] 1973. *Memories of My Life and Times in the Days of My Youth, 1857–1884*. Reprint. Calcutta: Bipin Chandra Pal Institute.

———. [1907] 1954. *Swadeshi and Swaraj*. Reprint. Calcutta: Yugayatri Prakashak.

———. 1916. *Nationality and Empire: A Running Study of Some Current Indian Problems*. Calcutta and Simla: Thacker, Spink and Co.

———. 1920. *The New Economic Menace to India*. Madras: Ganesh and Co.

———. 1923. *The Soul of India*. Madras: Tagore and Co.

Pandey, Gyanendra. 1978. *The Ascendancy of the Congress in Colonial North India*. Delhi: Oxford University Press.

————. 1990. *The Construction of Communalism in Colonial North India*. Delhi: Oxford University Press.

————. 2001. *Remembering the Partition*. Cambridge: Cambridge University Press.

Panikkar, K. M. 1963. *The Ideas of Sovereignty and State in Indian Political Thought*. Bombay: Bharatiya Vidya Bhavan.

Pant, Rashmi. 1987. "The Cognitive Status of Caste in Colonial Ethnography: A Review of Some Literature of the North West Provinces and Oudh." *Indian Economic and Social History Review* 24, 2: 145–62.

Parker, Andrew, and Doris Russo, eds. 1992. *Nationalism and Sexualities*. London: Routledge.

Perlin, Frank. 1987. "Money Use in Pre-Colonial India and the International Trade in Currency Media." In *The Imperial System of Mughal India*, ed. John Richards. London: Oxford University Press.

Phillips, C. H. 1961. *Historians of India, Pakistan and Ceylon*. London: Oxford University Press.

Polanyi, Karl. 1957. *The Great Transformation: The Political and Economic Origins of Our Times*. Boston: Beacon Press.

Poovey, Mary. 1994. "Figures of Arithmetic, Figures of Speech: The Discourse of Statistics." In *Questions of Evidence: Proof, Practice, and Persuasion across the Disciplines*, ed. James Chandler, Arnold Davidson, and Harry Haroounian. Chicago: University of Chicago Press.

————. 1998. *A History of the Modern Fact: Problems of Knowledge in the Sciences of Wealth and Society*. Chicago: University of Chicago Press.

Postone, Moishe. 1993. *Time, Labour and Social Domination*. Cambridge: Cambridge University Press.

Poulantzas, Nicos. 2000. *State, Power, and Socialism*. Trans. Patrick Cammiler. London: Verso.

Prakash, Gyan. 1990. "Writing Post-Orientalist Histories of the Third World: Perspectives from Indian Historiography." *Comparative Studies in Society and History* 32, 2: 383–408.

————. 1991. *Bonded Histories: Genealogies of Labor Servitude in Colonial India*. Cambridge: Cambridge University Press.

————. 1994. *After Colonialism: Imperial Histories and Postcolonial Displacements*. Princeton: Princeton University Press.

————. 1994. "Subaltern Studies as Postcolonial Criticism." *American Historical Review* 99, 4: 1475–90.

————. 1999. *Another Reason: Science and the Imagination of Modern India*. Princeton: Princeton University Press.

Prakash, Om. 1987. "Foreign Merchants and Indian Mints in the Seventeenth and

Eighteenth Centuries." In *The Imperial System of Mughal India,* ed. John Richards. London: Oxford University Press.

Princep, James. 1858. *Essays on Indian Antiquities, History, Numismatics, and Paleographic of the Late James Princep, to which are added his useful tables, illustrative of Indian History, chronology, modern coinages, weights, measures etc.* Ed. with notes by Edward Thomas. London: J. Murray.

Radice, Hugo. 1984. "The National Economy: A Keynesian Myth?" *Capital and Class* 22 (spring): 111–40.

Rae, John. 1834. *Statement of Some New Principles on the Subject of Political Economy, Exposing the Fallacies of the System of Free Trade, and of Some Other Doctrines Maintained in the "Wealth of Nations."* Boston: Hillard, Gray.

Rafael, Vicente. 1993. *Contracting Colonialism: Translation and Christian Conversion in Tagalog Society under Early Spanish Rule.* Durham, N.C.: Duke University Press.

Rai, Amrit. 1984. *A House Divided: The Origin and Development of Hindi/Hindavi.* Delhi: Oxford University Press.

Ramaswamy, Sumathi. 1997. *Passions of the Tongue: Language Devotion in Tamil Nadu, 1891–1970.* Berkeley: University of California Press.

———. 1999. "Catastrophic Cartographies: Mapping the Lost Continent of Lemuria." *Representations* 67:92–129.

———. 2000. "History at Land's End: Lemuria in Tamil Spatial Fables." *Journal of Asian Studies* 59, 3: 575–602.

———. 2001. "Remains of the Race: Archaeology, Nationalism and the Yearning for Civilization in the Indus Valley." *Indian Economic and Social History Review* 38, 2: 105–42.

Ranade, Mahadev Govind. 1902. *Religion and Social Reform.* Bombay: Thacker and Co.

———. 1906. *Essays on Indian Economics.* Madras: G. A. Natesan and Co.

———. 1990. *Ranade's Economic Writings.* Ed. Bipan Chandra. Delhi: Gian.

Rao, Narayana Velcheru. 1993. "Puranas as Brahminic Ideology." In *Purana Perennis: Reciprocity and Transformation in Hindu and Jaina Texts,* ed. Wendy Doniger. Albany: State University of New York Press.

Rao, Narayana Velcheru, David Shulman, and Sanjay Subramanyam, eds. 2001. *Textures of Time: Writing History in South India, 1600–1800.* Delhi: Permanent Black.

Rao, Shiva. 1939. *The Industrial Worker in India.* London: Allen and Unwin.

Rao, V. K. R. V. 1939. *An Essay on India's National Income, 1925–1929.* London: Allen and Unwin.

Ray, Rajat Kanta. 1995. "Asian Capital in the Age of European Domination: The Rise of the Bazaar, 1800–1914." *Modern Asian Studies* 29, 3: 449–554.

Robbins, Lionel. 1958. *Robert Torrens and the Evolution of Classical Economics.* London: Macmillan.

Rocher, Ludo. 1986. *The Puranas.* Vol. 2 of *The History of Indian Literature.* Wiesbaden: Otto Harrassowitz.

Ross, Kristin. 1994. *The Emergence of Social Space: Rimbaud and the Paris Commune.* Minneapolis: University of Minnesota Press.

Rothermund, Dietmar. 1970. "An Aspect of the Monetary Policy of British Imperialism." *Indian Economic and Social History Review* 7, 1: 91–108.

Rothschild, Emma. 2001. *Economic Sentiments: Adam Smith, Condorcet, and the Enlightenment.* Cambridge: Harvard University Press.

Roussakis, E. N. 1968. *Friedrich List, the Zolverein, and the Uniting of Europe.* Bruges: College of Europe.

Roy, M. N. 1999. *New Orientation: Lectures Delivered at the Political Study Camp Held at Dehradun, May 8–18, 1946.* Calcutta: South Asia Books.

———. 2000. *Selected Works of M. N. Roy.* Ed. Sibnarayan Ray. Vol. 1, *1917–1922.* Delhi: Oxford University Press.

Roy, Sripati Charan. 1911. *Customs and Customary Law in British India.* Calcutta: Hare Press.

Rudner, David. 1989. "Banker's Trust and the Culture of Banking among the Nattukottai Chettiars of Colonial South India." *Modern Asian Studies* 23, 3: 417–58.

Ruggie, John. 1993. "Territoriality and Beyond: Problematizing Modernity in International Relations." *International Organization* 47, 1: 139–74.

Rushdie, Salman. 1995. *The Moor's Last Sigh.* London: Jonathan Cape.

Sahlins, Peter. 1978. *Boundaries: The Making of France and Spain in the Pyrenees.* Berkeley: University of California Press.

Sarkar, Sumit. 1973. *The Swadeshi Movement in Bengal, 1903–8.* Delhi: Oxford University Press.

———. 1985. *A Critique of Colonial India.* Delhi: Oxford University Press.

———. 1997. *Writing Social History.* Delhi: Oxford University Press.

———. 2000. "Orientalism Revisited: Saidian Frameworks in the Writing of Modern Indian History." In *Mapping Subaltern Studies and the Postcolonial,* ed. Vinayak Chaturvedi. London: Verso.

Sarkar, Tanika. 1996. "Imagining Hindurashtra: The Hindu and the Muslim in Bankim Chandra's Writings." In *Contesting the Nation: Religion, Community and the Politics of Democracy,* ed. David Ludden. Philadelphia: University of Pennsylvania Press.

———. 2001. *Hindu Wife, Hindu Nation: Community, Religion and Cultural Nationalism.* London: Hurst and Co.

Sartori, Andrew. 2003. "The Categorical Logic of a Colonial Nationalism:

Swadeshi Bengal, 1904–1908." *Comparative Studies of South Asia, Africa and the Middle East* 23, 1.

Sassen, Saskia. 1998. Globalization and Its Discontents. New York: New Press.

Saul, S. B. 1957. "The Economic Significance of 'Constructive Imperialism.'" *Journal of Economic History* 17, 2: 173–92.

———. 1960. *Studies in British Overseas Trade, 1870–1914.* Liverpool: Liverpool University Press.

Sayer, Derek. 1987. *The Violence of Abstraction: Analytical Foundation of Historical Materialism.* London: Basil Blackwell.

———. 1991. *Capitalism and Modernity: An Excursus on Marx and Weber.* London: Routledge.

Schivelbusch, Wolfgang. 1986. *The Railway Journey: The Industrialization of Time and Space in the Nineteenth Century.* Berkeley: University of California Press.

Schneer, Jonathan. 1999. *London 1900: The Imperial Metropolis.* New Haven: Yale University Press.

Scholte, Jan Art. 1997. "Global Capitalism and the State." *International Affairs* 73, 3: 427–52.

Schwartzberg, Joseph. 1987. "South Asian Cartography." In *The History of Cartography,* vol. 2, ed. J. B. Marley and David Woodward. Chicago: University of Chicago Press.

———, ed. 1992. *A Historical Atlas of South Asia.* New York: Oxford University Press.

Scott, David. 1995. "Colonial Governmentality." *Social Text* 43 (spring): 191–220.

———. 1999. *Refashioning Futures: Criticism after Postcoloniality.* Princeton: Princeton University Press.

Scott, James. 1998. *Seeing Like a State: How Certain Schemes to Improve the Human Condition Have Failed.* New Haven: Yale University Press.

Seal, Anil. 1968. *The Emergence of Indian Nationalism: Competition and Collaboration in the Late Nineteenth Century.* Cambridge: Cambridge University Press.

Semmel, Bernard. 1961. "Philosophical Radicals and Colonialism." *Journal of Economic History* 21, 4: 513–25.

Sen, Amartya. 1981. *Poverty and Famines: An Essay on Entitlement and Deprivation.* New York: Oxford University Press.

Sen, Sudipta. 1998. *Empire of Free Trade.* Philadelphia: University of Pennsylvania Press.

Sen, Sunanda. 1992. *Colonies and the Empire: India, 1890–1914.* Calcutta: Orient Longman.

Sen, Sunil. 1976. "Marx on Indian Railways." In *Das Kapital Centenary Volume: A Symposium,* ed. Mohit Sen and M. B. Rao. Delhi: People's Publishing House.

Seth, Sanjay. 1999. "Rewriting Histories of Nationalism: The Politics of 'Moderate Nationalism' in India, 1870–1905." *American Historical Review* 104, 1: 95–116.

Seton-Watson, Hugh. 1977. *Nations and States.* Boulder, Colo.: Westview Press.

Sewell, William H. 1992. "A Theory of Structure: Duality, Agency, and Transformation." *American Journal of Sociology* 98, 1: 1–29.

———. 1996. "Historical Events as Transformations of Structures: Inventing Revolution at the Bastille." *Theory and Society* 25, 6: 841–81.

———. 1996. "Three Temporalities: Towards an Eventful Sociology." In *The Historic Turn in the Human Sciences*, ed. Terence Mcdonald. Ann Arbor: University of Michigan Press.

Shaikh, Anwar. 1979. "Foreign Trade and the Law of Value, Part 1." *Science and Society* 43, 3: 281–302.

———. 1980. "Foreign Trade and the Law of Value, Part 2." *Science and Society* 44, 1: 27–57.

Shirras, Findlay G. 1920. *Indian Finance and Banking.* London: Macmillan.

Shiva Rao, B. 1939. *The Industrial Worker of India.* London: Allen and Unwin.

Siddiqi, Assiya, ed. 1995. *Trade and Finance in Colonial India.* Delhi: Oxford University Press.

Simmons, Colin. 1985. "De-Industrialization, Industrialization and the Indian Economy, 1850–1947." *Modern Asian Studies* 19, 13: 593–622.

Singh, H. L. 1961. "Modern Historical Writings in Hindi." In *Historians of India, Pakistan and Ceylon*, ed. C. H. Phillips. London: Oxford University Press.

Singh, V. B. 1975. *From Naoroji to Nehru: Six Essays in Indian Economic Thought.* Delhi: Macmillan.

Singha, Radhika. 1998. *A "Despotism of Law": British Criminal Justice and Public Authority in North India, 1772–1837.* Delhi: Oxford University Press.

Sinha, J. C. 1927. *Economic Annals of India.* London: Macmillan.

Sircar, Dineshchandra. 1951. "Ancient Indian Cartography." In *The Indian Archives*, vol. 5. New Delhi: National Archives of India.

———. 1967. *Cosmography and Geography in Early Indian Literature.* Calcutta: Indian Studies, Past and Present.

———. 1971. *Studies in the Geography of Ancient and Medieval India.* Delhi: Motilal Banarsidass.

Sitaramaya, Pattabhi. 1969. *History of the Indian National Congress.* Vol. 1, *1885–1935.* Delhi: S. Chand.

Sivaramakrishnan, K. 1995. "Colonialism and Forestry in India: Imagining the Past in Present Politics." *Comparative Studies in Society and History* 37, 1: 3–40.

Smith, Neil. 1984. *Uneven Development.* Cambridge, Mass.: Blackwell.

———. 1993. "Homeless/Global: Scaling Places." In *Mapping the Futures,* ed. J. Bird, B. Curtis, T. Putnam, and T. Tickner. London: Routledge.

———. 1997. "The Satanic Geographies of Globalization." *Public Culture* 10, 1: 169–92.

Smith, R. S. 1985. "Rule-by-Record and Rule-by-Reports: Complementary Aspects of the British Imperial Rule of Law." *Contributions to Indian Sociology* 19, 1: 153–76.

Soja, Edward W. 1989. *Post-Modern Geographies: The Reassertion of Space in Critical Social Theory.* London: Verso.

Spengler, Joseph. 1971. *Indian Economic Thought.* Durham, N.C.: Duke University Press.

Spivak, Gayatri Chakravorty. 1988. "Can the Subaltern Speak?" In *Marxism and the Interpretation of Cultures,* ed. Cary Nelson and Lawrence Grossberg. Urbana: University of Illinois Press.

———. 1988. "Subaltern Studies: Deconstructing Historiography." In *Selected Subaltern Studies,* ed. Ranajit Guha and Gayatri Spivak. Delhi: Oxford University Press.

———. 1999. *A Critique of Postcolonial Reason: Toward a History of the Vanishing Present.* Cambridge: Harvard University Press.

Sporzluk, Roman. 1988. *Communism and Nationalism: Friedrich List and Karl Marx.* New York: Oxford University Press.

Stewart, Susan. 1993. *On Longing: Narratives of the Miniature, the Gigantic, the Souvenir, the Collection.* Durham, N.C.: Duke University Press.

Stokes, Eric. 1959. *The English Utilitarians and India.* Oxford: Clarendon Press.

———. 1978. *The Peasant and the Raj: Studies in Agrarian Society and Peasant Rebellion in Colonial India.* Cambridge: Cambridge University Press.

Stoler, Ann. 1992. "Rethinking Colonial Categories: European Communities and the Boundaries of Rule." In *Colonialism and Culture,* ed. Nicholas B. Dirks. Ann Arbor: University of Michigan Press.

———. 1995. *Race and the Education of Desire: Foucault's History of Sexuality and the Colonial Order of Things.* Durham, N.C.: Duke University Press.

Stone, Ian. 1979. "Canal Irrigation and Agrarian Change: The Experience of the Ganges Canal Tract, Muzaffarnar District (U.P.)." In *Economy and Society: Essays in Indian Economic and Social History,* ed. K. N. Chaudhari and Clive Dewey. Delhi: Oxford University Press.

———. 1984. *Canal Irrigation in British India: Perspectives on Technological Change in a Peasant Society.* Cambridge: Cambridge University Press.

Strachey, John. 1888. *India: Its Administration and Progress.* London: Allen and Unwin.

Strachey, John, and Richard Strachey. 1882. *The Finances and Public Works of India from 1869 to 1881*. London: K. Paul, Trench.

Subramaniam, Lakshmi. 1996. *Indigenous Capital and Imperial Expansion: Bombay, Surat, and the West Coast*. Delhi: Oxford University Press.

Subrahmanyam, Sanjay, ed. 1994. *Money and the Market in India, 1100–1700*. Delhi: Oxford University Press.

———., ed. 1990. *Merchants, Markets and the State in Early Modern India, 1770–1870*. Delhi: Oxford University Press.

Swyngedouw, Eric. 1997. "Neither Global nor Local: 'Glocalization' and the Politics of Scale." In *Spaces of Globalization: Reasserting the Power of the Local*, ed. K. Cox. New York: Guilford Press.

Tagore, Rabindranath. [1917] 1973. *Nationalism*. Reprint. Westport, Conn.: Greenwood Press.

———. 1921. *Greater India*. Madras: S. Ganesan.

———. 1966. "A Vision of Indian History." In *A Tagore Reader*, ed. Amiya Chakravarty. Boston: Beacon Press.

———. 1966. "From Greater India." In *A Tagore Reader*, ed. Amiya Chakravarty. Boston: Beacon Press.

Talwar, Kay, and Kalyan Krishna. 1979. *Pigment Paintings on Cloth*. Ahmedabad: Calico Museum.

Taylor, Peter J. 1994. *Political Geography: World Economy, Nation-State and Locality*. Longman: London.

———. 1996. "Embedded Statism and the Social Sciences: Opening up to New Spaces." *Environment and Planning A* 28, 11: 1917–28.

Thapar, Romila. 1965–66. *A History of India*. Vol. 1. Baltimore: Penguin Books.

———. 1989. "Imagined Religious Communities? Ancient History and the Modern Search for a Hindu Identity." *Modern Asian Studies* 23, 2: 209–31.

———. 2000. *History and Beyond*. Delhi: Oxford University Press.

Thapar, Romila, Harbans Mukhia, and Bipan Chandra. 1969. *Communalism and the Writing of Indian History*. Delhi: People's Publishing Press.

Thompson, E. P. 1978. *The Poverty of Theory*. London: Merlin.

Thorner, Daniel. 1950. *Investment in Empire: British Railways and Steam Shipping Enterprise in India, 1825–1849*. Philadelphia: University of Pennsylvania Press.

Thorner, Daniel, and Alice Thorner. 1962. "De-Industrialization in India, 1881–1931." In *Land and Labour in India*, ed. Daniel Thorner and Alice Thorner. Philadelphia: University of Pennsylvania Press.

Thrift, Nigel. 1990. "Transport and Communications, 1730–1914." In *An Historical Geography of England and Wales*, ed. R. A. Dodgon and R. A. Butlin. London: Academic Press.

Tilly, Charles. 1984. *Big Structures, Large Processes, Huge Comparisons*. New York: Russell Sage.

———. 1994. "States and Nationalism in Europe, 1492–1992." *Theory and Society* 23, 1: 131–46.

Tinker, H. 1974. *A New System of Slavery: The Export of Indian Labour Overseas*. Oxford: Oxford University Press.

Tod, James. [1826] 1920. *Annals and Antiquities of Rajasthan or the Central and Western Rajput States of India*. Reprint. London: Oxford University Press.

Todorov, Tzvetan. 1993. *On Human Diversity: Nationalism, Racism, and Exoticism in French Thought*. Trans. Catherine Porter. Cambridge: Harvard University Press.

Tomlinson, B. R. 1979. *Political Economy of the Raj, 1914–47: The Economics of Decolonization in India*. London: Cambridge University Press.

———. 1993. *The Economy of Modern India, 1860–1970*. Cambridge: Cambridge University Press.

Trautmann, Thomas. 1997. *Aryans and British India*. Berkeley: University of Press.

Tripathi, Dwijendra. 1991. *Business and Politics in India: A Historical Perspective*. New Delhi: Manohar Publications.

Tripathi, Maya Prasad. 1969. *Development of Geographical Knowledge in Ancient India*. Varanasi: Bharatiya Vidya Prakashan.

Trouillot, Michel-Rolph. 1995. *Silencing the Past: Power and the Production of History*. Boston: Beacon Press.

Tucker, R. P. 1983. "The British Colonial System and the Forests of the Western Himalayas." In *Global Deforestation and the Nineteenth Century*, ed. R. P. Tucker and J. F. Richards. Durham, N.C.: Duke University Press.

———. 1989. "The Depletion of India's Forests under British Imperialism: Planters, Foresters and Peasants in Assam and Kerala." In *The Ends of the Earth*, ed. D. Worster. Cambridge: Cambridge University Press.

Uno, Kozo. [1945] 1980. *Principles of Political Economy: Theory of a Pure Capitalist Society*. Trans Thomas T. Sekine. Reprint. Brighton, Sussex: Harvester.

Vandergeerst, Peter, and Nancy Peluso. 1995. "Territorialization and State Power in Thailand." *Theory and Society* 35:385–426.

Van der Veer, Peter. 1994. *Religious Nationalism: Hindus and Muslims in India*. Berkeley: University of California Press.

Verdery, Katherine. 1996. "Whither Nation and Nationalism." In *Mapping the Nation*, ed. Gopal Balakrishnan. London: Verso.

Visram, Rozina. 1986. *Ayahs, Lascars and Princes: Indians in Britain, 1700–1947*. London: Pluto.

Viswanathan, Gauri. 1989. *Masks of Conquest: Literary Study and British Rule in India*. New York: Columbia University Press.

Wade, Robert. 1996. "Globalization and Its Limits: Reports of the Death of the National Economy Are Greatly Exaggerated." In *National Diversity and Global Capitalism*, ed. Susanne Berger and Robert Dore. Ithaca, N.Y.: Cornell University Press.

Wakefield, Edward Gibbon. [1834] 1967. *England and America: A Comparison of the Social and Political State of Both Nations*. Reprint. New York: A. M. Kelley.

———. 1849. *A View of the Art of Colonization, with Present Reference to the British Empire*. London: J. W. Parker.

Wallerstein, Immanuel. 1980. *Mercantilism and the Consolidation of the European World Economy*. Vol. 2 of *The Modern World System*. New York: Academic Press.

———. 1983. *Historical Capitalism*. London: New Left Books.

———. 1991. *Unthinking Social Science: The Limits of Nineteenth Century Paradigms*. Cambridge: Polity Press.

Washbrook, David. 1990. "South Asia, the World System and World Capitalism." *Journal of Asian Studies* 49, 3: 479–508.

Watson, John, and Kaye Wilson, eds. 1868–75. *The People of India: A Series of Photographic Illustrations, with Descriptive Letterpress of the Races and Tribes of Hindustan*. Vols. 1–8. London: India Museum.

Watt, George. 1889–1902. *A Dictionary of the Economic Products of India*. 7 vols. London: W. H. Allen and Co.

———. 1908. *The Commercial Products of India*. London: John Murray.

Weber, Eugene. 1976. *Peasants into Frenchmen: The Modernization of Rural France, 1871–1914*. Stanford: Stanford University Press.

Weber, Max. 1961. *General Economic History*. Trans. Frank Knight. New York: Crowell-Collier.

———. 1978. *Economy and Society*. Vol. 1. Berkeley: University of California Press.

———. 2002. *The Protestant Ethic and the "Spirit" of Capitalism and Other Writings*. Trans. Peter Baehr and Gordon C. Wells. New York: Penguin Books.

Westwood, J. N. 1974. *Railways of India*. Vancouver: David and Charles.

Whitcombe, Elizabeth. 1972. *Agrarian Conditions in Northern India: The United Provinces under British Rule, 1860–1900*. Berkeley: University of California Press.

Wilde, Oscar. 1908. *Complete Writings of Oscar Wilde*. Vol. 2. New York: John W. Luce and Co.

Wilford, Francis. 1805. "An Essay on the Sacred Isles of the West." *Asiatick Researches* 8.

Winichakul, Thongchai. 1994. *Siam Mapped: A History of the Geo-body of the Nation*. Honolulu: University of Hawaii Press.

Wink, Andre. 1986. *Land and Sovereignty in India: Agrarian Society and Politics under the Eighteenth Century Maratha Swarajya.* Cambridge: Cambridge University Press.

Wolf, Eric. 1990. *Europe and the People without History.* Berkeley: University of California Press.

Yang, Anand. 1998. *Bazaar India: Markets, Society, and the Colonial State in Bihar.* Berkeley: University of California Press.

———, ed. 1995. *Crime and Criminality in British India.* Tucson: University of Arizona Press.

Young, Louise. 1998. *Japan's Total Empire: Manchuria and the Culture of Wartime Imperialism.* Berkeley: University of California Press.

Yuval-Davis, Nira, and Flora Anthias. 1989. *Women, Nation, State.* London: Macmillan.

Zaidi, A. M. 1985. *A Tryst with Destiny: A Study of Economic Policy Resolutions of the INC Passed during the Last One Hundred Years.* Delhi: Prakashan.

Zimmer, Oliver. 1998. "In Search of National Identity: Alpine Landscape and the Reconstruction of the Swiss Nation." *Comparative Studies in Society and History* 40, 4: 637–65.

INDEX